George Foster Talbot

Jesus - His Opinions and Character

The New Testament Studies of a Layman

George Foster Talbot

Jesus - His Opinions and Character
The New Testament Studies of a Layman

ISBN/EAN: 9783743388413

Manufactured in Europe, USA, Canada, Australia, Japa

Cover: Foto ©Lupo / pixelio.de

Manufactured and distributed by brebook publishing software (www.brebook.com)

George Foster Talbot

Jesus - His Opinions and Character

JESUS

HIS OPINIONS AND CHARACTER

THE NEW TESTAMENT STUDIES
OF A LAYMAN

By GEORGE FOSTER TALBOT

"Art thou he that should come, or do we look for another?" — MATT. xi., 3

BOSTON
GEO. H. ELLIS, 141 FRANKLIN STREET
1887

CONTENTS.

CHAPTER I.

SOURCES OF EVIDENCE, 11–43.

Brief *résumé* of what is known of the life of Jesus, 11, 12. He did not write, nor authorize the writing of his life, or of his doctrine, 12. Few traces of the human career or character of Jesus in the Pauline and other canonical Epistles, 13, 14; in the "Acts of the Apostles," 15, 16. Distinct and irreconcilable traditions of Jesus in the first three and in the fourth Gospels, 16. Story of Jesus as told in the latter, 17–22. Story of Jesus as told by Matthew, 23–28. These narratives but questionable *data* of history; intrinsic improbability of the events told in them, and their inconsistency with other events in the same narratives, 29. Hence an unreasonable scepticism as to the existence of Jesus, 29. Influence of Christianity upon civilization a personal influence, and implies a Christ, 30. Slight impression of deeds and sayings of Jesus on the mind of Paul, 30. Slight mention of him by Josephus, 30. What the historic Gospels, the apostles, and primitive disciples concur in imputing to Jesus probably formed a part of his faith and philosophy, 31. Reasons why the Fourth Gospel cannot be considered historical, 32. Question of miracles an embarrassment, rather than an assistance to modern faith, 33. Substantial variances between the First and the Fourth Gospels, 34. Jesus gained more influence by intellectual than by magical powers, 35. Matthew Arnold's adhesion to the Fourth Gospel considered, 36–38. Few points of agreement, many points of disagreement, between Fourth and Synoptic Gospels, 38. Arrest and condemnation of Jesus as told in Fourth Gospel incredible, 38–40. Mainly concurrent statements of Synoptic Gospels concerning the same natural and probable, 41, 42. The general historic credibility of the Synoptic Gospels assumed, 43.

CHAPTER II.

DOMINANT IDEA OF JESUS, 44–69.

Ideas and character of Jesus must be considered in their relation to his *dominant idea*, 44. His dominant idea, the *kingdom of heaven*, 45. Prominence of this idea in his preaching, 45. His ethical precepts relate to it, 45. The kingdom of heaven at hand the sole message of his sent-out disciples, 47. Significance of his title of *Son of Man*, 47, 48. *Kingdom of heaven* the chief theme of the parables, 50. Disclosures in the conversation at Cæsarea-Philippi, 51. Symbolic character of the procession of palms, 52, 53. Literal exposition of the doctrine of the *kingdom of heaven* in Matthew xxiv., xxv., 54–56. Kingdom of heaven most prominent in the discourse of Jesus, 56, 57. The idea not wholly original with him, 57. The expectation of the people of his time with reference to it, 57, 58. Derived from the national prophecies, 58. Passages in the law and in the temple songs considered Messianic, 58, 59. Restored kingdom and power of Israel mentioned by Isaiah, 59. By Jeremiah, 59. By Ezekiel and other prophets, 60. The promised era of peace was the peace of conquest — of the subjection and punishment of enemies, 61–63. Real nature of the prophetic writings political and didactic, and relating to the exigencies of the times, 63–65. Not predictions of future events, 66. The prophetic king to come not immortal, 67. The Jews of the time of Jesus believed the prophecies to be predictions of a restored monarchy, and of a domination by their nation of other people, 67, 68. How far Jesus shared the belief, 68, 69.

CHAPTER III.

DOMINANT IDEA OF JESUS, CONTINUED, 71–96.

Didactic method of Jesus, 71. His Messianic character gradually and diffidently assumed, 71. The conquering and the suffering Messiah of the prophets, 72. Jesus considered that there were not two Messiahs, but two comings of one Messiah, 72. Popular idea an empire of Israel; Jesus' idea an empire of the elect, 73–75. The popular expectation was of material prosperity, that of Jesus of spiritual, 76. The retribution in the dispensation of Jesus was more complete than in the prophetic. The former had no mercy for enemies who submitted, 76, 77. The prophetic kingdom a kingdom of the priesthood and of the permanence of the Mosaic laws, that of Jesus ignored the priesthood and the ecclesiastical laws, 77. Why Jesus believed the *kingdom of heaven* at hand, 78. Are the prophecies of Jesus capable of a purely spiritual interpretation? 79–81. The sense in which His first followers believed those prophecies, 82. The *kingdom of heaven* in the writings of Paul, 82–86. Paul's peculiar theory of the resurrection, 86. The *kingdom of heaven* in the Epistle to the Hebrews, 88. In the Epistle of James, 88, 89. Of Peter, 89, 90. Of John, 90, 91. Fuller details of the *kingdom of heaven* in the Apocalypse, 91–93. Wherein it differed from the original tradition, 93, 94. Disappointment of the Christian expectation, 95. Recapitulation of the argument that the *kingdom of heaven* was the *dominant idea* of Jesus, 95, 96.

CHAPTER IV.

POLITICAL IDEAS OF JESUS, 97–126.

Indicated generally in his *dominant idea*, 97. He repressed the struggle for life, 98. Radical character of his reforms, 99. His hostility to existing governments, 100. His national prejudices not strong, 100, 101. Did not sympathize with popular aspirations for independence, 102. His ideas of poverty and wealth, 103; as disclosed in his precepts and parables, 104–106. Not mere sentiments, 106. He practised his own principles, 107. He required their practice from his followers, 108. The wealthy young man, 109. His antipathy to the rich reappears in the Epistle of James, 109. Sentiment of justice not strong in Jesus, 110. Real import of parable of Dives and Lazarus, 112, 113. Worldly occupations of men seemed impious to Jesus, 114. His ideas of property quite consistent with and explicable by

CONTENTS   iii

his *dominant idea*, 115-118. Necessity of returning to secular pursuits and cares after defeat of expectation of the end of the world, 117. Paul the first to abate the rigor of the political ideas of Jesus, 118. Communistic character of the first Christian society, 120. The Church at Jerusalem maintained by subsidies from heathen converts, 121. Traces of the early communism surviving in monastic establishments and the minor sects, 122. Reversed attitude of the modern Church, 123. Effect of poverty and wealth upon personal character considered, 123-125. Antagonism betwixt ideas of Jesus and those of his own race, 126.

CHAPTER V.

ETHICAL IDEAS OF JESUS, 127-160.

Absence of a systematized statement of his ethical ideas, 127. His generalizations sometimes inconsequential and contradictory, 128. Instances given, 128-130. Two aspects of divine beneficence, 131, 132. Difficulty of reconciling the two characters, 132. Blessedness of sorrow, 133. Salutary influence of this lesson, 134. Blessedness of forgiveness, 135. Strict ideas of sexual purity, 136. Counter influence of Mohammedanism, 137. Jesus no ascetic, 138. Influence respectively of the temperance of Islam and the chastity of Christianity, 139. Murder and all personal injuries condemned in the malice that incites them, 140. Difficulty of controlling anger, 140. Not always himself true to his lesson, 141. Effect on character of indiscriminate almsgiving, 142. Provisional application of this lesson, 143. Jesus ignored the rights of property, which were the basis of the older cultus, 145. Major and minor morals distinguished, 146. The proscription of all oaths considered, 146, 147. Uncertain attitude toward the Mosaic ritual, 148. Omissions in the ethical code of Jesus, 148. Patriotism, 149. The marital, parental, and filial duties, 149. Defect supplied in ethics of Paul, 150. The Teutonic influence on manners, 150. Pity and tenderness toward animals not characteristic of the ethical system of Jesus, 151. Rule of-conduct toward brethren different from the rule toward other men, 152. Rise thence of ecclesiastical government, 153. How far the ethical ideas of Jesus were original, 153. The sect of the Essenes and their origin, 154. Respects in which their ideas differed from those of Jesus. Their regard of the old scriptures and the Sabbath, 154; of labor, 155. Their strong sentiment of justice, 155. Their separation from the wicked, their prayers, 156. Their washings and baptisms, 156, 157. Their hostility to war and slavery, 157. Their veneration of age, 158. Respects in which their principles agreed with the doctrines of Jesus, 158. Their requirement of virginity, 158. They forbade oaths, 159. They inculcated love of God; they confined their most esoteric doctrines to the brotherhood; they required the extirpation of anger; they forbade scientific studies; they expected the *Messiah*, and the *kingdom of heaven*, 160. Jesus accepted, modified, and gave currency to the ideas of the *Essenes*, 160.

CHAPTER VI.

PHILOSOPHICAL IDEAS OF JESUS, 161-186.

Difficulty of generalizing them, 161. The poetic and philosophic temperament incompatible, 162. Jesus taught that God was beneficent according to the human standard, 162. The fatherhood of God a psychological fact, 163. Difference between his and the Jewish idea of a divine paternity, 164. Courses of nature the appointment of God, 164. Opposite view of nature in Johannic Gospel, 165, 166. Doctrine of Holy Ghost suggested, not developed, by Jesus, 167. Exigencies developing the doctrine, 167, 168. How the word "spirit" is used by Paul, also by John, 169. New occasions required new revelations, 170. Christian ideas not derived from Jesus, 171. Words, which denote the intrinsic character of men, 172. The aversion of Jesus for bad men; his tolerance of publicans and sinners, 173. He believed in devilish possession, 174. Illustrations of his belief from the Gospels, 175. His scheme of nature, 176. The evil in the world due in part to devilish possession, 177. Wicked men children of the devil, 177, 178. The fatherhood of God as held by Jesus and by the Israelites, 179. His feeling toward men not disciples, 180. His opposition to the distinctions of rank, 181. No service of duty entitled to reward, 183. Self-depreciation and self-consciousness how regarded by him, 184. The import of all serious speech, and the indications of the moral sympathies, 185.

CHAPTER VII.

RELIGIOUS IDEAS OF JESUS, 187-208.

Whether there be gods a question of philosophy,— how to placate them a question of religion, 187. Worship corresponds to the conception of God, 187. With the beginning of the moral sense, righteousness became a service of worship, 188. Pagan idea of God human and cheerful; Hebrew idea, pure and stern, 188, 189. Scepticism as to Israel being the chosen people in certain of the old scriptures, 190. Jesus thought the relation of Israel to God was a conditional and temporary one, 191, 192. His assumption of authority over the Mosaic law, 192. His neglect of Sabbath observance, 193. His position as to the Mosaic code uncertain, 194. Prayer not a service of worship, 195, 196; but a familiar intercourse, 197. His aversion to fasting, 198. His slight regard of baptism, 199. His memorial service called the Last Supper, 200. His form of prayer considered, 202. The thoroughness of his precepts, 203. The forgiving and vindictive aspects of the divine character, 205. He placed no obstacles in the way of passing from the evil to the good character and state, 206. How the apprehension of the end of the world modified his religious ideas, 207, 208. Sudden conversions come to impetuous natures; growth the general law of righteousness, 208.

CHAPTER VIII.

HIS IDEAS OF A FUTURE LIFE, 209-236.

The question of a future life a question of philosophy, 209. The final destiny of men not beyond ultimate discovery, 210. Why religion has asserted exclusive jurisdiction over this subject, 211. The Jews had originally no ideas of immortality, 212. The Jews acquired belief in immortality during their captivity, 215. An established belief before the time of Jesus, 216. Popular opinions concerning immortality among the Jews and among the Greeks and Romans contrasted, 216, 217. Traces of the beliefs of the time of Jesus among his own people, outside of his own teaching, 217-220. Idea of day of judgment and its origin, 220, 221. Ideas of Jesus as to the future life traced in his literal and allegoric teachings, 221, 222. The resurrection a terror to all but the righteous, 223. Deplorable condi tion of the non-elect dead, 224-226. Imagination and tradition the source of all our knowledge of a future life, 227-229. Jesus' method of investigating the question philosophical and human, 229. In the Fourth Gospel, his teachings are from intuition and direct knowledge, 230, 231. In the Synoptic Gospels, quite otherwise, 232. Paul's revelations much more detailed and particular, 233. The colloquy with the Sadducees concerning the resurrection, 234, 235. The scheme of a future life in the mind of Jesus modified and supplanted by his dominant idea of a kingdom of heaven, 236.

CHAPTER IX.

LEGEND OF THE MIRACLES, 237-276.

Considerable part of events related in Synoptic Gospels improbable, 237. The miracles, if performed, must be proved by testimony of the highest validity, 238. Paul's character as a witness, 239. Did he witness the crucifixion? 240. Controversy in the early Church as to his apostleship, 241. His silence upon the miracles, 242. Did the divine power attributed by Paul to Jesus imply a power to work miracles? 243, 244. Silence of Paul concerning miracles irreconcilable with the Johannic miracles of Jesus in Jerusalem, where Paul lived, 244, 245. No mention of Jesus' miracles in the canonical Epistles, 246. Testimony of the Synoptic Gospels. Matthew and Mark evidently copy each other, 247. None of the Gospels extant while Paul lived and wrote, 248. At best, the evidence of the Gospels is of a low grade, 249. Detail of miracle-working as given by Matthew and Mark, 250-252. Difficulties encountered in giving it credence, 253-255. Detail of miracle-working as given by Luke, 255-257. Discrepancies in the testimony,— how far they are explicable, how far irreconcilable, 258-260. Paley's principle of weighing testimony applied to the testimony of the evangelists, 261. The miracles of the Fourth Gospel explained, 262-264. How the evangelical narratives were created, 264. Multiplicity of Gospels, and rule of selection among them, 265, 266. Such miracles as the evangelists record would, if performed, have obtained some mention in secular history, 267. They would have produced greater effects upon the communities where performed than the evangelists describe, 268-270. Jesus probably had a certain magnetic power of allaying nervous disorders, out of which the story of the miracles grew, 270-272. What the exorcization of devils actually was, 273. The raising of the ruler's daughter — the foundation of all the stories of raising the dead — not miraculous, 275. The inconsistent reasons given for the cessation of the miraculous powers of Jesus, 276. The real reason surmised, 276.

CHAPTER X.

ARREST, TRIAL, AND DEATH OF JESUS, 277-331.

Whatever may have been the providential plan, causes of his death to be sought in the order of known events, 277, 278. How came he to be obnoxious to his nation, 278; not as a healer of the sick, 279; not as a teacher of a sublime system of ethics, 279, 280; not by his claim to be the Messiah, 281-283. Tolerant attitude of scribes and Pharisees toward Jesus, 284. His intolerant attitude toward them, 284-286. His first contact with them in Galilee, 286. Jesus in no peril while he stayed in Galilee, 287. He went to Jerusalem, in fulfilment of prophecy, to be put to death, 287-290. Offensiveness to the priests and rulers of the procession of palms, and the driving out of the sellers of victims from the temple, 290, 291. The spirit in which Jesus prosecuted his controversy with the rulers and elders, 292, 293. Mode of life of Jesus and his company in Jerusalem, 294. Strange confusion of identities in the story of the woman with her offering to Jesus, 295. The chief priests and elders, ignorant of the person of Jesus, are compelled to hire a disciple to point him out among the strangers, 295, 296. Uncertainty as to the feeling toward him of the Jewish populace — consequent caution of his enemies, 296. The populace take sides against him; subsequent boldness of his enemies, 297. The narrative of the crucifixion most probable part of the synoptic narratives, 297. How the facts were probably learned by the writers, 298. Had the council of the Sanhedrim power to try and punish Jesus? Political condition of Jerusalem and Palestine considered, 299, 300. The Sanhedrim had power to try and punish at least all ecclesiastical offences, 300. The trials of Peter and John and Stephen, 301. Two essays in the *Contemporary Review*, on "Trial of Jesus," briefly reviewed, 302, 303. Only one trial, and that before the Sanhedrim, 303. The matter only came to Pilate to get his warrant for the execution, 304. Two reasons given why the Sanhedrim wished to involve Pilate in the responsibility of putting Jesus to death, 304, 305. Proceedings against Jesus violent and illegal, 306, 307. The adjuration by the High Priest, and how Jesus made it the occasion of insuring his own condemnation, 308. The probable course of the proceedings, 309, 310. Was the judgment against Jesus one which a just Jew might approve? 310, 311. Jesus had in fact claimed divine powers and authority, 311. Strictness of the Hebrew law of blasphemy, 312. His claim, however, would not have subjected him to prosecution, if he had refrained from provoking the priests and elders, 313. Laws against blasphemy ought to be executed with discrimination, 313. If Jesus had divine attributes, he studiously concealed them from his judges, 314, 315. His bravery and reticence at his trial and under his torture, 316. Totally different account of the arrest and trial in the Fourth Gospel, 317. They took place according to it before the Passover, 318, 319. The trial not before the Sanhedrim, but before Pilate, 319. Undignified bearing of Jesus before the latter, contradictory of his noble silence, as told by the Synoptics, 319-324. Slight variance in Luke from the story of Matthew and Mark not to be followed, 325. Complete isolation of Jesus in Jerusalem, 326. Indignities heaped on him during his trial and execution, 326-329. Matthew and Mark's picture of his last hours compared with Luke's, 330, 331.

CHAPTER XI.

HIS PERSONAL PRETENSIONS AND CHARACTER, 332-381.

To be considered in answering these questions: *What he thought of himself? What his age thought of him? What was he?* 332. Implication of name *Son of Man*, 333. Jesus claimed divine inspiration and authority from the first, 334. Impression that he was the Christ not original with him, and not at first accepted by him, 334. Crisis of self-consciousness at Cæsarea-Philippi, 335. Recapitulation of the conversation there, 335, 336. Obscure origin of all such self-consciousness, 337. Prevalent sadness of his temper, 338. Opinion concerning Jesus among his fellow countrymen, 339. Indifference of the people of Nazareth and Capernaum, 339. Probable alienation of his own family, 340. Paucity of his followers, and slight allegiance of the twelve, 341. Number of adherents at his death, 341. Number in Jerusalem and Judea, 342. Effect of excessive eulogies of Jesus to obscure his personal traits, 342. General accuracy of the synoptical descriptions of his mental peculiarities, 343. The parables and apothegms of Jesus easy to retain long in the memory, 343. Not easy to remember his longer metaphysical discourses, 344. Wit, wisdom, and moral emphasis of many sayings of Jesus, 345. He appreciated wit in others, 346. His fondness for intellectual puzzles, 347. Figurative character of his common speech, 348. How far he shared the false beliefs of his age, 349. His belief in angels, 349. In devils and a prince of devils, 350. Blending of truth and poetry in his mind and teaching, 350. The Hebrew scriptures to him a divine revelation, 352. The divine oversight of the world to him arbitrary and moral, 353. His courage more conspicuous than his meekness, 354. Thoroughness of his ethical methods, 355. Purity of his character, 356. His chaste ideas of marriage, 356. The highest modern conceptions of love not wholly the fruit of Christianity, 359. His rigorous rule of repression of anger, 360. Not himself true to it in his treatment of the Pharisees, 360. General upright character and salutary influence of the Pharisees, 362. Testimony of Paul, 363; of Josephus, 363. Early prejudice of Jesus against the Pharisees, 364. How it increased and expressed itself before his arrest, 366. Justice of his invectives, 367. Stress laid by him, in his *later* teaching, on faith and discipleship, rather than on righteousness, 369. His early and his later delineation of the day of judgment and the grounds of its sentences, 369. His indifference to common men, his antipathy to the heathen, 371. Character of Jesus to be studied, not in its typical and prophetic ideal, but in its historic significance, 373. His benevolence, 374. Capricious and propagandist exercise of the miraculous power attributed to him, 376. His reproach of Peter, and imprecation against the fig-tree, 377. His expectation of a *kingdom of heaven* not realized, 378. He inspired a new religion, 379. His religion and himself compared with the other great religions, and the men who revealed them, 380.

CHAPTER XII.

LEGEND OF THE RESURRECTION, 382-426.

Best supported by evidence of all the miracles, 382. Two distinct explanations of the resurrection in the New Testament, 384. Great stress laid by the Galilean tradition on disappearance of the body, 385. Grave differences in the attending circumstances as told by the evangelists, 385. They all insist that the appearances of Jesus were material, 386. The more spiritual conception of Paul, 387. The Pauline idea of the resurrection explained, 389. Its inconsistencies, 390. Events following the death of Jesus; his burial, and the visits to the tomb, 393. Who visited it, at what time, what did they see and hear? substantial discrepancies in the report, 394. The communication by angels, as told by Matthew, by Mark, by Luke, 395. The Galilean and the Judaic tradition, origin of each, 396. Did Jesus after his death show himself alive to any *man* at Jerusalem? 399. Did he show himself to Mary Magdalene or to any woman? 399. The showing of Jesus to the two travellers to Emmaus, 401. The showing of Jesus to his disciples in Galilee, 403. Fatal differences in the accounts of it, 404. Immense consequence of Jesus' last words, and improbability of their being forgotten, 404. Entire disagreement in form and substance in the three evangelical narrations, 405. Legal effect of such difference in the probative character of the testimony illustrated by a verbal will devising property, 405. The message, as told by each evangelist, recapitulated and considered, 407. How local prejudices among the disciples affected the report, 408. How the story of the resurrection gathered details in the telling by the evangelists, 408. Further details given in *Acts*, 409. Paul's account, 410. Singular failure of the early Christians to agree about the manner of the resurrection or the communications of Jesus, 410. Summing up of the five different accounts, 411. Cross-examination distasteful to uncritical minds, 412. A resurrection not in the apparent plan of Jesus, 412. Did he foretell it? 413. Explanation of the sign of Jonas, 414. If he had foretold his resurrection, it would have been expected by his disciples, as it evidently was not, 415. Vapidity of ghostly messages, 416. Those ascribed to Jesus not an exception, 418. The substance of the message was that the gospel was to be preached to all nations, 420. The early Christians disclosed that they knew nothing about any such message, 420. In the case of the centurion Cornelius, 420. In the controversy about admitting the heathen to the promises of the gospel, 421. Singularity of the opinions attributed to Jesus after his death, 423. His doctrine of baptism, 423. Of the Trinity, 423. Different schools of believers have injected their favorite dogmas into communications ascribed to Jesus after his death, 424. What was real in the resurrection of Jesus, 425.

CHAPTER XIII.

INFLUENCE ON HISTORIC CHRISTIANITY OF PAUL AND JOHN, 427-471.

Much of what is called Christianity the accretion of thought of the Christian ages, 427. Primitive Christianity to be studied in its scriptures, 428. The Synoptic Gospels unauthorized reports of unlearned men, 429. Primitive Christianity found, after Jesus, two men of marked ability to construct and propagate it,— Paul and the author of the Fourth Gospel, 429. In the expected crisis, no adequate provision made to record the life or sayings of Jesus, 430. Paul,— his ability, training, and mental and moral traits, 431. His genius, as disclosed in his speeches and letters, 431. Epistle to Romans his body of theology, 432. His speculations upon the resurrection, 432. His homily upon charity, 433. Two fragments of his speeches preserved in Acts, 434. His defects, 435. His false philosophy and bad logic, 435. His Jewish narrowness, 436. How he fitted the personality of Jesus to his scheme of the divine providence, 437. Paul the author of the Christian theology, 437. His scheme essentially Jewish, 438. Exalting Jesus to Heaven, he takes his place on earth as teacher of the Church, 438. His courage and love of leadership illustrated by his shipwreck, 439. Summary of the Pauline theology, 441. Paul did not learn of Jesus, 441. How he varied the ethical teachings of Jesus, 442. His attitude toward the State, 442; toward the rich, 442. He supplemented the teachings of Jesus, 442. Jesus a recluse and iconoclast, Paul a man of the world and compromiser, 443. Paul's ideas of woman and of marriage, 445. Advantage he gained over Jesus by getting into literature, 445. His influence, thwarted by the *pillar apostles*, revives after his death, 446. Greatly dominant in Protestantism and since its rise, 446. With Paul's interpretation alone, Christianity a barren dogmatism, 446. A man of mystic insight and capable of poetic emotion required to give it impulse, and found in so-called John, 447. Purpose of Fourth Gospel didactic and not historic, 448. A development of Pauline ideas, 448. Not written by John the apostle, 449. Its eschatology unlike that of the Synoptics, 451. It composed controversies among the Christians, 452. More than Paul, the writer idealized Jesus, 453, 454. Like Paul, he apologizes for the Pharisees, 454. Vividness of its descriptions, 455. Deficiency of its dramatic power, 455. Defects of its style. Superfluous statements; instances given, 456.

Vulgar expletives,—instances given, 457. Quite foreign to the manner of Jesus, 457. Irrelevant and inconsequential reasons given for statements; instances, 458 Mixed metaphors; instances, 459. The writer incapable of true allegory, 459. Rudeness of language; instances, 459. Paucity of ideas and wealth of sentiment, 460. The writer quite capable of the best thoughts he imputes to Jesus; instances, 461. If Jesus said what the Fourth Gospel reports, he could not have uttered the Sermon on the Mount and the parables, 461. Theologic and philosophic ideas of Fourth Gospel, 462. Circumstances that enhanced its reputation, 463. A parallel in Shakspeare's dramatic "Henry VIII.," 465. It presents the heart of Jesus, 466. It was in the New Scriptures what the Psalms were in the Old. The author the forerunner of the mystics, 467. His work a free-handling of the annals of the Synoptics,—the beginning of all the rehabilitations of Christ, 468. Jesus the fountain-head of Christianity, Paul and John its two great rivers, Tigris and Euphrates, 468. Their methods to be adopted rather than their conclusions, 469. The form of Christian doctrine must not cramp the Christian spirit, 469. Christianity interrogated on the side of intelligence and of morality. It must answer wisely on both sides, or give place to a gospel that can answer, 470, 471.

PREFACE.

It had been for many years a cherished purpose of the writer of the following chapters to examine, without prejudice or prepossession, the authentic documents in which are found the traditions of the origin of Christianity, and to ascertain what they indicate in reference to the character, opinions, and controlling purposes of Jesus. Engrossing occupation in professional employments, while requiring the postponement of the undertaking, better qualified for its successful performance, by knowledge acquired of the most approved methods of analyzing and formulating evidence, and of determining its probability and strength and the conclusions of fact which it compelled. The leisure of the last few years brought to the writer the opportunity to attempt the realization of a task which may perhaps be deemed beyond the scope of his scholarship and critical powers.

The many books upon the same subject that have appeared within the last few years in this country and in other countries, where thought is active and free, indicate that, so far from being exhausted, the life of Jesus has only begun to be studied. Most of these books have been written with the purpose, more or less confessed, of strengthening and confirming the devout prepossessions by which they were inspired. Of the fewer of them written in a historic spirit, and regarding Jesus, his character, teachings, and influence as normal developments of a civilization that has advanced, not only by steady growth, but by strong impulses given to it by the incursion of great men and the spring-tide of great epochs, some have been marred by lack of method in their study and of consistency and probability in the character they have delineated; some by arbitrary marshalling of the traditions to support a fanciful mythical theory; and still others by the confession, everywhere virtually expressed in them, that the barren compliment of sentimental adulation was to be offered to a dethroned Deity in compensation for degrading him from the height of worship where reason had ceased to recognize him.

What seemed to be called for was a judicial and critical study of the traditions of Jesus, which should find, in the nobleness of his character and in the peculiar national sentiments of the race to which he belonged, a reason for the daring ambition that drove him to the accomplishment of his destiny; which should explain how a new religion, the element of excellence and permanence in which was its system of esoteric ethics, should have subjected its author, through the general disaffection of his countrymen, to a premature and cruel death, and what peculiar conditions of the world and what co-operating agency of kindred minds contributed to give new vitality to that religion, after it had been, apparently, overthrown by his murder and the scattering of his disciples. If the present attempt has to any extent outlined a chief person of human history, the incidents and issue of whose life flowed naturally, as other men's do, from the force of his character and the direction of his activity, whose dominant idea once understood gives a general consistency and symmetry to all his ideas and to all his conduct, some approach has been made to the naked veracity of history, even if men like Matthew Arnold, to whom what is rational and intelligible seems to be suspicious, should satirize the method as "*rigorous and vigorous.*"

The range of investigation, though narrow, is fairly within the scope of the inquiry undertaken, it having been confessed by the most accomplished scholars, that there is next to nothing that can throw light upon the character and work of Jesus outside the canon of received Scripture. Nearly all the discussions, from a rationalistic point of view, of the supernatural phenomena asserted to have produced or attended the introduction into the world of the Christian faith, have impugned, to a greater or less degree, the trustworthiness and credibility of the Christian documents. The genuineness of those documents has been assailed and their imputed authorship denied, whereby the evidence which they contain has been degraded from the first hand testimony of eye-and-ear witnesses of the events they undertake to narrate to the second or third hand report of what artful partisans have heard others say.

The writer of these papers — beginning with the assumption that the Christian documents are authentic and a *bona fide* setting forth of the career of Jesus, as it was believed by the writers of them to have occurred, and that the question of authorship, arising, as it does, between Matthew, Mark, and Luke, and certain later adherents of Jesus unknown, but not a whit less obscure, illiterate, or unauthorized, is a question of secondary importance — has set himself to the task of ascertaining what the documents themselves seem fairly to prove.

His method of procedure was to draw up, by reference to the original texts of the Synoptical Gospels, every declaration reported to have been made by Jesus during his life, together with such of the *res gestae* as might be considered, along with his language, as expository of his thought. After an exhaustive list of these had been accumulated in the order of their narration, an attempt was made to classify and arrange them by subjects, placing in the same category whatever Jesus was believed to have said upon each special subject, or that might seem legitimately to relate to it. Finally, a finding or summing up — such as is imposed upon the judicial mind in determining, from a mass of notes of oral testimony or of documents and papers, what are the facts upon which, under the proper rules of law, the rights of litigants are to be determined — was undertaken, and a statement drawn up of what Jesus seemed to have believed and taught.

The only prepossession the writer is aware of in approaching the study of which these chapters are the record is that the great, dominant purpose of Jesus was to proclaim and prepare for the kingdom of heaven, although the nature of that kingdom and when it was to be expected to begin only became apparent after a complete review of the testimony. Upon all other points, the writer confesses he had no prepossession, and was himself, in many ins'ances, surprised at results that contradicted the prejudices in which he had been educated, though his later reading has shown him how widely these conclusions have been arrived at by other minds and how little claim he has to any priority of discovery.

At the very outset, the alternative presented itself between the validity of the Fourth Gospel and that of the other three. All attempt at reconciliation and harmony of the two conflicting narratives, for reasons fully set forth in the text, was necessarily abandoned. In electing to follow, generally, the statements of the three witnesses and to discredit the one, the writer believes he has followed not only the judgment of the most conscientious and competent scholars, but complied with one of the fundamental canons of the law of evidence.

So far as any criticism or adverse judgment has been ventured in reference to what seemed to have been the opinions of Jesus,— especially as to the speedy end of the world, to the incompatibility of property with personal salvation, and of marriage with the perfection of righteousness, as to indiscriminate almsgiving, to absolute non-resistance, to the hostility of political society to the order of the kingdom of heaven,— it is no personal criticism or private judgment: it is, rather, the deliberate judgment of Christendom against Christ. It is the sober second thought of the educated and fully developed age in reference to the enthusiasms and overfaith of the mind that introduced it.

The following propositions in reference to Jesus, believed to have been established by the investigation, may be considered as well verified as any events of ancient history. They are stated in the order of the validity and cumulation of the proofs upon which they stand : —

1. There lived in the beginning of the present era, in Palestine, in Syria, a teacher, prophet, and holy man, from whom the great world-religion, called Christianity, is named; and who, though not the author of its prominent ideas and doctrines nor the inventor of its dogmatic form, was, in some sense, its inspirer and source. He was put to death by his countrymen, who mainly rejected his personal claims and repudiated his peculiar doctrines.

2. He believed and taught that the end of the world, both as to its internal economy and physical constitution, was impending; and that, after his own death, which, if he did not provoke, he took no pains to avert, he would return to establish on the ruins of the old order a new kingdom of the righteous to endure forever.

3. He taught the blessedness of poverty, the incompatibility of wealth with the spiritual well-being of mankind, and that to enter the kingdom of heaven men must forsake and surrender their possessions, and forego all care for their physical existence.

The first of these propositions is based upon the concurrent testimony of the four extant written versions of the original tradition published somewhere after the year 55 and before the year 180 of the Christian era, upon the extant writings of the first Christian missionaries of whom Paul is the best known: it is asserted in secular history, and the reputation of it would have survived to our times without any mention in history.

The second proposition has all the same supports, except that secular history takes no notice of it; and its tradition is only preserved among obscure sects.

The third proposition, maintained in the most reliable traditions, is not supported by the Fourth Gospel nor by the adhesion of Paul, though the other apostolic writings, emphatically that imputed to James, affirm it.

The following propositions, not absolutely verified, are fairly probable and only deniable by a severe and rigorous scepticism : —

1. Jesus taught rules of personal conduct requiring, among other things, universal and indiscriminate beneficence, the absolute forgiveness and sufferance of injuries, simplicity and directness of

speech, avoidance of censoriousness, chastity and self-denial to the point of extirpation of natural instincts, and the repression of ambition.

These rules, however, are given with fundamental discrepancies in but two of the Gospels, and are wholly omitted in the other two. It is not certain that they are quoted in any of the writings of the apostles, whose rules and sanctions for personal conduct are somewhat different. Finally, they were not always conformed to by Jesus himself.

2. He had a certain power of allaying and curing mental maladies and those physical disabilities resulting from impaired nervous action. The great miracles of raising the dead, multiplying food and wine, walking on the sea, and whatever else is imputed to him outside the known scope of human powers, are not proved, on account of the material variances in the testimony of the evangelists concerning them; of the settled *consensus of the competent* to reject all miracles, when told in connection with other religions or as occurring in any age later than the first century, upon testimony more concurrent and trustworthy than that upon which the New Testament miracles have been believed; and on account of the feeble and doubtful confirmation they receive from the apostolic writers, and of the impossibility that the Jewish people, or any people, could have contemptuously rejected and cruelly slain a person who had, in their sight or knowledge, done such awe-inspiring works of divine power. On the other hand, some mysterious power must be attributed to Jesus to account for the influence he had over a certain class of simple and illiterate men, not likely to be attracted by the uncompromising severity of his ethical doctrines.

3. He did not originate nor give any special stress to the doctrine of personal immortality. It was believed in by the leading classes of his people and by the nations of Asia and Africa ages before his time; and the details of the life of men after death are given with much more minuteness and vividness by Paul, who never heard Jesus, than by Jesus himself. His scheme of a future life was swallowed up in his scheme of an impending kingdom of heaven.

4. As to the doctrines of the trinity of the Godhead, the complete and natural depravity of man as such, the condemnation of the human race for the sin of the first created pair, the expiation of the sins of those who believe in Jesus by the divinely appointed sacrifice of the Son of God, though germs of such ideas appear in the apostolic writings and later in the Fourth Gospel, they are nowhere discoverable in any accredited sayings of Jesus.

CHAPTER I.

SOURCES OF EVIDENCE.

"We must look for the apostolic root of the whole movement in the Synoptical Gospels, and more especially in those of Matthew and Mark; for Luke already betrays an approach to the Catholic tendencies of Paul. Here, we get the truest idea of Christ and his works as historical verities."— *John James Tayler.*

NEARLY nineteen hundred years ago there appeared in Galilee, a province of Palestine, then subject to Rome, a man whose teaching and character, aided by certain adventitious circumstances, powerfully affected the human race, and opened a new epoch in its history. After he became famous, it was claimed for him that he was a lineal descendant of David and the early Jewish kings; but the genealogies given in two of his brief biographies are too contradictory in their details to establish the royal lineage of Joseph,— a fact of no account, as those biographies maintain that Joseph was not his father. The imputation of his parentage to the Holy Ghost is robbed of its grossness, when it is considered that it was the effort of a reverent imagination to account for the phenomenon, by no means rare in human history, of a man born into the world whose grandeur of genius transcends all the apparent capabilities of his ancestors.

The name which he has given to history was Christ; but that Greek title, which obtained among his followers, seems to have been little used in his lifetime, he being known in his family and among his people as Jesus,[a] which signifies Saviour, but which is the same name as Joshua, and, like other words indiscriminately used to designate indifferent individuals, would soon lose in the popular apprehension all association with ideas. He seems to have belonged to quite a large family[b] among the artisan classes, and, until he assumed the character

[a] Matt. 1., 25.   [b] Mark vi., 3.

of prophet, is said to have followed his father's vocation of
a carpenter. The amazement which his wisdom excited
in the popular mind was increased by an impression that
he was illiterate, and had never been taught to read.[a]
Whether this were so or not, a devout Jew, brought up
in attendance upon the weekly reading and explaining of
the Jewish law, ritual, and history in the synagogue, is not
to be considered uneducated.

His whole career, after he emerged from the industrious
obscurity of his early manhood, is not claimed to cover a
period of more than three years; and the events of authentic occurrence, which are told in a consecutive order
in what are called the Synoptic Gospels, might all have
occurred, and apparently did all occur, in a single year.

What Jesus was, what he thought and believed, what
he taught, and what he did in that brief career, the whole
world are intensely eager to know. And, to satisfy this
intense craving, it has recourse mainly to three brief
histories, which, so far as they agree, seem to have been
copied from each other, the authorship of which is doubt-
fully imputed to obscure persons, whose relation to Jesus
is so remote, and whose authority to publish his faith is
so questionable, that everything in them, probable even
in itself, must be read with misgiving as to its actual
occurrence.

There is a fourth biography, imputed to a confidential
friend and disciple of Jesus; but this gives us a character
and history so wholly different from the other three, that,
instead of throwing light upon a subject already obscure,
it enhances the doubt and perplexity that surround it.

Mohammed and Confucius carefully committed to writing a summary of their respective doctrines. Socrates,
coming in an enlightened age and among an enlightened
people, was happy in the discipleship of two cultivated
men, Plato and Xenophon, who gave to the world the
different phases of his philosophy. Even Sakya Mouni
was more fortunate than Jesus, in that he finished his
career, and lived to see his ideas practically adopted by
great communities of men, and to give his own sanction
to the teachings of disciples. But Jesus was interrupted
by a violent death in nearly the beginning of a prophetic

[a] John vii, 15; Luke iv., 22.

course; nor does he seem to have had in his mind a completed system of religion and philosophy, such as Christianity, as it came to be developed in the hands of his followers. It will be necessary to discover, if it can be done by a careful study of his ideas, why no other provision was made for an authorized exposition of his doctrines than the volunteer biographies imputed to Matthew, Mark, Luke, and John, and why the propagation of the gospel among the Gentiles was intrusted to the apostle, who never had seen Jesus alive, and who, in all his writings, has scarcely mentioned any of the incidents of his life.

The personality of Jesus seems to have made but little impression upon Paul. He is to Paul not so much an historical person as a celestial *functionary*, performing an office, mainly through the efficacy of his death and blood, in the accomplishment of the salvation of the elect. The crowning fact, all the fact deemed worthy of consideration by the dogmatic apostle, is the resurrection; and, upon that fact, he predicates the whole scheme of a new *cultus* and a new order of the universe. Accordingly, we fail to find in any of Paul's writings the remotest allusion to any wonders of healing or other miracle-working done by Jesus, or to any of his acts of human charity and beneficence. The sententious and striking utterances by which Jesus was wont to command the ready attention of men everywhere, the vivid imagination which enabled him to embody, in allegories and parables, a metaphysical idea or a didactic lesson, are never quoted nor imitated. And though, like Jesus, Paul develops a system of ethics, and gives minute directions as to outward conduct and the control and development of the interior temper, his system is, in form and substance, unlike that of Jesus, and not only contradicts it in fundamental respects, but is based upon different sanctions.

Equally unsatisfactory is our search through the other apostolic Epistles to find definite data, out of which to complete our picture of the personal traits of Jesus or the incidents of his life. If these writings are properly attributed to Peter, James, and John, his trusted disciples and kinsfolk, this absence is quite remarkable. Paul, a Jew, born in Tarsus in Cilicia, but brought up in Jerusalem,— who does not claim to have seen Jesus, except after his death, in a vision, writing, when the memorabilia of Jesus, now embodied in the Gospels, were only traditions communicated from one believer to another,— might have chosen to ignore all those traditions. He seems even to have done it studiedly and with a purpose. The spiritual Christ, in his fervid soul, had so overshadowed the Christ after the flesh, that he did not care to recur to an image which had become to him carnal, earthly, and temporal. But why should not Peter and John and James, if they were indeed the authors of the canonical Epistles attributed to them, have given us some of the impressions, which intimate association with a presence so attractive as their great Master's was must have made upon their vivid memories? Why, using copiously the words and deeds of patriarchs and prophets to illustrate in their sermons and letters the lessons they taught the new Church, did they so nearly omit the acts and sayings of Jesus himself, so much more edifying and authoritative for the same purposes? Paul, indeed, alludes to the ceremony of the symbolical eating of bread and wine enjoined by Jesus, and imputes to him words not differing so much from those reported in the Third Gospel as they differ from those reported in the First and Second Gospels.[a] James gives with emphasis the prohibition of all oaths and of all indirectness of speech, in phraseology like the Sermon on the Mount, but strangely omits to enforce the lesson by attributing the prohibition to Jesus.[b] The writer of the Second Epistle of Peter[c] corroborates the account given in the Synoptic Gospels of the voice from heaven, to affirm the divine origin of Jesus upon the mount of transfiguration. But, when the writer of the First Epistle of Peter[d] has occasion to cite the example of Jesus to be followed by his disciples, instead of giving his own recollections of what he had seen or heard, or any tradition of him that afterward found place in the Gospels, he contents himself with a prophetic sketch derived from the Old Testament, supposed to foreshadow his functions as a Redeemer. In the First Epistle imputed to John are repeated several of the declarations which the same

[a] I. Cor. xi., 24, 25.   [b] James v., 12.
[c] II. Peter i., 17, 18.   [d] I. Peter ii., 22-24.

writer as an evangelist imputes to Jesus; but this identity has another import, to be considered hereafter.

In the narrative called the Acts of the Apostles, purporting to be the production of the writer of the Third Gospel, we should naturally look for some vivid pictures of the human life of Jesus. But there, as in the Epistles, we find Christ in his office of mediator, intercessor between man and God, and bringer of salvation from sin and eternal life to those who believed on him, rather than Jesus the man, the teacher, disclosing new conceptions of the relations of man to God, reinforcing virtue by new motives and sanctions, and prescribing for conduct a wider and deeper conformity to an ideal righteousness. As in the Epistles, the great stress is laid upon the efficacy of his blood and death, and the vindication by his resurrection of a power effectual to the salvation of all believers.

Peter indeed, on the occasion when the new believers assembled together on Pentecost day were kindled with an enthusiasm that seemed so marvellous to themselves, speaks thus to the people of the man they had a few days before scornfully rejected and crucified: "Ye men of Israel, hear these words: Jesus of Nazareth, a man approved of God among you by miracles, wonders, and signs, which God did by him in the midst of you, as ye yourselves also know: him being delivered by the determinate counsel and foreknowledge of God, ye have taken, and by wicked hands have crucified and slain."[a] In this declaration, the manhood of Jesus is emphasized, and his miracles are spoken of as done through him by God. Later, welcoming to the hopes of Christianity the devout Roman soldier Cornelius, the same apostle asserts that Jesus of Nazareth was anointed by God "with the Holy Ghost and with power"; that he "went about doing good, and healing all that were oppressed of the devil"; and that he, Peter, and his fellow-disciples are witnesses of all the things which Jesus did in the land of the Jews and in Jerusalem.[b]

Paul is represented as quoting, in an address to the Jews at Antioch, John Baptist's testimony, that Jesus was greater than he.[c] Exhorting the converts at Ephesus to be diligent in laboring, that they may have some-

[a] Acts ii., 22, 23.   [b] Acts x., 38, 39.   [c] Acts xiii., 35.

thing to support the weak, he reminds them of a saying he imputes to Jesus, though none of the Gospels report it,—"It is more blessed to give than to receive."[a]

Of Jesus, it was said that he spake as one having authority, and not as the scribes ; and the evangelist represents him as speaking of the fundamental precepts of the Mosaic law in the decalogue as traditions of them of old time, and either false or inadequate. But his disciples, including even the bold and eloquent Paul, speak of Jesus in an apologetic tone, and scarcely mention his acts and never his distinctive words. Doubtless, they were compelled by the hostile prejudices and inveterate bigotry of the Jews to find for Jesus a place in the Hebrew dispensation as its supplement or fulfilment, and to claim faith in him rather on the score of prophetic foreshadowing of his character and office than for his living work and words. Believing, as they did at first, that the gospel which Jesus brought was for the Jews, they everywhere appealed to the Hebrew Scriptures as setting forth his character, his death, and his resurrection, and asserted that the kingdom which he was coming with his angels to establish on earth was the consummation which Israel had been for ages waiting for. This strictly national and sectarian aspect in which his immediate followers seem everywhere, in this fragment of the Acts of the Apostles, to have presented the phenomenon of Jesus, is not a complete negation of the stupendous acts and the new ideas which the evangelists impute to him ; but it is an unmistakable index of how little impression those acts and ideas had at that time made upon the multitudes that dwelt in Judea and Jerusalem, and upon the Jewish communities scattered through the Greek cities.

When we come to the gospel narratives as sources of information concerning the history and character of Jesus, we are met at the outset with the general similarity and concurrence of the first three and the independent and conflicting details of the last.

The author of the Fourth Gospel does not mention the birth of Jesus or any incident of his life earlier than his baptism by John. He calls him Jesus of Nazareth,[b] and speaks of Joseph as his father, Mary as his mother, and

[a] Acts xx., 35.   [b] John i , 45, 46.

names his brothers. According to this writer, John the Baptist was baptizing in Bethany, a place somewhere upon the eastern side of the river Jordan in the wilderness or wooded country about its banks, when Jesus came first to him. The following day, John saw Jesus again walking, and pointed him out to those who were with him as the Lamb of God, upon which testimony two men, one of them Andrew, one of the twelve apostles, attached themselves to Jesus as disciples. Andrew immediately procured his brother Simon, afterward famous as Peter, to join the new prophet also. The day following, Jesus went into Galilee. So that it is fairly inferrible that this first sight of Jesus by John and this adhesion of two chief apostles happened in the wilderness country beyond Jordan and somewhere between the Sea of Galilee and the Dead Sea. Nathaniel, who with Philip became his disciple, on his return to Galilee calls him Jesus of Nazareth; and his residence in that city seemed well enough known in the neighboring cities to give him a special identity among the many persons of the Jewish race, who in all that region bore the very common name of Jesus.[a]

Returning to Galilee from the Jordan wilderness, Jesus next appears as a wedding guest at a marriage in the city of Cana, at which his mother and probably his brothers were also present. There, it is told of him that, when the wine failed, he miraculously changed water into wine of such excellent quality that the governor of the feast specially complimented it, while reminding the bridegroom that a poorer article would have complied with all the requirements of custom in the latter stages of the drinking.[b] Then, the narrator affirms, " This beginning of miracles did Jesus in Cana of Galilee, and manifested forth his glory; and his disciples believed on him."[c] As disciples, they have hitherto believed in him as a prophet. Henceforth, he is to them the representative and Son of God,— the Christ who was to come. From Cana, in company with his mother and brothers, he came to Capernaum, but continued there not many days. The Jewish passover being at hand, Jesus went up to Jerusalem, and expelled from the temple those who were there according

[a] John i., 28, 35-42, 45.   [b] John ii., 1-10.   [c] John ii., 11, 13-17, 23.

to wont and to a permission of the Mosaic law to sell
beasts and birds for temple sacrifices to the worshippers
coming from a distance. While at Jerusalem on the feast
day, it is asserted that he did miracles and gained many
disciples. This statement is confirmed by Nicodemus, a
leading Pharisee, who during this first visit to Jerusalem
visits Jesus by night, and opens the conversation by
avowing that "no man can do these miracles that thou
doest, except God be with him."[a] After these things,—
that is, after the coming to Jerusalem to the passover,
the casting out of the money-changers from the temple,
the unnamed miracles at Jerusalem, which had gained
disciples and attracted Nicodemus to him,— Jesus goes
from Jerusalem into the country of Judea apparently eastward and northward; for he goes to Enon [b] on the Galilean
border of the Jordan. And although it is asserted that
they, Jesus and his disciples, were baptized there, the
whole testimony of the evangelist fairly implies that only
the disciples were baptized, Jesus having been baptized
before; for John Baptist had testified that he was the
Lamb of God, while asserting that he knew that only
from the fact, that the dove had lit upon him at his baptism, which must thus have already taken place.

Following the slender thread of narrative with which
the writer of the Fourth Gospel illustrates his monologue
of Jesus, we learn next that Jesus pursued his northward
journey through Samaria to Galilee,[c] holding a remarkable conversation with a woman at Jacob's well. Here,
he exercised a power of thought-reading or divination,
such as is claimed by modern spiritualists; for he told the
woman incidents of her past domestic life not altogether
reputable, and gained not only from her, but from her
friends, the reputation of being a prophet.[d]

Two days later, Jesus comes to Galilee, where he is represented as, up to that time, not being of any great
repute. But it is told that the Galileans received him, or
accepted him, not on the score of anything done among
them, but *having seen all the things that he did at Jerusalem at the feast, for the Galileans also went unto the
feast.*[e] This declaration accords perfectly with what had

[a] John iii., 2.   [b] John iii., 22, 23.   [c] John iv., 3-5, 16-19.
[d] John iv., 39.   [e] John iv., 45.

been told previously. He had done but one miracle in Galilee, the vinifaction of the water at the wedding, which was unknown to all but the servants; and Jesus' impatient exclamation to his mother implies that he wished to have this miracle concealed. But he had done conspicuous miracles in Jerusalem. To make this more explicit, the evangelist proceeds to tell the healing of the nobleman's sick son in [a] Capernaum ; and then, to do exact and numerical justice to Galilee, as the theatre of the works of the great prophet,— about which, it is easy to believe, there were dissensions among the believers, each party claiming distinction for their own country,— he adds these words : "*This is again the second miracle that Jesus did, when he was come out of Judea into Galilee.*" [b]

After this the occurring of another Jewish feast,[c] the passover brought Jesus again to Jerusalem, and there he healed a lame man lying at the pool of Bethesda [d] on the Sabbath day. Although he was at first obliged to hide himself from the Jews, who threatened punishment for a violation of the Sabbath, he reappeared, showed himself in the temple, boldly avowed his act, appealed to the works which he had done as the credentials of a divine mission, and told the Jews that, if they really believed Moses, they would believe in him, for that Moses had foretold him.[e]

He next returns to Galilee, and in the neighborhood of the Sea of Tiberias so multiplies a few loaves of bread and two fishes that they feed to satisfaction five thousand people.[f] The multitude who saw this miracle believed that he was the prophet promised to their nation. In their enthusiasm, they wanted to make him a king ; but he withdrew into a mountain,[g] and the night following, walking on the surface of the sea, rejoined his disciples, who had embarked to row to Capernaum across the lake, and terrifying them with the fear that he was a spirit. We are next told of a discourse he held, suggested by the miraculous feeding in the synagogue at Capernaum, with the people who had followed him from the other side of the lake.[h] In the face of the palpable miracle, they

---

[a] John iv., 46. [b] John iv., 54. [c] John v., 1.
[d] John v., 9, 10. [e] John v., 36-46. [f] John vi., 10-13.
[g] John vi., 15, 19. [h] John vi., 25.

demand a sign ; and he tells them he is the manna of heaven [a] sent down to give them life. Many, who had been his disciples here, turned from him ; and he expressed doubts about the fidelity of the twelve.[b]

He avoided visiting Jerusalem for some days after his disciples went thither to the Feast of the Tabernacles and tarried in Galilee ; [c] and it is told that, even after these four Galilean miracles, his brothers did not believe in him.[d] In the midst of the feast, which lasted several days, Jesus himself appeared in Jerusalem, and taught openly in the temple.[e] It was notorious that the leading Jews sought his life. He himself had avoided Jerusalem for fear of them ; and the only reason the writer gives why his enemies did not take him, when he appeared among them, was that his time was not yet come.[f] He is represented as making some impression upon the people of the chief city by this discourse, since many asserted that he must be the Messiah ; but to the assertion of the orthodox Jews, that there was no Scripture warrant for receiving a Galilean as a Messiah, it was nowhere, by any adherents, maintained that he was in fact born in Bethlehem,[g] nor is such fact ever asserted by this biographer.

It is next related that Jesus went to the Mount of Olives, but returned early in the morning to the temple, where, after he had released from her accusers the woman taken in adultery, he held another discussion with the Pharisees, in which he gave offence to some of the Jews who believed on him by telling them that they were not the children of Abraham, but the children of the devil. The Jews became so exasperated at his claim, as they understood it, to have been contemporary with Abraham, that they were about to stone him; and he hid himself, and escaped from the temple.[h] On his way, Jesus met a blind man, and restored his sight. As this was done on the Sabbath, many Jews insisted that Jesus was not of God; but others asked, How can a man that is a sinner do miracles ?[i] The colloquy with the Jews proceeded ; and the time and place are given as in Solomon's porch of the temple, and in winter time. It thus appears that

[a] John vi., 32, 41.   [b] John vi., 60, 64.   [c] John vii., 1, 2.
[d] John vii., 5.   [e] John vii., 10, 14.   [f] John vii., 25, 26, 30, 31.
[g] John vii., 42, 52.   [h] John viii., 1, 2, 11, 31, 33, 44, 50, 59.   [i] John ix., 1, 6, 7, 16.

Jesus had come to Jerusalem in the midst of the Feast of Tabernacles, which was in October, and had remained there till winter.[a] But now, being again in danger of arrest, he betook himself to the Jordan wilderness, where John at first baptized.[b] Some indefinite time after, it must have been a short time,— for the disciples speak of these attempts of the Jews to stone him as events of late occurrence,— Jesus again comes into Judea,[c] and at Bethany performs the miracle of raising from the dead — in the presence of his sisters and many Jews, their friends who had come from Jerusalem to condole with them — the man Lazarus, who had been four days buried. The effect of this miracle in winning converts among the Jews was said to have been so great that the chief priests and Pharisees in council feared he would seduce the nation from its allegiance to Cæsar, and bring on a war that would destroy it; and, from that time, they studiedly plotted the death of Jesus.[d] The catastrophe was avoided by his withdrawal to the city of Ephraim, in the neighborhood of the wilderness, and within the limits of Samaria, where he stayed with his disciples.

Now approached again the Feast of the Passover, which occurred in April. There had been three of these annual feasts during the public career of Jesus; and he had not failed to be present in Jerusalem at any of them, besides going up in the autumn of the previous year to the Feast of the Tabernacles. His coming to these feasts was so well known that the people speculated whether the known purpose of the Pharisees to compass his death would induce him to break a punctilious habit. He came, however, but evidently depressed with a manifest foreboding of his death. When Mary, whose brother Lazarus he had restored to life, anointed his feet with a costly ointment, he said it was for his burial.[e] Many Jews believed on him, on account of the miracle of Lazarus; and, on his riding into the city, they met him with palm-branches and shoutings of Hosanna to the king of Israel.[f] The people that had seen Lazarus resuscitated testified of the fact; and the Pharisees, in despair, exclaimed that they prevailed not at all against him, and that the whole world

[a] John x., 22, 23.   [b] John x., 39, 40.   [c] John xi., 7, 8.
[d] John xi., 17, 43-45, 47, 48, 55, 56.   [e] John xii., 7, 8.   [f] John xii., 9, 12, 13.

was gone after him.[a] This success did not reassure him. The shadow of coming death broods over his spirit, and gives an indescribable pathos to all his last acts and words. He withdraws more and more to the society of his trusted disciples. After the feast, while they were yet seated, he rose, and, girding himself with a towel, with his own hands washed his disciples' feet,—as he assured them, to give them a lesson of humility and affectionate service.[b] He then proceeds to exhort them in those words of simple and touching eloquence which have been cherished and repeated with reverent gratitude, through eighteen centuries, by generations of devout disciples, as the affectionate expression of the divine compassion; and finally, having comforted and strengthened his followers by a memorable prayer, he submits to the soldiers, who, under the authority of the high priests, present themselves to his privacy, and hurry him away to his hasty trial and terrible death on the cross.[c]

Here is related a career covering the recurrence of three annual passovers, or more than two whole years, mainly passed in Judea and Jerusalem. It is said that Jesus made three visits to Galilee in that time; but it is denied that his abode in Capernaum, where Matthew asserts that he lived, continued for many days.[d] While in Galilee, he did the miracles of making water into wine, of healing the nobleman's son, of walking on the sea, and of feeding the five thousand people with five loaves and two fishes. Only the last of these was so public and indisputably supernatural as to coerce general attention; but, after them all, his own brothers did not believe his prophetic pretensions.[e] It is asserted that the Galileans, who believed on him, believed only on the report of miracles done in Judea[f] and Jerusalem. In the latter region, it is not only related that he did many miracles, which won converts, which were conceded by the people, and which the high priests who conspired against him did not deny, but that, with the utmost publicity and before many reputable Jews, he healed the impotent man at the pool of Bethesda, restored sight to one born blind in the neighborhood of the temple, and called Lazarus alive from

[a] John xii., 17–19.   [b] John xiii., 1–10.   [c] John xiv., xv., xvi., xvii., xviii.
[d] John ii., 12.   [e] John vii., 5.   [f] John iv., 45.

his grave, after he had been buried four days, in Bethany. Besides this, all his principal discourses, both with the people and his disciples, were at Jerusalem.

Turning to the narrative of Matthew, the history of Jesus appears to be as follows: He was born in Bethlehem in Judea, of Mary, betrothed but not yet married to her husband Joseph.[a] Herod, the king of Judea, instructed by a Hebrew prophecy of his advent, had all the children of Bethlehem murdered;[b] and the parents of the infant, under a warning in a dream, escaped into Egypt, and remained till Herod's death. Returning afterward, on learning that his brother Archelaus had succeeded Herod, they quitted Judea finally, and went to live in Nazareth in Galilee. There, the young child grew to manhood.[c] When John the Baptist appeared in the wilderness of Jordan,[d] Jesus went to him and was baptized; but, after John's imprisonment, he came into Galilee, and changed his residence from Nazareth to Capernaum.[e] Then, he went about all Galilee, teaching in the synagogues, announcing the kingdom of heaven at hand, and healing all manner of sickness and all manner of disease among the people. His fame went abroad throughout all Syria, and they brought to him *all* that were taken with divers diseases and torments, and those that were possessed of devils, and those that were lunatic, and those that had the palsy; and he healed them. And there followed him great multitudes of people from Galilee and from Decapolis and from Jerusalem and from Judea and from beyond Jordan.[f]

Seeing these multitudes, and apparently to avoid them, he went up into a mountain, and, seating himself, pronounced to his disciples the immortal Sermon on the Mount.[g] Coming down from the mountain, the multitude again beset him; and he cured a leprous man, that from the crowd invoked his power. Then, he came to his residence, Capernaum; and a centurion besought his aid for a servant sick of the palsy, and he healed him at a distance by his spoken word. He cured Peter's wife's mother of a fever; and, when it was even, they brought many persons possessed of devils to him, and he cast[h]

[a] Matt. i., 18. [b] Matt. ii., 16. [c] Matt. ii., 13, 14, 21–23. [d] Matt. iii., 13.
[e] Matt. iv., 13. [f] Matt. iv., 23–25. [g] Matt. v., 1, 2, 3. [h] Matt. v., 5, 13–16.

them out, and healed all that were sick. Passing across the Lake of Galilee, he was asleep while a storm arose which terrified his disciples; but, being aroused, he rebuked the storm, and a calm succeeded.[a] Arrived on the other side, he cast devils out of two possessed men; and, conjuring the dispossessed spirits into a herd of swine, the herd rushed into the lake and were drowned.[b] Coming back to his own city, he healed a palsied man, and held a colloquy with certain Pharisees, also with some of John's disciples.[c] While still speaking, a certain ruler came to ask his intervention in behalf of his daughter, who had apparently died; and he went and took her by the hand, and recalled her to life. On his way to the ruler's house, a woman diseased with an issue of blood obtained immediate relief by touching his garment as he passed.[d] The fame of the raised daughter of the ruler filled all the land. Going out of Capernaum, after having given sight to two blind men who followed him, and cast out a devil from a dumb man, he renewed his preaching the kingdom of heaven and teaching. He healed also of every sickness and every disease among the people, and obtained the following of a multitude of people.[e]

The next event in the career of Jesus, as told by Matthew, is the sending out of the twelve apostles. No other message is given them but to declare the kingdom of heaven at hand. Besides this, they are to heal the sick, cleanse the lepers, raise the dead, and cast out devils. They are to make no provision for their support, but to subsist upon the voluntary bounty of those who receive them. In giving them this commission, he exhorts them to boldness, and assures them that their fidelity shall be rewarded in the kingdom of heaven.[f]

After this sending out, Jesus himself went into the cities apparently of Galilee, to renew his preaching; and he is declared to have appealed for proofs of his Messiahship to the facts generally known, that the blind receive their sight, the lame walk, the lepers are cleansed, the deaf hear, and the dead are raised.[g] He also spoke of three Galilean cities, Capernaum, Chorazin, and Bethsaida, as distinguished above others as the theatre of many and

[a] Matt. viii., 23-27.   [b] Matt. viii., 28-34.   [c] Matt. ix., 1-7, 10-13, 14-17.
[d] Matt. ix., 20-26.   [e] Matt. ix., 35.   [f] Matt. x.   [g] Matt. xi., 1, 5.

conspicuous miracles.ᵃ On a certain Sabbath, he justified to the Pharisees the conduct of his disciples, in plucking and eating the growing corn,ᵇ and cured a man whose hand was withered.ᶜ The Pharisees deemed these acts unlawful, and sought to destroy him; and when Jesus disappeared, to avoid their machinations, the multitudes followed him, and he healed them all.ᵈ They brought to him a man possessed of a devil and dumb; and he cast out the devil, and the patient's speech returned to him.ᵉ He next went to the seaside, and from a ship told the multitude on the shore many parables, among them that of the sower and the seed, of the mustard-seed, of the leaven, of the hidden treasure, of the costly pearl, and of the net and the fish, all in illustration of his dominant idea of the kingdom of heaven. When he had finished these parables, he returned from his seclusion, apparently to his own city, Capernaum; and there he confessed that his prophetic claims had not been honored by his fellow-citizens, and refrained from doing many mighty works because of their want of faith in him.ᶠ

Now occurred the cruel death of John the Baptist, whom Herod had kept for some time in prison; and when Jesus heard of it, apparently under apprehensions for his own safety, he went by ship to a desert place apart, still followed it is said by the multitudes, and still exercising upon all their sick his wonderful gifts of healing.ᵍ In this desert place, where there were five thousand people unsupplied with food following him, if not with belief, with wonder, he performed the miracle of multiplying the five loaves and two fishes, and came walking on the sea to his disciples, who were in a ship, as told by the writer calling himself John. Sending the multitude away, Jesus came by ship to the east side of the Lake of Galilee, and there healed by the touch of his garment all the sick that came to him.ʰ Some Pharisees of Jerusalem now came to him; and he held a controversy with them about purification, insisting that defilement was a thing of the heart, and not the neglect of outward wash-

---

ᵃ Matt. xi., 20–23.   ᵇ Matt. xii., 1, 2, 3–8.   ᶜ Matt. xii., 10–13.
ᵈ Matt. xii., 14, 15.   ᵉ Matt. xii., 22.   ᶠ Matt. xiii., 54, 57, 58.
ᵍ Matt. xiv., 3, 10, 12, 13.   ʰ Matt. xiv., 15–21, 25, 34–36.

ing. After this, Jesus went into the coast of the old Phœnician cities, and not only healed the daughter of a Canaanite woman, but great numbers of lame, blind, dumb, maimed, and many others, to the amazement of the multitude. There, also, he repeated the miraculous feeding of a large company, who had been three days without food, upon seven loaves and a few little fishes.[a]

We next find Jesus on the coast of Magdala, a city on the Galilean lake, south of Capernaum. Some Pharisees and Sadducees there asked him to show a sign; and he told them no sign should be given them but the sign of Jonas, the prophet. At Cesarea Philippi, in the upper Jordan, he sounded his own disciples as to what they deemed him to be; and, after Peter had declared that he was Christ, the son of the living God,[b] he announced to them that he must go to Jerusalem, be killed there, and be raised the third day.[c] Six days afterward, Jesus withdrew into a mountain, with only Peter, James, and John; and there two angelic forms seemed to converse with him, and a voice out of the clouds declared him to be "*my beloved son.*" Returning to the multitude, he restores sanity to a lunatic. Still tarrying in Galilee, Jesus made his disciples exceeding sorrowful by renewing to them the prophecy of his delivery into the hands of men, his violent death, and his resurrection. He was, however, still at Capernaum, his own city, when the tribute was levied, which, after some hesitation, he concluded to pay. From this time, he appears to seek no longer the multitude, and to confine his teaching to the little band of his disciples. These he instructs, both by direct precept and by parable.[d]

Journeying now toward Jerusalem, he comes into the Jordan wilderness; and again the multitude resort to him, and he heals their sick. The Pharisees accost him with questions about divorce, and he gives to his disciples his ideas of the true relation of the sexes. The coming to him of the young rich man gives him an occasion to explain his ideas of the incompatibility of wealth and the kingdom of heaven.[e] He tells also the parable of the laborers in the vineyard.[f] Still going toward Jeru-

[a] Matt. xv., 17-20, 21-30, 37, 39.   [b] Matt. xvi., 4, 13, 16.   [c] Matt. xvi., 21.
[d] Matt. xvii., 1-8, 14, 18, 22-27.   [e] Matt. xix., 1-12, 16-30.   [f] Matt. xx., 1-16.

salem, the foreboding of his death growing stronger, he again, in the most direct and intelligible language, tells the disciples of his crucifixion and of his resurrection. Arrived at Jericho, two blind men importuned him as the Son of David to open their eyes; and he touched them, and their sight came to them.[a] At Bethpage, he orders an ass to be taken; and, being placed thereon, he rides into the holy city, the company of disciples casting their garments and branches of palms under the feet of the animal, and shouting, "*Blessed is he that cometh in the name of the Lord!*" Then immediately followed the driving out of the money-changers and sellers of victims from the temple, which the Pharisees, though sore displeased, could not resent; for the very children kept up the cry with which his disciples had entered the city, "*Hosanna to the Son of David!*"[b] Jesus himself took no timid or apologetic course, but boldly proclaimed himself the Son of God, about to establish the kingdom of heaven on earth, and offering its grace and glory to the descendants of Israel first, but determined to reject Israel and give the kingdom to the Gentiles, if its new king were rejected. These declarations he covered in the parables of the man and his two sons,[c] of the householder and the husbandmen, and of the king's marriage feast; but the Pharisees saw the implications clearly enough to be greatly incensed. They, however, first sought to lessen his influence with the multitude by perplexing him with difficult questions, which he not only triumphantly answered, but, in his turn, plied them with questions which they were not able to answer.[d] Then, he launched against them that terrible invective in the twenty-third chapter of Matthew, perhaps never equalled in severity in any known human speech, in which he denounced the men, whose claim to sit in Moses' seat he had acknowledged, as hypocrites, oppressors, extortioners, murderers, children of hell, a generation of vipers destined to damnation.[e] When his disciples came to him after the oration, he told them of the destruction of the temple, and, in answer to their importunity, explained the future events which they were to consider signs of the destruction of

[a] Matt. xx., 17-19, 30-34.   [b] Matt. xxi., 1-11, 12-16.   [c] Matt. xxi., 28-41.
[d] Matt. xxii., 1-14, 15-46.   [e] Matt. xxiii.

Jerusalem, of his own coming, and of the end of the world; asseverating that that generation should not pass till all these things should be fulfilled, and adding that, though heaven and earth should pass away, that declaration of his should stand.[a] Rising into that allegorical treatment which seemed the confirmed habit of his mind, he went on to depict the coming of the Son of Man as Judge, in the parable of the wise and foolish virgins, and of the lord and the servants intrusted with his money; and declared everlasting life the reward of those who had ministered to him and to his followers, and everlasting punishment the fate of those who had rejected and neglected them.[b]

During these last few days, it seemed to have been the habit of Jesus to withdraw for the night to one of the outlying villages, generally to Bethany, where Mary and Martha lived; but, though the anointing by the former is told substantially[c] as by John, the fact that she was a sister of Lazarus, and that he had died and was called out of his grave alive by Jesus in the presence of a concourse of sympathizing visitors, on one of those very days that preceded the arrest of Jesus, is strangely omitted by Matthew, as it is also by Mark and Luke. Indeed, the latter intimates that the woman who in the house of Simon anointed Jesus' feet with precious ointment was a disreputable person, whose character Jesus, if he were a prophet, ought to have known.[d]

The eating of the passover with his disciples; the lonely and ejaculatory prayer in Gethsemane, so different from the fervent and long prayer reported by John; and the coming of the officers of the law, guided by the treacherous Judas, follow, and the hasty trial and public crucifixion close the scene. The incidents of the life of Jesus as told by Mark are substantially the same. The variances in the Third Gospel need not now be considered.

The first impression which these narratives, including the Fourth Gospel, make upon the sincere mind, is of their unreliability as data of authentic history. There is in the telling of these stupendous events such an absence of detail as to time and place as would create doubt as to alleged occurrences in themselves less improbable. Then

[a] Matt. xxiv. [b] Matt. xxv. [c] Matt. xxvi., 6–13. [d] Luke vii., 39.

how can we reconcile the statements made in one place with what, with equal positiveness, is affirmed in another? Let a few examples of this inconsistency be cited. How could a man have gone about all the cities of Galilee, followed by a multitude from Galilee, Decapolis, Jerusalem, and Judea, and from beyond Jordan, and healed all the sick, cured all the deaf, blind, and lunatic, and in one or two instances restored the dead to life, the fame of such miracles extending through Syria, and yet his own brothers, as John states, have remained without faith in his prophetic pretensions? How could the people of the city where he lived, and where such mighty works had been done, have contemptuously rejected him? If Jerusalem and all Judea and all the region round about Jordan betook themselves to John the Baptist, and received his baptism confessing their sins, as Matthew declared, how could Jesus have afterward asked the Pharisees in Jerusalem, "Why then did ye not believe in John the Baptist"? In what age of the world and among what people could a man have been shamefully crucified by the civil government under the accusation of the ecclesiastical authority, and with the fierce concurrence of the populace, who had done such works as were by either of these writers ascribed to Jesus?

There seems to have been in all the ages, beginning with the apostolic times, a sweeping and impatient scepticism, that upon these or some other grounds has denied the historic existence of Jesus, and has insisted that his life, character, and works, as handed down by tradition, are the creation of the fervid imagination of the early Christians. Such a doubt, however, seems to have been pushed beyond the verge of reason.

That there was manifested in the world, somewhere about the beginning of the present era, a faith for which martyrs endured persecution and death, and, if not positively new conceptions of duty, new sanctions for and an increased devotion to virtue, is accredited by records left in literature and secular history, and by such monuments of a tidal wave of world-enthusiasm as the Christian Church, with what human genius under a devout impulse has done in art and architecture to make it and its teachings impressive. There is no great enlightenment of the race, no forward starting in the movement of civilization, no incursion of great ideas that have not been due to the advent of some man of transcendent genius.

The French astronomer, Leverrier, predicated the existence of the planet Neptune upon certain irregularities in the motions of Uranus; and not only its existence, but also its probable place in its orbit, its distance, and its mass. The appearance of the conjectured body in the place assigned to it, and its observed motions, fully confirmed the *a priori* conclusions of science. In the uncertainty of tradition, one famous figure stands conspicuous and assured in the very age to which the marvellous career of Jesus is assigned,—that is, Paul of Tarsus, the zealous missionary of a new faith that has nearly conquered the world, the mould of whose mind and character in his still extant letters literature preserves. The most obvious fact about Paul is that he was surcharged and saturated with an immense admiration and deference for a person whom he called the Lord, Jesus Christ. How largely this person was ideal, how few reminiscences he had of his actual sayings and deeds while he lived, Paul himself most distinctly discloses. But the ideal points to an actual, the affection and reverence to a veritable object; and we have no more reason to deny the existence of Jesus, and make him to Paul what Egeria was to Numa or Jehovah to Moses, than to conclude that Socrates was the venerable dæmon in whose name Plato and Xenophon taught philosophy to the Athenians.

But there is another unquestionably historic personage in the very position to have been powerfully affected by such a character as Jesus: Josephus, whose writings are still extant. He was a man of evident probity. He lived in Galilee a few years after Jesus, and wrote a history, giving a minute account of the prominent personages and events of his age. He is nearly silent about Jesus; for the only direct notice of the great prophet now found in his works is believed to be an interpolation, and is altogether inadequate to the impression Jesus must have made on his times, if he was the widely known miracle-worker followed by crowds through all the cities of Galilee, as told by the synoptics, or the eloquent disputant at Jerusalem, who raised the dead to life and gained converts among the priesthood and rulers, as told in the Fourth Gospel.

What the conditions require is a Jesus that shall win the faith of Paul, but not of such commanding power as to disturb the candid indifference of Josephus. To be still more precise, there is demanded a Jesus whom Paul shall first recognize only as an impostor and blasphemer to be persecuted, but who shall be able to win the respect, admiration, and life-long devotion of his better sentiments and better instructed mind.

Asking after this personage, whose light gleams through the ages, who and what manner of person he was, there are some strong grounds for maintaining that his proportions exceeded all the conceptions of him held by his disciples; that, as he was an apparent enigma to them while he lived with them,— they always mistaking his spirit and misapprehending his language,— so necessarily, after his death, they could but travesty a character and career wholly above their comprehension. To carry this method to its logical result, however, is to deprive the human life of Jesus of all historic reality, and in idealizing to lose his personality. If we may consider him better and greater than the words he is said to have spoken and the acts he is said to have done, we create him from our ideas, and, instead of a normal place and office in human history, he becomes an ever-enlarging influence running through history, toward which all progress tends. Paul betrays mental tendencies toward such a conception of the Christ, and it largely affects the theologic philosophy of modern Christianity. An ideal of excellence and wisdom separated from all that men have believed of Jesus is a phenomenon difficult to account for, since nothing can be found in the world except that conception itself; and the basis of that conception must be the evangelical tradition of Jesus, however freely it may have been handled, and however much its grossness and imperfection may have been tempered by devout fancy.

It may on the whole be safely affirmed that what the gospel histories, that are *really* histories, the Apostles and the early Church all concur in imputing to Jesus, formed a part of his faith and philosophy, and that, when these sources of testimony do not concur in any statement with reference to his thought or deeds, that statement is not historically verified.

We come back then to these narratives, from the necessity of the case, and accept them with all their inaccuracies, all their indefiniteness, their extravagances of statement, their irreconcilable details, not to speak of the coolness with which they assert things in themselves incredible as the only historical data we have of the life of Jesus.

Is the narrative called John's Gospel to be included in this category? To exclude it relieves our inquiry of the chief difficulty. The career of Jesus, as sketched by the writers now known as Matthew, Mark, and Luke, had for its theatre Galilee, with occasional excursions into the Jordan wilderness, across the lakes of Gennesaret to the other side, and northward and eastward to the borders of Phœnicia. He goes to Judea and Jerusalem only to fulfil the prophecies that declare that he must be rejected of his nation and crucified. John, on the other hand, gives us a life of more than two years passed mainly in Jerusalem and Judea, with three excursions into Galilee during that time. The synoptics declare that Jesus went through all the cities of Galilee, healing all manner of sickness and disease, restoring the blind to sight, restoring the lame to wholeness, casting out devils, and raising the dead. Besides this assertion of miracle-working in a comprehensive way,— boldly challenged by himself as proof of his divine mission, and acknowledged by his enemies,— there are given in detail, for nearly every day of his public preaching, individual cases of supernatural power put forth by him, including two cases of the restoration to life of persons who were believed to have died. All this occurs in Galilee, or *outside of Judea*. Approaching the latter country, his miraculous power seems to pass from him with the healing of the two blind men at Jericho, unless we give credit to the story told only by Luke of the cure of the servant Malchus, whom a disciple had mutilated with a sword at the time of the sudden arrest of Jesus. He not only does no miracle in Jerusalem, where of all the places it was desirable that he should work divine works to show his divine origin, but, when asked to show a sign, he says emphatically that no sign should be given to that wicked generation but the sign of his own resurrection.

John enumerates but two miracles done by Jesus in

Galilee, but afterward details two others, four in all, and asserts that the Galileans received him as a prophet on the occasion of his returning to them from Jerusalem, hearing of the miracles he had done in Jerusalem and Judea. On the other hand, John declares that many persons believed on Jesus at his first going to Jerusalem to the passover, when they saw the miracles he did there. And he enumerates and particularly describes the healing of the impotent man, the restoration of sight to the man born blind, and the raising from the dead of Lazarus, as done in the presence of many Jews, and well known to all the people of Jerusalem.

But it is apprehended that there are few candid and well-instructed believers in Jesus, who will not confess that, while they defer to the veracity of the Christian Scriptures so unreservedly as to accept as credible the account of the miracles in all the Gospels, they feel embarrassed by this demand upon their faith. The story of the miracles they will acknowledge, so far from being the ground of their faith in Jesus, or even helping toward it, is the weak point in the case, the part of the doctrine to be apologized for and explained. Had the miracles been done in the presence of the people of Galilee or of Judea, or were the historic evidence of their having been done indubitable, they would powerfully support the supernatural pretensions of Jesus. But, coming to us in the very records that avouch their improbability, they compromise the character of Jesus, just as it would compromise the character of Socrates, if all the authentic biography we had of him narrated that he talked with the devil on the top of the Acropolis; just as the legend of Mohammed riding through the air to Jerusalem closes our minds to the wisdom of much that he said and wrote. So that a judgment on the two distinct biographies of Jesus contained in the Gospels, based upon the question of miracles alone, would incline to favor the Johannic rather than the synoptic, because the wholesale healing of every manner of sickness throughout populous Galilee, in the latter, shrinks in the former to four miracles in Galilee and three in the vicinity of Jerusalem. But discrepancies of a more serious kind turn the scale of decision quite to the other side,— discrepancies involving the presentation of two distinct personalities, holding different ideas, possessing different intellectual and moral traits, and leading different careers in different countries.

Matthew says the Sermon on the Mount and all the principal parables were spoken in Galilee, where also Jesus preached and explained in all the synagogues his characteristic doctrine of the kingdom of heaven. At Jerusalem, indeed, he is brought in contact with the Pharisees; but the controversy is not of his seeking. He answers their questions; but he turns from them to address his disciples and the multitude that follow him, and never lays aside his allegoric method nor forgets the great burden of his prophecy, *the kingdom of heaven.* John gives us no Sermon on the Mount, no parables, no special gospel of a kingdom of heaven, but exhibits Jesus holding long disputations with the Pharisees in the temple, which were succeeded by pathetic and confidential conversations with his disciples interrupted by his arrest and trial.

How different as a dramatic representation is the Jesus of John from the Jesus of the other Gospels is manifest at the most cursory glance. Mention has been made of the disposition of Jesus, as represented in the synoptics, to conceal his didactic purpose under figures and imagery,— a disposition which seems as characteristic of his intellect as the dialectic method was characteristic of the intellect of Paul. It was truly said of him that without a parable spake he not unto them. In all but his later conversations there is but little self-assertion: he stands behind his message. His word of wisdom strikes direct to the human reason and conscience, and wins its sway over both by its intrinsic truth rather than by authority. Against all traditions, even the tradition of the fundamental law of the tables, he opposes the reasonableness of a deeper or larger law upon the simple authority of *I say unto you.* There was a certain vigor, clearness, comprehensiveness of thought, admirably embodied in language that was direct, and forms of expression that had the relish of wit, which made his answers so effective, and gave rise to the saying of his time, Never man spake like this man. In this later age, the sovereign man, the man who commands a hearing and gains adherents, is the man who with pen or tongue can most aptly embody the dominant thought, the intellectual tendency of his age. In the age of Jesus, as in the age of Socrates, men were not allowed the deliberation of studied and premeditated speech. The great man was challenged as he walked; and he must solve the riddle of life to the first asker, and from his own resources, without time to consult an oracle or a volume, or to verify his conjectures by the authority of a great name. On *a priori* grounds, it may be fairly inferred that the influence which Jesus gained among his contemporaries was more due to those traits of genius and intellect by which he responded to the demand of his time for a wise word, than to any thaumaturgic works by which he impressed their devout imaginations.

One can but be struck with the absence of all these intellectual traits in what John gives us of Jesus' conversations. He talks much, he multiplies words, often enfeebling and obscuring some obvious idea. It is difficult to disenchant words that have been reverently repeated by thousands of devout lips through eighteen centuries of the glamour of inspiration they have drawn from deeply moved souls. If that could be done, we should ask ourselves whether there were real eloquence in those formally balanced sentences, whether there was any logical order in those sequences only of sound, whether details often trivial did not mar the simple dignity of the thought, and whether the inferences and conclusions, connected with the antecedent statement by a *for* or a *wherefore*, did not introduce elements of strangeness and confusion.

Matthew Arnold, in his *God and the Bible*, while clinging to the Gospel of John as the truest indication of the mind of Jesus, admits that its historical data are nearly valueless, and contends that, though the form and style of the discourses imputed to Jesus in that Gospel are those of the Greek redactor who wrote the book, the ideas — elaborated and often misunderstood by the editor, and intermixed with his own irrelevant and unauthorized comments — are *logia*, or sayings, of Jesus reported by his confidential disciple John.

Why does Mr. Arnold cling to his prepossession against the conclusions of the most careful English and German scholars? Simply to give effect to the tradition, first found in the so-called Canon of Muratori, dating about A.D. 175, in this form: "The fourth of the Gospels is by the disciple John. He was being pressed by his fellow disciples and bishops; and he said: Fast with me this day and for three days, and whatsoever shall have been revealed to each one of us let us relate to the rest. In the same night, it was revealed to the apostle Andrew that John should write the whole in his own name, and that all the rest should revise it." Clement of Alexandria, who wrote later, says: "John last, aware that in the other Gospels were declared things of the flesh and blood, being moved thereto by his acquaintances, and being inspired by the Spirit, composed a spiritual Gospel."

Must the good sense and good scholarship of Christendom surrender themselves without question to this unauthenticated fragment of an idle legend? What is more natural than that these ancient writers should be easily persuaded by the dramatic illusion, under which the writer of the Fourth Gospel succeeded in veiling his dogmatic purpose? In an illiterate age, when the very data of history were unattainable, the fervid admiration of a speculative and mystic convert might easily impute marvellous deeds as well as the subtilties of his own thought to Jesus as a part of his history and doctrine. How easy it is already to idealize the characters and actions of Washington and of Napoleon, and that, too, in an enlightened age, and when all historical documents are so carefully recorded and so critically studied!

Even if the tradition be accepted as testimony, it gives little countenance to Mr. Arnold's conclusion, that the nucleus of the Johannic Gospel is the record of real sayings of Jesus preserved and disclosed by John. Why should John, if he had such sayings in his memory, have withheld them till his old age, and then made them known, as it were, upon compulsion? Was he not a witness of Jesus, under orders to tell among all nations what his master had said? Why should a faithful witness of the truth have maintained silence, while all manner of unauthorized volunteers, who knew nothing at first hand, were filling the young Church with unedifying gossip about the revered teacher whose memory he loved? Above all, why should the tried and tempted and persecuted brethren in Asia, Africa, and Europe, be kept from the strength and consolation which the touching and tender words of Jesus before his arrest would have given them in their sufferings?

While believing the tradition, Mr. Arnold in effect repudiates it, when he acknowleges that a gospel, instead of being written by John, dictated by the Spirit, and revised by the survivors of the twelve apostles, has no historic validity, is in its rhetorical form the composition of a Greek scholar other than John, and is largely made up of the comments and explanations of that scholar; and that such sayings of Jesus as it contains are not in the form or language that Jesus used. Why should John and Andrew have given their sanction to the minutely told story of the raising of Lazarus, which, if Mr. Arnold is correct, they must have known to be a pure invention?

Finally, the tradition itself virtually asserts that the Fourth Gospel is not a veritable narrative of incidents in the life of Jesus, held to old age in the memory of one of his three confidential friends, but the fruit of a special spiritual revelation. John is not represented as sitting down to recall what he could of Jesus' sayings and acts, but as proposing that he and his fellow-disciples shall fast three days, and see what after that *would be revealed to them*. The book was such revelation. Clement confirms this in saying, "In the other Gospels were declared things of flesh and blood." They alone were the real "*flesh-and-blood*" life of Jesus,—his actual life. "John, inspired by the Spirit, wrote a *spiritual* life," or, to use terms of modern significance, an idealized life of Jesus. Not only is this the popular significance of the contrasted phrases *flesh and blood* and *spiritual*, but, singularly enough, almost similar contrasted phrases are used in the Third Gospel in the same sense, wherein Jesus, after his resurrection, is made to say, "It is I myself," my flesh and bones, and not a spirit.[a]

So that the oldest tradition about the Fourth Gospel is that it is not an actual, but an ideal life of Jesus, as these chapters maintain. True, it attributes the authorship by implication to John, the apostle; but Mr. Arnold himself

[a] Luke xxiv., 39.

acknowledges that that apostle had neither the talent nor culture for such a work, while the prologue and the First Epistle, evidently the author's own achievement, show that such a creation lay within the scope of his powers.

In the Jesus of John, we find no love or even notice of the works of nature, no doctrine of the blessedness of poverty nor of the incompatibility of wealth with the order of the kingdom; no doctrine of meekness, non-resistance and self-denial, or of giving all possessions to the poor; no superiority to the narrow ideas of the Hebrew *cultus*. But we do find Jesus standing within those Hebrew ideas, and urging upon the Jews that more liberal interpretation of the national prophecies which would permit the recognition of himself as the Messiah therein foreshadowed. We find a doctrine of regeneration by baptism of water, of Jesus purchasing salvation for men by his death, of the Holy Ghost and his office and relations; and exhortations to love as the great test of genuine discipleship, always coupled and contrasted, however, with an intimation, that death, condemnation, and darkness are the doom of those who reject the grace offered to them in Jesus. The book is redolent of the controversies of the Church that sprang up in the lifetime of disciples that had seen Jesus; and the unmistakable peculiarity of style and mode of thought characterizing the three Epistles attributed to John show that it has with them a common authorship. It is the work of a man who, putting his thought of Jesus into a dramatic form, is not able to give him or any other character a distinct personality, but makes him repeat the writer's own sentiments in language that betrays their origin; for no matter who speaks, Jesus, John the Baptist, or the disciples, one and all express themselves in the unmistakable, mystical, involved, and illogical dialect of the Greek convert, the author.

The Jesus of John is an essentially different character from the Jesus of the three other evangelists — as different as is Paul, Moses, or Mohammed from him and from each other. The sketches are alike, in that they portray a person, who was reputed to be a Galilean, and the son of Mary; who was a master with twelve chief disciples, though their names and identity are not agreed upon;

who performed miraculous works, who allowed himself to be called the Son of God, and claimed divine appointment as a prophet, messiah, savior, and founder of a new order on earth or in heaven; who provoked the hostility of the Jewish rulers, and was by their procurement put to death, and was believed to have shown himself alive after death. Here, the agreement ends. John's Jesus is wholly unlike Matthew's in his intellectual traits, in his style of speech, in the philosophy that he held, and the doctrines that he taught, in all the principal incidents of his personal history, and in the very region of the earth, in which he made himself known to his fellow-countrymen.

But the chief objection to the acceptance of the narrative called John's, as historic, is that, according to it, the arrest, condemnation, and crucifixion of Jesus are utterly unaccountable. According to this narrative, Jesus had been a very familiar figure in the streets of the sacred city, and in the precincts of the temple for two or three years. He had charmed a credulous and devout populace with many conspicuous works of healing, and even, in one instance, had raised from the dead an individual, who became almost as popular with the multitude as himself. He had interrupted the solemnities of the national worship by long discussions with the chief priests concerning his own Messianic pretensions. In the main, those discussions had been on his part deferential toward their legitimate authority to sit in Moses' seat as the civil and ecclesiastical magistrates of the nation; and only once, in the bitterness of his spirit, had he declared explicitly that they were the children of the devil. His most questionable proceeding, that of whipping the money-changers from the temple, had happened years before, and had been forgotten; and the breach of the Sabbath, in healing the blind man, had been condoned,—excused, as it was, by many of the orthodox. He had fairly outlived his unpopularity; and the raising of Lazarus had effected so powerful a diversion in his favor, that his enemies confessed they could make no headway against him, and that the whole people seemed inclined to believe on him. And yet, in the very flush of that popularity and success, the evangelist surprises us with the recital, that Jesus was beset by the police, captured without an attempted rescue or the slightest demonstration of resistance on the part of his friends and was carried away, condemned and crucified, because that very populace, upon whom he had made such a favorable impression, fiercely demanded his death, after the executive power had strenuously sought to effect his pardon and release! The council of the chief priests and elders, with some show of fairness, deliberated over his accusation, and arrived at the conclusion, with no appearance of dissent, that he was worthy of death; although a large body of intelligent citizens, some of whom may have sat in the council that condemned him, had been present a few days before, when a man four days buried had come forth from the grave alive at the invocation of the man put upon his trial, and although it was generally believed in Jerusalem, at the time of his arrest and trial, that he had done this stupendous and beneficent miracle. If it is required to believe that these things were done as a part of a supernatural machinery, which brought about the death of Jesus for foreordained heavenly ends, we are not required to consider human probabilities. The possibilities of human conduct, when ordained by the supernal powers, are infinite. But, if human nature is substantially the same in all ages, and human conduct is governed by intelligible motives, then it is impossible to understand how the death of Jesus was brought about under such conditions. The Jewish people, who sat in the Sanhedrim, and who composed the multitude that clamored for the crucifixion, in fine who created the public opinion which made it impossible for even the authority of the Roman governor to effect the deliverance of the victim, must be considered to be no more sceptical and no less susceptible to superstitious influences than are ordinary men. If it had been believed that one of the prisoners put to trial during the Reign of Terror, a few days before his trial, had in the environs of Paris restored a dead man to life, neither could the revolutionary tribunal have condemned him, nor would the mob have permitted his execution. It cannot be believed that there is a government so impious, or a mob so cruel, or a horde of robbers or savages so degraded, as not to be awed with reverence or paralyzed with terror by the very presence of one who had shown himself capable of raising the dead to life.

On the other hand, the mainly concurrent testimony of Matthew, Mark, and Luke, presents a perfectly probable and intelligible explanation of the judicial murder of Jesus. According to them, he was a Galilean, a dweller in a remote and disreputable province. If he had been born in Judea, it was during a visit of his mother, which under no circumstances could give him a right to claim that province as his country. He had passed his whole lifetime in Galilee. Though a rumor of his miracles had reached Jerusalem, and the ecclesiastical rulers had sent a deputation down to that region to inquire about them, the conclusion the messengers arrived at, that all the miracle-working was by the power of Beelzebub, showed that, in the inveterate prejudice of the orthodox Jews, Jesus was less, rather than more, esteemed at Jerusalem for these questionable practices. Heresies and fanaticisms had been no unusual phenomena of the times, and Galilee had before been the theatre of them. Josephus relates several popular religious and political outbreaks; and the learned Gamaliel recites, in the fifth chapter of Acts, how Theudas and Judas of Galilee had successively come forward with Messianic pretensions, and much larger following than Jesus had, and had been brought to nought.

At length, this unknown provincial fanatic, with a feeble following of illiterate fishermen and women, not all of them quite respectable, ventures to come to the sacred city itself. His person is unknown, he has no friends in the city and cannot even lodge there over night. He may have done miracles in Galilee. He does none here. Challenged to do them, he peremptorily declines. He enters the city with a most offensive ovation,—a clamor of the Galilean converts, mostly children, proclaiming him the son of David coming in the name of the Lord. Of course, the implication of this cry was revolutionary in the extreme. It was a threat both to Cæsar and to the High Priest and the rulers. What, to the astonished Jews, must have looked like a mob, at once blasphemous and fantastic, proceeded in open day to the temple itself, where Jesus, armed with a whip, drove out the money-changers and sellers of doves. When we consider how little he had to do with the ceremonies of the national worship, that he was believed to have spoken contemptuously of it and of its priesthood, and that the very practice of selling victims for sacrifice was not only a necessary and decent convenience for those worshippers who came from a distance, but was specially sanctioned by the written Hebrew law itself, the anger which this proceeding aroused among the leading Jews becomes quite intelligible. Jesus, however, was in no mood to let their anger cool. His evident purpose in coming to Jerusalem was to precipitate this controversy. He takes care of his life and liberty by going out at night to find safe lodgings in the country, only that he may declare to the full the denunciation that had been for many days swelling in his heart.

His next demonstration is in the temple itself, where he chided the Pharisees for their rejection of John; told against them the parable of the two sons, of the wicked husbandmen and of the rejected wedding guest; and wounded their self-love by a triumphant answer to all the knotty points of legal casuistry, in which they sought to entangle him. After they had thus been fairly put to the worst, and had left him master of the situation, holding the very temple itself, from which the people were wont to receive in silence from their lips the authoritative expositions of the will of God, Jesus launched against them that masterly invective of the twenty-third chapter of Matthew, unequalled for its severity in the literature of the world. Of course, the whole city were on fire with indignation and passion. Public sentiment turned decisively against the Galilean reformer. His very disciples forsook him; and those who had come up from a remote province to see their master take possession of the throne of David, and give them honored seats on his right hand and on his left, denied that they ever knew him. For such a state of popular feeling, it is easy to see that Matthew and his copyists give an adequate reason; and under that feeling, sweeping all before it, it was perfectly easy for the Sanhedrim to get Jesus arrested without any attempt at rescue, to get him condemned in a hasty and illegal way without a dissenting vote of a single ruler, and even to draw the populace around the Roman palace, to defeat by their fierce hatred the avowed purpose of Pilate to release him.

Enough has been said in this preliminary chapter to indicate why such historical data, as will be appealed to in this discussion, will be taken exclusively from the Synoptic Gospels; while the Fourth Gospel, an undoubtedly genuine and legitimate literary creation of the awakened thought of the first and second centuries, will be sometimes cited, as a drama, poem, or review might be to-day, as giving a better exposition of an historical situation or character than the annalists, who had more literally followed the incidents or the documents. In presenting in detail the ideas of Jesus, further confirmation will be found of the position already taken, while a more careful critique of the Fourth Gospel itself, as indicating that culture and tendency which has adapted Christianity to expanding civilization, will be added to complete the whole subject.

CHAPTER II.

THE DOMINANT IDEA OF JESUS.

"Whoever can read the New Testament with a fresh eye must be struck with the prominence everywhere of the Messianic idea. It seems to be the ideal framework of the whole,— of history, parable, dialogue, of Pauline reasoning, of apocalyptic visions. *'Art thou he that should come?'* This question gives the ideal standard by which on all hands, and on the part of disciples, relations, enemies, of Saul the persecutor and Paul the apostle, the person and pretensions of Christ are to be tried. His birth, his acts, his sufferings, are so disposed as to fulfil what was spoken by the prophets, so that the whole programme of his life would seem to have pre-existed in the national imagination."— *James Martineau.*

"The Messianic faith is the soul of the entire New Testament, giving unity to the Gospels, Epistles, and Apocalypse, and making Christianity a vital organism." — *Francis E. Abbot.*

EVERY great historical personage, to be understood, must be studied in connection with his dominant idea. While a man puts into his dominant idea a certain force and quality of his own genius, it in turn reacts upon and modifies his character. No one would undertake to comprehend the distinctive character of Luther, without making himself acquainted with the controversy into which Christendom was drawn between him and the Pope, and with the protest made in the interest of a reformed religious faith against the doctrines and practices of the Catholic Church. Copernicus, Laplace, and Newton without their investigations and discoveries in reference to the mechanism of the celestial bodies, Shakspere without his dramas, Beethoven without his music, Wilberforce and Garrison without the abolition of slavery, would be characters of no historical significance and of no definite identification.

The dominant idea of Jesus, by which all his ideas are to be examined and entertained, and by which his character and pretensions are to be estimated, was his *doctrine of the kingdom of heaven*. Not to understand, at least in some general way, what his system was of a new order of things to begin in the world, known to his thought as the *kingdom of God* or the *kingdom of heaven*, is not to understand his true function in history; and until this central idea of his, around which was grouped all that he said and taught, is appreciated, only confusion and incertitude will be attained in trying to master his system of ethics, or his theory of the future destiny of the world and of mankind, or to properly determine the order of being to which he belonged.

Of all the words recorded by Matthew as having been uttered by Jesus in his lifetime, more than one-fourth are directly upon the subject of *the kingdom of heaven;* and much of what is original and peculiar in his ethical teaching can only be understood or made capable of practice, by accepting it as the law, not of the human society of his time or of our time, but of that new order which he believed himself about to inaugurate in the place of such society. When it is considered how much of the conversation imputed to him related to incidents of his daily experience, how much of it was in answer to persons interrogating him upon subjects prominent in their thought, rather than in his, it becomes more apparent how spontaneously his mind reverted to the theme which seemed to possess and inspire it.

Of this doctrine of *the kingdom of heaven*, the earliest writers of the Gospels have more to say than the later. It almost disappears from the narrative of John. When the time had passed, plainly indicated by Jesus for the kingdom of heaven to begin, with unmistakable signs of great physical catastrophes, the believers naturally began to accommodate their faith to a scheme of things allowing a greater security, and a longer endurance of the old order of the world, and to lay less stress upon what related to the coming *kingdom of heaven*. The expectation remained, but it was less vivid; and cares for other and urgent things diminished its pressure upon attention. As all the narratives of the evangelists are supposed to have been written, after the expectation, created by the words of Jesus of a change, which should put the secular power more into the hands of believers, had been weakened by frequent disappointments and delays, it is probable that those narratives contain less rather than more of what Jesus actually said relating to his dominant idea.

When Jesus left the privacy of his humble life as an artisan and went out among his countrymen in the capacity of a prophet, this is what he is reported to have said, not in one place or at one time, but as the comprehensive summary of what he said in all places and at all times: "*Repent, for the kingdom of heaven is at hand.*" Afterward it is said, he went about all Galilee, teaching in their synagogues, healing diseases indeed, but preaching the *gospel* or good news of *the kingdom, i.e., of heaven*.[a] When he taught his disciples apart upon the mountain, his opening declaration was that the poor shall possess the kingdom of heaven.[b] The beatitudes which follow all relate to reward and compensation in heaven and in the heavenly state, oftener called kingdom. Continuing the same discourse, he speaks of ranks of eminence in the kingdom of heaven, of the standard of rectitude which will qualify to be received into it.[c] In the prayer he dictated for use by his disciples, the petition for the coming of the kingdom of God is the first and chief petition.[d] The abstention from anger, the reconciliation of all enmities, no matter if purely the fault of another, the termination of all controversies are required; the obliteration, if necessary, by excision, of all lustful desires, the absolute forgiveness of injuries, the meeting of all exaction and extortion and affront by concession and courtesy, an absolute carelessness of all that concerns the sustenance of life, an omission of all thought and foresight, are demanded, on the ground, that in the kingdom of heaven there is ample reward for all suffering, ample compensation for all loss and wrong, and in the large economy of God all the physical wants are amply provided for.[e] The kingdom of heaven, however, is not for the crowd. Jesus preached no doctrine of the virtue of the people; and his kingdom was not open for the masses, whom revolutions and seditions have always flattered. The way into it was by a narrow gate, which only a few found, while a broad road led to destruction.[f] Many even of his nominal disciples would be driven from its portals as workers of iniquity, and in the near end the rains, floods, and winds,

[a] Matt. iv., 24; ix., 35; Mark i., 21, 39; Luke iv., 15, 43, 44.
[b] Matt. v., 3.   [c] Matt. v., 19, 20.   [d] Matt. vi., 10.
[e] Matt. v., vi.   [f] Matt. vii., 13, 14.

emblems of some secular catastrophe, would sweep to their final fall all who had listened to his words without obeying them.[a]

When the Roman centurion, whose servant was sick, told Jesus, that he might cure the invalid without incurring the trouble of a personal visit, he was so pleased at such an exhibition of faith, that he declared that strangers and aliens from the East and West should come and sit with the patriarchs in the kingdom of heaven, while the children of the kingdom should be thrust into the outer darkness.[b] Again, when he saw multitudes thronging to his proclamation of the kingdom, he wished for more helpers to proclaim it,[c] and, fired with this thought, immediately afterward commissioned his twelve chief disciples, and, besides giving them power to heal all kinds of disease, authorized them to declare only what had been the burden of his own preaching,—"*The kingdom of heaven is at hand.*"[d] He gave them no other message. He told them they need not meditate beforehand what they should say, if brought before the civil tribunals as seditious persons.[e] He told them they should be ridiculed, hated, and persecuted; that they must not resist, but flee from city to city, always bearing the proclamation of the impending heavenly order. And he comforted them with the assurance that their heavenly Father would care for them, and, if slain in his cause, would recognize and honor them, when his kingdom was established; and he asserted that, in their fleeing from persecution from city to city, as advised, they should not have gone over the cities of Israel before the Son of Man should come,— that is, in his kingdom.[f] This title, Son of Man, by which he began to designate himself, was used by the prophet Ezekiel throughout his prophetic rhapsody as the medium by which Jehovah communicated in vision his purposes. It was also used by Daniel, a prophet then and ever since held in highest repute, because, more definitely than any of his class, he is believed to have possessed the power of soothsaying, always a most fascinating talent, to have foretold with rare precision the successive ascendency and destruction of the Assyrian, Persian, Greek, and Roman

[a] Matt. vii., 21-23, 24, 27.   [b] Matt. viii., 11.   [c] Matt. ix., 36-38.
[d] Matt. x., 7.   [e] Matt. x., 17-19.   [f] Matt. x., 22, 23, 26-33.

empires, and to have stated in some cabalistic and insoluble figures the term of the whole present order of the world. Daniel, however, does not mean by Son of Man a prophet, but some angelic, immortal, and divine being, greatly honored by the Ancient of Days, and to whom was given dominion and glory, an everlasting and indestructible kingdom over all nations and all languages. It is difficult to determine in which sense Jesus used this title; and it may have been in both senses, and under the belief that he was at the same time the true-sighted prophet, to whom Jehovah communicated his purposes, and the coming king, whose authority all nations were to acknowledge.

The more Jesus talked with his disciples upon his inspiring theme, the loftier rose his confidence and enthusiasm. He told them not to expect peace and acquiescence, but dissensions, hatreds, wars, and martyrdoms.[a] They were not to be dismayed even by death itself. To lose life in such a cause was to find it again in the coming kingdom, in which even those who had given a disciple a cup of water were not to be without their reward.[b] He assured them that whosoever believed them believed him, and that to take up the cross and follow him was the only way to make themselves worthy of him. This so aptly described the modes of thought by which the disciples of the earlier centuries must have comforted and strengthened themselves under the martyrdoms and persecutions of the Jews and of the Roman emperors, long after the death of Jesus, that there is a strong suspicion that these words, particularly this allusion to the cross, were injected into the conversations of Jesus after the crucifixion. But as this suspicion, carried into its details and its consequences, as has already been shown, will rob us of nearly all historic data concerning Jesus himself, it must be repressed.

Jesus had already with fulness and detail unfolded his ethical ideas in the hearing of his disciples. But the principal apostles gave afterwards such lamentable exhibitions of their utter misconception of his spirit and incapacity to understand his philosophy, that he would only have compromised himself by intrusting them with the

[a] Matt. x., 34, 39. [b] Matt. x., 41, 42.

discretion of teaching them; and their attempts on several occasions to apply his principles and communicate his doctrines had involved him in difficulties that had tried his temper.[a] But any messenger could communicate the startling intelligence that the *kingdom of heaven was at hand*, and that a catastrophe was impending over the human race, against which precautions that required an amendment of character were processes altogether too slow. Taken all together, this commissioning of the apostles indicates a firm prepossession in the mind of Jesus of a conflict between the order of the kingdom of heaven and the secular order, internecine and irrepressible, in which his personal friends were to be active agents, and which was to end in the triumph of his adherents, and their reward in that period in which they lived.[b]

A short time after these events, Jesus declared to the multitude about him that John Baptist, then awaiting death in prison, was the last of the old prophets; and that with him terminated the old order; and that, greatest as he was of all prophets, the least in the kingdom of heaven was greater than he; and that from John's time till then men are rushing into the kingdom of heaven and making its blessedness their own by a kind of violence.[c] As all the qualification of the messengers seemed to be to have tongues to tell the startling message, so, he said, all the qualification of the listeners was to have ears to hear it.[d] Remembering how the respectable and intelligent people, who in his own home, Capernaum, and in the neighboring cities, Chorazin and Bethsaida, had coldly disdained his pretensions and the glories of his coming kingdom, he declares that, in the day of judgment they shall be brought down to hell.[e] He blessed the simple ones, who had been able to see what the wise and prudent overlooked; he invited to him the laborers and the oppressed, and declared that all things were given to him of God, and that he only had the true knowledge of God, and could communicate it to whom he would.[f]

When certain Pharisees attributed to demoniac agency his manifest power to cast out devils, he assured them

---

[a] Matt. xv., 16. [b] Matt. x., 7–23. [c] Matt. xi., 7–14. [d] Matt. xi., 15.
[e] Matt. xi., 20–24. [f] Matt. xi., 25–30.

that Satan would not be likely to cast out himself, and that, if he (Jesus) had cast out devils by the power of God, then it was manifest that the kingdom of God had come unto them,— the heavenly order had indeed already begun.[a]

When afterward the multitude thronged about him, he took his stand upon a small vessel, and addressed them, grouped upon the shore, in a series of allegories, all representative of the kingdom of heaven, its incidents and leading features.[b] These parables were not all intelligible, even to his disciples; and he condescended to give them personally some explanations; for, he said, it was lawful to communicate to them the mysteries of the kingdom of heaven. As to the multitude, he declared his purpose not to enlighten them; and he said they were the people doomed by the prophet Isaiah to blindness and dumbness, lest God should convert and heal them.[c] In these allegories, those who heed his proclamation of the kingdom of heaven, and for that blessed estate joyfully sacrifice every other advantage, are called the children of the kingdom: they are also called the just and the righteous, as the rest of mankind are called the wicked and the children of the wicked one. His disciples are not to be disheartened by the present aspect of all the world being against him. Small as the leaven is, it will leaven the world; and, from the little seed he is planting, a tree shall grow, in whose branches the birds of the air shall lodge.[d] Quietly as these two classes now live together, and so much alike that only the discriminating eye of the Judge can detect whose are his, in the near end of the world they shall be separated like tares from the wheat, like bad fish from among the good, and those who are not his shall be cast into a furnace of fire, where shall be wailing and gnashing of teeth. "Then," he declared, quoting from a vision of the prophet Daniel, "shall the righteous shine forth as the sun in the kingdom of their Father." It is not absolutely necessary to infer that Jesus had in his thought a conception of a gross and material destruction by fire of those, who at his coming had not believed his message; but when, after the assurance of a purpose to explain confidentially to his friends

[a] Matt. xii., 24-28.   [b] Matt. xiii., 1-3.   [c] Matt. xiii., 11-17.   [d] Matt. xiii., 18-52.

what he had avowed he intended to disguise from the multitude, he uses language that he knew would convey to them images only of a physical and summary destruction and punishment, there is only an *a priori* prepossession, upon which to entertain the conjecture that he had nothing in his mind but a picture of a purely spiritual condition. Of some impending changes (and he doubtless had in his mind that coming of the Son of Man with his angels during the lifetime of some of his auditors), he thought there were so many palpable signs, that he told the Pharisees, if they were as prescient, as they were about the harbingers of the weather, they would readily discern them.[a]

Some undeclared time after the telling of these parables, Jesus was with his disciples at Cesarea Philippi; and there he is said to have disclosed to them his purpose to go to Jerusalem. But he announced that the chief priests and elders would persecute and put him to death. He told his followers, as he had before, that they must not be afraid of death, nor try to save their lives, but must follow him, if necessary, in his crucifixion; to save their lives was to lose them, to lose their lives for his sake was to find them,—*i.e.*, in his kingdom. For what profit is it to gain the whole world, he asked, and lose one's own soul? For the Son of Man—that is, himself, who was to be killed at Jerusalem a few days hence—shall come again in the glory of his Father, with his angels, and then shall reward every man who had made sacrifices for him; and truly, he said, closing this impassioned exhortation, there be some standing here which shall not taste of death till they see the Son of Man coming in his kingdom.[b] This mood of exultation and expectation did not leave him; for, a few days later, he expressed impatience because his disciples could not cast out a devil, and assured them, if they had faith, they might say to a mountain:[c] *Be moved to yonder place*, and nothing should be impossible to them. The kingdom in his fervid thought had already come; and the powers which he would confer in the new order to do great works, to lay down and take up life, would be given now by the new king to those who had great faith.

[a] Matt. xvi., 3.   [b] Matt. xvi., 13-28.   [c] Matt. xvii., 16, 17, 20.

When his disciples asked him who was greatest in the kingdom of heaven, he told them whoever should humble himself and believe on him as a little child was the greatest, and that whoever should offend such a trustful believer had better have been cast into the sea with a millstone about his neck; that to enter his kingdom they must not hesitate to sacrifice an eye, a hand, or a foot; and that every little one of his had an angel in heaven always looking upon the very face of God.[a] He commended those who for the sake of the kingdom of God had been celibate; he told his disciples it was scarcely possible for the rich to enter that kingdom; and soothed his disciples, who asked what reward they should have for leaving friends and property and all things for his sake, by promising that, when he should sit in the throne of his glory, they should sit on thrones judging the twelve tribes of Israel, and should, for all the possessions they should give up, receive back a hundred-fold and inherit eternal life.[b]

Fired by the ever-present vision of the kingdom of heaven, this question of the disciples roused his spirit to new disclosures of its scenes and solemn compensations. For, said he, continuing the conversation, the kingdom of heaven is like a man who was a householder, that has no true scale of wages, but gives to the latest laborer the same reward as to the earliest, and allows no man to claim, in the day of recompense, that he was the earliest convert or the oldest disciple.

On his way to Jerusalem, he again declared his death and resurrection; and, when the mother of James and John came to ask that her sons might be viceroys of the new kingdom, he did not deny that there were such places to be filled by those for whom the Father had prepared them; but he said the scale of rank in his kingdom, unlike the kingdoms of the world, was the scale of service, and not princes, but servants, obtained chief precedence in it.[c]

Besides the direct way of promulgating an idea or declaring an event about to happen, besides Jesus' characteristic way of foreshadowing these in a parable, there was what may be called the national way. The old

[a] Matt. xviii., 1-11. [b] Matt. xix., 3-30. [c] Matt. xx., 1-28.

prophets were wont to resort to physical demonstrations by way of making their warnings and vaticinations more impressive to their hearers. Thus, Zedekiah, in the time of King Jehoshaphat, made horns of iron, as it turned out, only to give rhetorical emphasis to his prediction, that the king should prevail against Syria. "Thus saith the Lord," was his message, "with these thou shalt push Syria, till she be consumed."ᵃ Hosea declared, on two different occasions, that he was commanded to cohabit with an adulterous woman, that he might illustrate the falsity of Israel in leaving Jehovah, her true husband.ᵇ And now Jesus, not with any serious expectation of ushering in the kingdom of which he was to be king,—for he seems to have believed his rejection by the Jews and his temporary death are to precede that event,—but to give an impressive physical demonstration of what he had been repeating to a stolid and indifferent people, prepares the triumphal entry into Jerusalem, and has himself announced to the daughter of Zion as her king, coming meek and sitting upon an ass, and a colt, the foal of an ass. The narrative does not attribute to Jesus the details of this affair.ᶜ But as he directed the animal to be procured upon which he intended to ride, as he entered cordially into the character assumed by him of the prophetic king of Zion, and as Luke narrates that he justified his disciples for this ostentatious ovation in language which showed that he was acting under the pressure of an intense enthusiasm, it is just to infer that the whole demonstration was premeditated by him, to give impressiveness to the message he was bringing to the sacred city itself of the coming of the kingdom of heaven.ᵈ He must have been somewhat disappointed. To the decorous and conservative Pharisees, the spectacle was offensive, and prejudiced them in advance against the gospel he came to promulgate. From this time to the end, he evidently anticipates his rejection, and withholds a message that he has assured himself will only be despised. The temper of the city is such that, after the imposing entry into it, followed up by his driving from the temple the money-changers and sellers of victims, he

ᵃ II. Chron. xviii., 10.   ᵇ Hosea i., 2-3; iii., 1-3.   ᶜ Matt. xxi., 1-16.
ᵈ Luke xix., 39, 40.

deemed it not safe to remain there over night, and up to the day of his arrest went every night into some outlying village to lodge.[a] To the Pharisees and their adherents, he declared afterward only the punitory and destructive aspects of the coming of the kingdom of heaven. He told them, the publicans and the harlots go into the kingdom, while they refused,[b] that in persecuting and slaying him they were killing the son of the husbandman, just as they had slain his servants, the prophets; and that they were drawing down upon themselves a miserable destruction.[c] "The kingdom of God," he said, "shall be taken from you and given to a nation bringing forth fruits thereof." To his own disciples, he spoke with exceeding bitterness against the scribes and Pharisees, whom he charged with keeping themselves out of the kingdom of heaven, and not suffering others to enter it. He declared that the damnation of hell awaited them, that all the evil deeds of themselves and their fathers would be visited upon them, and that the woes he had uttered should come upon that generation. Invoking Jerusalem in tones of mingled indignation and pity, he announced that the city should not see him again till it should say, "Blessed is he that cometh in the name of the Lord," evidently reflecting with some disappointment that the city had not joined in that hosanna, and believing that when he came again in the clouds with his angels, in the glory of his kingdom, every knee would bow, and every tongue would confess him.[d]

Relieved of the contradictions and contempt of the Pharisees, by which his spirit seemed much disturbed, Jesus, on the eve of events which he felt assured and which even to any intelligent observer betokened his speedy death, reverts to the society of his followers, and in answer to a direct request by them, to tell them what should be the sign of "thy coming, and of the end of the world," proceeds to unfold with great fulness and precision the whole scheme of the kingdom of heaven, as it was then shaped in his anticipation.

The twenty-fourth chapter of Matthew has been sometimes considered a prediction by Jesus of the destruction of Jerusalem, which took place about forty years after

[a] Matt. xxi., 17, 18.   [b] Matt. xxi., 28-46.   [c] Matt. xxii., 1-15.   [d] Matt. xxiii.

his crucifixion. Concerning this, it must be said, however, that Jesus never manifested the slightest interest in secular history. Nothing that he ever said indicated that he had any knowledge, outside the annals of his own people, of the changes of empires in the past, or that he built any hopes upon beneficent political changes to occur in the future. His destitution of patriotism and of the national feeling, his profound indifference to the shame of being subject to the Roman sway, and his light estimate of the glories of the earlier times and of greatness of the prophets, kings, and patriarchs, were rather conspicuous. Then there was nothing remarkable about the capture of Jerusalem, which was not so much destroyed by Titus as it had been by Nebuchadnezzar; in fact, it has never been destroyed, but always has been inhabited as a city. The destruction of Carthage, of Babylon, of Nineveh, of Tyre, of Sidon, of Memphis, of Baalbec, of Ephesus, and of very many Greek and Roman cities, was far more complete and summary than that of Jerusalem. Jesus himself warned his disciples that it was not mere secular revolutions, such as are always going on, such as were rife in his age and in that following and preceding it, of which he wished them to take note. " Ye shall hear of wars and rumors of wars. Nations shall rise against nation ; there shall be famines, earthquakes, pestilences,"— he might have added, as there always have been,— but the end is not yet. It is not of these events or their like that I wish to speak, but of that consummation indicated by the abomination of desolation standing in the holy place, which is the sign, which he that readeth may well understand,— the sign for instant, precipitate flight, the sign of the coming on of tribulation, such as never was since the beginning of the world, and from which the elect of God can hardly be saved. Heed not those who shall then proclaim Christ to be here or there, and go not forth to find him ; for, as the lightning cometh out of the east and shineth unto the west, so shall the coming of the Son of Man be. Immediately after, the sun shall be darkened, the stars shall fall from heaven, all the heavenly powers shall be shaken, and the Son of Man, coming in the clouds of heaven, shall gather his elect from the four winds of heaven ; and he declared, with the most solemn form of asseveration he ever used on any occasion, "*This generation shall not pass away till all these things be fulfilled.*"[a] Heaven and earth may pass away: this, my word, shall not pass away. His very hearers, the men then living and standing with him, he conjured to be vigilant; for they could not tell when he, their Lord, should come, and he promised that the faithful servant, found watching for the coming of his Master, should be made ruler over all his house. Then, resuming his allegoric method, he said: The kingdom of heaven shall be likened unto ten virgins waiting by night for the bridal procession of their Lord, the prudent ones, who had provided themselves with oil, to be let in to the marriage feast, the improvident ones, whose lamps had gone out, to be refused admission.[b] It is like a proprietor leaving his property to trustees, and returning after a journey to reward the thrifty with gifts and honors, but to punish the slothful and wasteful by consignment to dungeons and torture. And finally, dropping his allegory, he declares that, when he so comes in his glory and sits upon the throne of his kingdom, all nations shall be gathered before him, and that he will separate them as goats are separated from sheep, the sheep being those who received and ministered either to him or his followers, the goats those who had rejected or neglected them. The sheep he will receive into immortal life, the goats shall go away into an endless punishment. In drinking wine with the twelve just before his arrest, Jesus said that he would not again drink of the fruit of the vine until that day when he should drink it new with them in his Father's kingdom; and, when interrogated by the High Priest, this was his reply: "*Hereafter shall ye see the Son of Man sitting on the right hand of power, and coming in the clouds of heaven.*"[c]

From this recapitulation, it becomes apparent how much the expectation of the kingdom of heaven was in the thought of Jesus, and how large a topic it was of his discourse. Are we not fully justified in the inference that it was his *dominant idea?* It was the theme upon which all his characteristic teachings were based, the underlying image which all his parables disclosed to the faithful and childlike disciples, but designedly concealed from the apprehension of the critical and the wise. It

[a] Matt. xxiv.   [b] Matt. xxv.   [c] Matt. xxvi., 29, 64.

was the favorite subject, to which, when left to the promptings of his own mind and not diverted by the questions of those about him, he always recurred. As he began his public career by announcing that *the kingdom of heaven is at hand*, so he closed it by declaring to his affectionate and devoted followers with touching pathos what was equivalent to saying, The next time I eat and drink with you, it will be in the kingdom of my Father; and to the chief of his enemies, the High Priest, You who condemn me to death now shall see me sitting on the right hand of power and coming in the clouds of heaven.

It is very rare, perhaps it is impossible, for a single person to import into the world a wholly new idea. Before the seed of a great thought can take root and bear fruit, the ground must be prepared. Every great discovery, every germinal truth, proclaims itself in the anticipation of seekers, in the blind gropings of those who feel after it without quite apprehending it. Newton's discoveries in physics were foreshadowed and anticipated by his predecessors and compeers. Columbus discovered America through the provocation of other adventurous voyagers in unknown seas. Garrison demanded immediate emancipation after the humanitarian spirit had begun to permeate modern civilization.

It is not surprising that the dominant idea of Jesus is not found to be wholly original with him, but to have been anticipated by men who lived before him, and to have been shared by his countrymen and contemporaries. John the Baptist preceded Jesus in the specific proclamation, "*The kingdom of heaven is at hand.*"[a] Luke mentions a priest, Simeon, as a just and devout man, waiting for the consolation of Israel; and a prophetess, named Anna, who conferred with those in Jerusalem, looking for redemption.[b] And Mark speaks of Joseph of Arimathea, by whose liberality the body of Jesus obtained honorable sepulture, as one waiting for the kingdom of heaven.[c] The two disciples walking to Emmaus after the crucifixion are represented by Luke as speaking of Jesus, as the one they had hoped would redeem Israel.[d] They might have derived this hope from what he had said; but there is evidence that, besides all he taught,

---
[a] Matt. iii., 1-2.   [b] Luke ii., 25, 36, 38.   [c] Mark xv., 43.   [d] Luke xxiv., 21.

the expectation of some deliverance for the Jewish nation and its sudden elevation to great glory, accompanied by the overthrow of the Gentile powers, had widely pervaded the popular heart. There had been fanatics and adventurers, who had taken advantage of this national feeling to incite sedition, and to make themselves leaders of popular revolutions.

The golden age of the Greek was in the remote antiquity. The Jews, like the modern peoples, saw their golden age in the future; and that which in the devout mind paints itself as *the millennium*, and which comforts the popular heart under trials and privations as the *good time coming*, to the Jews of all ranks was the sceptre of David restored to a prince of his house, under whose sway God would restore them to prosperity, and punish with destruction all their enemies.

The expectation which we find affecting the priesthood, the common people, the devout and enlightened classes, John the Baptist, Jesus and his disciples, was based upon the vaticinations of the national prophets, whose writings in highly ornate and poetical language, a unique collection among the literature of antiquity, were carefully preserved, and read and chanted as a part of the national worship every Sabbath in the synagogues.

There was a certain extravagant method of interpretation adopted by the Christians of the first and second centuries, and which appears in the evangelists, by which passages from the Pentateuch and from the Psalms came to be considered as predictions of the coming and office of Jesus; but the most casual reading shows that they had no such purpose or significance. In fact, it is open to debate whether the Messianic expectation in the form in which it was held by Jesus and his followers, or as held by his countrymen, the Jews, had any reliable basis in prophecy. It is certain that some of the so-called Messianic prophecies and what the early Christians, the evangelists, and apostles, and Jesus himself, confidently considered predictions of the Messiah, clearly related to early historic persons, and to political events nearly contemporaneous with the time of their writing.

Making all allowance for the extravagance begotten of the fierce controversies between the adherents of the new faith and the orthodox Israelites, by which even Moses was claimed to have foretold Jesus, and temple songs in honor of Jehovah attributed to David were assumed to be pre-recognitions of Christ, there still remained among the priesthood and the common people a well-defined expectation of a glory to come to their nation, a restoration to it of more than its primitive prosperity, the subjugation and defeat of the powerful heathen empires that had successively oppressed it, and a sovereign of the lineage of David brought back to reign in Zion, who, if not personally immortal, was to have a kingdom, to which there should be no end.

Isaiah had sung that Jehovah should choose again Israel, and set him in his own land, and that there he should hold captive those who had held him captive, and have rest from sorrow, fear, and bondage.[a] At the blowing of a trumpet, they who were ready to perish in Assyria, and the outcasts of Egypt, should worship Jehovah in Zion in Jerusalem.[b] The ransomed of Jehovah should return to Zion with songs and perpetual joy.[c] The feeble nation should become strong.[d] Israel should eat of the riches of the nations, and boast himself in their glory; and aliens and strangers should become his servants.[e] Jehovah should delight again in Jerusalem, and take from her the voice of weeping. In great prosperity, her citizens should build houses and plant vineyards, and live, saint and sinner, a full lifetime of one hundred years.[f]

The gloomy and unpatriotic Jeremiah, who had been put in prison for falling off to the Chaldeans, and depressing the national courage by his counsel to make no resistance to the hosts of the Assyrians, had indicated a time, when Israel should not speak of Jehovah as his deliverer from the slavery of Egypt, but as he who led him out of the North country, and from all countries whither he had driven him, to dwell again in his own land.[g] Jehovah should bring him again from Chaldea to his own land, and plant him there not to be plucked up.[h] Jehovah should gather Israel as a shepherd gathers his flock. Israel should rejoice on Zion in the plenitude of wine, of oil, of

---

[a] Isaiah xiv., 1-3. [b] Isaiah xxvii., 13. [c] Isaiah xxxv., 10.
[d] Isaiah lx., 22. [e] Isaiah lxi., 5, 6. [f] Isaiah lxv., 19-22.
[g] Jeremiah xxiii., 6-8. [h] Jeremiah xxiv., 5-7.

the young of flocks and herds. The priest should be satiated with fatness, and the people with the goodness of Jehovah.[a] Israel should be to Jehovah again a name of joy, and all the nations should fear and tremble for the goodness and prosperity his God should procure him.[b] Ezekiel had declared, speaking in the name of Jehovah, "I will take you from among the heathen, and gather you out of all countries, and will bring you into your own land"; and ye shall dwell therein, and be my people, and I will be your God.[c] Amos had written that Jehovah should bring again the captivity of his people Israel, that they should prosper greatly in the land whence they should never again be expatriated;[d] and Zephaniah that the restored and ransomed people should be a name and a praise among all the people of the earth.[e]

In spite of the contemptible character of many of their kings, the Jews had always looked back to their monarchy with longing regret, and could not consider themselves as either free or prosperous under any other government than that of their own sovereigns of the lineage of David. Their sacred writings expressed and kept alive this national aspiration. A child should be born upon whose shoulders the government should be, to be called "Wonderful, Counsellor, the mighty God, the everlasting Father, the Prince of Peace," whose kingdom should increase forever, and who should sit upon the throne of David to establish it forever and ever.[f] The days should come when Jehovah would raise unto David a righteous branch, who should reign a king and prosper, and execute justice in the earth.[g] My servant David, Jehovah had said, shall feed my flock and be their shepherd; and I will be their God, and my servant David shall be a prince among them.[h] Israel and Judah shall be one, and they shall have one king and one shepherd, even David, my servant.[i] The kingdom to come was to be an everlasting kingdom, not to pass away or be destroyed; and its king all people, nations, and languages should serve.[j]

There was to be an era of peace, the peace of glory, prosperity, and content for the Israelites, the peace of

[a] Jeremiah xxxi., 10-14.   [b] Jeremiah xxxiii., 9.   [c] Ezekiel xxxvi., 24, 28.
[d] Amos ix., 14, 15.   [e] Zephaniah iii., 20.   [f] Isaiah ix., 6, 7.   [g] Jeremiah xxiii., 5.
[h] Ezekiel xxxiv., 22, 23.   [i] Ezekiel xxxvii., 22-24.   [j] Daniel vii., 14.

subjection and docility for all the other nations. Out of Zion in Jerusalem, the destined king should judge nations and rebuke many people; and they should beat their swords into ploughshares and their spears into pruning-hooks, and learn war no more.[a] Of the peace his reign should inaugurate there should be no end. The very wild beasts should lose their ferocity, and nothing should hurt or destroy in all the holy mountain.[b] Violence should no more be heard in the land, nor wasting nor destruction.[c]

The peace, however, was to be the peace of conquest, the peace after a struggle, victory and triumph over all enemies. This was quite in accord with the savage temper of the times, the fierce spirit which the exterminators of the Canaanites continued for ages to cherish. Here is the way this feeling flashes out of the sombre, national literature. David had been a man of blood whom the sacred poetry of his people represented as singing praises to Jehovah for teaching his hands to war and his fingers to fight. In his old age, the blood he had shed, not always even in legitimate warfare, sat heavy on his soul; and his tender conscience restrained him from building and consecrating a temple to the God of righteousness. So the new David was to be a warrior, and was to sit down upon the right hand of power, after he had made his enemies his footstool.

The kings of the earth take counsel against Jehovah, and against his anointed (king), saying: Let us break their bands and cast off their cords. Jehovah shall laugh, and sitting in the heavens, shall have them in derision. He calls the anointed his Son, and promises to give him the heathen for an inheritance, the uttermost parts of the earth for a possession, that he might break them with a rod of iron, and dash them to pieces like a potter's vessel.[d] Jehovah at the right hand of the anointed, sitting with his feet on the neck of his enemies, shall strike through kings in the day of his wrath. He shall judge among the heathen, he shall fill the places with dead bodies, he shall wound the heads over many countries.[e] Say to them of a fearful heart, Be strong, fear not, your God shall come

[a] Isaiah ii., 3, 4.   [b] Isaiah xi., 6–9.   [c] Isaiah lx., 18.
[d] Psalms ii., 2–9.   [e] Psalms cx., 5, 6.

with vengeance and retribution.[a] It was the Messiah, clad in garments glorious with blood, who was represented as declaring: "I will tread them in mine anger, and trample them in my fury; and their blood shall be sprinkled upon my garments, and I will stain all my raiment. For the day of vengeance is in my heart, and the year of my redeemed is come."[b] "For, behold, Jehovah will come with fire, and with his chariots like a whirlwind, to render his anger with fury, and his rebuke with flames of fire. For by fire and by his sword will Jehovah plead with all flesh; and the slain of Jehovah shall be many."[c] "He shall smite the earth with the rod of his mouth, and with the breath of his lips shall he slay the wicked."[d] "Every battle ... is with confused noise, and garments rolled in blood; but this shall be with burning and fuel of fire. For unto us a Child is born," etc.[e] The harvest is ripe, the press is full, the vats overflow; for their wickedness is great. The day of the Lord is near in the valley of decision. The sun and moon shall be darkened, and the stars withdraw their shining. Jehovah shall roar out of Zion, and the heavens and earth shall shake; but Jehovah shall be the strength and hope of the children of Israel.[f] The day of the Lord cometh; for, said Jehovah, I will gather all nations against Jerusalem to battle, and it shall be taken. Then shall Jehovah go forth and fight against those nations. His feet shall stand on Mount Olivet, which shall be cleaved by a great valley running east and west. It shall be light in the evening as in the day. Living water shall go out by Jerusalem, half to the Mediterranean, half to the Dead Sea. All the south land shall become an elevated plain, and the land of Israel shall be peopled and never more destroyed, and Jehovah shall be king over the whole earth. And this shall be the plague wherewith Jehovah will smite all the people that have fought against Jerusalem: their flesh shall consume away while they stand upon their feet, and their eyes shall consume away in their holes, and their tongues shall consume away in their mouths. A great tumult from Jehovah shall be among them, and they shall lay violent hands on each other. And Judah shall fight at Jerusalem, and

[a] Isaiah xxxv., 4.   [b] Isaiah lxiii., 2-4.   [c] Isaiah lxvi., 15, 16.
[d] Isaiah xi., 4.   [e] Isaiah ix., 5.   [f] Joel iii., 13-16.

gather there the wealth of the heathen — gold, silver, and apparel — in great abundance. And every one that survives of the nations, that went against Jerusalem shall become worshippers of Jehovah, and come up there yearly to celebrate his feasts; and whosoever among them shall not come up to these feasts shall be punished with drouth upon their lands. Everything, even the bells of the horses, shall be consecrated to Jehovah: among the nations, that come up to the house of Jehovah to celebrate his feasts, however, the accursed Canaanite shall be forever excluded.ᵃ "The day cometh that shall burn as an oven; and all the proud, all that do wickedly, shall be stubble." "Ye shall tread down the wicked; for they shall be ashes under the soles of your feet, in the day that I shall do this, saith the Lord of hosts."ᵇ

So fixed in the prophetic mind was the idea of a grand retribution, convulsion, and reversal of situations between the chosen people and their powerful and numerous enemies, whose prey and spoil they had been so many years, that they came to mention it as *that day*, the grand assize, the judgment and condemnation of the nations, the vindication of the right of Jehovah to be worshipped as the chief among the gods, — an idea which, modified by Christian eschatology, became the modern day of judgment.

It may not be strictly pertinent to this discussion to inquire what is the real value and significance of this prophetic literature. The prophets appear to have been a school of devoted patriots, who adhered more to the monotheistic idea and the ritual of national worship, than they did to the fortunes of the reigning kings, or to the tendencies of the popular sentiment. Of this lower type of patriotism they were, as a class, quite destitute. Jeremiah had incensed and disheartened his countrymen with his melancholy vaticinations of defeat and subjugation. Indeed there seemed ample reason for his gloomy forebodings in the magnitude of the Assyrian empire, and in the petty resources of the miniature kingdom of Judea, as well as in the fate that was known to have befallen nations much more able to resist so great a power. All the prophets were too plain-spoken and too little flatterers of the national pride to be popular. They had suffered

---
ᵃ Zechariah xiv.   ᵇ Malachi iv., 1-3.

more or less persecution, and some of them had been put to death. Their writings, however, were true to the national spirit: they all recognized what every Israelite believed, that his fathers Abraham, Isaac, and Jacob were chosen men of God, and that their lineage was favored among the races of the earth as the chief beneficiaries of the Deity, the only nation that he had not given over to work evil and inherit destruction. They all flattered the national hope — born of their calamities, defeats, and enslavements — of a restoration to more than the glories of David, more than the wealth and prosperity of the patriarchs. So that, when the generation which the prophets had denounced for their vices and idolatries was dead, and especially when a remnant of the captives returned from Babylon with chastened hearts and more enlightened minds to rebuild Jerusalem and re-establish the national worship, it is not surprising, that the prophetic writings came to be cherished by the people, and their poetic fervor to be ascribed to the direct inspiration of Jehovah.

It is a modern conception that the world is subject to general laws, and that society and government develop their existence and are maintained by a compliance with certain principles. The ancient mind, if capable of forming such an hypothesis, had scarcely data enough upon which to base it. To the ancient observer, if one country, kingdom, race, and city prospered, grew rich and populous, and subdued its neighbors, it was not because it was peopled by a more brave and intelligent race, or had advantages of soil, sea-coast, or mines, or a stronger and better organized government, but because it had a more powerful god than its neighbors, or had been careful to propitiate him by a more punctilious performance of worship. This idea runs through the whole ancient literature of the Jews, is in fact the one doctrine taught and reiterated in it all.

The writings of the Hebrew prophets possess for us the quality, which all serious literature has in a greater or less degree, of supplying incentives to piety and virtue. They are, as Paul aptly expresses it, "profitable for correction and instruction in right living." But we shall best understand the influence and function of these poet-prophets in the development of the national character of the people for whom they wrote, if we perceive that they were primarily political writers. They wrote upon political subjects. Their inspiration was their patriotism, and their object the public good. As the French or American political pamphleteer believes that universal suffrage, legislation by a popularly elected government, free-trade, common schools, public morality, are all essential elements of national prosperity, so he will write, with what eloquence and zeal he is capable of, in advocacy of these measures. Such views, in the age of Isaiah, Hosea, and Ezekiel, were quite inconceivable. The only assured opinion to which they had come was that national prosperity, abundant harvests, wealth of gold, silver, and raiment, brave and victorious armies, conquests over rivals and enemies, were the gifts of Jehovah, made generous and propitious by worship, sacrifices, and decorous conduct. Accordingly, they advocated a faithful adherence to Jehovah, in a style suited to the rude temper of the times and the rude fervor of their own spirits. Their style to a cultivated taste seems extravagant, the everywhere obtrusive illustration of the worship of alien deities indecent, and the callous indifference of the writers to the most horrible suffering and absolute extermination of all people, who were not Hebrews, and would not become their servants, as inconsistent with the merciful instincts of good men. But we look in vain for the humanitarian spirit of our time among this primeval people, whose literature is to be studied in connection with a study of the people who produced it, and the age in which it was produced.

Returning to the illustration of the patriotic pamphleteer, who devotes his pen to the advocacy of education, popular morality, and good government,—as he draws illustrations and examples from the past, so he does not hesitate to forecast the future, without claiming any enlightenment other than what comes of a close observation of the course of history and the natural results of human conduct. He feels authorized to declare with as much assurance as if the truth had been revealed to him by a divine oracle, or the voice of God speaking out of a cloud, that a government systematically ignoring the interests and rights of the people, as represented in a legislative assembly, will inevitably become an oppressive despotism; that the neglect of popular education will be followed by a loss of liberty, and that, through the decay of the national morality, luxury, effeminacy, corruption, conquest, and subjection ensue, and consume a nation. The prophets had a single remedy for all the evils of their times, a single safeguard against all the perils of the future; and, so far as the faithful service of Jehovah related to conduct, and to the practice of such virtues as temperance, chastity, industry, frugality, honest dealing, and truthfulness, the remedy and the safeguard were certainly efficacious, and the truth of their revelations absolute. They did not work out their teachings in an ethical, didactic way. If they had attempted that, they would have been more unheeded by their countrymen than they were. They gave them in a poetic form, to seize the imagination of their hearers. They concealed their didactic purpose and ethical implications under vivid pictures of the material prosperity that should attend a patriotic attachment to the national religion, and of the horrors of slavery, slaughter, and mutilation that should befall them in the invasion of heathen nations — become the ministers of Jehovah's vengeance for the rebellion of his people.

It is by no means probable that the prophetic writers among the Hebrews claimed any knowledge of the future, other than of this kind. The changes of empire in the East had been so rapid and summary that it is as safe to predict the downfall of a luxurious, populous, and corrupt city or kingdom, as to predict of youth, exulting in the plenitude of its powers, that old age will weaken and death destroy its strength and beauty.

All the more remarkable and precise prophecies, which have been claimed by the early and later Christians to be applicable to the Messiah, are plainly applicable to persons and events contemporaneous with their utterance. Those prophecies, which, like the visions of Daniel, have been considered foreshadowings of the course of world-history, may correspond in some general way with what is now known of the prominent events of the age, and before the age, when they are believed to have been written. All semblance of accord, however, between these vague and indefinite visions and the actual sequel of events during the Christian era wholly disappears. The changes of empire from Chaldean to Persian, from Persian to Greek, are sketched with tolerable accuracy. The prophetic eye, in peering into the modern world, saw only dim shapes which the most devout ingenuity has utterly failed to find even typical representations of the growth and decay of states that have succeeded the Roman Empire.

It may likewise be remarked that giving to the prophetic declarations, of which a concise summary has been in these pages recapitulated, the full force of a divine prediction, they do not necessarily imply a divine or even immortal king of the new kingdom which was to overthrow and make subject all other kingdoms. Isaiah had indeed said, he shall be called — not shall be — Wonderful, Counsellor, the great and mighty God. Such epithets were quite consonant with Oriental exaggeration, with the adulation and deification of kings among the Egyptians, Assyrians, and even the Romans. The kingdom was to be an everlasting kingdom. The king was to be born, was to be a child, was to be of the lineage of David; but, as it is plainly said that men were to live out their days to a hundred years, it is implied that there was to be a perpetual succession of wise and good kings, each gathered to his fathers in a good old age, after a glorious and prosperous reign. Indeed, while the Persians on one side of them and the Egyptians on the other, in their literature and their monuments, were indicating how much the thought of a future life and a judgment, which fixed the fates of men in it, affected their daily conduct; while even the pleasure-loving Greek had his sad and pensive moods, in which he bewailed the brevity of youth and life,— the practical Hebrew, from his great lawgiver, Moses, down nearly to the advent of Jesus, contemptuously ignored all such considerations, and insisted, even in his most spiritual moods, that life was good enough, if there was enough of it, and if he could have a fair chance in it, quite content after such fortune to be gathered to his fathers.

But what is chiefly to be considered is not what the significance of the prophetic writings is, but what it was held to be by the countrymen of Jesus at the time he lived. Everything in the New Testament indicates that the belief was general that these writings were predictions, made upon the authority of the Supreme Being, of events that were to occur. All these prophecies, so far as they related to a restoration of the Israelites to their own land, and the glory of their new kingdom, were uttered after the principal part of the nation had been carried into captivity; and the more explicit and definite prophecies were uttered during the continuance of the captivity of the remnant of the nation in Assyria. The feeble political existence which the restored Jews maintained for a few years, under the sovereignty of the successors of Cyrus until the conquest by Alexander, was too transient and too wretched to be accepted as the realization of the extravagant promise of an everlasting dominion, established at Jerusalem over all people and nations and languages, though this was the restoration which the exiled patriots had in their mind, and pictured in the glowing imagery of their hopes and of their indomitable pride of race. So they waited for the consolation and redemption of Israel, and have waited through all the succeeding centuries till the present day, the most touching and pathetic, but not the only instance in history, of a race cherishing from generation to generation an aspiration which often becomes the enthusiasm and force by which it is realized.

Jesus himself evidently shared this expectation of his countrymen, and derived it from them. The phrases, *kingdom of heaven* and *kingdom of God*, are not found in the Old Scriptures, that set forth the glories of the golden age to which the Israelite looked forward. But as the kingdom is represented to be set up by God himself, and as the sovereign was to be the Son of Man coming in the clouds of heaven, the name *kingdom of heaven* was of very natural derivation, and probably had become a popular term before John the Baptist used it or Jesus adopted it from him. The kingdom of heaven by that name must have been everywhere familiar in the popular thought, or the disciples in the very earliest stages of their discipleship would not have been commissioned to go and make everywhere proclamation that it was at hand. It is fairly inferrible that the Jewish people had as distinct idea of it as Christendom has to-day of the *millennium*.

It must then be considered that Jesus derived from his times the name *kingdom of heaven*, and that it represented a sequence of secular events, among which were prominent the recognition of a chosen people by Jehovah, their establishment in a perpetual kingdom which should dominate the kingdoms of the world, with Jerusalem for the seat of empire, the hostility of the nations against this kingdom, their total defeat and overthrow, with a remnant saving their lives by submission and servitude and by the adoption of the true religion.

CHAPTER III.

THE DOMINANT IDEA OF JESUS.

"No less remarkable is the over-faith of each man in the importance of what he has to do or say. The poet, the prophet, has a higher value for what he utters than any hearer, and therefore it gets spoken. The strong and self-complacent Luther declares with an emphasis not to be mistaken that 'God himself cannot do without wise men.' Jacob Boehmen and George Fox betray their egotism in the pertinacity of their controversial tracts, and James Naylor once suffered himself to be worshipped as the Christ. Each prophet comes presently to identify himself with his thought, and to esteem his hat and shoes sacred. However this may discredit such persons with the judicious, it helps them with the people, and it gives heat, pungency, and publicity to their words."—*Emerson's Essays, second series. Essay on Nature.*

IN endeavoring to learn how much Jesus remodelled in his own mind the national aspiration for the kingdom of heaven, we must not disregard certain indications that he came gradually to his own conceptions, and that he accepted with hesitation and diffidence the impression that at last forced itself upon him, that he was himself the Son of Man, the heir of the kingdom of the world. It is in the early part of his career, and mainly in the Sermon on the Mount, that what Matthew Arnold denotes as the characteristic of the mind of Jesus, "his sweet reasonableness," becomes apparent. He seemed to the people to speak with authority, but that was because he appealed directly to their moral sense and did not quote Scripture, which seemed to be the peculiar didactic method, they had been accustomed to in the preaching of the scribes. He did not make himself prominent, nor exact any homage to or belief in himself. So peculiar is this method in contrast with his later teachings that we hesitate to accept as a part of what he actually said, "Many will say unto *me* in that day, Lord, Lord,"[a] and believe it may have been injected afterward into a discourse so wholly impersonal and self-forgetful.

[a] Matt. vii., 22.

Still, it must have been not only the inspiration that the kingdom of heaven was near, and that he must join John the Baptist, and reinforce himself with disciples, and go everywhere and be its herald, that urged Jesus in his remarkable career, but the conviction that he himself had some larger function to perform in the stupendous events about to strike the world with awe.

It was with real diffidence that he received the frank declaration of Peter, that he believed him to be the Christ, the Son of God, that he rebuked the possessed persons, who loudly imputed to him a divine nature,[a] and that he begged his disciples to tell no man that he was the Christ.[b]

It is hard to account upon rational principles for any high enthusiasm, or for the determination of the soul toward any special study or achievement. It comes to the spirit of men by those mysterious movements of the spirit which have been called genius and inspiration. In Jesus, the conviction that he was a divine and providential person, which he undoubtedly had, may have sprung from the consciousness of a substantial exemption from the sensual appetites and sordid ambitions that determine the ordinary quality of humanity, of a clear insight of moral truth, and of an eloquence in illustrating and conveying it which all who listened to his speech seemed to have attested, and lastly of a certain power over depressed and nervously diseased and enfeebled persons to relieve and cure them, out of which the legends of the miracles grew.

In coming to the conclusion that he was the national Messiah,— a claim, by the way, other men made before him and after him,— the mental processes might have gone on thus: How can a man who was born of human parents, who remembers his uneventful, humble, laborious youth of thirty years, whose brothers, sisters, and mother all the people know, be the person whom Jehovah calls *my Lord*, and invites to sit at his right hand? How can he be the Son of Man, brought to the Ancient of Days upon the clouds to be the crowned king of the nations? How can a man who has patiently borne all insult, and whose faith it is to resist not evil, come up

[a] Luke iv., 34, 35.   [b] Matt. xvi., 20.

from Edom with garments gloriously red with the blood of enemies he has trampled to death in his fury?

But Esaias had declared: My servant, my elect, upon whom Jehovah has put his spirit shall not strive nor cry, nor cause his voice to be heard in the street; but the isles shall wait for his law.[a] "He is despised and rejected of men; a man of sorrows, and acquainted with grief." He was despised, and we esteemed him not. He was wounded for our transgressions, and bruised for our iniquities. Jehovah hath lain upon him the iniquity of us all. He was oppressed and afflicted. He is brought as a lamb to the slaughter. He was taken from prison[b] and from judgment. He was cut off from the land of the living, and his grave was made with the wicked. Daniel, too, had explicitly announced that Messiah should "be cut off, but not for himself."[c] And Zechariah, whose descriptions of the kingdom of heaven had been fuller of details than the writings of any of the prophets, had in prophetic vision invoked the daughter of Jerusalem to behold her king coming to her, just, and having salvation; lowly, and riding upon a colt, the foal of an ass.[d] And, again, he had summoned the sword to awake against the shepherd and companion of Jehovah, and smite him, so that the sheep should be scattered.[e]

So, then, there is a Messiah coming in the clouds, coming red with the blood of his enemies and in the heat of his fury, and a Messiah coming lowly upon an ass's foal, a man of sorrows, to be oppressed and afflicted, to be tried and imprisoned, and cut off from the living, and buried with the wicked. Are there, then, two Messiahs? No, Jesus reasoned, but two comings of one Messiah. And, as the glorious king cannot be rejected and slain *after* he has come in the clouds to sit on the throne of an everlasting kingdom, his life of sorrow and death of shame must *precede* all that glory.

Jesus told the Pharisees in Jerusalem a few days before his arrest a parable which discloses with great particularity his idea of the connection between these two comings. Jehovah was a householder, who had a vineyard, with a wine-press enclosed with a hedge, and defended with a

---

[a] Isaiah xlii., 1, 2, 3.   [b] Isaiah liii.   [c] Daniel ix., 26.
[d] Zechariah ix., 9.   [e] Zechariah xiii., 7.

tower. The Jews were certain husbandmen to whom
he let the vineyard, expecting to receive its income. The
prophets were his servants, whom he had sent from time
to time to collect the dues, whom the wicked husbandmen had beaten, stoned, and slain. Jesus himself was the
husbandman's son, whom they caught, cast out of the
vineyard and slew, but who should be the head stone of
the corner in the new kingdom of heaven, falling on his
enemies and grinding them to powder.ᵃ The Messiah
comes first to do the same office as the prophets, and to
invite to repentance. He meekly submits to obloquy
and death, and makes no appeal to his divine power;
but, rejected, he becomes the avenger and punisher of his
persecutors.

It was an essential feature in the popular idea of the
kingdom of heaven, that it was to be the empire of Israel.
All the prophets, who were believed to have predicted the
event, assigned its glory and prosperity to the favored
nation as their heritage and recompense. Daniel, speaking in a Syriac tongue, and before the Babylonian court,
had affirmed that the people of the saints of the most
high God should possess the kingdom; but, as Jehovah
obtained in the royal proclamation of the Assyrian mon-
archs the title of the "*Most High God*,"ᵇ it is probable
that his auditors understood by Daniel's language the
sacred, elect, consecrated people of Jehovah, or, in other
words, the Jews, excluding from the promise, perhaps,
those who had in the captivity lapsed into the worship of
other gods.

It was quite alien to what is told of the character of
Jesus that he should entertain an anticipation so narrow
and national. Though he told the Syro-Phœnician woman
that he was sent only to the lost sheep of the house of
Israel,ᶜ that was evidently to test the strength of her faith.
His real sentiment was early expressed in the declaration: "Many shall come from the east and west, and
shall sit down with Abraham and Isaac and Jacob in
the kingdom of heaven;ᵈ but the children of the kingdom shall be cast out." He had but little patriotism:
the national pride and exclusiveness of his countrymen

ᵃ Matt. xxi., 33–45.   ᵇ Dan. vii., 27; iii., 26; iv., 2.
ᶜ Matt. xv., 24.   ᵈ Matt. viii., 11.

excited his contempt. The Roman domination he had no controversy with. He paid taxes to it, fully recognized its secular authority, treated its officials with a courtesy and respect which he habitually withheld from the accredited successors and representatives of the old hierarchy, that held to the national traditions and maintained with great strictness the national worship. He never, by word or deed, gave the least sanction to those seditious risings of over-zealous patriots, which vexed the peace of the country, and of which his own native province, Galilee, had been the principal theatre.

With such sentiments, it is not surprising that the teachings of the prophets became at length considerably transfused by his own ideas, and that, if in the beginning he believed, that Scripture could only be fulfilled by a kingdom universal and perpetual given to the people of his nation, he came later to the belief of the utter repudiation and rejection of his nation, and of a kingdom transferred to those who should accept him as a deliverer and sovereign. Nor was this idea at all alien to the general tenor of the Hebrew Scriptures. All the Hebrew writings had represented the choice of Israel as provisional, and conditional on his obedience and faithful devotion. Rejection had been the steady discipline, by which the idolatry of the earlier ages had been punished. Every successful invasion, every waste of territory, the domination of Philistine, Egyptian, Syrian, Assyrian, Greek, and Roman powers, was always represented as Jehovah's resentment of their falling away from his worship. Moses himself was represented in Deuteronomy — though the book is now believed of comparatively modern composition — to have set before the Israelites a blessing, if they obeyed the commandments of their God, a curse if they went after other gods. This is the one lesson of all the historians, the inspiration of the poets, and the burden of the prophets.

In the memorabilia which are preserved of Jesus, he does not seem to have given to what may be called the national party a *locus penitentiae*. Toward the Pharisees and Sadducees he always demeaned himself, as if he had adopted the intolerant thought of his master, John the

Baptist, who had said to those classes, "*O generation of vipers, who hath warned you to flee from the wrath to come?*"[a] It is one of the indicia of the unreliability of the Johannic Gospel, that it represents Jesus as holding long and feeble controversies with the scribes and Pharisees at Jerusalem, for the purpose of maintaining his claim to a place in the divine dispensation in reference to the peculiar people; while the other evangelists represent him as hostile to the Pharisees from the first, and meeting even their courteous overtures with suspicion and denunciation. Arrived at Jerusalem, he weeps over it, and says: If thou hadst known the things that make for thy peace, but *now* they are forever hid from thine eyes. The judgment has already come, the rejection of the daughter of Zion is complete.[b]

But shall the rejection of Israel prevent the establishment of the divine kingdom on earth? Not at all. My oxen and fatlings are killed: the wedding feast is prepared, and let the servants scour the highways and hedges, and compel everybody they meet to come in, that my house may be furnished with guests. "Children of Abraham, indeed!" exclaimed, in his indignation, the clear-sighted John: "God can make out of the common dust, out of these stones on the surface of the wilderness, children of Abraham."[c] "The poor have the gospel preached to them." The babes see that to which you wise and prudent are blind, said Jesus; and every one is blessed that does not take offence at me.[d] So, instead of the Israelitish nation taking the kingdom of heaven, and ruling the remnant of the nations forever, the Israelitish nation, by rejecting him, their shepherd and king, have filled the measure of their iniquity; and the kingdom is given to the poor, to babes, to the children of the kingdom, to the righteous, to those who have received Jesus and ministered to him, or to the *little ones* that believe on him.[e]

A scarcely less radical modification of the prophetic conception, as kept alive in the popular feeling, is traceable also to the known character of Jesus. The glory of the restoration was long life, peace, power over the

[a] Matt. iii., 7. [b] Luke xix., 41, 42. [c] Matt. iii., 9.
[d] Matt. xi., 5, 6. [e] Matt. xi., 25.

heathen — the wealth of the nations in gold, silver, and raiment poured into Jerusalem. To Jesus, life was nothing. He held his own ready to lay down for his hope. He roused the dull souls of his followers by telling them, "He that saveth his life shall lose it: he that loseth his life for my sake shall save it.ᵃ Fear not them that kill the body: fear only him who can kill both soul and body in hell."ᵇ He cared nothing for wealth. The first words of his Sermon on the Mount were a beatitude upon the poor. He denied that a rich man could enter his kingdom of heaven. He told a young man, whose correct morals won his love, that he must give away all his possessions to have treasure in heaven.ᶜ He gloried in having no property, not even what the birds and foxes had, — a place to lay his head.ᵈ Power over other men was to him a snare and a reproach: the great man was he who was servant of all.ᵉ Accordingly, Jesus eliminated from his doctrine of the kingdom of heaven all the elements of secular prosperity, and gave no pictures of its wealth and luxury to excite a merely sordid and sensuous imagination. Some ideas of recompense for the privations they had suffered, some recognition of his persecuted disciples sitting in judgment on their persecutors, evidently lingered in his promise of a hundred-fold more houses and lands than they had given up, and of the twelve thrones, on which his twelve chief friends should sit, judging the twelve tribes of Israel.ᶠ

Terrible in vengeance and fire and blood as was the great day, which all the prophets had foreseen in vision, not all the enemies of the chosen people were to be destroyed. The heathen nations were to be ruled over by the victorious Israelites, and only those, who had fought against Jerusalem and Jehovah, were to be miserably destroyed. The rest of mankind were to become proselytes, and yearly to come up to Mount Zion to perform rites in recognition of the world-sovereignty of Jehovah. We look in vain in the scheme of Jesus for this mitigation and mercy. Though the redeemed, the saved, the blessed of his Father were the poor, the little ones, that had believed on him, and though to this class no hard test of

---

ᵃ Luke ix., 24. ᵇ Luke xii., 4, 5. ᶜ Matt. xix., 16, 26. ᵈ Matt. viii., 19, 20.
ᵉ Matt. xxiii., 10, 12. ᶠ Matt. xix., 27-29.

discipleship was applied, no searching analysis of the genuineness of conversion, no metaphysical inspection of a grace, the counterfeit of which eludes the careful scrutiny of all but divinely aided experts,— nothing, in fine, but giving a cup of water to one, or ministering to the physical wants of one, because he is a disciple of Jesus,— yet nowhere in all the conversation of Jesus is any purpose disclosed to exempt those, who shall disbelieve on him, or neglect to minister to him or the humblest of his followers, from complete rejection and perpetual punishment and destruction. After the judgment, their submission was declared to be too late.[a] They are not to be servants even in the new kingdom.[b] Their doom, like the kingdom prepared for the blessed of the Father, is prepared for them from the foundation of the world.[c]

The chief feature of the prophetic restoration was the re-establishment of the Mosaic worship, the honor of the priesthood, and the punctilious observance of the feasts and sacrifices of the temple. But, of these, Jesus entertained a very light estimate. According to his three more credible biographers, he never went up to Jerusalem to the annual feasts until on the eve of his death, and then with quite other views than to be a humble communicant. The priesthood he held in such contempt, that his animosity toward the order is the one riddle of his character; and of the laws of Moses, even of the ten commandments, he spoke slightingly, as the traditions of them of old times.[d] Accordingly, there is no glorified Jerusalem, no temple worship to which all nations come up, and no priest nor priestly order, no scribe nor Pharisee in his kingdom of heaven.

It is thus apparent how much the genius of Jesus had modified the national anticipation of a glorious epoch, which was believed to be foretold by the poet-prophets of an earlier age. It is not surprising that the great body of well-taught scribes and, following them, the mass of the Jewish people, failed to see in Jesus any similitude of their hero king and deliverer; rejected his idea of two comings of the Messiah, neither of them bringing any restoration *to Israel* as such, or making the worship revealed through

[a] Matt. xxv., 10-13.   [b] Luke xiii., 25.   [c] Matt. xxv., 34, 41.
[d] Matt. v., 21, 27, 33, 38, 43.

Moses the cultus of the subdued Gentiles; and would not accept, as the salvation promised to *their* race, what was offered on such cheap terms to wayfarers in the highways and hedges, and to the Israelite only as he virtually fell off from Moses and the Jehovah of their fathers.

Why did Jesus believe the kingdom of heaven to be at hand, and, though he declared he did not know the day nor the hour when the Son of Man should come in the clouds to establish it, yet stake his whole veracity upon the prediction that that generation should not pass until all that he had affirmed in reference to it, should be fulfilled?[a] We can discover two reasons which probably contributed, with other impressions too private and subtle for conjecture even, to this fixed prepossession of his life. John the Baptist had preached repentance as a necessary preparation for the *kingdom of heaven*, which he declared to be at hand. Those who came to his baptism — and they were undoubtedly many, even if we consider Matthew's statement that Jerusalem and all Judea and all the region about Jordan were baptized by him,[b] an obvious exaggeration — believed his prediction at the time. When afterward Herod laid hands on him, kept him in prison at his will, and had him murdered without any popular commotion, without any tokens in earth or sky of the displeasure of heaven, the fickle multitude, ready to be alarmed, easy to be reassured, doubted if anything unusual was about to happen. Not so Jesus: in his sincere and earnest soul, that revered John as a prophet, a conviction once fastened would abide. He believed in his old master none the less loyally after the ruling powers had suppressed him, and after his treacherous converts had forsaken him.

When once he had accepted the belief, that the prophetic era of a reign of righteousness was on the eve of beginning, upon the faith of John's declaration, there was much in the character and opinions of Jesus to confirm and intensify that belief. Jesus had lived a blameless life. Free from the taint of sensuality and sordidness, he had preserved a tender moral feeling, highly sensitive to the contact of evil. When he came out of the seclusion, in which his youth had passed, in pious meditation and devout communion with what was to him the personal

[a] Matt. xxiv., 34, 35.   [b] Matt. iii., 5, 6.

presence of the paternal God, and with a marvellous intuition of character looked upon worldly men,—the corrupt, licentious, and extortionate Roman place-holders, courtiers and soldiers with their base retinue of male and female profligates, the priesthood zealous and punctilious in the performance of worship, but formal, undevout, and uncharitable, if not extortionate, oppressive, and vicious,—when he came to learn, that everywhere reputable and honorable men gave themselves shamelessly to the practice of acts which he had found it easy to exclude from his thought, it is not surprising that he came to believe that humanity had sunk to its dregs, that the last stages of wickedness had been reached, and that the sin-drunken world was staggering to its doom. Thus ever does the observation of life in its excesses of evil sadden and shock that rare feminine type of purity to which he belonged; while the experience of years, travel, and especially familiarity with the history and literature of other ages corrects our despair of our own age, and either makes us cynical in the familiarity with conditions which seem to affect society nearly alike everywhere, or philosophical in the confidence that, in the midst of outcropping crime that ruins individuals, humanity, by slow accretions, is gaining in virtue and moral sanity. Had Jesus visited Alexandria, Athens, Rome, had he known by familiarity with the history and literature of earlier times the refinements and debasements of iniquity, that had distinguished the luxurious capitals Babylon, Nineveh, and Memphis, he might have believed that the industrious, frugal, and devout people of his own provincial Galilee were not the wicked and adulterous generation[a] of whose evil ways the heavens had grown weary.

It is, perhaps, generally believed in the Christian Church, now that nearly nineteen centuries have intervened without any coming of Jesus in the clouds of heaven with a retinue of angels to gather his chosen into an everlasting kingdom, and to consign all other men to an everlasting punishment, that Jesus did not mean by the words he uttered with so much emphasis of asseveration to indicate any outward and physical changes in the constitution of nature or the order of human society. It

[a] Matt. xii., 39.

is held that the kingdom of heaven is a highly figurative expression, and denotes not so much a catastrophe or new order of civilization, as the introduction into the old order of a new and spiritual force, whereby the world is, through long and gradual processes, to be renovated and made the fit abode of regenerated and purified men. Such passages as these are cited in support of this view: When he was asked by the Pharisees when the kingdom of God should come, he answered, " The kingdom of God cometh not with observation: neither shall they say, Lo here! or Lo there! for, behold, the kingdom of God is within you."[a] The parable of the mustard-seed and that of the leaven are also believed to typify the gradual and quiet evolution of the kingdom of heaven. The conversation of which the first declaration forms a part, according to Matthew, was not held with the Pharisees, but with his own disciples.[b] A detailed account of the method and time of the end of the age given to his disciples by Jesus in answer to their specific question, is broken into two narratives by Luke, and part told to his disciples and part to the Pharisees in answer to their demand when the kingdom of God should come. The probabilities seem to favor Matthew's correctness. The Pharisees are not shown ever to have reached a stage of docility and confidence, to make it probable that they would ever ask such a question. His determination to exclude from a knowledge of the mysteries of the kingdom of heaven all to whom it had not been given to know them, would prevent Jesus from making such disclosures to the Pharisees. If he used such language to any questioner, it must be reconciled with what he said before and afterward. Luke declares that he went on to say: As the lightning shineth from one part of the heaven to the other, so shall the Son of Man be in his day. Every eye shall see him. But still the kingdom cometh not with observation, or, as it has been better translated, *with outward show of its coming*. This translation accords with what he emphatically insisted upon. Even I do not know the day or the hour. There is no premonition that I can give. It comes like lightning from the sky, like a thief in the night: the only safety is to be always watching and ex-

[a] Luke xvii., 20-37.   [b] Matt. xxiv., 3-5.

pecting it. Only Luke reports that he said the kingdom of God is *within you*. Another translation gives *among you*, and this makes the statement harmonize with what Jesus said on another occasion: "Behold, a greater than Solomon is here";[a] and on still another occasion to the Pharisees: "If I cast out devils by the spirit of God, then the kingdom of God is come unto you."[b] Even if he said to the Pharisees, The kingdom of God is within you, it might well have been with the significance, Until you are changed within, for you no kingdom of God is possible. If it was said to his disciples, it might have been to rebuke their interest in mere outward splendors, and in the glory and authority they would have under the new order, and to insist, as he always did, that the right heart, the devoted faith, were the essential condition of their salvation, without wishing to disaffirm what he had promised them of honor and dominion in his kingdom.

The growth of the mustard-seed and the leavening of the meal were both quite rapid processes, and might well express the progress which his new religion had made and was to make under the preaching of his apostles, from the time they were appointed, until their Lord should come to bring them their reward and make them rulers of his household.

Finding a belief in the speedy occurrence of a great catastrophe, that would involve the world in its social order and in its physical constitution, common among the first believers in Christianity, the hypothesis is possible that they, in attempting to report the conversations of their master, injected into them their own prepossessions. He himself might have been a man of such transcendent genius, and his philosophy, so much beyond their comprehension, might have been so purposely veiled in the enigmatic form of his usual teaching, that his disciples ignorantly mistook a scheme of a gradual amelioration of mankind in personal character and social conditions, under a physical order of things substantially like what it had been from the beginning, for a violent crisis, judgment, and segregation of mankind into good and evil, and a sudden and complete and lasting destruction of the latter class in a general overthrow and reconstruction of the

[a] Luke xi., 31.   [b] Matt. xii., 28.

visible universe. Such a method of reasoning, however, utterly defeats every sincere effort to discover a proper historical basis for the character and for the existence of Jesus. If we may believe that all that the New Testament narratives impute to Jesus, as his doctrine of the kingdom of heaven, was never said by him, or was said in a sense entirely different both from the obvious import of the language and from the significance of it in the minds of those who heard it, then we may with equal reason believe that his teachings of non-resistance, of the blessing of poverty, were all misapprehensions of his apostles, and that he himself was hot-tempered, hasty to avenge injuries, avaricious, and subservient to the rich. Nay, we may hold that all his intellectual and moral traits were the creation of his biographers, and that he himself was dull, commonplace, envious, and ignoble.

Immediately after the death of Jesus, a body of men and women go out from Jerusalem, and in a few years penetrate into nearly every region of the then civilized world, proclaiming that the world is about to come to an end. They accompany this message with expressions of devotion and subjection to Jesus, to whom they award an authority and character substantially divine; and they say that they make this declaration mainly on the faith of what he had told them in his lifetime. They differed about many most fundamental things, such as the validity of the Mosaic law and revelation, and as to whether good conduct or faith alone was the essential agency in effecting salvation. But that the day of the Lord, the day of judgment, the coming of the Son of Man with his angels, the separation of the saints from the wicked, was at hand, all sects and schools of the early believers seem to have taken for granted.

Paul had written to the converts at Rome, describing the sinner as treasuring up wrath against the day of wrath and revelation of the righteous judgment of God, who will render to every man according to his deeds, in the day when God shall judge the secrets of men by Jesus Christ, according to the gospel which Paul had preached.[a] He had comforted them with the assurance that, having suffered with Jesus, they should be glorified with him,

[a] Romans ii., 6, 16.

and had described their earnest expectation of the manifestation of the sons of God and of the redemption of their bodies.[a] He had, in allusion to what Jesus had so earnestly urged, that they should watch all night for his coming, that might be at midnight and might be at cock-crowing, apprised them, that it was high time to awake out of sleep, the night was far spent, the day was at hand, and their salvation was nearer than when they believed.[b]

To his Corinthian converts, he had written as those waiting for the coming of our Lord Jesus Christ, who should strengthen them, to the end that they might be blameless in the day of our Lord Jesus Christ.[c] He told them not to judge him in reference to conduct he deemed it unnecessary to explain, in fine to judge nothing before the time, until the Lord came, who should bring to light the counsels of all hearts.[d] He used the phrase, "*the day of the Lord Jesus Christ*," as if its import as the day of his final coming was already familiar, as it doubtless was in the minds of all believers, from the frequency with which its approach had been impressed upon their minds. He warned them that the time was short: married or not married, in affliction, in pleasure, possessing this world's goods or not, it mattered not; the fashion of this world passeth away.[e] All the relations and interests of a state so transitory were of trivial account. The ends of the world, he said, had come upon him and his contemporaries.[f] By the communion of the bread and wine, he told them they showed forth the Lord's death "*till he come.*"[g] In a fuller detail of his views of the resurrection, he explained that Christ was the first fruitage or product of the resurrection, and that after him all that were his at his coming would rise, and then the end should be, when death should be destroyed, and Jesus, having put down all rule, authority, and power, and all enemies under his feet, should deliver up the kingdom to God. This consummation was in his view so near that he spake of himself, though now verging upon old age, and of his Corinthian correspondents, as likely to be alive at the time, and to be changed without dying into the

[a] Romans viii., 17, 19, 23.   [b] Romans xiii., 11, 12.   [c] I. Cor. i., 7, 8.
[d] I. Cor. iv., 5.   [e] I. Cor. vii., 28–31.   [f] I. Cor. x., 11.   [g] I. Cor. xi., 26.

immortal and incorruptible form.[a] Indeed, though Paul, writing from his prison in Rome, sometimes anticipated his own death, as well he might under such a cruel and capricious tyranny as that of Nero, yet he as often spoke of living to the general resurrection and of going up from active life to meet the Lord in the air.

He exhorted the Philippians to be sincere and without offence till the day of Jesus Christ:[b] he said he should rejoice over them as fruits of his no vain labor *in that day*.[c] Our conversation, he writes, is in heaven, whence we look for the Saviour, the Lord Jesus Christ, who shall change our vile body, and fashion it like his glorious body,[d]—which is another anticipation of the coming of the Lord before his body shall have wasted in the grave. Finally, he urged them to be moderate, to care for nothing, because, he assured them, that "*the Lord was at hand.*"[e]

He begged the converts at Colosse to be thankful that, they had been deemed worthy to be partakers of the inheritance of the saints in light, and avowed that he was the minister to them of a mystery hid for ages, but then revealed by him, which was the hope of glory in Christ,[f] and charged them to be faithful and hearty in their service of the Lord, as they expected to receive of him the reward of the inheritance.[g]

Writing to the church at Thessalonica, he commended them for turning from idols to the true and living God, and to wait for his Son from heaven, whom he raised from the dead, even Jesus who delivered us from the wrath to come.[h] "What," he asks, "is our hope, or joy, or crown of rejoicing? Ye are in the presence of our Lord Jesus Christ at his coming."[i] He told them not to be in hopeless sorrow for those of their members, who had died; for he assured them on the word of Jesus himself that, when he should descend from heaven with a shout, with the voice of the archangel and the trump of God, the believers who had died should rise, and then that himself and the living disciples would be caught up with the raised saints to the clouds to meet the Lord in the air, and ever afterward be with him.[j] As to the time

[a] I. Cor. xv., 24, 51, 52. [b] Phil. i., 6, 10. [c] Phil. ii., 16. [d] Phil. iii., 20, 21. [e] Phil. iv., 5. [f] Col. i., 12, 27. [g] Col. iii., 24. [h] I. Thess. i., 9, 10. [i] I. Thess. ii., 19. [j] I. Thess. iv., 14–17.

when this stupendous event would take place, he reminded them that they knew perfectly "*the day of the Lord cometh as a thief in the night,*"[a] words of Jesus well known to the whole Christian community. It would come suddenly, and the destruction of the wicked outside world could not be avoided: wherefore he charged them, just as Jesus had charged his disciples, to be sober and watch. He closed his letter with a devout prayer that their whole spirit and soul and body (evidently expecting that the body in which they lived on earth would survive to partake of the transformation) be preserved blameless, until the coming of the Lord Jesus Christ.[b] In a second letter to the same church, he comforts them under persecutions with the assurance of rest with him, when the Lord Jesus shall be revealed from heaven with his mighty angels in flaming fire, taking vengeance on them that know not God and that obey not the gospel of our Lord Jesus Christ, who shall be punished with everlasting destruction from the presence of the Lord and from the glory of his power, when he shall come to be glorified in his saints and to be admired by all that believe. Aware that they might have been troubled by his first letter with the apprehension that the coming of the Lord might be momentarily expected — and such indeed was its import, and his own impression when writing it — he tells them that there is to be a falling away first, a man of sin, a son of perdition to come.[c] There had been an apostasy among the believers. Things looked less prosperous in the young church. False teachers had come in. It was the custom of the zealous apostles to deal in no mild terms with men, who viewed the Christian scheme or the Christian history differently from themselves; and the terms *anti-Christ*, son of perdition, man of sin, were the vigorous epithets, which they applied to these heretics. Jesus, in his details of the process of the kingdom of heaven, had told his disciples there should be false Christs, false prophets, doing great signs and wonders, almost deceiving the very elect.[d] Several of the apostles seemed to have shared with Paul the expectation of this time of trial. But he evidently expected that this interval would be short, for the mystery of iniquity, he said, doth already work; and he who hin-

[a] I. Thess. v., 1-3.   [b] I. Thess. v., 23.   [c] II. Thess., ii.   [d] Matt. xxiv., 23, 24.

dereth the coming of the man of sin will be taken out of the way, when the man of sin will be revealed, whom the Lord will consume with the breath of his mouth and with the brightness of his coming.

Writing to his own disciple, Timothy, he exhorted him to abstain from covetousness and to follow after righteousness, and to keep that commandment without spot or rebuke until the appearing of our Lord Jesus Christ, which in his time the King of kings would show.[a] In a second letter, he probably quotes words of Jesus as then reported, when he says, "If we be dead, we shall live; if we suffer, we shall reign; if we deny him, he will deny us."[b] He exults in the near prospect of the crown of righteousness which the Lord shall give to him in *that day*, and to all that love his appearing; and he declares that, when Jesus appears in his kingdom, he will judge the living and the dead.[c] To Titus, he declares that his looking for the glorious appearance of the great God and of our Saviour Jesus Christ is his blessed hope.

Paul seems to have maintained with much pertinacity and eloquence a peculiar theory of the resurrection. To Paul, the resurrection was a power or process achieved wholly by Jesus through his death. By descending into the world of the dead, he had overcome Death and won from him the power of eternal life, first for himself, afterward for his elect. Hence, Paul everywhere declares his gospel a gospel of life and immortality brought to the world by his master, Jesus. That Jesus had overcome death was proved by his own resurrection. So completely did Paul stake the whole scheme of faith and salvation upon the actual physical resurrection of Jesus that he declares, if Christ be not risen, there is no resurrection and faith is vain.[d] These views he asserted against nominal disciples, some of whom affirmed that there was no resurrection of the dead, and some that the resurrection was already past. Christ's rising, Paul asseverated, was the cause of all resurrection. In Adam all die. Only in Christ are all made alive.[e] This may be called peculiar, because as a Pharisee Paul should have believed with his sect in spirits, and in the spiritual existence of the right-

[a] I. Tim. vi., 14, 15. [b] II. Tim. ii., 11, 12. [c] II. Tim. iv., 1, 8.
[d] I. Cor. xv., 12, 13, 17. [e] I. Cor. xv., 22.

eous dead; and because, upon the Pauline hypothesis, the argument by which Jesus sought to prove to the Sadducees the continued life after death of Abraham, Isaac, and Jacob, had no basis whatever.[a] According to Paul, Abraham, Isaac, and Jacob, had, like the good dead of his own age, slept with Jesus, and were to be brought with him into his kingdom, made alive after his resurrection.

The hand of Paul or some of his school is plainly seen in a gloss given to Matthew's account of the phenomenon of the bodies of many of the saints rising under the general shock which the earth felt at the instant of the death of Jesus on the cross. How could Jesus' resurrection be the cause of the resurrection of dead men? How could he be the first product of the resurrection, if certain buried saints actually rose from their graves on the Friday afternoon preceding the Sunday morning when Jesus rose? It would have been discreet, like Mark and Luke, to have omitted the legend. But it was too dear to the wondering converts. So it appears, with the clumsy addition, "Many bodies of saints which slept arose, and came out of the graves *after his resurrection*, and went into the holy city, and appeared unto many."[b] Alas poor ghosts! Their graves were opened and they rose, but decorously waited upon the etiquette of precedence, two days, to come out of their graves and appear to their friends in the holy city.

The Epistle to the Hebrews, which purports to be written by Paul, but which careful scholars have found reason to impute to some other of the earlier disciples, speaks of Jesus' crucifixion, as having taken place in the end of the world,—that is, in the world's last days,—and declares that, to those that look for him, he will appear the second time without sin unto salvation.[c] It describes the then status of Jesus himself, crucified and believed to have passed into the heavens, as seated at the right hand of God, and expecting continuously till his enemies be made his footstool,[d] or, in the very condition in which Jehovah is supposed in the Psalm to have addressed him, of waiting for the catastrophe, which was to bring his enemies under his power. It advises the Hebrew converts to exhort each other to good works, and so much

---

[a] Luke xx., 37. [b] Matt. xxvii., 52, 53. [c] Heb. ix., 26, 28. [d] Heb. x., 12, 13.

the more as they see the day approaching,[a] evidently considering that even unenlightened persons could discern in passing events signs of the coming on of the end. It begged them to hold fast their confidence and to be patient, that after doing God's will they might receive the promise, "for yet a little while, and he that shall come will come, and will not tarry."[b] Before this remarkable Epistle ends, it gives with great precision an embodiment of the conception which the believers of the first century derived from the prophecies, particularly those of Zechariah as modified by the explanations of Jesus and his apostles. In the vividness of the description, the day so near is considered already come, and it is affirmed: "Ye are come unto Mount Zion, and unto the city of the living God, the heavenly Jerusalem, and to an innumerable company of angels, to the general assembly and church of the first born, which are written in heaven, and to God the Judge of all, and to the spirits of just men made perfect, and to Jesus the mediator of the new covenant." When Jehovah spake to your fathers from Sinai, his voice shook the earth. When he speaks from Mount Zion, it shall not only shake, but overthrow the earth; and only the uncreated things, that cannot be shaken, shall remain. Wherefore, receiving a kingdom which cannot be moved, they were to serve God with reverence and fear, who was to be a consuming fire to all who served him not.[c]

Thus far have been traced the opinions which Paul held in reference to the second coming of Jesus and the end of the world, and which the Pauline adherents of Christianity in Asia and Europe must have received on the faith of his writings. Let us now see whether substantially the same opinions were entertained by those propagandists of the new religion, whose head-quarters were at Jerusalem, and who looked at Paul with suspicion and seriously, and with some bitterness, controverted the dogmas, which he taught with such confidence of conviction.

James, who was Jesus' brother, in the only Epistle preserved of his, urges the converts among the twelve tribes to be patient unto the coming of the Lord, to be patient as the husbandman who waiteth for the coming up of his

[a] Heb. x., 25.   [b] Heb. x., 37.   [c] Heb. xii., 22-29.

planted seed, *"for the coming of the Lord draweth nigh"* ; to have no controversies nor unkind feelings against brethren, for behold the judge standeth at the door,[a] evidently having in his memory the words of his brother : "Be ye like men that wait for their Lord, . . . that, when he cometh and knocketh, they may open unto him immediately."[b]

Peter, the confidant of Jesus, in a letter to the converts among the heathen in Asia Minor, affirms that he and they are begotten unto a lively hope to an incorruptible inheritance in heaven, reserved for them, in the anticipation of which they rejoiced through present trials, and that their faith would redound to their glory at the appearing of Jesus Christ.[c] This salvation for which they hoped, he declared, the prophets had predicted, and the very angels had interested themselves in; but they must hope for it with soberness till the revelation of Jesus Christ.[d] He declares that Jesus is then ready to judge the living and the dead, and that the dead have had the gospel preached to them, that they may be judged by the same standard as men then living.[e] Peter evidently did not share Paul's peculiar views about the resurrection. To him, as to his countrymen generally, including Jesus, the patriarchs and kings and prophets and people of Israel were alive in the underworld, were spirits in prison, to whom it would be just to carry the intelligence of the coming of the kingdom of heaven, which all that were worthy would accept and rejoice in. The end of all things is at hand, he asserts: be therefore sober and watch. He says, however, a fiery trial is to try them: the falling away is to come, the false Christs: all but the elect will be deceived, but they will only be partaking of Christ's sufferings, and, when his glory shall be revealed, their joy shall be exceeding. The time *has come* when judgment must begin at the house of God; and, if the righteous are barely saved, what must be the fate of the sinner? He calls his converts the flock of God, and assures them that, when the chief Shepherd appears, they shall receive an unfading crown of glory.[f]

[a] James v., 7-9. [b] Luke xii., 36. [c] I. Peter i., 4, 5, 7.
[d] I. Peter ii., 12, 13, 17, 20. [e] I. Peter iv., 5, 6. [f] I. Peter iv., 5, 7, 12, 13, 17-19.

In a second letter, the authenticity of which, however, is questioned among Biblical critics, Peter maintains that he was not following cunningly devised fables, when he made known the power and coming of the Lord Jesus Christ, that he himself heard a voice declaring Jesus the beloved Son of God; and that they have in the Scriptures spoken by holy men, moved by the Holy Ghost, even a surer word of prophecy than that attestation of his.[a] The frequent disappointment of the expectation of the Church, strained to utmost tension by these notes of warning everywhere sounded by the preachers of the new religion, had begotten its natural fruit. Scoffers and sceptics had come, saying: Men live and die, and the world goes quietly on as it was wont from the first; and where is this promise of his coming? Ah! just so quietly went on the old antediluvian world, sleeping between the great surrounding oceans with no premonition of change, till it perished suddenly in the engulfing water. By the same token, he says, these heavens and this earth are kept in store, reserved unto fire against the day of judgment and perdition of ungodly men. The day of the Lord will come as a thief in the night, in which the heavens shall pass away with a great noise, and the earth and its works shall be burned up. Expecting that catastrophe, he exhorts them to holy conversation and godliness, and declares that he and the disciples of Jesus (on *his* promise) look for a new heaven and a new earth, wherein righteousness shall dwell.[b]

The Epistles of John betray a common authorship with the evangel standing in his name. By whomsoever they were written, they indicate how extensive was the expectation of the immediate return of Jesus from heaven; and, if they were not written till the second century, they indicate how tenaciously that expectation was cherished by believers, after all the events to attend that return had long happened or become impossible. "Little children," the Christian father writes, "it is the last time; and, as ye have heard that *antichrist* shall come, even now are there many antichrists, whereby we know that it is the last time."[c] "Abide in him, that, when he shall appear, we may not be ashamed before him at his

[a] II. Peter i., 11, 16, 19.   [b] II. Peter iii.   [c] I. John ii., 18.

coming."[a] "It doth not yet appear what we shall be; but, when he shall appear, we shall be like him, for we shall see him as he is."[b]

Scholars have agreed that the Revelation, so called, is a genuine and early product of the literary spirit that kindled with the first Christian reformation. Like the twenty-fourth and twenty-fifth chapters of Matthew, it is an elaborate exposition of the kingdom of heaven. But it is not, like those chapters, by a master hand; and, in place of the severe simplicity and solemn dignity of the conceptions of Jesus, we have much trivial detail, many extravagances, that are more grotesque than awful, redeemed, however, in the last few chapters, by soothing and pathetic descriptions of the rest and consolations of the righteous, that have always deeply affected the human heart. There is less creative power in this curious prose poem than at first seems apparent. A fervid convert, susceptible to the sublime imagery of the Hebrew prophets, thoroughly imbued with those terrific and exultant expectations of convulsions, falling heavens, deluges of fire, slaughter and torture of unbelievers, which the early Christians must have recounted in their assemblies to each other with blanched cheeks and glowing eyes, might have woven together in his sleeping and waking visions just such fancies. The seven golden candlesticks were borrowed from Zechariah, the description of the Son of Man was taken from Daniel, Ezekiel, and Isaiah. The description of the throne, of the book, of the four beasts, of the slain lamb, of the four horses, are all reproductions of the symbolisms of the same prophets. The beast with seven heads and ten horns had appeared before in the visions of Daniel; Isaiah had told of the downfall of Babylon; and Ezekiel had given the topography and measurements of the holy city. In fine, this composition of a man of inferior genius takes, imperfectly remembered and understood, the ideas of Jesus, of a kingdom of heaven, that involved the destruction of the world, the punishment of the wicked, and the gathering into renovated Jerusalem of the saints, collated with the poetic exaggerations of the prophets, and sets them forth as verities of the future. The fact that it was written,

---

[a] I. John ii., 28.   [b] I. John iii., 2.

was read and cherished and wondered at, shows how deeply the idea of the end of the world possessed the early Christian mind.

It purports to be a revelation made through John from Jesus Christ of things which must shortly come to pass. "Behold," he says, "he cometh with clouds; and every eye shall see him: and they which pierced him: and all kindreds of the earth shall wail because of him." He sends messages to several churches, and announces that he is coming like a thief in the night, and they must watch. Him that overcometh he will acknowledge before God and the angels, and clothe in white raiment, will write on him the name of the holy city and his own new name, and make to sit down with him on the throne of his kingdom. Then follow details of the plagues of the earth, the destruction of its inhabitants, the stars falling, the sky rolled together like a scroll, the islands and mountains displaced, the selection of the saved,— a specified number from each of the tribes of Israel, an unnumbered multitude from other nations, who had been persecuted for Jesus' sake,— the opening of the bottomless pit and the woes that issued from it; the wicked earth, although the heavens have been rolled up and the stars are fallen, still keeping up the warfare against the heavenly powers, and suffering fearful slaughter and torture. At last, the Lamb appears on Mount Zion; and, after the contest between him and the kings of the earth, in which they are aided by the beast with seven heads and ten horns and by the old serpent or dragon, and by the woman city Babylon, Satan is imprisoned, and the souls of the martyrs who had been faithful to Jesus live with him on earth a thousand years. After this, all the dead are raised, and all who are not inscribed in the book of life are consigned with the dead to a lake of fire. The new Jerusalem comes down from a new heaven to a new earth, where God shall reign with his saints in a world where there shall be no more death, sorrow, crying, or pain. It is difficult among the incoherences and grotesque horrors of this composition to find even this consecutive order of events; for details, often trivially minute and unimportant and utterly irreconcilable with any chastened imagination, are given in chapters, that are evidently recapitulations of what had been told before. The pictures are like those which harass a sickly sleep, when no person or thing retains its identity, and a locust becomes a horse with the head of a man and having his chief power in his tail. The two resurrections with an interval of a thousand years are an idea for which the prophetic descriptions, the delineations of Jesus, and the traditions of the apostles furnish no authority. So marked a distinction, even among the elect, might well have fired the heart of the persecuted Christians to bear with patience and welcome with exultation the martyrdom, which was to be so indemnified and honored in the kingdom of heaven. After the coming of the Lord, and after his victory over the rebellious race of man had become so complete as to have Satan bound and cast into the bottomless pit, he is again let loose to deceive and seduce the world to their final terrible doom; but this gratuitous improvidence on the part of the heavenly powers is not reconcilable with any scheme of eschatology hinted by Jesus, his disciples, or their forerunners, the prophets.

The controversial force of such a work in a superstitious age must have been considerable. The idol worshippers, pleasure-seekers, mere busy, worldly men, the pagan philosophers, the obstinate adherents of the old religion as well, as the heretical teachers of the new, are denounced, punished with plagues, and finally consigned to the lake of fire and brimstone, it being implied that they are the great majority of the human race, with an absence of all commiseration and of all feeling except exultation, that shows that the author was very little touched with the better spirit of the humane character of Jesus. Slight honor is it to Jesus to make him the conspicuous champion and contriver of the cruel tortures for mankind, which are only not harrowing to read, because by their coarse grotesqueness they excite the ludicrous side of human sensibility. It must be said, however, that the hell of the Apocalypse, the hell of Paul and of Jesus, and the catastrophe that befalls the Gentiles in this prophetic forecasting of the coming of the Messiah, merciless and indiscriminating as they are, will not compare in unthinkable horrors with the physical hell of Dante, of Milton, and of Robert Pollok, nor with the hopeless, never-ending mental agony, which is accepted as the fixed fate of a large portion of mankind by refined and educated modern evangelicism.

According to Jesus, the righteous only were to be received into eternal life, while the wicked were to go away into everlasting fire prepared for the devil and his angels; but this language carries with it the implication that the fire is to be effectual to their everlasting destruction. Paul declares that those who obey not the gospel shall be punished with an everlasting destruction, which fairly implies, that from that destruction there shall be no remanent life or resurrection. So in the fire-pictures of the writer of Revelation, only Satan, the beast, and the false prophet are to be tormented day and night, forever and ever; while the mass of men, whom they had deceived, were to be cast into the lake of fire, and there experience a second death. It accorded doubtless with such an idea of a complete and just retribution, as even a Jew in the first century might entertain, that only the ringleaders in a rebellion against the new sovereign of earth and heaven should be tortured forever,— perhaps because they were endowed with a nature not capable of death,— but that the great crowd of their mortal, defeated followers should be summarily destroyed by fire, an agency intimately connected with the coming of the Lord in all the Old and New Testament prophecies.

It has thus been seen, by a careful examination of the authentic Christian records, how deep and paramount and universal was the conviction in the minds of the witnesses and confidential friends of Jesus, who became for the world and the Church the media of communicating the traditions of his life and doctrine, that the *kingdom of heaven*, drawing after it, in a series of supernatural and stupendous events, the end of the order of the world, the overthrow of all secular governments and societies, the destruction of the opponents of the gospel, and the establishment of an everlasting kingdom of the saints, reinforced by the resurrection of the good among the dead, was so near its fulfilment, that the great duty of every man was to watch in prayer and soberness for its sudden appearance. While so many passages are found in the writings of all the apostles and New Testament contributors directly affirming this conviction, it is the underlying sanction of all their exhortations to virtuous conduct, the secret fire, at which all their zeal for the new doctrine was lighted, the solution of the otherwise incomprehensible patience and exultation, with which they encountered persecutions, beatings, imprisonments, and cruel deaths.

As Jesus had discouraged all industry, all forethought to make provision for the wants of the body, refused with disdain to interest himself in disputed rights of property, spoken disparagingly of the ties of family relationship, and challenged those, who would be greatly honored in the kingdom of heaven, to arrest, so far as they could, the generation of the human race; so Paul thought, in the narrow margin of time that was left, it was entirely inexpedient for the unmarried to marry or for the married to be divorced. Had Paul been assured that the world was to go quietly on, as it had from the beginning of history, for two thousand years, that wars were to continue, kingdoms, dynasties, and republics to rise and fall, intelligence, virtue, and civilization to ebb and flow over different regions and among the different races of the world, that nations that had never accepted or had apostatized from Christianity, and men that disowned it, would live as virtuously and as prosperously, and contribute as much to the civilization of the world, as the nations and men that were true to his traditions of Christianity, he might have exclaimed with his accustomed impetuosity, "*Then is my preaching vain and your faith vain.*"

The historical fact, that the early Christians expected the end of the world in their lifetime, few intelligent persons will deny. But it will be denied that this expectation had a justification in the teachings of Jesus, rightly understood, or that it stands now in any prominent view in a comprehensive summary of the doctrines and opinions of the New Testament. It will be said, that it was an unimportant misapprehension of those who undertook to report the words of Jesus, in no wise compromising his omniscience or divinity; that it was, even if they accepted it, a mere blemish of their human intelligence, which did not incapacitate them from being instruments of a divine revelation to the world of the truths of the gospel, which are in no wise complicated with this misapprehension.

Does it not rather seem that this expectation of the end of the world was derived by the first believers from what Jesus had himself taught? He had not taught it casually or incidentally. It was his kingdom of heaven, to proclaim which he believed himself appointed; it was his dominant idea, to which every thing else in his mind and in his teaching was made subordinate. To accept Jesus as a revelator of the will of God, as the introducer of a new order into the world, and then to reject his revelation; to deny the new order to have come or that it is ever to come, what is this but to be disobedient to his gospel, and to incur the fate which Paul declared awaited that class? A historical theory is possible and has been asserted that accepts Jesus, but denies his doctrine of a kingdom of heaven. A like daring of sceptical criticism acknowledging the existence of Christopher Columbus might insist that he was a professor at Salamanca, who had such a horror of the water that he could never be induced to set his foot in a vessel or a boat; or yielding to the force of the evidence that there was a German, who lived in the sixteenth century named Martin Luther, might maintain, that all that is said about his controversy with the Papacy is a fiction, he having been all his life a devout Jesuit and advocate of Papal infallibility and supremacy.

CHAPTER IV.

POLITICAL IDEAS OF JESUS.

"To me, it is much more animating and encouraging to see that, in natural course and by ordinary operation of universal faculties, prophets and saviors arise, and will doubtless continue to arise, than to believe that, by a special intervention, one Redeemer was once sent whose influence has certainly thus far not been adequate to so singular an occasion and office."—*Harriet Martineau's Eastern Journal.*

THE social relations of men, the rights and duties which the marital, family, tribal, and national ties imply, and the instincts, affections, sentiments, and principles which they develop and inspire, have very largely contributed to the culture and growth of the human mind, and to the progressive evolution of civilization. Accordingly, the laws of the social relations, the principles, which underlie the structure of communities, cities, and states, and by conformity to which, public order, the ascendency of justice, the protection of the weak, the security to the greatest number possible of the substantial and prime goods of life, can be preserved, have always deeply engaged the thoughts of the most liberal and highly endowed men.

The political notions of Jesus have already been indicated in his dominant prepossession of an immediately impending kingdom of heaven. His scheme of a perfect social order was summary and comprehensive. It was to tear down the effete, decayed world, the rejected Jerusalem, and to receive from heaven a new Jerusalem, a city having foundations, whose builder and maker is God.

Government is the application of political economy, the law of the house or of the social order to the struggle for life, whereby the strong, while taking, in the right of their strength, a superior share of the goods of life, shall not deprive the weak of their smaller share. Jesus not only rebuked the greed and violence of the strong, but he sought to repress the very struggle for life itself. He said: Take no thought for your life, what ye shall eat, what ye shall drink, with what ye shall be clothed. Live like the birds, which the heavenly Father feeds; enjoy your life like the lilies, careless of what may befall them; leave the care for property to the Gentiles, the world's people, who have always troubled themselves about such things, and seek only the kingdom of heaven, in which the supply of the bodily wants is the minimum of the divine foresight.[a]

Of what use is political economy in such a faith? Why should law be invoked to make men contend fairly with each other for food, drink, and clothing, and all the fortune that is an equivalent for them? "Who made me," he asked impatiently, "a judge or a divider over you?"[b] If thy brother has cheated thee out of thy share of a paternal inheritance, do not appeal to the law: only the Gentile, the law-loving Roman, the modern Englishman, whose highest idea is fair play, care for justice.[c] Give him an acquittance of the whole inheritance. Has a thief entered thy hall and taken thy Sunday overcoat? Seek him out,— not to hand him over to the police, but to bestow upon him thy blessing and thy cloak. Not only resist no evil, but seek no indemnity for it afterward. If thou art knocked down by the blow of a ruffian, if it was upon the right cheek, offer to his not yet appeased wrath the left cheek also. And wealth,— useless in itself in the approaching destruction of all things,— what does it represent but the lawless striving and worldly thrift that went into the getting of it? It is as impossible, with such a burden, to enter into the kingdom of heaven, as for a camel to enter the eye of a needle. Sell all that thou hast and give it to the poor, and thou shalt have treasure in heaven.[d]

When it is considered that human society, like the complicated communism of ants, bees, and beavers, and the looser aggregation of all the higher animals, so far as it has not been superseded by the care or broken up by the hostility of man, has for its prime object the procurement of subsistence and the common defence against

[a] Matt. vi., 24–34.   [b] Luke xii., 13, 14.   [c] Matt. v., 38–48.
[d] Luke xii., 33; Mark x., 21, 25.

attack from without, it will be seen, how revolutionary is a political scheme, that makes it a prime principle not to seek subsistence and not to resist attacks. When it is remembered, that out of society have grown all the sentiments and affections of men that are developed beyond beastly instincts, out of resistance to evil have proceeded a sense of justice, many of the ideas of right and wrong, together with nearly all the patriotism and enthusiasm, which have made human life in all ages heroic, it can be seen how complete was the challenge of Jesus to all the virtue of the world.

A reformer he most certainly was, but not a reformer who acknowledged, that any good had been achieved before him, or that, by any of the methods, by which the world had seemed to have progressed, any further progress was possible. If he never spake the words imputed to him in John's Gospel, they fitly describe his exclusive spirit,— "All that ever came before me are thieves and robbers."[a] He was the most uncompromising of innovators. He demanded new forms for the new spirit, new bottles for the new wine, no patching of the old garments with new cloth. So far as mankind had gone, it had gone all wrong. It must be born again. The old order must perish. The ideal city, the perfect political state, could not grow up out of a corrupt mankind, or be built of any materials the growth of the bad earth. It must come down from heaven; and happy were those, who, listening to him and believing, should be thought worthy to be made citizens of it.

Nothing was farther from his thought than to work with the spirit of his age, or of any age — to promote as much as possible all the good tendencies of the times. The spirit of the age, the tendencies of the times, were all toward evil and toward doom; and the earth, replete with wickedness, was waiting for the manifestation of the wrath of God in its destruction. Suppose ye, he once exclaimed, that those Galileans whom Pilate slew in the midst of their sacrifices, or those eighteen upon whom the tower of Siloam fell and killed them, were sinners above other men, because they suffered such things? "I tell you, Nay: but except ye repent, ye shall all likewise perish."[b]

[a] John x., 8. [b] Luke xiii., 1-5.

The hostility of Jesus to the existing political order is manifest in many of his reported words. In sending his disciples forth to teach, he said they were sheep going among the wolves. The wolves, who would devour them, were "the councils, governors, and kings" before whom they would be brought. He begged them to be wise and harmless, and assured them that their persecution should be a testimony against the nations and governments.[a]

In the earlier period of his career, Jesus seems to have shared with moderation the national prejudices of his countrymen. He charged his disciples, in sending them out to proclaim the approach of the kingdom of heaven, to avoid the houses and cities of the Gentiles, and even of the Samaritans; and it is quite certain that, during his lifetime, he did not afterward remove this interdict, or by precept or example disclose, that his message of repentance had any relevancy at all for other people than the Jews.[b] After his death, Paul justified his preaching to the Gentiles, not by any tradition of Jesus, but by a direct commission from the resurrected Master, who met him journeying to Damascus; and Peter, by words that he heard from heaven in a vision he had at Joppa. When Jesus was in Phœnicia, though this must have been not quite serious, he told the woman whose daughter he healed that the Phœnicians were dogs only, while the Israelites were Jehovah's guests, seated at his table.[c]

But the cool incredulity of the learned and clerical classes, who controlled the intelligent public opinion in Galilee, and still more in Judea, contributed to weaken these prejudices, never very strong. To the Jew of his time, Moses was a great leader and law-giver, who, like the greatest of the prophets, had passed into heaven without having suffered death; Abraham, Isaac, and Jacob were great princes, who had held familiar conversations with Jehovah; David was an heroic king, and an inspired poet, beloved of the Lord. For the books of the law, especially the ten commandments, there was everywhere a veneration amounting to absolute awe. The Psalms and the prophecies were only in slightly less repute. We, who consider it nearly sacrilegious to speak otherwise than

---

[a] Matt. x., 16–18. [b] Matt. x., 5. [c] Matt. xv., 24, 26

with respect of Washington and his compatriots, who hold to the Declaration of Independence as embodying axioms of absolute truth, and for whom a citation of the Constitution is an end of all political disputation, can understand how, when to the Jews the Church and State were one, and the principles of government were at the same time a standard of faith and a rule of conduct, the memory of the great leaders of the nation, the sanctity of their State papers and civil codes, and the authority of their politico-ecclesiastical annals and literature should have grown in reverence in ten or more centuries of their national existence, far more than the corresponding attachment for our heroic men, heroic annals, and national documents has grown in a single century.

Jesus seems to have been considerably emancipated from this veneration. In the Sermon on the Mount, he quotes two of the fundamental precepts of the decalogue, the prohibition of murder and of adultery, not as the laws of God, not even as laws of Moses, or as imperative statutes of the national code, but as traditions of them of old time. He puts them in the same category with the direction to hate one's enemy, which is not a precept of the Hebrew law at all, only an implication and inference, which an orthodox Jew would probably have denied and resented, even in his time. It is true he declared, in the same discourse, that he came not to destroy the law, and that not a jot or tittle should be taken from it; but he asserted that he came to fulfil it,— a process that must have seemed to his hearers quite as revolutionary, and which, coupled with the sweeping implications of the utter inadequacy of even the moral features of it to influence character and form correct conduct, must have seemed eminently unpatriotic and sacrilegious to the conservative Jews. Doubtless, he shared John the Baptist's contempt for the exclusiveness arrogated by the children of Abraham, and broke up the prestige, which was accorded to the patriarchs in the kingdom of heaven, by intruding upon their select privacy a crowd of aliens from the four corners of the world.[a] He was called the son of David.[b] He never so styled himself, and his frank avowal that he held himself greater than Solomon may indicate what he

[a] Matt. viii., 11, 12; iii., 9.   [b] Matt. xv., 22; xx., 30, 31.

thought of that royal lineage.[a] While allowing that the scribes and Pharisees sat in Moses' seat and that the observances they required were fairly binding upon the conscience of the Jewish citizen, he denounced their personal characters: he denied that, though Moses' representatives, they were to have the title or obedience of Rabbis,—himself being the real master. He satirized their excessive devoutness, and the minute and formal character of their worship, which was only minute and formal, in the fidelity with which it followed the pattern laid down, as they believed, by Moses himself.[b]

The Jews bore the Roman yoke as impatiently as they had borne any earlier foreign domination. There were among them in Jesus' time, and before and afterward, strong aspirations for the restoration of their ancient autonomy, which had passed away forever, not so much on account of their especial corruption or lack of intelligence and bravery, as because the fashion of the world had been constantly changing. The earlier legends of the Hebrews represent the Semitic people as under kings whose kingdoms were only a single tribe or city. Greece, in the time of the Trojan war, was dominated by as many kings as it had principal cities. It was the tendency of progress for these separate sovereignties to melt into the greater empires of Egypt, Assyria, Greece, and Rome, each in succession enlarging and extending its sway, till the old civilization perished under the incursions of the barbarians. Barbarism manifested itself again in disintegration, and in the multiplicity of sovereigns and governments, and only in modern times is the old process of coalition and absorption resumed. The Jew had in his national literature an unusual stimulus to revolt against any attempt to subjugate him to the power or the law of other nations. He was naturally seditious; and the priesthood, his natural leaders, aided his revolutionary purposes, whenever they had the faintest prospect of success.

Jesus kept himself wholly aloof from this feeling. To the Pharisees, he was obnoxious as destitute of love of country. Their question to him of the lawfulness of paying tribute to Rome was evidently designed to prejudice him with the mob as an unpatriotic citizen.[c] His evasion

[a] Matt. xii., 42.   [b] Matt. xxiii.   [c] Matt. xxii., 17, 21.

of it has always been commended for its readiness and sagacity, rather than as a logical solution of a difficulty. On the other hand, it is plain that the Roman aristocracy never considered him other than a Jew, and doubtless as ripe for sedition. Pilate, at the crucifixion, seemed at first to have been considerably influenced by the insinuations of the chief priests to believe that Jesus' real object was political, and insisted, against strong remonstrances, in affixing to the cross the superscription, *"Jesus of Nazareth, the king of the Jews."*[a] This suspicion of both parties of him showed how fairly he had maintained his neutrality, the solution of which is already given in his doctrine of *the kingdom of heaven*, and gives further confirmation to the impression, that that was his dominant idea. He was not of the Jewish party nor Cæsar's friend, because, as he is declared to have told Pilate, "If my kingdom were of this world, then would my servants fight"; but it is not thence.[b]

It seems proper to class with his political opinions the ideas of Jesus concerning wealth and poverty. Political economy has been fitly termed the science of wealth; and a large part of the functions of civilized governments are those which pertain to the protection of men in their acquisition and possession of property. Jesus opens his earliest discourse, if the chronological order of Matthew be followed, with a benediction upon poverty. *"Blessed are the poor,"* he said, *"for theirs is the kingdom of heaven."*[c] Matthew reports it, indeed: "Blessed are the poor *in spirit.*" Poorness of spirit or poor-spiritedness has always been considered contemptible among mankind, who require of a man to be always superior to his fortune and, however narrow and restricted his possessions may be, demand that his soul shall be large and affluent. It is not to be believed that Jesus intended to pronounce a benediction on a quality, that all noble minds have agreed to consider despicable. Adding the words, "in spirit," the ordinary explanation of commentators is that the *poor in spirit*, whom Jesus blessed, are the humble, the meek, those who had overcome all pride and self-estimation. But, as he pronounced a benediction on the meek, and on those who patiently suffered persecution, it is not

[a] John xix., 19-22.   [b] John xviii., 36.   [c] Matt. v., 3.

to be supposed that he intended to mar the rhetorical excellence of these striking apothegms by such obvious tautology. Luke undoubtedly gives the true version of this saying, when he reports: "*Blessed be ye poor, for yours is the kingdom of God*," and makes it certain what class was meant by adding the converse, "*Woe unto you that are rich! for ye have received your consolation.*"[a] In Luke's hands, the beatitudes become altogether more practical; and outward conditions are more regarded than metaphysical qualities. The poor in spirit, the pure, the merciful, the meek, those hungry for righteousness, are not mentioned; but the poor in property, the hungry for food, those who weep and are hated and persecuted, are comforted with the assurance, that their reward in heaven shall be great, and that the rich, the sumptuously fed, the prosperous and gay, shall exchange conditions with them.

While it has been agreed among the most careful scholars that the general details of events, as given by Matthew and Mark, conform most nearly in sequence of occurrence with the facts, it is not so generally believed that the fragmentary manner in which Jesus' conversations are distributed through his career by Luke — the Sermon on the Mount being partly uttered, when he first began to preach, partly midway of his ministry, and a portion of it at Jerusalem just before his arrest — may not be the true arrangement. It seems more probable that Jesus avoided long discourses, as less effective than brief colloquies. A love of system seems to have guided Matthew or his editor in putting together all his ethical teachings, which were not pertinent to some incident of his life, and in arranging in a consecutive order the parables spoken to the disciples, and those spoken to the scribes and Pharisees, after it had become impossible to determine the special time or occasion when they were in fact delivered.

Jesus charged his disciples not to be thrifty or careful to accumulate property. Lay not up for yourselves treasures upon earth, but rather lay up for yourselves treasures in heaven; for your hearts will be where your treasures are.[b] There was to be no compromise about this, no diligence in business *and* fervency of spirit,[c] as Paul after-

[a] Luke vi., 20, 24.   [b] Matt. vi., 19-34.   [c] Rom. xii., ii.

ward taught, no looking for the wealth of the kingdom of heaven with a prudent care for the things of this world. No man, he said, can serve two masters. If you love Mammon, you will hate God. Therefore, I say unto you, Take no thought for your life, to preserve which all property is sought. The life is the essential thing, food and raiment are the mere adjuncts of life. Take no thought even for life itself, nor for what you shall eat, drink, or wear. Do the fowls of the air sow, reap, and harvest crops? yet your heavenly Father feedeth them. Do the lilies toil or spin? yet they are more beautiful than Solomon in his glory of royal vesture. What utter lack of faith to think the grass of the field, which blooms for a day, is thus cared for, and ye, the children of God, are not cared for! Let the people of the world seek such things. Leave to your heavenly Father the provision for you, and seek first the kingdom of God and his righteousness, and all such things shall be given besides. Do not even prepare for to-morrow, which will take care of itself. The illustration of the birds was not quite satisfactory to him. The fowls of the air, though they are not anxious for the morrow, are certainly exceedingly diligent, not to say sordid, in their pursuit of what to eat during the entire day; and, if they do not gather into store, as the thrifty squirrels and many of the rodents do, for winter supplies, they take thought of the morrow so far as to migrate from cold to warm regions, long before actual scarcity of food compels them. Men must be more absolutely careless even than that: only the lily, rooted to the ground, cares not for the juices that shall nourish it, nor forebodes the scythe that shall consign it to the oven. This must be the true type of the children's confidence in the bounty of their heavenly Father.

But meantime, until the kingdom of heaven shall have come, what are his disciples, who have left all their industries and discontinued their foresight for to-morrow's wants, at his invitation, to do? He had considered that too. They are to ask whatever they want of the heavenly Father. Ask, he said, and ye shall receive; seek, and ye shall find; knock, and it shall be opened unto you. This he reiterated and emphasized. It is really, he believed, the method now. It is not the diligence of the bird, that finds the casual food in the lonely forest. Never entertain such a godless supposition. It is God, who, caring for the birds, his creatures, has with viewless hands scattered the food in the way of their guided flights. Are not men of more account than birds? Every one that asketh receiveth; he that seeketh findeth; to him that knocketh, it is opened. If a child asks bread of a father, he will not give him a stone. If men, who are evil, still give to their children good things, shall not the heavenly Father give good things to his children for the asking?[a]

These were not, as has been generally regarded, mere sentiments of Jesus: they were the fundamental practical ideas of his living as well as of his philosophy. He found some of his disciples engaged in earning their livelihood by fishing. They left their nets, and followed him. This he seems to have required.[b] Whosoever forsaketh not all that he hath cannot be my disciple.[c] Why should they go back even to take care of the nets? They will need nets no more. He will make them catch men, and save them in the kingdom of heaven.[d] Let the people of the world care for the nets, and pursue their old acquisitiveness. The disciple has learned a new and easier road to more enduring wealth.

He directed his disciples to sell their possessions and to bestow the proceeds in alms, to provide for themselves money-bags which would never grow old and a treasure in heaven. The abnegation of all worldly possessions, the cessation from all care for their accumulation, even for the daily necessities of living, was to be immediate and complete.[e] When one inchoate disciple wanted leave of absence to attend his father's funeral, and another to take leave of his family and household, he would not accept their adhesion to him upon such terms. No man, he said, is fit for the kingdom of heaven who postpones it for any service however dutiful, or any leave-taking of affection however tender. It is putting one's hand to the plough and looking back with regret.[f] He invited men away from their bodily toils to share his methods of living, like the birds of the air, upon the provided bounty of God to

[a] Matt. vii., 7–12. [b] Mark i., 16–20. [c] Luke xiv., 33. [d] Matt. xix., 27–30.
[e] Luke xii., 13–40. [f] Luke ix., 59–62.

be had for the asking. Come unto me, ye that are burdened with labor, and find rest. Take my yoke upon you, which you will find light, and my burden, which is easy.ᵃ

He himself seems to have lived in strict conformity to these principles. He had no house, no home, no property. He made it a boast that, in respect to possessions, he was worse off than the birds and the foxes. These had nests and holes: he had not where to lay his head. It is said of the band of devoted women who followed him out of Galilee to Jerusalem previously to his arrest and crucifixion that they ministered to him of their substance.ᵇ It is probable that, after he abandoned his father's service and vocation and became a prophet, his friends charged themselves with his maintenance; and the woven garmentᶜ mentioned in the story of the cross was doubtless the gift of the affectionate admiration of the Galilean women, who clung to him with a fidelity exceeding that of his chosen apostles.ᵈ The curious provision of nature which leads one animal to befriend and provide for another of its own or even some other species, when blind, lame, or in infancy, happily characterizes the associations of men. Some men have tastes so delicate or ambitions so lofty, that they disdain the ordinary prudence and thrift, that seem an instinct of the race. Jesus was one of these, and admiring and liberal patrons felt themselves honored and compensated in charging themselves with the sustenance, which an absorbing enthusiasm had made to him contemptible.

When the apostles were sent out to preach the coming kingdom of heaven, the question of subsistence came up in his mind. True to his principles, he makes it an absolute condition of their mission that there shall be no provision of money, food, or raiment.ᵉ He had sedulously charged his disciples, in language which he thought it necessary to repeat and emphasize, that they should take no thought of their lives or for what they should eat, drink, or wear. Shall he shrink now from a practical application of his own principles? He has no such purpose. Enter with boldness any house, no matter whose. Salute it with a benediction of peace, and there remain,

---

ᵃ Matt. xi., 28–30. ᵇ Luke viii., 3. ᶜ Luke xxiii., 49, 55; John xix., 24.
ᵈ Matt. xxvi., 56. ᵉ Matt. x., 9.

eating and drinking such things as the inmates give you; for the laborer is worthy of his hire.[a] The least reward they can give for the tidings of the kingdom of heaven, and how to obtain an entrance into it, is to feed and lodge the messengers. Doubtless, the disciples did not readily adopt these suggestions. It is a part of the instinctive nature of man to make some provision for journeying among strangers; and it required some emphasis and some repetition to satisfy these peasants, who had perhaps prided themselves on paying in honest toil for all that they had consumed, that the direction "*Put money in thy purse*" had become superfluous, and that they were to live freely upon the bounty of those, whose guests uninvited they should constitute themselves. Jesus seems himself to have challenged them to acknowledge the complete success of his commissariat. "When I sent you," he asked at Jerusalem, "without purse and scrip and shoes, lacked ye anything? And they said: Nothing."[b] Still, though they did not quite regret the throwing away for the kingdom of heaven's sake their property and their family ties, they were disposed to exaggerate a little the meritorious sacrifice they had thus made. Peter on one occasion thought fit to remind his master of his obligation; and Jesus, with a delicate and generous consideration for the infirmities of his followers, exclaimed: "Verily I say unto you, there is no man that hath left house, or parents, or brethren, or wife, for the kingdom of God's sake, who shall not receive manifold more in this present time, and in the world to come life everlasting."[c]

It is related that a young man of singularly blameless character came once to him, and asked what he should do to obtain the eternal life. Jesus first told him to avoid those sins which are prohibited in the law, and which, in that time, as in our time, the great body of reputable people find it easy to avoid. The young man professed that he had never stolen, nor borne false testimony, nor committed adultery nor murder; and that he had loved and honored his parents and dealt fairly with his neighbors. Then Jesus told him that, to enter the kingdom of heaven, he must sell all his property and give the proceeds to the poor, and come and follow him, and obtain

[a] Luke x., 5-8. [b] Luke xxii., 35. [c] Matt. xix., 27-29.

treasure in heaven. The young man, who was rich, withdrew in sorrow.[a] Here is a very plain and practical direction that, to be a disciple of Jesus, a man must dispossess himself of his property in favor of the poor. It is generally said by many, who claim special reverence for and allegiance to Jesus, that, in this declaration, he was not serious; that the young man was a hypocrite, and Jesus, who saw through him, wished to rally and expose him. There is not the slightest foundation for suspecting the young man's integrity. Jesus did see through him, and, believing in his sincerity, loved him, and sought not to repel him, but to win his discipleship. It is entirely foreign to that serious enthusiasm, which characterized the mind of Jesus, to suspect him of mere levity under circumstances, which should call out only the most fervent and sincere feeling. The truth is, Jesus was unusually earnest and serious. The interview affected him, as it had the young man. After he had gone, Jesus said with great deliberation to his followers: "*Verily I say unto you*,"—a form of speech he always seemed to use when he wished to say something fundamental and memorable,—"that a rich man shall hardly enter into the kingdom of heaven." And still dwelling upon the theme, though no one meantime had spoken: "Again I say unto you, it is easier for a camel to go through the eye of a needle than for a *rich* man to enter into the kingdom of God."[b]

The same hostility to the rich, and rejection of them as candidates for subjects of his kingdom, appear in several of the prominent parables, particularly in some told only by Luke, who, from the prominence he gives to all the anti-property opinions of Jesus, may be called the evangelist of the poor. Indeed, the rich, as a class, are more frequently made the subjects of his satire than any other class, not excepting the Pharisees. It is not at all surprising that James, who was his own brother, and must have been conversant with his antipathies, uses this vigorous language in his Epistle: "Go to now, ye rich men, weep and howl for your miseries that shall come upon you! Your riches are corrupted, your garments moth-eaten: your gold and silver are cankered; and the

---

[a] Matt. xix., 16-22; Mark x., 21.   [b] Matt. xix., 23-26.

rust of them shall be a witness against you, and shall eat your flesh as it were fire. Ye have heaped treasures together for the last days."ᵃ*

In the parable of the sower and the seed, some seed fell among thorns, or, as was explained to the disciples, among men occupied with the cares of life, or, as Paul would say, quite respectfully, diligent in business; and the deceitfulness of riches, the canker of gold and silver, choke the seed, and it will not bring forth the fruits of righteousness.ᵇ

It seemed to Jesus a grievance, not worthy of the interference of a just man, that one should be defrauded by his brother out of his father's inheritance; and the dishonest heir must have derived much satisfaction from the rebuke, which fell upon the brother who had suffered, rather than upon the brother, who had committed the fraud. *It is of no consequence*, thought Jesus; and went on to say: There was a certain rich man, who, when he had harvested a great crop, said to *himself* (not even to his intimate friend): I have not room for my fruits. I will pull down my barns, and build larger; and I will say to my soul, Thou hast much goods laid up for many years, take thine ease, eat, drink, and be merry. To whom God said: Thou fool! this night shall thy life be required of thee. Whose, then, shall be those things thou hast provided?ᶜ This parable plainly implies that, to Jesus, all providence for the future, all satisfaction in business prosperity, however fair and just, were not only wrong, but impious.

Indeed, we are compelled to entertain the suspicion that the sentiment of justice was only feeble in Jesus, and greatly encroached upon by his general sentiments of pity for the weak and the poor. He told a story of a dishonest steward, who had committed defalcations upon the trust property of his master, which he was employed to manage, who, when he was detected, sought to make friends with his master's debtors by falsely altering the

---

ᵃ James v., 1–3.

* Luther, and many others in the Church of scarcely less eminence, have doubted the authenticity of this Epistle. To such as share their suspicions, these words can of course bring only the authority which a writer, evidently of the school of James, and sharing fully the ideas he is known to have maintained antagonistic to the teachings and tendencies of Paul, deserves to have.

ᵇ Matt. xiii., 22.   ᶜ Luke xii., 13–23.

ledgers to their advantage. It is even said that Jesus commended the shrewdness of this proceeding, without condemning its injustice, and uttered by way of improvement that puzzle of all preachers and commentators: "And I say unto you, make to yourselves friends of the mammon of unrighteousness; that, when ye fail, they may receive you into everlasting habitations."[a]

It is but just, however, to say that, in Jesus' rules of conduct, the question of justice, of what is exactly due to another, has but little place. To petty, rigid justice, he opposes, not injustice, but loose and liberal charity. It is as if he should say: You are exceedingly careful to render to every man his due. Render him more than his due. Overpay your debt. Shame his narrow scale of exactitude by your overwhelming bounty. In liberal natures like his, the sentiment of justice is apt to be feeble. Hence, to him, the servant that kept his lord's talent wrapped in a napkin, neither lessening nor spending it, was an unprofitable servant, to be bound hand and foot, and cast into outer darkness. His master was hard and extortionate; but it was by bounty, and not by justice, that his obdurate heart was to be touched.[b]

He said the courtesies and civilities of society were not to be extended to those that could return them. Gifts did not create obligation. Debt and credit are not to be kept in beneficences. When thou makest a feast, invite not thy friends, brothers, kinsmen, nor rich neighbors, for they will invite thee in turn, and thy good deed will have been cancelled; but invite the poor, the maimed, the lame, and the blind, who cannot recompense thee, and thou shalt be recompensed at the resurrection of the just.[c]

To the wedding feast,— his frequent illustration of the kingdom of heaven,— were invited a prosperous landholder, a large owner of cattle, and a bridegroom, all types of the successful and the wealthy classes. Too much occupied with their good fortune, they sent polite excuses. Then, the angry master of the feast hurried in the poor, the maimed, the halt, and the blind, and, as there was still room, actually compelled the loiterers in the high-

[a] Luke xvi., 1-12.   [b] Luke xix., 12-27.
[c] Luke xiv., 12-14.

ways and by the hedges to come in.[a] The rich came in by the favor of invitation, the poor in the right of their poverty; and there is a still lower class, upon whom the honor is actually thrust.

To the covetous Pharisees, he told the parable of Dives and Lazarus.[b] This parable is still told with fearful impressiveness to the tender apprehension of childish minds, on account of the vivid picture it has of the dismal condition of those who are punished in hell. This, however, is a mere incident of the story, and by no means its chief lesson. Doubtless, Jesus accepted the traditional, conventional idea of hell, which his countrymen generally held. It seems to the sensitive modern mind incredible that the Hindu, the Jew, and the Christian should, in their several methods, entertain a vague idea of a place of indescribable and perpetual misery, and, in their thought, coolly regard it as the inevitable fate of their neighbors or their enemies, of, in fact, the whole race of mankind outside of the circle of their sympathy and fellowship. But history compels us to believe, that the human mind can entertain such a conception without forfeiting its instinctive cheerfulness. Jesus was telling his story in his, and in the vivid Oriental way. The story, like all his moral allegories, needed a catastrophe : it was not important what the catastrophe should be. And so he took the conventional hell of his age, just as Shakspeare in the drama of " Hamlet " takes the conventional purgatory of mediæval Catholicism, that he may inspire fresh pity for the murdered king condemned to such a fate. In either case such dramatic use of a popular notion does not of itself imply the author's faith in it. The real animus of the famous parable is its imputation against the rich and its comfort for the poor, whom it is intended to console with the assurance of compensation. It puts into an allegory what stood before in an apothegm: " Blessed be ye poor, for yours is the kingdom of God. Woe unto ye that are rich! for ye have received your consolation."[c] Of Dives, it is simply said he was a rich man, who clothed and fed himself according to his condition. It is not said that he was a vicious man, an impious man, an oppressive or even a proud man. The

[a] Luke xiv., 16-24.   [b] Luke xvi., 14, 19-31.   [c] Luke vi., 20, 24.

fact that he suffered a poor wretch, whose diseased condition made him a disagreeable and even loathsome object, to lie at his gate and be fed with fragments from his table, indicates rather more humane feeling, than is found in the average religious man of our time, who would contrive to rid himself speedily of Lazarus' presence at his front door by having him removed to a public hospital or almshouse. The artistic structure of this allegory not only exhibits the genius of Jesus, but there gleams through the lurid horrors of the picture flashes of the humor, with which, to a certain extent, the grave enthusiasm of his character was tempered. For in hell Dives is made to exhibit traits of character that fairly coerce our admiration. It is one of the marks of a gentleman that he shall not magnify his personal inconveniences, and shall accept with thanks the most trivial alleviations. Could anything exceed the modesty of his request that Lazarus, who he doubtless thought would go with alacrity on such an errand to please his old patron and benefactor, should be sent with a drop of water to cool his tongue? With a cool tongue, with which to continue the conversation, he will be too polite to think of remonstrating against the other considerable discomforts of his situation. When this small indulgence, purely, as it seems, on the score of physical impossibility, is denied, he does not roar nor blaspheme, nor, for a single moment, lose his heroic patience or cheerfulness. With a disinterestedness which, in his situation, is perfectly sublime, he passes at once to thinking of his five brothers, who have doubtless inherited his dangerous wealth, and bethinks himself how they may be warned of their liability to the same place of torment. Abraham, who henceforth befriends Lazarus in heaven, as Dives was wont to do on earth, explains to the amazed rich man how the change has come about. "Son," he says, —there was a palpable sarcasm in thus making him a devout and orthodox Israelite, whom even Abraham recognized as of his seed,— "Son, remember, that thou in thy lifetime receivedst thy good things, and likewise Lazarus evil things; but now he is comforted, and thou art tormented." Dives is in hell, because he was one of the rich, who could not enter the kingdom of heaven any more than a camel could pass through the eye of a needle. On the other hand, Lazarus, who is sheltered in Abraham's bosom, is not described as a good man, a pious man, or even a believing man. Blessed are ye poor, for yours is the kingdom of heaven, in virtue of your poverty. The poor have the gospel preached to them. The rich, who cannot enter the kingdom, need not even be invited.

It is not difficult to trace the consecutive order of Jesus' thought. He had been telling his disciples that, they must forsake, nay, even hate, father, mother, wife, children, brothers, sisters, all their possessions;[a] that they must do this deliberately, carefully, counting the cost beforehand. Then, he had told three parables, which indicated, that he preferred repentant prodigals, men who had come back from deep experience of dissipation and excesses, to the just persons that need no repentance, to the careful and prudent who had saved their patrimony by economy and self-denial.[b] From this, he had passed to speak with qualified commendation of the steward who had plundered his master, who was rich, but had made himself friends by fraudulently understating the debts of those who owed him, because they were poor.[c] And when the Pharisees, who were covetous, derided him, he startles them with this exaggerated picture of the compensations, which, in the kingdom of heaven, are provided for the rich and for the poor respectively.[d]

To the mind of Jesus, the ordinary avocations of human life, to which men go by the uncontrollable instincts of their nature, were impious. In his description of the suddenness of the opening of the new order of things, he said, it would be as in the time of Noah's flood, and of Sodom's destruction by fire and brimstone, when men ate and drank, bought, sold, planted, builded, married and were given in marriage. Like the rich man in the parable, the calamities fell upon these ancient people, not more to punish *their sins*, than to punish their *secular carefulness* about life and property. And so, above all, he counselled them against that human instinct, which, in fire and shipwreck, prompts every hand to save

[a] Luke xiv., 25-33. [b] Luke xv., 11-32. [c] Luke xvi., 1-12. [d] Luke xvi., 14, 19.

what is possible of possessions.[a] He that is on the housetop, and his stuff in the house, let him not come down to take it away, nor he who is in the field return to save his treasures.[b] It is impossible to overlook the fact that Jesus warred strenuously against the property instinct in man, as hostile to that state of mind, which was a fit preparation for the kingdom of heaven; and that this teaching is a fundamental principle in all his teaching.[c]

Outside of the circle of his disciples, and in portions of Palestine where he had never been, his gospel seems to have been understood as a gospel of poverty. When he was passing through Jericho on his fatal journey to Jerusalem, a rich publican named Zaccheus, who might have been a Jewish proselyte, but was not probably a descendant of Abraham, was moved to become his disciple. Jesus hears of his purpose, and visits him at his house. Zaccheus does not wait to be challenged, as the young man had been: *"Sell all that thou hast, and distribute unto the poor, and thou shalt have treasure in heaven; and come, follow me."* He apparently understands from public rumor that this is the everywhere prescribed condition of discipleship. He makes tender at once of all his property. One-half, he says, I give to the poor forthwith; out of the other half, let restitution be made fourfold, if I have taken anything by false accusation, as, in his odious office, he doubtless believed he had. Jesus accepts the offer, and declares that he is a true son of Abraham, and that the salvation which was promised to Abraham's seed has come to him and to his family.[d] Nowhere in the record is found such an absolute commendation of a convert. It was because no convert had so wholly embraced his ideas.

The harmony and interdependence of the ideas of Jesus now begin to be quite apparent. From the belief that the world itself, in all that relates to the structure of human society, in the condition and destiny of its human inhabitants, is about to be suddenly brought to an end, naturally proceeds the conclusion, that all care for subsistence is superfluous, and that wealth, which is the result of past labor and prudence, and the assurance of future subsist-

[a] Luke xvii., 26-30.   [b] Luke xvii., 31.   [c] Matt. vi., 32, 33.   [d] Luke xix., 1-10.

ence, is no longer desirable. Jesus seems to have concluded that there was wealth enough, already earned, to last the world till its dissolution, and that all devotion thereto was a distraction, which wholly unfitted men for the preparation to meet the catastrophe. He admitted the necessity of food, clothing, and shelter; but he had two resources, either of which was an ample provision. His first resource was the free bounty of the heavenly Father, whose gifts were to be had for the asking. Will even an unkind father give bread to his children, and will not a good and perfect God? Will the beneficent God feed the birds of the air, and clothe in beauty the grass doomed to the scythe, and will he not feed and clothe his children?[a] Besides this, the destitute were to share the free gifts of the rich,[b] who, coming into the kingdom of heaven, must show the sincerity of their repentance by forsaking all things,[c] selling their possessions,[d] and bestowing the proceeds upon the poor, already in the kingdom in virtue of their poverty.

If such a catastrophe as Jesus apprehended was impending, no prudence, or forethought, or industry was necessary to provide for the wants of the brief interval of human life. The catastrophe, which he had asseverated with a *verily, verily*, would occur in the lifetime of that generation,[e] did not occur, and up to this last period of the nineteenth century has not occurred. If Jesus came again after his death, it was not with a glittering escort of angels, the splendor of his appearing flashing from one side of the heavens to the other. He came not to shake,[f] still less (as the apostle believed) to remove the earth, preparatory to the new earth and new heavens, in which righteousness should dwell. If he came at all, it was in no official character, clothed with no divine powers, doing no more any works of healing or dispossession of evil spirits, and, what is most perplexing of all, without that fine power of uttering pithy and vigorous words which characterized his human intellect. He does not confront the High Priest, nor awe with the glories of his risen state the high social and ecclesiastical circle of Jerusalem, that had disdained him as a Galilean enthu-

[a] Matt. vii., 7-12.   [b] Matt. v., 42, 45; Luke vi., 30-34.   [c] Luke xiv., 33.
[d] Luke xii., 33.   [e] Matt. xxiv., 34, 35.   [f] Heb. xii., 27.

siast. Like a poor ghost only, he manifests himself, chiefly to susceptible Mary Magdalene; or, most privately, to a small circle of his chosen followers, and some even of them did not hesitate to express their doubt that they had indeed seen him at all.[a]

But whatever occurred in the invisible world, or in the policy or counsels of the heavens, of which nothing can be known, it is certain that the secular order went on. The sun rose in the east as before, not darkened nor changed into blood.[b] Not a star was missing in its place. The quiet movements of the heavenly bodies revealed no shock, and no sympathy with any new force or will in the mechanism of the universe. That mysterious power, call it nature, call it law, call it God, by which all things subsist and by which all things are controlled, utterly declined to be turned out of its ancient courses and to forsake its long-observed methods, to promote any new order of things, or to usher in with imposing scenic phenomena a new era of human or angelic society. It is only in a poetic sense that the sun, moon, and stars, and the aspects of the sky, sympathize with the profound sorrows or the profound yearnings of the deeply moved human spirit. It is the extravagance of enthusiasm that commands the sun and moon to stand still, that the great struggle we have on our hands may go on to victory.

What became alike necessity and duty under the changed expectation? Evidently, just what not only the world, but the disciples and worshippers of Jesus, actually did. They returned to their work; they prudently saved the earnings of their labor; they planted, they builded, they married and were given in marriage, and gradually the sense of impiety in so doing faded away.

There may be genial regions of the globe where the free bounty of nature invites man to repose, and abates the intensity of the struggle, by which mankind have maintained their existence against the encroachments of various and petty forms of inferior life, and against the rigor of climate. Palestine, where the fig and olive grew wild, and where wild honey and edible insects abounded in the wilderness, doubtless offered life to men on much easier conditions than does Europe and America to-day.

[a] Matt. xxviii., 17.   [b] Matt. xxiv., 29.

But how does the precept, *Take no thought of the morrow* mock the wretched tenants of crowded northern cities, whose whole life is a painful thought of to-morrow's subsistence, and how to make adequate to it the scanty income of to-day? How applicable is the economy of the kingdom of heaven to the dwellers within the arctic circle, who, in an atmosphere that inflicts sudden death upon all not shielded by the skins of the most cunning animals, or not warmed by intense fires, which, in that treeless zone, only animal oils supply, must brave the perils of ocean and frost to gather every day their food and fuel? The law of life is substantially the same everywhere. It is only by taking intense thought for life that men can preserve it. Not all the ravens are fed. If the sparrows do not fall to the ground without the heavenly Father, they do nevertheless fall. With all the power of associated man to help his race, with the great advantage which the social state, rising into the more complex structures of cities and governments, gives to individual men in systematizing and making effective their diligence to obtain sustenance; with the large surplus which industrious people accumulate; with the organized charities which form a part of the voluntary or legal institutions of all civilized communities, men do starve to death in Ireland as well as in America, India, and China. Cover it up with what sentiment we may, there stands for all men the primeval law,— *In the sweat of thy forehead shalt thou eat bread.*

Paul himself, with an admiration for his master almost idolatrous, was one of the first of his followers to awake from the dream of a life without labor, and a subsistence as precarious as the birds. Peter, true to the maxim of Jesus that the laborer was worthy of his hire, that they who preached the good news of the kingdom were not to provide purse, nor scrip, nor extra clothing, but were to be fed by the bounty of converts, so far enlarged that bounty as to share it with a wife and a sister, made companions of his mission. Paul nobly relinquished altogether this perquisite of apostleship.[*] He found time, while exhorting to faith and repentance, to work at his trade, and not only to support himself, but to have something to give to relieve the necessities of the sick and

---
[*] I. Cor. ix., 5, 6, 15.

disabled. He urged his followers diligently to work, that they might have something to bestow upon the distressed, and might escape the scandal that would fall upon idleness and dependence. Those among the disciples that would not work he denounced as disorderly and busybodies.[a] He thought less of men that did not earn the bread that they ate; and, so far from encouraging the habit of taking no thought for what they should eat, he acknowledged that his remedy for such an unscrupulous way of living upon the bounty of others was to cut off the supplies of every able-bodied man, who thought himself exempt from the condition of labor.[b]

Paul does not seem to have shared James' antipathy to the rich, nor to have held, with Jesus, that they could not enter the kingdom of heaven without dispossessing themselves of their wealth. Wealthy men had accepted his gospel, and been received by him among the believers; and these, in a letter to Timothy, he fully recognized as heirs of the promise of the kingdom. "Charge them that are rich," he writes, "in this world, that they be not high-minded, nor trust in uncertain riches, but in the living God, who giveth us richly all things to enjoy; that they do good, that they be rich in good works, ready to distribute, willing to communicate."[c] Thus, wealth, instead of being an impediment to salvation, was God's own gift, richly given, freely to be enjoyed.

While the apprehension of the overthrow of all things was vivid in the minds of the early Christians, as it continued to be during the lifetime of the apostles, the contempt of labor and the repudiation of property, as something offensive to the coming king, continued among them. It is related that, after the death of Jesus, the disciples were together and had all things in common, and sold their possessions and goods, and parted them to all as every man had need, and continued every day with one accord in the temple, and breaking bread from house to house, eating their food with gladness and singleness of heart.[d] After they became a multitude, they remained of one heart and mind, neither said any of them that aught of the things which he possessed was his own; but

---
[a] II. Thess. iii., 8-15.   [b] I. Thess. ii., 9; II. Cor. xi., 9; Acts xx., 33, 34.
[c] I. Timothy vi., 17, 18.   [d] Acts ii., 44-46.

they had all things in common. Jesus' methods proved confessedly successful, even after the little flock had grown a powerful community. After his death, they were constrained to answer the question, which, in modest self-reproach, they did not answer when he put it: "When I sent you without purse, and scrip, and shoes, lacked ye anything?"[a] The new economy is successful. There were none among them *that lacked anything;* "for as many as were possessors of lands or houses sold them, as Jesus had commanded them," and brought the prices of the things that were sold, and laid them down at the apostles' feet; and distribution was made unto every man according as he had need.[b]

The church at Jerusalem seems to have been established and maintained upon the plan of confiscating the property of the rich converts for the benefit of the poor.[c] When this resource failed, as in the nature of things it soon must have done, the believers subsisted upon the donations of those gathered into the faith in the populous and wealthy Greek and Roman cities, mainly through the successful propagandism of Paul. And, indeed, suspicious as the leaders at Jerusalem were of the dogmas and practices which Paul held and taught — as is most manifest from the New Testament records — or in reference to his indecorous habit of working as a mechanic, to his admission of rich men to the communion of the saints without compelling them to surrender their wealth to be divided among the poor, and to his frequent exhortations to converts to labor diligently for the purpose of having something to bestow upon the needy, they could not very consistently condemn what redounded to their own advantage. For the Jerusalem church, under the strict *régime* of Jesus himself, seems to have come into an eleemosynary relation with all the other churches, and to have been supported all through the apostolic period by collections gathered wherever a new Christian community was planted. It is not known whether this relation was maintained until the capture of the city by Titus, and the scattering of the Church, or whether the Gentile converts under the teachings of Paul — in which a vein of satire is not wholly absent — grew weary of supporting their idle

[a] Luke xxii., 35. [b] Acts iv., 32-35. [c] Luke xiv., 33.

brethren, and at last applied to them the rough method which he ordered adopted at Thessalonica, — "If any will not work, neither shall he eat."[a]

For a world not suddenly ending, as had been confidently believed, but persisting in going on, and going on in much the old way, the Christians found it necessary to modify the strictness and scope of the command of their master, to forsake and hate houses, lands, and all their possessions, to become his disciples. The common believer might, and, as Paul insisted, must be *not slothful in business.* He might even propose, as an end of his diligence, the reward of money even to the extent of wealth. He might accumulate property to give of its income and surplus to the necessities of the saints.[b] He would be worse than an unbeliever, if he did not accumulate sufficient to provide for his own household.[c] Rich men came into the churches without scandal; and it was not long before the churches, instead of levying from them at the very door the surrender of all their riches, flattered and courted them for their patronage; and Lazarus fed from the crumbs of the table of Dives, without the rude reminder that, after death, the former should rest in the bosom of Abraham and the latter howl in torment.

But so fundamental a part of the system which Jesus sought to establish, and died to consecrate, could not be lost. The Christian priesthood gradually rose. The missionaries of the gospel, to the earliest of whom great reverence and authority were accorded, as the witnesses of Jesus' words and works while alive, and of his resurrection after his crucifixion, were universally considered to be elevated above the drudgery and degradation of toil. Let the preachers of the gospel at least live of the gospel. Even sturdy Paul would not give up this prerogative of his profession. Besides this class — quite large when compared with the body of believers — all who, as Jesus had said, would be perfect, all who would insure their entrance into his kingdom, when it should come, continued to adopt his ideas about property, as they did also his ideas of the relation of the sexes. They became

[a] II. Thess. iii., 10.
[b] Acts xi., 30; xxiv., 17; Rom. xv., 25, 26; I. Cor. xvi., 1-3; II. Cor. viii., ix.
[c] I. Tim. v., 8.

monks and nuns, making themselves celibates for the kingdom of heaven's sake, having their goods in common, and were supported by the donations of those, who were awed by the austerity of their piety.

The attitude of the modern Christian Church toward property and wealth is quite the reverse of that of the early Church. All through mediæval time and down to the present, Christianity has been the great bulwark of property, and pronounces benedictions upon the rich. It has not in terms transposed the beatitudes of Jesus, and said: Blessed are ye rich, for yours is the kingdom of heaven; but it has practically said so. A sentiment is still cherished, which respects the virtuous poor, and the places of Christian worship are nominally open to them; but, more and more, the fellowship of the Church confines itself to the prosperous classes. The old meeting-houses, such as were open fifty years ago to all classes in New England, have one after the other fallen into decay; and their places have been supplied by small and costly temples, whose whole interiors are occupied with expensively finished and upholstered pews, where the weekly accommodations for a family cost more for persons of small means than the rental of a dwelling-house. The poor are not excluded from these religious assemblies, but no seats are provided for them. The whole aspect of the place as effectually excludes them as would an opera house or a private club house or a wedding in an aristocratic family, where not only the cost of admission, but the rigid etiquette of dress and manners, interposes barriers which the sensitive poor cannot pass.

In assemblies from which the classes, that made up the wedding feast, the type according to Jesus of the kingdom of heaven, are carefully excluded, the preacher of the gospel, such as eighteen centuries of contact with the influences of civilization has made it, cannot repeat with any fervor or directness the denunciations of the rich, which form so considerable a part of the recorded discourses of his master. He is expected, with rhetorical ingenuity and delicate tact, to refine and explain them away. How can he denounce, as outside of the kingdom of heaven, those who, already in possession of its outworks, hold the purse and scrip, and can testify their disapprobation by withholding his support, and leaving him no resource but that which Jesus said was sufficient, — to ask of the heavenly Father whatever was needed?

The communistic principle, which, as has been seen, was the natural outcome of the property ideas disseminated by Jesus, has lasted considerably longer than those ideas themselves. From the primitive Church, it passed to various monastic orders, that still perpetuate it in connection with celibacy. In modified forms, it has appeared in the economy and creed of several Christian sects, like the Moravians and the Shakers. But the generally accredited Christianity comes more and more to disown and antagonize it; and to-day, both in Europe and America, the bodies of men who hold the tenets of Jesus in reference to property, and who are seeking or have sought to embody them in a new social order recognizing the complete equality of men, are generally decried as antichristian and atheistic.

This departure of the ostensible followers of Jesus from the principles which so widely formed the structure of his system, so far as it was a system fit for a subsisting world, is not mentioned to condemn it. There have been, since the first century of our era, a great many generations of men, upon whom the effect of the passion for possessing property in its influence upon character has been carefully watched and noted. If the successors of Jesus lack the prescient accuracy of his judgment, they have judged upon much larger data, and with the opportunity of correcting a too hasty generalization by deliberation and concurrent consideration.

There are certain faults of character which the possession of wealth seems to aggravate. Pride, arrogance, indifference to human suffering, are apt to attain a rank growth in the over-prosperous man; while two dangers beset his path,— either, that the sordid habits he formed while he was painfully and with self-denial accumulating money by grovelling labor or narrow saving, shall pinch his soul and make it hard and base, or, that the consideration of having much goods laid up for many years shall invite to sensual indulgence. Ordinarily, the first danger becomes fatal to the men who themselves, by slow industry and painful methods, acquire wealth: the latter besets especially those, who inherit it, or come to it by fortunate enterprise.

On the other hand, more insidious and more deadly perils beset the poor. The poor, especially in the presence of the pomp and luxury of the rich, become morose, vindictive, envious, and censorious, a prey to more subtle vices, and harder to eradicate from the soul, than sensuality, often a taint of the blood. In the struggle for life, the steadily unsuccessful grow exasperated; and the most upright principles yield many times before the pressure of an adversity, that is suggestive of a malignant ill-will, provoking to retaliation. The daily necessity for labor to the full extent of the bodily powers, to support the necessities of life, is, for myriads of human beings, an effectual guarantee of temperance and chastity. The self-denial which men begin to exercise to acquire food for their offspring becomes a habit, a strength, a conscious power of the soul. The man who can labor after fatigue and pain learns first what duty means. He says, *I wish* I could do this, but *I must* do that. The more he does what he must, rather than what he wishes, the more of a civilized, moral, religious creature he becomes. When he has followed duty in one direction against inclination, he has learned the mystery of noble living, and is in the royal road to all virtue. These high influences sanctify labor, and make the beginnings of the acquisition of wealth salutary and even sacred. Nor the beginnings alone; for, carefully to note our own observations, their net result would be that more men are made generous, public-spirited, refined, lovers of pure and simple pleasures by becoming rich, than are made humble, patient, magnanimous, and upright by long and hopeless poverty. This is proved by the statistics of most civilized countries, in which, though the prosperous, particularly the suddenly prosperous, classes would be found tainted with crimes of oppression, fraud, and profligacy, the great army of the criminal classes, with which society has constantly to maintain a warfare to insure its own preservation, is recruited from the ranks of the poor. The best wisdom of his race was not at all in accord with that of Jesus, when it uttered from the lips of a cynical king the prayer, "Give me neither poverty nor riches; feed me with food convenient for me, lest I be full, and deny thee, . . . lest I be poor and steal, and take the name of my God in vain."[a]

In nothing, however, did Jesus show the original force of his own mind, and its impatience of dominant, national and conventional ideas, more than in his opinions concerning property. As Moses, brought up under the intense *other-worldliness* of the Egyptians — than whom, it is probable, no race of men ever lived with death, judgment, and the retributions of eternity so awfully impressed upon their imaginations — came to have a supreme contempt for a faith that had palpably failed to make men either virtuous or happy; and determined to base a new religious cultus on sanctions, limited wholly to the life of this world, so Jesus, a man also of transcendent genius, determined to strike at the very root of the religious cultus of his race and time. The Jews preserve to this day the dominant trait of the national character in their devotion to wealth. Abraham was great in the extent of his fields and pastures, in silver and gold, in flocks and herds, in dependants and servants. Jacob, out of the line of the first-born, the father of the nation, was great in the ingenious contrivances of his thrift. All the law of Moses was built upon the sanction, not of rewards and punishments in an after-life, but of large possessions, and prosperous fortunes in a long human life, if men should keep its precepts; but if they failed to keep them, of famines, drouths, pillage and enslavement. The very ten commandments were promulgated mainly in the interest of property. It is of the nature of the reformer, that he is profoundly disappointed in the results of the culture that has gone before him, and distrustful of the ideas that underlie that culture. Behold the fruit of the Mosaic dispensation, — of the soul of man oblivious of the life to come, turned sordidly upon this world, wealth and long life its chief goods! Let the pendulum swing again to the other side. What is the value of life? Of what advantage is it to gain the whole world? He that seeketh his life shall lose it. A man's life consisteth not in the abundance of the things that he possesseth. Jesus sought to restore to life its mystery, its seriousness,

[a] Prov. xxx., 8, 9.

its awful import, as a threshold of an immortal life, the gate of entrance to the kingdom of heaven. The Christian cultus, almost lost now in the accretions of an insidious civilization, that it could not resist, is the fruit of his enthusiasm.

CHAPTER V.

ETHICAL IDEAS OF JESUS.

"Let us beware of awarding to the founder of the Church any honor which a subsequent time may be compelled to recall. The only service the human race can render such a being as Jesus is to study the actual facts, and not the desirable facts, of the great historic page of his life."—*Prof. David Swing.*

CLOSELY connected with the political ideas of Jesus, and in some directions blended with them, are his ethical ideas, the principles which he declared should regulate conduct. It were most desirable to present them in a system, to indicate the axioms, upon which they rest, and the scheme of an ideal life of which they formed the elements. If we could find, in the memorabilia of Jesus' life, his system unfolded by himself, if he had declared the primal truths, upon which his soul rested, and to which he confessed allegiance, it would be very easy to express his ethical precepts in a creed or in a philosophy, and to consider them under his weighty and august authority. That his mind was capable of such generalization his conversations plainly imply. For, while commending virtuous conduct rather upon its reasonableness than upon his own, or the divine authority, his habit seemed to be to find the underlying principle consonant to the human reason, which is the sanction of the virtue enjoined.

Thus, in the Sermon on the Mount, when he pronounces a certain condition of life or state of the heart good or blessed, as the poor, the sorrowing, the meek, the pure, and the persecuted, he feels called upon to give, as a reason for his estimate, the temporal or spiritual advantage, that shall befall them in consequence of such condition or affection. They shall enjoy the kingdom of heaven, they shall be comforted, they shall see God, they shall inherit the renown of the persecuted prophets. He said his followers were to be heroic in their suffering of evil, ascetic in the repression of appetite and resentment; and that they were to meet violence, not by resistance or remonstrance, but by inviting new assault, because the grade of goodness taught and practised by the strictest piety of his time was not a qualification for entrance even into *the kingdom of heaven.* Daring and sublime must be the flight of the soul in the higher atmosphere of an ideal nobleness to reach the heavenly blessedness, and no easy or commonplace conformity to the standard of the scribes and Pharisees, or of the philosophers, could be accepted as a commutation of the rigid self-denial, the vivisection of all the instincts of the animal nature, which he made the discipline of a soldier of the cross. He said that enemies were to be loved, because God gave the blessing of light and rain to bad and good men alike; and that men must be perfect — that is, sublime in their love of those who injured and hated them — in order to be like God. Prayer and alms were to be in secret, that God, and only God, should openly reward them. Treasure was not to be laid up on earth, lest men's hearts should tend earthward to their treasure, instead of heavenward to God. No anxiety was to be had for subsistence, because God supplies it to men as to birds. The strait gate was to be sought, not because it was open to all, but because it was narrow and obscure, and only a few intense strivers would ever be able to find it. This disposition of Jesus to confirm and illustrate all his ethical precepts, by a reason based upon the absolute verities of the universe, may fairly be assumed as the characteristic of his mind and the peculiarity of his ethical system.[*]

Why, then, may we not adopt his own generalizations, and deduce his moral system from his own accredited words? Because we are perplexed by the inconsequential and contradictory character of these generalizations. A few of the more striking instances will justify this assertion.

Jesus had enunciated the doctrine that enemies were to be loved, that blessing was the due return for cursing, and kind wishes and prayers for cruel usage, because, in

[*] Matt. v., vi., vii.

that high strain of perfect love, men put on a likeness to
the heavenly Father, whose equal gifts of light and rain
to good and evil expressed his equal love to all, not less
to the disobedient than to the obedient.[a] When asked
afterward how many times an injury was to be forgiven —
a real and intentional injury being referred to — and if
seven times would meet his requirement, he promptly
answered, Forgive seventy times seven,— that is, indefinitely.[b] And this men are to do, because God does it.
Plainly, this generalization implies that God forgives
wicked men even, and not only forgives, but blesses
them. But later, in the same conversation, Jesus declares that his heavenly Father will say in some near
future day to many who had prayed to him, and in some
way derived power to work miracles in his name: Depart
from me, workers of evil,[c] — a sentence which he afterward supplemented with the indication of the place of
their departure — into everlasting fire prepared for the
devil and his angels.[d]

Indeed, this forgiving and universally blessing Deity of
the Sermon on the Mount is not the permanent conception of Deity which Jesus dwells upon. Much oftener,
particularly in the later part of his career, God is presented as a being to be feared, because he can destroy
soul and body in hell.[e] Indeed, taking the whole thought
of Jesus and attempting to reconcile the being, who is
imitated by rendering blessing for cursing and good for
evil, with the being who says: Depart, ye accursed, into
everlasting fire prepared for the devil and his angels, we
find a suggestion in the words of Jesus himself, which
gives something like consistency to his conception. In one
of his parables, he represented good and evil men under
the figure of wheat and weeds growing together in a field.
When it was proposed to root up the weeds, that was forbidden, lest the wheat should suffer. The forbearance
with the weeds was not at all on their account; for afterward, as soon as they could be separated, they were mer-
cilessly burned. So, Jesus affirmed, should it be at the
end of the worldly order and the beginning of the heavenly.[f] The unjust then have the rain and the sunshine,

[a] Matt. v., 15, 16. [b] Matt. xviii., 21, 22. [c] Matt. vii., 22. [d] Matt. xxv., 40.
[e] Luke xii., 5. [f] Matt. xiii., 24-30, 36-43.

because, being with the just, they cannot be prevented from participating in a good condition designed only for the latter. But that very incongruity demands a separation, so that the evil shall receive, not sunshine and rain, but fire and the outer darkness, which is their fitting allotment.

The Christian ages, reverencing Jesus as divine, and accepting as absolute truth all he is believed to have said, have been seriously perplexed by this twofold presentation of the divine character, as something to be imitated. Must we imitate the heavenly Father returning good for evil, or returning evil for evil? or imitate him in returning good for evil for a time, and indemnify ourselves afterward by the completeness and excess of our vengeance? One order of souls, endowed with natural pity, have, in all ages, learned the earlier lesson. Another order, in whom the sentiment of justice overweighed natural pity, have insisted that evil-doing shall be rigorously punished. It can hardly be claimed that the humane instincts of mankind have been, on the whole, stimulated in the direction of mercy and beneficence by the whole doctrine of Jesus, or that they who have deferred specially to his authority have been distinguished among mankind for the mildness of their methods with offenders against the social order of the world.

To take another example. Jesus, in enjoining secrecy and brevity in prayer, had declared, as if from an intimate knowledge of the Deity, that he knew already what men needed, and so was not informed or influenced by much speaking.[a] But, later, he declared that men ought to importune God for what they needed; and that, though he would not grant their requests to their necessities, of which he had knowledge, or from his benevolence, he would grant them, to rid himself of the annoyance of their persistency.[b] Wherever a low and a lofty conception of the divine character is presented to the immature minds of men, it is not surprising that they should seize and appropriate the former. So we see that it was the anthropomorphic idea of a God capable of being wearied by much speaking, rather than the more dignified idea of a God knowing beforehand the wants of men, and giving

[a] Matt. vi., 5-7. [b] Luke xi., 5-8; xvii., 1-8.

heed to their prayers on the side of his affection and pity, as expressions of their confidence and piety, that has determined the devotional practice of Christendom. For the liturgies of every form of Christian worship have ever abounded in much speaking. Repetitions, the wearying power of which upon God can only be judged by their wearying effect upon the men that listen to them, form the body of prayers, so long and so often repeated, that to recite them has demanded a special order of functionaries, and fairly furnished them with regular employment.

Let us consider, as an instance of inconsequential generalization, the direction about the secrecy of alms and prayer. If men prayed in secret, Jesus affirmed God would reward them openly.[a] Why openly, and why reward? Is prayer, then, a grateful homage to the Deity, for which, as a courteous return, some reward is due?

Jesus also said, If we forgive not the person who has wronged us, neither will God forgive us for wrongs done toward him.[b] This thought he afterward elaborated in a parable, in which a certain master released a heavy debt to his servant, because he was poor. But, learning afterward that his released debtor had exacted by imprisonment a small debt due from a fellow-servant, he was angry, and ordered his debtor to the torture till he should pay the last farthing. "So," added Jesus to the parable, "likewise shall my heavenly Father do also unto you, if ye from your hearts forgive not every one his brother their trespasses."[c]

Does God then render evil for evil, when men do likewise? Is his beneficence caprice or character? Does it not degrade God to think of him, whose perfection all rational souls are to imitate, as an imitator of the cruelty of the evil, and as delighting in the severity with which he can surpass them in retaliation? Jesus had declared that it was a small effort of the soul to love only them that loved us, to salute those who saluted us. The publicans even, men who made no pretensions to a high grade of nobleness, could do as much as that;[d] but, to be perfect like the heavenly Father, we must love those who do not love us, we must forgive the trespasses of

---

[a] Matt. vi., 6.　[b] Matt. vi., 15.　[c] Matt. xviii., 25-35.
[d] Matt. v., 46.

those who do not forgive our trespasses, nor those of our fellow-men.

There is an immense challenge to the spirit of man in this imitation of God in the perfectness of love. Jesus never spake anything so far-reaching in its implications. Christianity does not contain an idea so sublime. But the older conception fairly crowded it out, even, of the poetic mind that uttered it. The older conception was, "*Vengeance is mine, I will repay.*"* Not that vengeance is not due and is not to be taken, but that it is to be waited for at the hands of its lawful minister, who only can make it summary and effectual. So the world, stirred for a moment by the daring presumption, that by a complete forgiveness it can imitate God, recoils from the splendor which opens before it, and, while uttering an earlier and lower inspiration, comes to believe that, in the vengeance with which it punishes and retaliates the trespasses of evil-doers, it is itself forgiving, while acting as the minister of a heavenly Father who will not forgive the unforgiving.

In no part of the study here undertaken is the temptation stronger to repudiate the statement of general principles as given in the gospel narratives. The writers of those narratives might perhaps be trusted to give the historical incidents of the life of Jesus, they might faithfully reproduce his parables and his direct ethical precepts; but, when they undertake to disclose his philosophy, the primal ideas upon which he based his ethical precepts, there, if anywhere, their acknowledged incapacity to comprehend him would be most likely to mislead them. All, therefore, already said, or that may be said, in criticism of this underlying philosophy of the Great Teacher, must be said with modesty, and with the misgiving that the record is not true to the integrity of his thought. It can only be insisted, that the method of investigation proposed requires just this treatment; and that, upon any other assumption than that of the substantial accuracy of the language imputed in the Synoptic Gospels to Jesus, we have no data from which to determine his character or his doctrine or, in fact, upon which to predicate his historical identity. No other course is

---

* Rom. xii. 19; Deut. xxxii., 35.

then left for the sympathetic critic, who has not come to the study under the prepossession of discipleship, but to state the ethical ideas of Jesus as nearly as possible in his own words, as historic tradition gives them, modified, limited, or contradicted only by himself.

Such of the precepts of Jesus as related to poverty and non-resistance have already been elaborated in a previous chapter as coming under the category of political ideas, though they have an intimate relation with the specific subject of the present chapter.

Jesus affirmed also that a state of sorrow was a blessed and wholesome condition. Blessed, he said, are they that mourn, for they shall be comforted. Blessed are ye that weep now, for ye shall laugh. Woe unto ye that laugh now! for ye shall mourn and weep.[a] Undoubtedly, the ministry of sorrow, if not too long and hopeless, is salutary to the soul. It chastens pride; it moderates desire; it abates the standard of enjoyment to the measure of a rational contentment; it disciplines and refines the passionate instincts of the heart; it gives entrance into the deeper secrets of the moral and spiritual life, by making the sufferer a participator in the higher experiences of his race, since it is mainly by suffering, and the striving which it stimulates, that human nature has passed upward from bestial conditions and satisfactions to the realms of pure thought and spiritual power. Since the whole sentient world has for all the ages lain, and still lies, under the shadow and discipline of sorrow, Jesus spake no word that has thrilled more deeply the universal human heart; and this tone, once struck by his gentle touch, vibrates through all the Christian ages, its purity and pathos prolonged in echoes that bid fair to outlast the world. Fresh as the agony of bereavement, the languor of prolonged sickness, the weariness of imprisonment and exile, the pang of constantly defeated effort, the long aching that comes of monotonous toil or care, is the tonic word that even conventional Christianity has not forgotten to repeat in its pristine power, "*Blessed are they that mourn.*"

Not that Jesus believed that sorrow was the normal condition of the human soul. "For they shall be comforted." All sorrow is suffering, and all suffering is evil. His

[a] Luke vi., 21, 25.

scheme of compensation embraced a reversal of all conditions. Just so much joy, so much grief. Those that laugh now must weep hereafter, while the weepers shall laugh in the assurance that God shall wipe away all tears from their eyes; and there shall be no more death, neither sorrow nor crying, neither shall there be any more pain: for the former things are passed away.[a]

In this blessedness of sorrow, in this consecration and deification of suffering, made memorable by the pathetic story of the cross, and the man of sorrows that agonized upon it, we may find the principal power of the religion, which has named itself after the name of Jesus. History may be said to have disclosed two methods by which society has striven to elevate itself and enlarge its capacities and achievements. One is the revolutionary method, which seeks to ameliorate external conditions, which promises to man emancipation from his rulers, more rights, larger liberty, greater possessions, and happiness. The other may be called the religious method, prominent and distinctive in Christianity, but present, too, in the great Oriental religions that preceded it, and the secret of their success. This method comes to comfort and cheer men, not by delusive hopes of escaping the inevitable woes of life, the sufferings out of which man has gained his moral nature, but by strengthening him to bear them; and it is on this side, and not on the side of its doctrines or disclosures of the fate of men in a future life, that Christianity has not only maintained itself, but retained the allegiance of the noblest and purest minds.

Jesus pronounced the pitiful blessed.[b] One of the chief accusations he brought against the scribes and Pharisees was that they were over-punctilious in bringing the lesser offerings — mint, anise, and cumin — while neglecting to be merciful.[c] The cruel servant, who, in the delay of his master's coming, beat his fellow-servant, was cut asunder suddenly by his enraged lord, and consigned to a place of weeping and gnashing of teeth.[d] He would receive into the blessedness of the Father's kingdom those whom, to their modest surprise, he had separated to his right hand, because they have been pitiful to those

[a] Rev. xxi., 4.   [b] Matt. v., 7.   [c] Matt. xxiii., 23.   [d] Matt. xxiv., 49, 50.

of his followers who had been sick, poor, and imprisoned.[a] He recognized, as modifying the divine justice, the element of mercy, and taught men to pray for the forgiveness of their sins, assuring them that God would forgive, at least the forgiving.[b]

He characterized the cultus under which his nation had been trained as something radically different from this. The old idea had been an eye for an eye and a tooth for a tooth; but his word was: "Resist not evil."[c] But to us, who have the Christian and Hebrew systems in their written records, the contrast between them is less striking. Along with that characterization of Jehovah as a jealous God, visiting the iniquities of the fathers upon the children to the third and fourth generation of them that hate him, which is an original commentary upon one of the ten commandments, is the converse declaration,— showing mercy unto thousands of them that love him and keep his commandments.[d] The pity of the Deity is as emphatically expressed in the Old, as in the New Testament, and it is in the former that we find that touching expression of the kindness of God, "*As a father pitieth his children, so the Lord pitieth them that fear him.*"[e] The old idea was that the jealous God, visiting iniquity with punishment, involving the children and grandchildren of the wrong-doer, pitied and forgave those who feared him. And this substantially is the idea of Jesus, who declared with severity: "If ye forgive not men their trespasses, neither will your heavenly Father forgive your trespasses."[f]

Purity of heart, according to Jesus, brings man to the consciousness of the divine presence; and in this idea we come to a feature of Christian ethics in sharp contrast with the cultus that had preceded, and in advance of the moral standard of modern civilization. The older religion of the Jews had introduced the Deity as pronouncing a blessing upon the reproductive function. The first counsel, according to its teaching, given to the newly created man was:[g] "Be fruitful, and multiply and replenish the earth." A marriage barren of offspring was regarded as a token of the disfavor of God, to be averted by prayers

---

[a] Matt. xxv., 33, 34.   [b] Matt. vi., 14, 15.   [c] Matt. v., 38, 39.   [d] Ex. xx., 5, 6.
[e] Ps. ciii., 13.   [f] Matt. vi., 15.   [g] Gen. i., 28.

and sacrifices; while children swarming around the family table were considered olive branches, alike the ornament of human life and the pledge of the loving partiality of Jehovah. The word of Jesus was: He that looketh upon a woman to desire her hath committed adultery with her in his heart.[a] He said the only defilement of which a man was capable was the defilement of adulterous and wicked thoughts.[b] The natural affections, out of which the relations of the sexes grow, were to be repressed as sins. To the plea that they are human and assert themselves with the sanction and strength of nature, he said: Well, then, extirpate nature itself. If thine eye offend thee, pluck it out and cast it from thee. It is better to enter into life one-eyed than, having two eyes, to be cast into hell. He commended those, who, for the sake of the kingdom of heaven, had applied to themselves this process of extirpation, and declared that, in the new and heavenly order which he was about to introduce, human beings would be like the angels, and neither married nor were given in marriage. This declaration had no force to meet the dilemma of the woman who in her human life had had in succession seven lawful husbands, if it did not imply that in the resurrection state not only no new marriages are contracted, but all pre-existing marriages, with all the special relation and affection which belong to them, are ignored and blotted out. In strict conformity to these ascetic ideas, he himself, though of a tender and affectionate disposition, which attracted to him the companionship and confidence of women, never in word or action indicated that the kinship of marriage was compatible with his modes of thought and feeling.

Jesus went no further than to affirm that sexual desire was inherently evil, and that sexual relations did not belong to the perfect man. He recognized marriage as a condition of the earthly, human life; and, while challenging those, who would be perfect, to celibacy in thought and life, he only stipulated that those who married should not be divorced for other cause than fornication.[c]

Historic Christianity has been, on the whole, faithful to the principles of Jesus in this department of nature,

[a] Matt. v., 28-30. [b] Matt. xv., 11, 18-20; xxii., 29, 30; xix., 10-12.
[c] Matt. xix., 9.

although stopping far short of his ideal. Out of his pure precepts have grown monogamy, and a resolute opposition to divorce, which fairly distinguish the Christian ages and races, as well as that prescribed celibacy, for those who are the recognized teachers and exemplars of religion, and the general honor in which absolute chastity is universally held. Against monastic vows and the practice of celibacy, mainly perpetuated by a large body of men and women who have inherited the singular purity of Jesus, there have been many powerful protests and reactions. Mohammed, exhibiting in himself that by no means unusual blending of the sensual and devout — a type highly favorable to poetic susceptibility and power, like what was exhibited in Israel's favorite king — gave to his disciples an ideal of a kingdom of heaven as unlike as possible to the state in which they neither marry nor are given in marriage. The completeness with which his lower ideas supplanted those of Jesus in the very countries to which his gospel came, and by which it was first received, shows how much more thoroughly human Mohammed was than Jesus, and how much better he understood the capacities and tendencies of the Semitic races.

The same reversion to primitive and natural notions, the same reactionary resentment of the rigorous yoke, which Jesus endeavored to throw upon animal instincts, reappears in Mormonism, and in those groups of eccentric Christians, who in communities have sought to combine a recognition of the supremacy of right, with the recognition of such law as human nature discloses.

When it is thoughtfully considered how much social misery and personal degradation have grown out of the ill-regulated appetites of man, and that his superiority over the beasts, and over the savage types of mankind, from which he has progressed, consists mainly in the moral power he has gained by imposing restraint upon instincts before which they are helpless, it cannot be denied that Jesus was profoundly right in what he believed and taught; and that the heavenly order, if not to be reached by the rapid and summary transformation, which he anticipated, is only to be attained by the daring of self-denial and sacrifice, rather than by the effeminacy of indulgence; and that all schemes of social regeneration are but steps downward, and in the direction of degradation, that do not propose for individual man a higher law of purity.

Still, Jesus is not to be considered as an ascetic. He went to feasts, and never seemed to have annoyed his entertainers with scruples either of appetite or conscience as to his entertainment.ª It is fairly inferrible that the rule he gave his disciples was the one that regulated his own conduct as a guest. He told them to tarry at the houses, to which they might be invited, eating and drinking such things as were set before them.ᵇ John's Gospel, to which we do not have recourse for authentic history, tells of him that at a marriage feast where he was present, when the wine failed, rather than have the harmless hilarity suspended, he miraculously produced wine of a quality and quantity which more than met the demands of the occasion.ᶜ The story would not have been told, if scruples on his part about wine-drinking itself had obtained any currency in his times. Indeed, his habits and principles upon this point are fairly disclosed by his own authentic declaration that, whereas John's asceticism had fallen on that age like the lamentation of a mourner, his own liberal manners were as merry as the notes of a piper. He did not resent, or declare libellous, the saying of his countrymen, which he himself reported, that he had come eating and drinking like a gluttonous man and a winebibber. The wisdom of his free living and of John's abstemiousness, however, he said, the wise would know how to appreciate.ᵈ

Two forms of sensuality have infested and degraded humanity, the one leading to drunkenness, the other to licentiousness. The religion taught by Mohammed seems to have set for itself the task of eradicating the former, while tolerant of the latter. The religion inspired by Jesus turned its pure eye in stern reprobation of sexual desire, while it chose as the emblem of its saving grace, the instrument of its only distinctive ceremony, the liquor which Islam proscribed as accursed, and which has been in all ages the principal stimulant of intoxication. Alco-

---

ª Matt. xi., 19; Luke xi., 37; xiv., 8.   ᵇ Luke x., 8.
ᶜ John ii., 1-11.   ᵈ Matt. xi., 16-19.

holic drunkenness has ever been the moral stain and weakness of the Christian peoples; and, when the danger and misery which it wrought came to be appreciated by the awakened humane sentiment of a recent age, good men were perplexed to find how equivocal were the teachings of the Christian scriptures upon the subject, and how little sanction for total abstinence was furnished in the example of the founder of Christianity himself.

Fairly to present the ethics of Jesus in reference to the purity which he practised and blessed, it must be said that he disclosed it rather as an ideal than a practical attainment. He challenged men to follow him in a strain of virtue that he admitted to be beyond the attainment of all but the loftiest spirits.[a] Paul, who came after him, may be said to have supplemented his delicacy with plainer speech, to have accommodated the ideal virtue of his master more nearly to the decent practices of civilized society, and to have found in the permitted order of the world a place for an instinct, which, according to Jesus, obscured in the soul of man the vision of God. If it be said that the faith of Mohammed was more powerful in countries over which it prevailed in repressing drunkenness, than the faith of Jesus has been in Christendom to repress licentiousness, let it be remembered that drunkenness is an invention of a comparatively recent civilization, while the sexual appetite springs from the methods of human existence, and strengthens itself by relations with the whole progress of animal life. Let it be remembered, too, how much the ideal purity, which Jesus enjoined and exemplified, has done, through the centuries since he lived, to exalt the sentiment of human love, and to introduce into the social relations of men the chaste satisfactions of an angelic state.

In considering offences against persons, Jesus thought the proscribing of murder exceedingly inadequate and elementary. He disdained to enumerate the minor violences of mutilating, wounding, and beating, and every form of bodily harm or manual assault, and passed at once to combat the causeless resentments out of which all injuries flow. Whosoever is angry with his brother without a cause is in peril as a wrong-doer. If he ad-

[a] Matt. xix., 11, 12.

dresses him in terms of contempt, he is advanced a grade deeper in guilt and danger; and, if he insults him with the epithet *thou fool*, he is in danger of hell fire.[a]

It is not to be concluded that Jesus intended to condemn natural anger, and the just resentment that acts of cruelty or of treachery excite in all sensitive minds. He himself, as might have been supposed from the delicacy of his mental organization, was strongly susceptible to anger; and several instances are related when he gave his resentment expression.[b] While acknowledging that anger degrades and exposes the soul, and holding up self-control as the true law of blameless conduct, the difficulty has always been, in the sudden access of anger, to measure dispassionately the injury that provoked it. But meantime, while the judgment of reason is disturbed or overthrown, the act of retaliation has been done, the bitter, biting reproach has been hurled, and the enemy, who might have been conciliated and made magnanimous by love and forgiveness, has been provoked to a fresh aggression. Or, if the overt act or word has been suppressed by a supreme effort of patience or for want of opportunity, the pent-up anger, which utterance might have relieved, remains to torture and depress the soul, and shut out from it all the serene influences of virtue.

Jesus himself was not aware how hard he might find it, with his delicate and sensitive spirit, to bear the contradictions and malicious suspicions of those who took offence at him, and the stupid misapprehensions of those who thought they loved and understood him. We are compelled to adopt an explanation of his language that shall exclude the scribes and the Pharisees and all evil and indifferent persons from the category of kindness and forgiveness, and to say that Jesus forbids anger and opprobrious epithets only toward brothers, the brothers of natural kinship or the brothers of our faith and school; or else to conclude that, when he said afterward of the scribes and Pharisees that they were a generation of vipers who could not escape the damnation of hell,[c] he was not mani-

---

[a] Matt. v., 21-26.
[b] Mark iii , 5; Matt. xii., 27, 32, 34, 39; xiii., 15; xv., 1-20; xvi., 1, 4, 6, 12, 28; xvii., 17; xxi., 19.
[c] Matt. xxiii.

festing the spirit of the Highest, who is kind unto the unthankful and the evil, nor conforming to the principle of conduct he himself prescribed, when he said: "Judge not, that ye be not judged; for with what judgment ye judge ye shall be judged."[a] Even if we restrict to the narrow limits of relationship and discipleship the obligation of a forgiving love, and so sink the moral standard of Jesus far below the best pattern of virtue that older philosophers have given, and to which ordinarily good-natured men find it not difficult to conform, we cannot understand why he should hurl into the little circle of the brotherhood itself, and upon the head of the only too ardent and enthusiastic Peter, a name of so much more evil significance than *fool*. To call a man a fool is only to impute to him some unwisdom, and, unless he is very humble, to undermine his self-conceit. To call a man *Satan* is to charge him with hopeless and inveterate evil.

Later in his experience of mankind, Jesus might have learned, from watching his own spirit, how hard is the struggle of a virtuous purpose with those defects and insanities of the soul, which form types of character among mankind, and which are largely the effect of hereditary influence. A man may break away from an old external habit, as of drunkenness, gluttony, impure speech and action, neglect of worship of God, idleness, pursuit of pleasure, wealth, or ambition, without effort greatly disproportioned to his moral powers. But to obliterate a subtle envy, to soothe a fierce impatience, to counteract a profound melancholy, to combat successfully with evil inclinations that he never wittingly cherished, the discovery of which in his heart surprises and alarms him like the unbidden and unwelcome presence at his table of some foul and ghastly shape, to overcome morbid moral feelings, which, if he be wise, he finds to be a taint of the blood, since he has learned that they marred the fine quality of his ancestry,—this is a more difficult and longer task. Reasonably successful is that human life which has maintained a fair fight with these tormentors, and lessened their power of mischief. Out of the effort of virtue comes strength. The heroic man may hope to bequeath to posterity along with hereditary tendencies

[a] Matt. vii., 1, 2; Luke vi., 35; xvi., 23.

to evil, the full strength of the protest and resistance he has made against them; and may have the assurance, that, what the aroused will resolutely and persistently confronts, will at last be conjured from the slowly regenerated family of man.

Jesus enjoined an absolute, unconditional, and universal alms-giving. The effect of this practice upon society and the maintenance of the political order I have already alluded to in a preceding chapter. It remains to consider the precept of benevolence and free giving in its ethical effect upon the moral character of the giver and of the receiver.

How sweeping and absolute the precepts are, will be perceived by recapitulating the familiar words: "Give to every man that asketh of thee, and of him that taketh away thy goods ask them not again." Do good, and lend, hoping for nothing again. Lend to those from whom you do not hope to receive. "Give, and it shall be given unto you: good measure, pressed down, and shaken together, and running over, shall men give into your bosom."[a] The incongruity in the same juxtaposition of this giving to those from whom nothing is hoped in return, and giving that a fuller measure shall be given back to our bosom, seems somewhat difficult of explanation. In both precepts, the giving is enjoined for the sake of the reward. The reward is made very prominent; and the giving to the generous is distinctly discountenanced, because, when they return the donation, we are paid and can hope for no reward. It must have been the whole thought of Jesus that men should give freely and largely, not to the honest and just who would return their gifts, but also to the indolent, the thriftless, the dishonest, the fairly apparent impostor, who would not return, and who was not expected, to return the gifts. In the former case, they would be rewarded by the bounty of men whose generosity they appealed to: in the latter case, they would be rewarded by God in the kingdom of heaven. For it was a prominent consideration with Jesus that good deeds, even prayers, were to be offered, not so much from an impulse of feeling, as for the sake of the reward.[b] Indeed, he had given such prominence to this

[a] Luke vi., 30, 33-35, 38.   [b] Matt. vi., 1, 6.

consideration that we are not surprised when his disciples ask him, and he goes on, with the detail of one careful to be complete in his generosity, to tell them, what shall be the reward for the ardor of their attachment and the losses that had befallen their discipleship.[a]

No precept of Jesus, as has already been attempted to be shown, is so inapplicable as this to the maintenance of the present order of the world and the natural succession of human society. The obvious incompatibility of such inconsiderate beneficence with the welfare of mankind, with the preservation of the conditions respectively of the rich and poor, and with the perpetuation of the human race, has justly arrayed in protest against it, not the political powers, not the philosophic unbelief of the world, but the whole official sentiment of the organized believers in Jesus, at the head of whom stands his greatest disciple and apostle, Paul. It is Christianity itself that repudiates and protests against a primary precept of Christ.

In the expectation of the speedy end of the world, Jesus came, and said: Take no thought to make any provision for the sustenance of your earthly lives. Give without stint or expectation of return to every one that asks of you. He that forsaketh not all that he hath cannot be my disciple. His followers in a later age, while revering his sacred character, while even elevating him in their profound regard to the grade of a divine being, yet presumed to apply to these directions of their Lord and Master, the modifications compelled by the indefinite postponement of the expectation upon which they were given.

If the old order is to go on for some centuries and ages, it must go on in its old methods, and subject to its old laws. God scatters not upon the surface, but here and there, in places only accessible to toil and effort, not lavishly, but in limited supply, the sustenance of all living creatures. There are always living creatures enough to exhaust this supply. Nay, more, at the gates of life, of all life, stand an innumerable crowd of potential creatures, watching that limited supply, to see whether their potential life can become actual life, who are shut out from the crowded tables of God, because there is not room for a tenth of them. Every day, the inequality between the

[a] Matt., xix, 27-30.

guests and the supply must be readjusted by the painful process of death, and the dismissal of the superfluous. You may take your portion of this bounty of nature, and appropriate it to the sustenance of your life; you may generously bestow it upon another life and forego your own. When, for the mere asking, you take the bread that is to sustain your children, and give it to an unknown man to sustain his children, what assurance can you have that the universe has been enriched, and God's grand plans promoted by the gift? If you leave your food to the rats, have you improved the quality of life on the globe? Will the rats imitate in their turn your disinterestedness, and bravely choose starvation, that the race of ants may thrive and multiply upon their charity? If the ants in their turn, smitten with this fantastic politeness, pass the food still lower at the divine table, the fungi will revel in it, and build their cells and spores out of it, and the glad vegetables suck at its rich decay with eager throats. The struggle for life gives life to the strongest and the best; indiscriminate alms gives life to the weakest and the worst.

There is a sphere for pity and fellow-help, everywhere more and more recognized by the expanding benevolence of men. The patient workers who, by some natural calamity or political revolution, or the fraud or violence of others, have lost the wages of their toil, must be helped by the strong and the successful; but giving must be discriminate, and upon some better claim than want or the importunity of asking. "It is not meet to take the children's bread, and to cast it to dogs," was a later saying of Jesus, when dogs signified an alien race of men.[a] It is not meet to take what one man has saved by denying his lusts and laid in store to feed children that will inherit his chaste and temperate nature, and give it to another man to expend in gratifying his lusts, or to sustain a progeny that will perpetuate his sensuality. Strip life of its primal condition of labor and patience and self-denial, by which the spirit is chiefly strengthened and chastened, and "*give to every one that asketh of thee*," and who will take the long and thorny road to achievement and self-support, when the easy door of charity is open to every

[a] Matt. xv., 26.

one that has speech or gesture by which to beg? You destroy character, fatally and fast, at both ends of the process; and such a charity is least like that which blesseth him that gives and him that takes.

Is the rule for all? Then, if I give to-day all my store because my neighbor asked it, must he not to-morrow give it back to my asking? We have not increased the store by bandying it back and forth in a vain effort to make what was provision for one suffice for two, and have lost all the time not expended upon one side or the other in adding to the store itself.

It is easy to see that, given the necessity of labor to produce wealth, that is not only the justest but the most economic distribution of wealth which gives the property produced to the producer, and that this law of distribution most favorably affects the moral development of individual men.

Looking into any code of criminal law or into any complete treatise upon ethical science, we note how large a place laws in support of the rights of property occupy. That part of the Jewish law which was considered distinctively moral — the ten commandments of the Old Scriptures — was nearly all of it in defence of the right of property. Thou shalt not covet, thou shalt not steal, thou shalt not falsely testify against thy neighbor, are all prohibitions against invasion of property. Adultery was forbidden more in the interest of the right of the neighbor to the exclusive society of his wife, than in the interest of personal purity. In perfect accord with the ideas of Jesus about property, which have been fully considered in another chapter, he ignores the whole subject of these property regulations; and, in giving the law of adultery, gives that new statement of it, which regards the very aspect of the offence, which they of old time had wholly overlooked. How could he, even by indirection, give the sanction of his voice to that prevalent passion for possessions, which the whole Hebrew cultus stimulated and sanctified? It was at that very point that he antagonized the old ideas, and sought to introduce the new. So we find no prohibition against theft or false testimony or fraud. "Who made me a judge or divider over you?" he said impatiently.[a] Give way to the oppressor

[a] Luke xii., 14.

and the robber. If a man has relieved thee of thy possession, he has done thee no real disservice, but has opened for thee the door of the kingdom of heaven, into which he that hath riches can only enter by a possibility of which only God has knowledge.[a]

Thus far, the teachings of Jesus have been studied in the department of what may be called the major morals — that sphere of human conduct, where men are accredited as good or evil, as virtuous or vicious, in the judgment of the general human reason. The discussion must be pursued into the department of minor morals, — to those lines of conduct, where the sentiment of the world has uttered itself in a more uncertain way, — in fine, to those modes of action which belong rather to *manners* than to *morals*, and over which preside good taste and the sense of propriety rather than the paramount obligations of duty. Very confused must be the ideas of that mind which estimates the malicious murder of a man, as of the same turpitude with a profane or superfluous speech; which places in the same category of guilt the fraudulent breach of a public trust, and the profanation of a holy day; and thinks it as wrong to assume the obligation of an oath, as to tell a lie. It is with a different standard of moral valuation distinctly in view that the remaining ethical theses of Jesus must be considered.

He said oaths were not to be taken, either to fortify the will in performing some definite purpose, or to strengthen the truthfulness of some consequential, deliberate and official statement, or to give undue vehemence and emphasis to ordinary conversation. He swept away, with that integrity of application, which characterized his ordinary dealing with a rule or principle of conduct, the vow, which in earlier times formed so large and solemn a feature of the intercourse of men with the divine powers, the judicial oath, that enters so largely into all modern official procedure, and every form of rhetorical or vulgar exaggeration, that deforms and distorts literary expression and colloquial speech. He said it made no difference whether the oath or imprecation was to God, or heaven, or earth, or a man's own head; any invocation, anything beyond a simple assertion or

[a] Matt. xix., 23-26.

denial, came of evil.* Certainly, Jesus never said anything that was characterized with more thorough good sense, or more clearly disclosed a wise man's perception of the laws of the human mind, than these words. One is strongly moved to defend their sagacity and propriety against a disregard of them by the Christian world which seems almost contemptuous. For it is undoubtedly true that the use of oaths in judicial proceedings, and to sanction and strengthen the obligation of official trusts and official declarations, is chiefly due, not only to the religious sentiment in men, but to that type of religious sentiment which is distinctively Christian. In pleading against the practice of oaths, one must not only ask to have the proceedings in which they are used dissociated from the sanctions of religion, but that such proceedings shall be conducted in disregard of an obligation imposed by considerations which Jesus himself especially emphasized. It is claimed, against the authority of Jesus, that the office of the oath is to put men upon their fidelity and conscience, to make them serious and sincere, to bring into the performance of a human duty the consciousness and the law of God.

The attitude of Jesus toward the Mosaic forms of worship has been much discussed. It has been claimed for him by many, whose mental portrait of his character is drawn from the Christianity of Paul, and from still more modern conceptions of its central purpose and spirit, that Jesus came as a reformer and protestant against the formal and outward imposition of sacrifices, fasts, prayers, priestly interventions, ceremonies of dress, prescription of holy days and of clean and unclean practices, into which the simple Jehovah-worship of his nation had degenerated in his age. His denunciation of the scribes and Pharisees, his disregard of the Sabbaths, the stress he laid upon virtue, mercy, and faith, his insisting upon pure motive as alone the reality of a pure act, are cited in evidence of this protest.

All these acts and words are quite consistent with a decorous conformity to the whole letter and spirit of the ecclesiastical law of his time. He declared to John the Baptist that it became men who expected the kingdom

* Matt. v., 33-37.

of heaven, to fulfil all pious rites.[a] He carefully protested, that he had not come to destroy the law or the prophets, which would stand and be binding upon the human conscience while heaven and earth stood, and till they were perfected in his kingdom of the heavens. Meantime, he that should break one of the least commandments of the law, *and teach men so*, should be the least in the kingdom of heaven.[b] The scribes and Pharisees, he said, sat in Moses' seat, and, whatever they bid, men must observe and do.[c] If he seemed to speak sarcastically of the tithes of mint, anise, and cumin which they were so careful to pay, he told his disciples they ought to do these things also, while not neglecting the weightier matters of the law, justice, mercy, and faith.[d] His kinsmen and most trusted disciples scrupulously conformed to the ritual of the national worship; and even the erratic Paul, though boasting of the unsectarian spirit, — which he had maintained among the Greeks, that he might win them to discipleship,— when he came to Jerusalem, and saw Peter and Jesus' own brother zealously performing the vows and keeping the fasts and sacred days of the Jews, was constrained to succumb to their example.[e]

All the fundamental ethical precepts of Jesus have thus been considered save those, which can be more properly viewed as a part of his philosophy, to be discussed in a later chapter. They are not comprehensive of the whole sphere of human conduct, and there are conspicuous omissions in what may be considered the standard of the completed man.

It is already apparent why whole lines of human action could not be consistently entertained by Jesus. His expectation of the speedy ending of the social and political order necessarily rendered superfluous all political duties. Patriotism, bravery in the defence of one's country or its institutions, loyalty to the sovereign power, whether monarchical or republican, were virtues he disesteemed and ignored. If men learned and practised them, it was from other teachers and other inspiration than his; and, while enjoying the consideration and applause they

[a] Matt. iii., 15. [b] Matt. v., 17-20. [c] Matt. xxiii., 2, 3.
[d] Matt. xxiii., 23. [e] Acts xxi., 26.

won from secular minds, it was all the time with the misgiving that they were, in the estimation of Jesus, unsanctified virtues lightly esteemed of God. In the severe judgment of men wholly influenced by his spirit, the patriots who have died in defence of their country, the heroes who have led suffering and oppressed nations to independence and honorable peace, the faithful public ministers who have with good counsel and high integrity served their rulers or the state, the reformers who by their eloquence and constancy have rid the world of chronic political abuses, have misdirected their efforts, and earned only a pagan glory that will turn to darkness before the brightness of the coming of the Son of Man.

Scarcely less conspicuous is the omission of the marital, parental, filial, and fraternal relations of men, of the natural affections that pertain to them, and of the duties that grow out of them. Jesus was oblivious of natural ties. If we are not required to believe that he ever addressed his mother as John represents in the story of the wedding feast of Cana,[a] we can find in no part of the more reliable records any incident of his tenderness and respect for her; and we remember how, on a public occasion, he declined to be accosted by his mother and brethren, and in the elevation of his enthusiasm declared that he that did the will of God was his brother, sister, and mother.[b] Half-questioning himself the purity of ties that bind the human race in families, and affirming that they who would be perfect were not entangled in such ties, and that in the kingdom of heaven they are neither married nor given in marriage, how could he follow men into such temporary and questionable relations, and fix from his high ideal their laws and duties? It was Paul with his political training, with his secular spirit, with the feet of his common sense firmly planted upon the world, and with his determination to make it orderly and decent for the brief interval that it should stand, who exhorted husbands and wives, children and servants, to the practice of those virtues that their position demanded, and supplemented the meagre code of his master by a brief summary of political duties. It is Paul also who contributes to the form of the Christian doctrine nearly all the pre-

[a] John ii., 4.   [b] Matt. xii., 48-50.

cepts that it has, regulating the social intercourse of men,— all that fine courtesy, that delicacy of mutual consideration, which is the expression of a refined spirit — and which a chivalric nature like his readily takes on, by mingling with the morally well-educated. Jesus had said, *Love your enemies.* Paul remembered that love was none the less due to friends, and gave us that fine precept to regulate the social intercourse of equals. " Be kindly affectioned one to another with brotherly love, in honor preferring one another." [a]

The modern mind has no better word than gentleman to define its idea of perfected manhood. The idea is a composite one, having for its constituents the meekness and patience under injuries, the spirit that returns blessing for curses and offers the other cheek to the smiter, which are the inspiration of Jesus, the brotherly courtesy which gives the friend the preference of honor enjoined by Paul, and what may be called the Teutonic influence — that chivalric feeling which accepted the Christian cultus with essential modifications. Not abject or insensate under the affront of wrong, this chivalric feeling exhibits its magnanimity sometimes by the completeness of its forgiveness, sometimes by the moderation of its retaliation, sometimes by waiting for the violent deed to recoil of its own force upon the offender. Not hasty or vindictive in resenting personal injuries, this feeling inspires no restraint upon indignation provoked by attacks upon woman, upon children, upon the weak and the unfriended, and finds a place for the masculine virtues of courage in shielding from wanton cruelty those who cannot defend themselves.

In Egypt and in India there were types of religious faith which emphasized the relationship between men and the lower order of living creatures. The hunting and slaying of animals endowed with strength, cunning, or swiftness to stand at bay, or flee, or hide, while it gave the barbarous man a keen delight, ministered to the development of his cruel instincts, and kept him closely akin to the beasts he pursued. Even the more decent practices of civilization, that localize, specialize, and cover up the slaughters that inaugurate our feasts, leave us

[a] Romans xii., 10.

compromised with the reproach that our lives are largely supported by the violent and premature deaths of sentient creatures, whose rank in the order of nature below our own may have been fixed only by our own conceit.

The Israelite cherished no sentimental tenderness toward the lower animals. He honored the dumb races only by eating them, and looked with aversion upon those he deemed unclean,— that is, unfit for food. The aversion to dogs, which appears in the older and later literature of that people, is one entirely in keeping with a national trait, which is scarcely intelligible to those more sympathetic races who have made that sagacious and affectionate creature the companion of their toils and their pleasures. Jesus spake of the animals sometimes, to illustrate his thought, but never in a spirit discordant with the national antipathy. He spoke of aliens as dogs, and asked, How much better is a man than a sheep? Cast not your pearls before swine, which after trampling them will tear you. The legend of the devils and the herd of swine is an illustration in part of an unsympathetic aversion to brutes, in part of a local and partisan repugnance to the repulsive diet of an alien race, which must have characterized the school of men, who came under his special influence.

Germs of a civil polity for the community of the believers appear in Jesus' directions as to the treatment of offences by the brethren. His rule seems quite different from that given for offences received from persons outside the fellowship of discipleship. In the latter case, it was: "Whosoever shall smite thee on thy right cheek offer to him the other also.[a] If any man will sue thee at the law and take away thy coat, let him have thy cloak also. And whosoever shall compel thee to go a mile, go two miles with him."[b] For wrongs, affronts, and exactions received from ordinary men, from men not of your faith, the remedy is silent suffering, the meek surrender of yourself to their violence, the wearing out of their malice by your patience. But how about offences received from those who walk with you in the same meekness and blamelessness,— when they happen to give offence, what shall we do? They will not smite again,

[a] Matt. v., 39, 40.   [b] Matt. v., 41.

nor exact the cloak or the coat, nor compel us to walk even a furlong. The question was asked of Jesus, If *my brother* trespass against me and come with his penitent regret, how many times must I forgive him,—seven times? Yes, seventy times, said Jesus. But if he does not come to acknowledge his fault or to ask forgiveness? Then go to him, said Jesus, and rebuke him. The brother must not be left in his sin, as you leave the ordinary man. Rebuke him with privacy. If he is of the right spirit, he will see his fault, and you shall have saved his soul. But, if he is perverse and obdurate, do not give him up. Take one or two more with you, that from a disinterested point his offence may be shown him. Even if he will not hear the remonstrances of two or three, still let the whole brotherhood, the assembly of the elect, add their remonstrances; and, if the offending brother is still unmoved, let him be to thee a heathen and a publican. Cast him out of the category of discipleship.[a]

The necessity for these directions in the personal dissensions arising among the early Christians, must have been very imperative. The inclination is very strong to look upon their recapitulation as an interpolation of the biographers of Jesus; but the rule of selection heretofore adopted compels us to accept these as parts of his authentic teaching. The spirit of his followers was not, even in the brief period of their personal attendance upon him, so completely under his control as to make it improbable, that he was called upon to indicate some rule, by which their dissensions among themselves might be settled. What surprises us is the absence of reference to himself and his authority. If a brother had offended a brother, why should not there have been a reference in some stage of the attempted reconciliation, to the authority of the master? Or did Jesus give this direction late in his career, and when, in anticipation of his own departure, he wished to indicate some tribunal, that would remain during the interval of his absence? That he feared some outbreak of a quarrelsome temper among his own disciples, in that interval, is evident from his caution, *But if that servant " shall begin to smite his fellow-servants and to eat and drink with the drunken, the*

[a] Matt. xviii., 15-18, 21, 22.

Lord of that servant shall come in an hour that he thinketh not, and shall appoint him his portion with the hypocrites." [a]

Out of these few and doubtful words has sprung the whole complicated and imposing structure of the Christian Church, so terrible in its power and in its punishments, so minute and universal in its surveillance and jurisdiction. These words must be considered doubtful because they are so foreign to the general ideas of Jesus, that contemplate no organization of believers, and nothing like government or discipline, however temporary, before the new economy, which was to be from heaven, should create a new heaven and a new earth for the elect of God.

The same question occurs in reference to the general ethical ideas of Jesus as in reference to his dominant idea of the kingdom of heaven,— how far were they his own, how far do we find them or germs of them in the times that immediately preceded his own?

Besides the Pharisees and Sadducees, the two principal sects that divided the Jewish world, there was a smaller body of devotees called the Essenes, whose influence upon the ethics and practices of Jesus and his followers is now generally acknowledged. The origin of this sect is lost in obscurity. No distinct traces of them are found in the Jewish scriptures. Though thoroughly national in their attachment to the Mosaic ritual and in their vivid expectation of a Messiah, their manners and morals have in them something foreign. Very great must have been the germinal power of the doctrine of Sakya Mouni, the Hindu reformer, in the first fervor of conversion. We know that, besides powerfully affecting India, it spread Eastward, and became the dominant faith of China, Japan, and Thibet, as well as of many islands of adjoining seas. Although kept out of Persia by strong military and ecclesiastical authority, it is not impossible, that, the zealous propagandists that penetrated every part of Asia, in spite of opposition and persecution, might have indoctrinated some of the captive communities of Hebrews in exile under the Assyrian and Persian kings, and that these latter might have brought back to Palestine, along with

[a] Matt. xxiv., 48, 49.

their devotion to Jehovah and their attachment to Jerusalem and its stately worship, some of the ideas of the Hindu reformer. The tradition of Jesus is the story of a good man, born in a stable, whom the rulers of his nation had persecuted and crucified, but who through the power of God had risen from the dead, shown himself to his disciples and ascended to heaven. Belief in this tradition gave wings to the ideas and doctrines of Christianity, and set them flying over the world. It was the equally touching and romantic legend of a man born a wealthy and powerful prince, who was so deeply moved by the sufferings of the poor and the miseries that embittered human life, that he voluntarily laid aside his royal state, and in toil, poverty, and privation spent his life in alleviating the sufferings of the wretched, till in his old age he was rewarded with the supreme bliss of heaven, that sent a new faith — singularly destitute of promise or satisfaction to the human heart — buoyed up by the enthusiasm and martyrdom of its converts over two-thirds of habitable Asia.

Many scholars, however, insist that Essenism was an essentially national development, natural enough among a people whose genius was religion; and that the sect, which obtained notice from the writers of the first century, was a sect of the Pharisees — a later development of the devout and ascetic feeling, which tinged the character of several of the Hebrew prophets, and which was manifested in the orders of the Nazarites, Reccabites, and Chassidim of the ante-christian period.

From the distinct pictures of Essenism found in the works of Philo, Josephus, and other writers, it is easy to determine how much it contributed to the ethical system and to the philosophical ideas of Jesus.

The Essenes had a great reverence for the old scriptures, and were most strict in their observance of the Sabbath. It has been seen that Jesus read and quoted the Hebrew scriptures, and was evidently very familiar with them. He also persistently maintained that he had not come to destroy the least tittle of the law, and exhorted his disciples to do whatever the scribes and Pharisees taught or required as observances and ceremonies of worship. But he evidently anticipated that his teaching would be supposed antagonistic to the Mosaic code; and spoke of its most fundamental prohibitions, as of murder, as a tradition of them of old time, and of the whole moral law of the ten commandments as wholly inadequate to define the character of a righteous man, or to form a standard of conduct for the least in the kingdom of heaven. His attitude toward the Sabbath was unequivocally contemptuous;[a] and he asserted his personal authority to make the day the minister to his convenience and necessity.

The Essenes believed in labor. The community was industrial. Industry was as much insisted upon among them as devotion. It has already appeared that Jesus' prime direction, *Take no thought for your life*, abolished the incentive of labor; and that his invitation to his hearers was: Leave your toil, your care for subsistence; forsake houses and lands, and come to me, who have not where to lay my head, and you shall have rest.

The Essenes insisted upon strict justice to all men and faithful obedience to rulers. In Jesus, as has been shown, the sentiment of justice was feeble. He thought it a small matter, not worthy his interference or even rebuke, that a man should defraud his brother of an inheritance. His attitude toward rulers was equivocal. He paid taxes, while protesting that they were an unwarrantable exaction, because he would not offend. He thought Cæsar's coin, which an inheritor of the kingdom had no business to possess, and must give to the asker, might be given to Cæsar. But he nowhere helped the secular arm by the sanction of voice or act, and gave no exhortation to his followers which indicated, that he held what the Essenes held, and what Paul so emphatically taught, that the rulers held their power as the ministers of God.[b] To him, they were the wolves who would conspire to shed his blood; and who after his death would ravage the flock of which he was the shepherd.[c]

The Essenes discountenanced association with the wicked, and formed a separate community to avoid contact with the unclean. Jesus promulgated a higher principle. He held no man ceremonially unclean. To him the only defilement was the defilement of a wicked dis-

---
[a] Matt. xii., 1-8.   [b] Romans xiii., 1-7.   [c] Matt. x., 16-18.

position, and he did not sever himself from evil men. He obtained the reputation of associating with the publican and the harlot, the extortioner and the sensualist, the two types of evil of his time; and several of his most pronounced disciples were gained from these classes. Strong in his own integrity, he did not seem to have thought it necessary to impose upon weaker and baser natures a constraint and segregation, that might become necessary to maintain their feeble virtue.

The Essenes had substituted prayers for sacrifices. Jesus clearly taught that men were to ask freely and simply for whatever they needed; but he is not to be considered as insisting much upon prayer, and never as insisting upon it as an act of worship or expression of allegiance towards the Deity. When ye pray, he says to his disciples, Enter into your closet,—that is, if you pray, pray only thus; just as he had said, When thou fastest, anoint thy head and wash thy face. In neither case did he command men to fast or to pray.[a] Indeed, it appears that, up to a certain period of his teaching, he had not taught his disciples to pray; and that they reminded him of an omission in his doctrine by citing the example of John the Baptist.[b] In the sense of asking of God any good gift, Jesus taught that his disciples should have frank, open, and frequent access to the heavenly Father; but that God is not to be annoyed with repetitions. He knows what men want before they ask him; and prayer is never to be used ostentatiously, as an edifying exhibition of devoutness, or to impress others as a manifestation of piety. Jesus spoke of the long prayers of the Pharisees—probably much shorter than the modern Christian prayer of our public worship—as a pretext for extortion.[c]

The Essenes believed in bodily washings and baptism. Jesus seemed to have apologized for being himself baptized;[d] and there was some disfavor in his mind to the rite, which confirms the saying in the Johannic narrative, that Jesus left all the baptizing to his disciples,[e] and may have suggested Paul's boast, that he never baptized but a single family.[f] The saying of Jesus, that not eating

[a] Matt. vi., 3, 5-7. [b] Luke xi., 1. [c] Matt. xxiii., 14.
[d] Matt. iii., 15. [e] John iv., 2. [f] I. Cor. i., 14-17.

with unbaptized hands, but wicked and lustful thoughts, worked real defilement,[a] harmonizes with this estimate on his part of baptism.

The Essenes gave an emphatic testimony against war and slavery. The doctrine of Jesus, that men were to suffer with patience and meekness and without retaliation all injuries, is the extreme statement of the principle of peace; and must be taken as his rule of conduct not only for individuals, but for associations, communities, and nations. With what view he on one occasion directed his followers to arm themselves with swords, it is difficult to determine. He evidently contemplated no formidable physical demonstration, since, when but two weapons could be procured, he declared the armament sufficient; and when the enemies, whose arrival he had every reason to anticipate, actually appeared, he promptly forbade any forcible resistance. Whatever may have been the teachings of the apostles or the practice of the earlier Christians, the hostility of Jesus to all war and violence is clear and unmistakable. With regard to slavery, in his time an established usage of society, practised among his own people, his teaching was nearly silent. The ideas of brotherhood and equality, which he insisted upon as the social condition of the little band of disciples, his command to them to call no man master and to esteem him greatest who did the lowest forms of service, utterly excluded from the Church the claim of mastery or ownership. The outside world, however, was never reproached by him for oppressing, buying and selling fellow-men, with anything like the severity with which he denounced the merely rich. He never said that, to enter into the kingdom of heaven, it is necessary to emancipate one's slaves. It was quite consonant with the tolerance of slavery on his part for Paul to exhort converted slaves to be obedient, even to wicked and cruel masters, and to recognize them among the classes, whose duties he presented by the side of those of the other social conditions — husband and wife, parent and child.[b]

The Essenes cherished a special reverence for age, supplying to the aged celibates in their communities the tender consideration and affection which even children

---
[a] Matt. xv., 20; Luke xxii., 36.   [b] Eph. vi., 5, 6; Col. iii., 18-25.

are not wont to render toward superannuated parents. If Jesus taught any similar duty, his biographers have made no record of it. That peculiar sect hated every form of falsehood, and the speaking of truth under all circumstances was enjoined as a most imperative duty. Falsehood is the taint of all the decayed and hopeless races, the prime badge of their degradation. Cruelty and sensuality can be bred out of savage men by the slow culture of civilization, but falsehood is a degeneration that precedes national extinction. The Jews, who had their great law against bearing false testimony against the neighbor, had no prohibition against the lie helpful to one's neighbor or to one's self. The national character, which honored every form of advantageous duplicity, and which imputed to Deity itself the deceit of making false revelations to ensnare men into punishment, was not above the necessity of some new doctrine of truthfulness. In the comparatively trivial matter of the indirectness and exaggeration of the forms of speech, we are perplexed to miss the requirement of the essential matter, that, whatever be the forms, only truth must be spoken. Jesus himself indulged in indirectness of speech, and avowed the purpose of so uttering his most fundamental doctrines, that, all excluded from the knowledge of the divine mysteries, might make shipwreck of their faith.[a]

It may thus be seen in what respects Jesus taught either in direct opposition to the principles of the Essenes, or laid little or no stress upon doctrines which to them were essential. But, on the other hand, how closely he reproduced their ideas may be seen from the following recapitulation.

Like them, he taught that the sexual desires, if not absolutely sinful, were indicative of a low stage of virtue, and that all who would be perfect, who in purity of heart would attain the vision of God, must abstain from marriage.[b] It was an Essenic rule that the brotherhood must give up their property upon entering their community to be administered for the benefit of the whole, and that thereafterward the convert must not lay up any treasure for himself. What he had he must give to the brother asking for it, expecting nothing again. All traffic

[a] Matt. xiii., 11-15.   [b] Matt. v., 8, 28, 29; xix., 10-12; xxii., 29-30.

in the sect itself was unlawful. No man was to be master
or to be so called. There was no recognized priesthood,
no external sacrifices, no ritual of worship, other than that
which every humble believer might practise and conduct.
Jesus' rule of ecclesiastical discipline, already alluded to,
of first making a personal appeal to an offending brother,
then renewing it with the support of one or two associates, then submitting it to the assembly of the faithful,
and if all remonstrances failed to bring the offender to
penitence, casting him out as a heathen and a publican,
was the exact regulation of the Essenes.

They enjoined abstinence from all oaths, and, like
Jesus, said all speech that exceeded mere denial and
affirmation came of evil. Though scrupulous in their
washings and linen clothing as preparations for their
common meals, considered by them sacraments, they
required ordinary garments to be worn out before they
were changed or laid aside. Jesus forbade his disciples
to provide more than one coat, or one pair of shoes, or
any money for their journeys.[a] This, too, was a uniform
injunction upon the Essenes on similar occasions. Abstaining generally from marriage, they depended, like
the modern Shakers, upon waifs from other sects, mostly
children, to keep up their numbers. To these forlorn
children they were indulgent and affectionate, and were
wont to say before Jesus repeated it, "*Of such is the kingdom of heaven.*"

The blessing upon meekness, and the characterization
by Jesus of himself as meek and lowly, though singularly
undescriptive of the spirit of his later days, was Essenic.
The Essenes, too, placed love of God before worship and
sacrifice. Jesus made God dear to the human heart by
calling Him his, and our Father in heaven, and applauded
the saying of the wise scribe, who declared that to love
God with all the heart was better than all whole burnt-
offerings and sacrifices. It was unlawful among the
Essenes to promulgate their higher doctrines to persons
outside the sect; and, in strict accord with this idea,
Jesus declared that it was not given to the multitude who
heard his parables to understand the mysteries of the
kingdom of heaven, but only to his disciples. The

[a] Matt. x., 9, 10

Essenes enjoined an excision of anger and malice. Jesus declared anger endangered the soul, and that God would accept no worship from a heart cherishing malice toward a brother. Miracle-working, particularly curing diseased persons and casting out devils, power that extended even to raising the dead, was a claim of an advanced stage of Essenism. It was quite manifest that Jesus could gain no high estimate as a prophet and Messiah, until he had created for himself a similar prestige. The Essenes forbade scientific studies and all irreverent scrutiny into the laws of God, as destructive of salutary piety. Jesus boasted that not many wise men had been attracted by his preaching, only the simple ones and the babes in reason and intelligence." The doctrine of the Holy Ghost promulgated by Jesus, and which grew into such large proportions in the early Church, first appears among these forerunners of Christianity. Finally, it was the Essenes that, of all the Jews, had chiefly studied the Messianic prophecies, kept their promises alive in the national heart, and indicated in the reachings of their faith the nearness of the time for their expected fulfilment. So that when John first, and Jesus afterward, began to preach in Palestine, and to say, *Repent, for the kingdom of heaven is at hand*, they threw a spark into the vigilant hope of all devout souls which could but kindle into a vital and spreading enthusiasm.

Thus, it is seen that, in his ethical ideas, Jesus accepted and repeated the doctrines of a singular sect that he seems to have converted and absorbed,— accepted them as he had his faith in the coming of the kingdom of heaven, not blindly, as a mere convert and copyist, but putting his own original genius into them, modifying them by his own powerful thought, and giving them the wings of his own enthusiasm with which to fly across the world and down to the latest centuries.

a Luke x., 21.

CHAPTER VI.

PHILOSOPHICAL IDEAS OF JESUS.

"Systems of thought should be studied sympathetically, but critically,— from the outside as it were, and never from the stand-point of discipleship. Those philosophers who have had no distinct 'school' are best understood."— *From a summary of Wundt's Physiological Psychology in the Nation.*

IN a preceding chapter has been stated and illustrated the perplexity in which the sympathetic critic is involved in attempting to deduce a system of morals, an ethical philosophy, from the generalizations with which Jesus is reported to have explained his specific precepts relating to conduct. The perplexity mainly proceeds from the inconsequential and contradictory nature of those generalizations. To make the survey of the words and acts ascribed to Jesus complete, to embrace in the analysis of his character all the data that a reasonably probable tradition has supplied, the effort must be made to collect the prominent principles of his philosophy.

If he was an intellectually and spiritually complete man,— still more, if he was a being whose traits entitled him to a divine rank,— a harmonious conception of nature and of its meaning might be expected from him. It would be assumed that he had the knowledge of the truth, that all his authentic utterances were more or less complete expositions of a scheme of knowledge absolutely infallible. All seeming inconsistencies and errors in the words imputed to him would require to be attributed either to the incompleteness of his own declaration or to the misconception and mistakes of the report. But if it be assumed that Jesus was a man, it does not surprise us to discover, that he was affected by the beliefs of his age, and that his conceptions of nature and its laws were limited by the scientific knowledge of his times. It is not to be expected of a poetic mind kindled by an enthusiastic temperament, that it should also be either logical or comprehensive. Such intellectual types rarely meet in the same individual.

When, therefore, a chapter is devoted to the philosophical ideas of Jesus, it is not to be implied that he taught a distinctive philosophy, since the tendency of his thought seemed to be to discredit all philosophy, and to invite men to distrust their critical faculties, and to surrender their minds to the prepossessions of a childlike faith. It is rather a concession to our own logical faculties that can only consider a character or a system, as they bring it to the standards of those ideals and axioms, which the human understanding has established. When a poet, a prophet, a reformer, such as Jesus was, utters the vital message which burdens his soul, he thinks of some more instantaneous and powerful result than flows from any new philosophy. Jesus may never have used the words, nor reached the conception expressed by them, imputed to him in John's Gospel,—"The words that I speak unto you, *they are spirit, and they are life*":[a] but they admirably describe the influence of his teachings upon those who listened to him, and which has been perpetuated in the report of them. But though he had no thought of promulgating a mere system of philosophy, and felt the consciousness of a more direct spiritual power than such system could have, it is not impossible to construct a philosophy more or less complete out of the ideas and conceptions his words imply. Meagre and unsatisfactory as the data are, this is what the symmetrical portrayal of his character requires to be undertaken.

Jesus taught in general the Divine beneficence. He measured the goodness of God by the standard of goodness in men, and affirmed that, if men who were evil — that is, who were unpitying and indifferent and selfish — gave out of natural affection to their own children, much more God, who is good, pitiful, and self-forgetful, would give good things to those who asked him.[b] The old Jewish scriptures had affirmed the goodness of God, and had repeatedly spoken of the relation of God to his chosen people, as that of a father to his children. Very tenderly, too, had they given expression to the paternal affection of

---

[a] John vi., 63.   [b] Matt. vii., 11; xxiii., 9.

Deity in the saying: "*As a father pitieth his children, so the Lord pitieth them that fear him.*"ᵃ Still, to the Jewish mind, the fatherhood of God ever remained a figure of speech. It was never accepted as a real relation, but as only an illustration of the divine care and affection. To Jesus, it was evidently something more. The fatherhood of God to him, if not a physical, was a psychological fact. By his spirit, man was veritably a child of God; and he sought to emphasize the relation, and make it displace the human relation, which to him seemed only physical and secondary. He told his followers explicitly: "Call no man your father upon the earth; for one is your Father, which is in heaven."ᵇ This was in perfect accord with that ignoring of the ties of natural kinship, which he expressed in the declaration that, in the kingdom of heaven, the marital relation, the foundation of all the natural relations, would no longer exist,ᶜ with the impatience he exhibited when a man inclined to discipleship proposed first to attend his father's funeral,ᵈ and with his assertion, when on a public occasion his mother and brothers desired to speak with him,— "Whosoever shall do the will of my Father which is in heaven, the same is my brother and sister and mother."ᵉ

So far as possible, Jesus evidently wished that the affections to spring out of conscious sonship to God should take the place of the human affections. His followers were not to be children of their parents, kindred of their kinsmen, compatriots of their fellow-countrymen; but children of the Highest and brothers in the faith. The new faith was to plough through families, break domestic ties, and separate mother and daughter; and a man's foes should be they of his own household.ᶠ

The decorous and conservative Jew shrank from this realistic application of a metaphor. While Jesus taught his disciples to address the Almighty God as *our Father*, while he endeavored to habituate their thought to the relationship as one that was actual and not figurative, no offence was taken by the orthodox teachers of the old monotheism; but when Jesus began to speak

---

ᵃ Ps. ciii., 13. ᵇ Matt. v., 45; xxiii., 9. ᶜ Matt. xxii., 30.
ᵈ Luke ix., 59, 60.   ᵉ Matt. xii., 50.
ᶠ Matt. x., 34-39.

more frequently of God as his father,[*] and place himself in a relation to him superior to that of the prophets, as that of the son of the owner of the vineyard, while they were the servants,[a] when too, perhaps, his natural birth came to be denied by admiring disciples, and his descent from the spirit of God came to be told, as it might have been in his lifetime, the scribes and Pharisees conceived that the pretension had become criminal. They sought to make him commit himself explicitly to such a pretension; and, when they had on his trial provoked him to reiterate it, they thought they had found a sufficient warrant for condemning him as a blasphemer.[b]

Jesus taught that the courses of nature are the special appointment of God, and that a minute providence environs the lives of good and pious men. The rain and the sunshine, he declared, to be divinely directed; and the fact, that the just and the unjust alike enjoyed them, clearly manifested the care and love of God, not only for those who loved and worshipped him, but for those who hated and neglected him. It is, he said, the heavenly Father who feeds the fowls of the air and clothes the flowers of the field with beauty, and gives to all men what they ask of good things. Not a sparrow falls to the ground without the knowledge of the Creator, whose oversight is so minute that he does not suffer a hair to fall from the human head without noting and permitting it.[c]

These are fragments indeed of casual discourses; and it may not be wholly just to strain to all their logical conclusions the breathings of a trustful and sanguine spirit, overcharged with the reverence of a paternal God. It is legitimate, however, to indicate the corollaries and deductions from such inferences of the divine beneficence and paternity, without imputing the inferences to the authority of Jesus. A partial view of nature presents certain aspects in harmony with the theory that a beneficent agency controls it; and these aspects, seizing hold of devout and hopeful minds, lead them to affirm that

---

[*] It may be remarked that from the time Jesus disclosed to his followers his purpose to go to Jerusalem as the Messiah and son of David, he only twice spoke of God as the father of his disciples, though previously to that, in addressing his followers, he had sixteen times called the Highest *your father*. Only five times before that time had he called God his father, but thirteen times afterwards.

[a] Luke xx., 10-13. [b] Matt. xxvi., 63-66. [c] Matt. v., 45; vi., 26-28; Luke xii., 7.

nature is good. Sad and despondent men find other aspects, which drive them to the conclusion that nature is evil. Perhaps a more comprehensive view, from which the disturbing influence of personal feeling is carefully eliminated, leads to the conclusion that nature — neither good nor evil — utterly refuses to be estimated by a standard, which a morally trained man has been wont to apply to his own conduct.

We come upon another distinction here, which compels us to elect between the Johannic narrative and the three others in substantial agreement with each other. In the Synoptic Gospels, Jesus appears as assuming that the courses of nature, the general order of the world, are directly under the control of God, and that its aspects and changes represent and express his beneficence. In the Johannic Gospel, Jesus is represented as invariably surrendering the world to the enemy and to malign powers, that administer it antagonistically to God. It is therein declared that, though God made the world, when Jesus who is the true light came to it, the world knew him not.[a] Jesus is made to say that the world is under condemnation, and can only be saved by faith in himself.[b] The world hates him, because he had testified to its wickedness.[c] The spirit of truth the world, not capable of recognizing, can never receive; but Jesus will manifest himself to his disciples in the world, though not to the world.[d] The prince of the world, the ruling power in human society, has nothing in Jesus. The world hated Jesus: it will hate all those who abjure its spirit for the faith of Jesus.[e] But the world is to be reproved, and the prince of the world brought to judgment; and Jesus will overcome the world.[f] For the world, recognizing its necessary hostility to himself, Jesus will not even pray.[g] In the condemnation in which he finds it, he leaves it. It had been said of him by John the Baptist, "Behold the Lamb of God, which taketh away the sin of the world!"[h] Jesus himself does not so declare his mission, — not to take away the sin of the world, he says, but to save out of the world, for which he will not

[a] John i., 10.   [b] John iii., 16, 17.   [c] John vii., 7.   [d] John xiv., 17, 22, 27, 30.
[e] John xv., 18, 19.   [f] John xvi., 8-11; xvii., 6, 9, 14.
[g] John xvii., 9, 15.   [h] John i., 29.

even pray, those whom the world hate, because they are not of it.

The word "world" is sometimes used in English to denote the earth in its physical condition and under its organic laws. The word "nature" fitly embodies the idea expressed by it, save that nature, being applicable to the whole cosmos, has a wider signification. When so used, the world means the earth and its immediate environments of sea and atmosphere, together with all the living creatures, animate and inanimate, including man, belonging to it. But it is proper to use the word "world" to denote human society, the temper, influence, and character of the men of the world taken in the aggregate. It is easy enough to see that the antagonism of the Johannic Jesus to the world is not to the courses of nature, but to mankind taken in the mass. And yet in the Synoptic Gospels, though the implication is always that nature is orderly, harmonious, and good,— a manifestation in its changes of the beneficence of the Creator,— it is nowhere affirmed that human society is naturally and hopelessly antagonistic to God. Jesus utters indeed a woe upon the world, but only on account of the offences of evil men.[a] The world itself is good, but it will necessarily suffer in the punishment of the wicked.

It is not to be expected that the writers of those narratives kept in their minds the distinction between the world as nature and the world as society. The critical student is able to make the apparent antagonism between their conceptions less pronounced, by calling to mind a distinction, which it nowhere appears that they were careful to make, even if they entertained it. The philosophic idea underlying the teachings of Jesus, as given in the first three Gospels, seems to be that nature — that is, the earth, with its forces, and the living organisms upon it, from which man is not excluded — is in a state of harmonious conformity to the law and will of God. If man as a class seems to be outside of this harmony, he fell out accidentally, in a manner for which what appears to be the hypothesis of Jesus seemed to have offered an explanation. John represents Jesus as denouncing the world, as recognizing its utter and irremediable aliena-

[a] Matt. xviii., 7.

tion from God, and as saving his disciples from the evil in it, and to come upon it. While the evil, according to this writer's view, seems to be in society rather than in nature, the control of the divine beneficence over nature is nowhere asserted by him : no kindly or appreciative eye is ever once turned upon nature; and there is no reservation or exception of nature in the doom that is to befall the world, out of which the elect of God have been rescued by a miracle of the divine mercy.

The doctrine of the Holy Ghost or Holy Spirit may properly be considered among the philosophic ideas of Jesus. The full development of this doctrine can only be found in the primitive Christian literature. As all schools of the disciples seem to have received this doctrine, as it is a prominent feature of the Johannic Gospel — entitled to consideration as an expression of early Christian thought — its first suggestion may be fairly imputed to Jesus, though he did not develop it in any complete and systematic way. If we then find Peter and Paul and the writers of the apostolic Epistles and Gospels holding concurrently to a belief in the existence and agency of a Holy Ghost or Holy Spirit, it may be assumed that they derived that belief from the teachings of Jesus, though it is not quite so certain that he should be held responsible for the precise form in which the conception shaped itself in their minds.

After the death of Jesus, the body of his followers, no one of whom could rightfully claim precedence over the rest, and all whose efforts for a spiritual vice-royalty had been rigorously repressed by Jesus,[a] needed some sanction for the immense political, moral, and spiritual authority they soon found themselves compelled to exercise over the assembly or church of the believers. Under the inspiration of their master, they had learned to regulate their conduct, to a large degree by a law of righteousness. They had been taught to restrain anger, to control lust, to repress ambition, to live above sordid cares and anxieties for merely earthly goods. In their simple and guileless souls, the peace and moral power, of which, in these endeavors after pure and noble living, they had become conscious, had seemed to them like some visitant from

[a] Matt. xxiii., 8.

God. While Jesus was with them, they had disheartened him by their moral stupidity, their want of appreciation and spiritual discernment. But his terrible death, coming suddenly, after the most extravagant expectations of triumph and glory which they had hoped to share, touched their affectionate hearts with a new sensibility, and brought out in vivid lines the lessons of virtue, which seemed to him at the time of utterance to have fallen on dull ears. Never does the power of a good life manifest itself in the hearts of men so grandly as when that life is just ended. Every sensitive conscience, melted to tenderness by sorrow, vows to be the upright, faithful, and virtuous soul that has just become a divine image in the heart. This is man in his highest and best moods, and man at his best is divine. It is a noble self-abnegation of man, that he cannot believe his best thoughts and noblest choice come from himself, but are the prompting of a spirit of God. Jesus had taught his followers to call this influence the Holy Ghost, and that they were to trust and obey it implicitly.[a]

Accordingly, when he was dead, the Holy Ghost became sovereign in the kingdom of the watchers for the return of their real Lord. The manifestations of Jesus after his death seem to have been of a somewhat uncertain character. It came to be believed that his form had been seen and his speech heard; but this belief differed fundamentally, both as to modes and places of those manifestations, and as to the communications that had been received. That Jesus communicated with his followers after his death was firmly believed, and so they told that the commandments he had imparted to them were not by oral speech, but through the Holy Ghost. The Holy Ghost was to descend upon the believers as a baptism, giving them new powers to authenticate their mission as witnesses for Jesus throughout all the earth. The Holy Ghost had inspired the old scriptures, and made them a divine communication.[b] The gift of tongues was a gift of the Spirit, to descend upon all believers and be a sign of salvation from the impending destruction.[c]

This new power in the world was not a mere passive influence: it held judicial authority, and executed ven-

[a] Matt. x., 19, 20.   [b] Acts i., 2, 5, 8, 16.   [c] Acts ii., 17, 38–40.

geance on deceit and hypocrisy.[a] The Holy Spirit minutely controlled the movements of the early apostles, directing them in what cities they should preach, to what prominent men they should appeal, and even in what houses they should lodge.[b] It was the Holy Ghost that fixed the canon of morals, which it was agreed should be imposed upon the converts from the pagan communities, who, somewhat to the surprise of the disciples, began to come into the Church.[c]

Paul seems to have used the terms Spirit of God, Spirit of Christ, Holy Spirit, and Holy Ghost to designate divinely conferred influences never very critically analyzed in his own apprehension. Oftener, when he speaks of the Spirit or the Holy Ghost, he seems to refer to the internally manifested presence of the crucified Jesus. Thus, in a single Epistle, he declares the incongruousness of fornication in a regenerated person, whose body has become the temple of the Holy Ghost; and also that Christ is the soul that animates even the body of the true believers, in which, as in a shrine or temple, the divine Spirit is worshipped.[d]

In the dogmatic drama of John, the distinct identity of the Holy Ghost appears more clearly; for, although Jesus is represented as saying that the Comforter, whom he is to send, is himself, who is to come, he oftener speaks of the Spirit of Truth, as an influence and a personality other than himself, whose coming to, and stay in, the world is to be a substitute for his withdrawn presence.[e] This advanced development of the doctrine of the Holy Ghost, far toward the ultimate conception of the tripersonal Divinity to which the Church in a few centuries came, may be taken as another proof of the late production of the Johannic Gospel.

Nothing appears more natural and consistent than the growth in the Christian mind of this conception. There fell to the new movement a jurisdiction so much larger than Jesus himself seemed to have contemplated that new principles, new precepts, and an enlarged philosophy were necessary to give it completeness, and to organize it as

[a] Acts v., 3, 5, 9, 10.   [b] Acts viii., 29-39; x., 19, 20; xi., 12, 13; xiii., 2, 4, 9-11.
[c] Acts xv., 28; xvi., 6, 7; xix., 2-6; xx., 23; xxi., 4.
[d] I. Cor. iii., 16, 17; vi., 15.   [e] John xiv., 16-26.

a system of faith and life for mankind. The imperfect and provisional religion, which was sufficient for a world about to come to an end, was not adapted to a world developing into a larger civilization. More and more, its teachers and missionaries found themselves met by personal and social contingencies which Jesus had not contemplated. They had to enlarge his code, to supplement his ideas, to utter oracles that he had not spoken, and even to qualify, limit, and contradict many of his absolute commands. It may be said that it is the peculiarity and vitality of Christianity, that its ideas were never formulated in definite and irrepealable statutes, that it was a spirit rather than a code; that it was the awakening of the human moral sense, and sending it upon its long quest of truth, rather than the subjection of conscience to the authority of a revelation. The freedom which it gave was a freedom to question all authority, to criticise and to handle Jesus himself as he had handled Moses.

How shall Paul and Peter and the witnesses of the gospel of Jesus, carrying new doctrines over the world, authenticate their mission? Jesus had written no Bible, taught no complete system of philosophy or ethics, uttered no comprehensive canon of conduct. Of what he had taught, so far as tradition has preserved it, Paul seems to have been nearly ignorant. Yet he is never at a loss. He has eloquent and exhaustive discourses for all the different communities of the Roman world, in which he preached the gospel of Christ. To the Jew, he is a Pharisee of the Pharisees, blameless in all the requirements of the law.[a] In his intercourse with the cultivated and philosophic Greek, he lays open his liberal and comprehensive mind.[b] Before the common worldling, lover of pleasure, lover of wealth, he reasons of righteousness, temperance, and judgment to come.[c] He teaches the fervent disciples, and by his frequent letters edifies the faith of all the distant churches. How is all this original power consistent with his unbounded deference for the name of his crucified master? Did Jesus teach all that he preached and wrote? This is more than he could say,— much more than to us seems probable. His answer is: I teach as Jesus would have taught, if he were here. It is his spirit, the spirit of

[a] Acts xxiii., 6; xxvi., 5; Phil. iii., 5. [b] Acts xxii., 22–31. [c] Acts xxiv., 25.

God; for in spirit he was one with God, who inspires me. The gospel I bring is not mine, but Christ's, working within me his will and pleasure.[a]

More and more, as the new religion developed, Jesus exalted into the heavens became worshipped as divine; but, for the very reason that the worship of his disciples had elevated him to the heavens, it had banished him from the earth, and from practical control over their faith and life. The Spirit takes his place on earth, while the Church waits for his promised second coming; and now it begins to be discovered that the Spirit was always in the world; Peter finds that in all ages men who feared God and wrought righteousness were accepted of him;[b] Paul that they who are without law are a law unto themselves,[c] and the metaphysical poet, who wrote the Johannic drama, that Jesus was but a manifestation of the light that enlighteneth every man that cometh into the world.[d]

Now, it is not to be believed that this doctrine of the Holy Ghost, as it shaped itself in the creed of mediæval Christendom, or as it is disclosed in the speeches and letters of the apostles or in the later expressions of the Johannic Gospel, originated with Jesus, or scarcely had the sanction of his authority. The germs of it, however, appear in his discourses. There is a Holy Ghost, more awful in his sanctity than even God himself, of an ineffable dignity, with which the name of Jesus was not to be ranked, against whom it was fatal to the soul to commit sin; for that sin had no forgiveness in this life nor the life to come.[e] When he told his disciples that they need not be careful what defence they should make, if brought before rulers and kings, for their faith in him, that the spirit of their Father would speak within them,[f] it is not apparent that he wished them to believe that that spirit was a special influence, still less a divine personality, or any other than the communication by God himself, who is spirit, of the words the occasion might make fitting. So too, when he is made to say, The good Father is more ready to give the Holy Ghost to them that ask for it[g]

---

[a] Romans viii., 1; I. Cor. iii., 16; xv., 1-4; Gal. i., 9, 12, 15, 16.   [b] Acts x., 34, 35.
[c] Romans ii., 14.   [d] John i., 9.   [e] Matt. xii., 31, 32.   [f] Matt. x., 20.
[g] Matt. vii., 11; Luke xi., 13.

than earthly parents are to give bread to their children, it is probable the later prominence of the doctrine of a Holy Ghost has distorted the report, given more correctly by Matthew: "If ye then, being evil, know how to give good gifts unto your children, how much more shall your Father which is in heaven give *good things* to them that ask him?"

Jesus seems to have taught that character is determined by the ruling love, and that men are to be judged by their words. As the eye is the light of the body, so is the heart of man the light of his soul. The words "heart," "soul," "spirit," and "mind" were used by Jesus as they were by his more cultivated disciples, with none of the precision which modern metaphysical discussion has rendered necessary; and it is not always easy to determine what the exact conceptions of Jesus were in reference to the moral faculties of man. Taking into view all that he said, it seems probable that he recognized a radical difference in the moral attributes of men. The good man out of the good treasure of his heart brought forth good things, the evil man evil things. The good tree could but produce good fruit, the bad tree bad fruit. How can ye, being evil, he once asked, speak good things? He held, too, that the word was the expression of the character. It is not to be inferred that he underrated the power of self-control and hypocrisy, or was easily deceived by persons who came to him with professions of elevated and devout sentiments.[a] On the contrary, there are signal instances given where, with a keen insight, he detected the imposture of such assumptions, and exposed the evil principles underlying plausible professions. By words, by which a man was to be justified or condemned, he meant only genuine or sincere words,—perhaps more than this, the expression of conduct as well as of speech. By words in that large sense,—that is, by all the spontaneous expression of the character,—men were to be judged in the great day of judgment. For men tainted with moral evil, men blind to the influence of the divine light, and who in their perversity imputed good deeds and pure words to corrupt influences, he seemed to have had no hope of repentance.[b] He wished to withdraw himself from them, and to leave them to the fruit of their own evil growth.

[a] Matt. vii., 22, 23; xii., 33-37. [b] Matt. xii., 31, 32.

With instinctive and intense aversion to bad men, whose very presence inflicted a pang upon his sensitive spirit, we have to reconcile another class of declarations equally authentic, that he was a friend of publicans and sinners,[a] that he came not to call the righteous but sinners to repentance,[b] and that there is more joy in the heavens over a sinner repenting, than over many just men who need no repentance.[c] The joy over the repentance of a sinner may be accounted for because it is so difficult and rare an achievement, the natural and general law being for the corrupt tree to bring forth corrupt fruit, and the evil man to be incapable of doing good things. If we may consider the character of some of his disciples, it will probably become apparent that certain forms of sensuality, growing out of natural temperament, often a taint of heredity, might, in Jesus' estimation, more readily yield to remedies from without than the more subtle vices of the soul, such as envy, malice, ambition, and impiety. The judgment of the world corresponds to his, and notes that intemperance, licentiousness, and even a rash and angry temper may be controlled by moral considerations, by favorable influences, and by a resolute will; while those infestations of natural baseness return in force, after the strongest self-condemnation, and intrude themselves into the selectest privacy of the most favorable environments. In this connection, it is hard to reconcile a very marked prescience in Jesus to detect under professions of piety and virtue men who were really base with his indiscriminate preference for the poor, unless he had come to believe that the state of poverty was itself a state so congenial to virtue that only the good were to be found in that condition. It is hard to account for the harshness with which he repelled the advances of the Pharisees,— a sect so well accredited in history,— under whose influence such an eminent character as Paul had been reared.

Looking further for the philosophical ideas of Jesus, it is found that he believed in devilish possession, and that diseases and infirmities among men are due to the malicious agency of an evil spirit. It seems to have been the belief of the age of Jesus that insanity was a possession

---
[a] Matt. xi., 19.   [b] Matt. ix., 12, 13.   [c] Luke xv., 7.

by evil spirits or devils, the intensity of the diseased mental condition being due to the greater number of demons employed in the infestation. It has been claimed for Jesus that he did not share in this superstition, and that the narrative of his life, in dealing with his cures of the insane, necessarily conforms to the ideas of the nature of insanity prevalent in the world in his lifetime ; and that, if he seemed to give some sanction to those ideas in the language he sometimes used, it was only in deference to the popular mode of thought, and to make his beneficial agency intelligible to the persons relieved and to the people who surrounded him.

This explanation cannot fairly be entertained without doing such a violence to the veracity of the record, as to leave it an untrustworthy foundation for any definite conceptions of the character, opinions, and even of the existence of Jesus ; and, accordingly, it must be excluded from this study. It seems scarcely possible for those who believe his recorded words authentic, or those even who find themselves obliged to accept them as reliable data of his history, to doubt that he shared substantially the prevalent opinion on this subject of his countrymen and of his times. He declared in his Sermon on the Mount that many in the day of judgment would say, with apparent truth, that they had cast out devils in his name, whom he should not recognize as his followers.[a] He gave his sent-out disciples, who were in his name to proclaim the kingdom of heaven at hand, power against unclean spirits to cast them out, and charged them to heal the sick and cast out devils.[b] When the Pharisees heard of his power over people generally believed to be possessed with fiendish spirits, they imputed it to diabolic agency. The devil himself, they said, helps him. But Jesus turned most effectually their imputation, by asking: *Can Satan then cast out Satan?* Will the devil thwart himself?[c] — a saying that would have no force or pertinency, unless he himself believed in demoniac possession.

Luke tells that, once in a synagogue of Capernaum, there was a man who had in him the spirit of an unclean devil, — that is, according to our ideas, a form of insanity well known, under which the patient gave utterance to

---

[a] Matt. vii., 22. [b] Matt. x., 18. [c] Matt xii., 24-27.

obscene language. When this spirit invoked Jesus as the *Holy One of God*, he rebuked not the man, but the spirit in him, and bade him be silent and come out.[a]

The disciples whom Jesus had sent forth to cast out devils found a man conjuring by his name, and forbade the unauthorized worker; but Jesus rebuked them, and recognized as of his party all who were doing his work.[b] When the seventy disciples returned from their mission and reported to Jesus that, through his name, they found even the devils subject to them, he greatly exulted, and said: "*I beheld Satan as lightning fall from heaven!* Behold, I give unto you power to tread on serpents and scorpions, and over all the power of the enemy." But he told his disciples not to rejoice because the spirits were subject to them, but because their names were written in heaven.[c] On another occasion, he gave with minuteness some of the laws of demoniac possession. He said that a cast-out spirit betook itself by some weird propensity to dry places in quest of rest, and had longing to get back, as to its home, to the soul whence it had been expelled. Finding that soul empty, swept and garnished, it will associate with itself more wicked spirits — their number seven is specified — and returning to the doomed man make his last worse than his first state.[d] Scarce an instance can be found elsewhere in the recorded sayings of Jesus, where he seems to have undertaken the exposition of a general theory. Such a disclosure of the recondite rationale of spirit-infestation could hardly have proceeded from one who disbelieved it. When told that Herod was plotting to take his life, Jesus called him a fox, and said that for three days he must continue to do cures, and cast out devils, within which time it was not possible that a prophet could be destroyed. In vindicating himself for giving straightness to the woman who had a spirit of infirmity, a work done on the Sabbath, he said: *Ought not this woman, whom Satan hath bound these eighteen years, to be loosed from her infirmity on the Sabbath?*[e]

With these data, it is possible to construct in some of its details Jesus' conception of the divine providence in the

---

[a] Luke iv., 33–35.   [b] Luke ix., 49, 50.   [c] Luke x., 17–20.
[d] Luke xi., 24–26.   [e] Luke xiii., 16, 32.

world. The world is God's; its changes are his appointments; its laws, mainly beneficent, are the expressions of his goodness. He sends the sunlight and the rain. He gives to the flowers their beauty, and to the birds of the air their food, in the mere bounty of his beneficence.

These are indeed but glimpses of the universe as it looked to him; but they seem fairly to imply, that he thought of nature, as well under the control of an overruling benevolent will, and of living creatures, as following in their instincts the controlling purpose of God. He did not seem to consider men in harmony with this divine order. He never overlooks the radical distinction between good and evil men. From each proceed words and actions according to their kind. It is nowhere found that he held that God is the father of all men. It was to his disciples only, after he had withdrawn himself from the thronging multitudes, for whom the mysteries of the kingdom of heaven were not open, that he allowed the relationship, which permitted them to approach the Highest with the address, "*our Father in heaven.*"[a] There were many, even of those that strove, who would not enter into life;[b] and the multitudes crowded the broad thoroughfare to destruction. With those even, who so far recognized his mastery as to call him Lord, and who could cast out devils and do wonderful works in his name, he should in the end deny his relationship, as workers of iniquity.[c] Only they who were the light and salt of the earth, they whose righteousness exceeded that of scribes and Pharisees, were recognized by him as children of the Highest.[d] The poor were the children of God and inheritors of the kingdom, not solely on account of their poverty, but because he seemed always to impute to the estate of poverty a certain humility, meekness, and self-control, compatible with the heavenly state. The rich were not excluded, but the test of their sincerity was the surrender of their property; and from this class he almost despaired of winning subjects for the kingdom of heaven.[e] The sensual and intemperate were not despised. Conscious of the strength of his own purity, and almost exempt from the temptations that assailed them, he be-

[a] Matt. v., 1, 2; vi., 9. [b] Luke xiii., 24. [c] Matt. vii., 22; Luke xiii., 24.
[d] Matt. v., 13, 20. [e] Luke xviii , 22.

lieved that there were periods of moral revulsion from sensual indulgence, promotive of sincere repentance. So he sought the society of such persons to invite them, when under the compunctions of an aroused conscience, to virtue and temperance.^a For proud men, oppressors, the malicious, the evil-minded, for hypocrites and formalists, for the cunning and self-confident, he had only reprobation, sometimes expressing itself in language exceeding the moderation which he prescribed as a rule for other men.^b

The wickedness and evil which he could not fail to find in the world, it is certain that he imputed in part to the agency of evil spirits. He always associated the curing of disease with the dispossession of malignant powers. He believed that, in healing the sick and restoring sanity to the mentally deranged, he was warring with Satan, and bringing his kingdom to an end.^c It was Satan, and not, as modern devout thought would conceive in a like case, the mysterious providence of a good God, that had bound the daughter of Abraham for eighteen years with an inveterate infirmity.^d According to his theory, the physically diseased, the paralytic, the blind, and the maimed, are prisoners of the devil; and it is the mission of a divine redeemer to effect their relief.^e When multitudes are healed, when reason returns to the insane, he sees Satan as lightning fall from heaven, and the malignant spirits that had infested the world driven out before the power of the coming king. Thus, Jesus seemed to think that men had fallen out of the order that pervaded nature as a whole, partly because the mass of mankind were genetically wicked, partly because they were suffering from an infestation of evil spirits, whose malign influence manifested itself in physical infirmity and in mental derangement.

While it is fairly presumable that Jesus never sanctioned the extension of the divine fatherhood to the whole human race, it is equally probable that he believed evil men were children of the devil.^f Such became unquestionably the distinct Christian conception after his death. The Johannic Gospel, which may always be cited as an ex-

^a Matt. xi., 19.   ^b Matt. xxiii.   ^c Luke x., 18.   ^d Luke xiii., 16.
^e Luke iv., 18.   ^f John viii., 44, 49.

pression of the opinions of the Christian converts of the first centuries, distinctly imputes to Jesus the declaration that the Pharisees were children of the devil. John the Baptist had called the Pharisees and Sadducees, even when showing some purposes of repentance and righteousness by seeking his baptism, a generation of vipers,[a] and had declared that it did not lie within his mission to give them any warning against the wrath to come. Jesus had repeated this most denunciatory epithet on two different occasions, and in addition called the Pharisees serpents, whose escape from damnation of hell was virtually impossible.[b]

The serpent, the old serpent, the dragon, were names used by the New Testament writers to designate Satan,[c] the chief of the evil spirits, of which the Jewish people had had a distinct conception for several centuries before the time of Jesus. When, therefore, Jesus addressed the Pharisees as serpents and the progeny of vipers, he fairly imputed to them a devilish origin; and the Johannic drama did no violence to his thought, in making the relation as actual as the paternity of God in reference to the followers of Jesus, and in declaring that it was as natural for the Pharisees to do the lusts of their father, the devil, as it was for Jesus to do the works of his Father, God.

It is not quite apposite to this discussion to consider the conception of modern Christendom of the universal fatherhood of God, otherwise than to say it is an unauthorized inference from the teachings of Jesus and of the New Testament writers, and that the universality of the relationship necessarily destroys it. Of a father, we have no other idea than of one exercising toward his children that special preference and favor that grows out of natural affection. When the relationship of father becomes so broad as to include all men, the possibility of preference and favor, which are of the essence of paternity disappears. But we are compelled to enlarge the regard and affection of the supreme will, so as that it shall cover all sentient beings, and to consider it impartial. What nature thrusts everywhere upon intelligent observation is the impartiality of God,— that God does not prefer men to sheep, that he allows the struggle for life to go

[a] Matt. iii., 7. [b] Matt. xii., 34; xxiii., 33. [c] Rev. xii., 9; xx, 2.

on between the meanest and noblest forms of creation without intervention, giving to the latter not always the advantage, never an advantage not due to their superior equipment of faculty. Mankind, sedulously studying the problem, has not yet been able to determine that the good man competing with the bad man has any extrinsic success, any reward or help not an adjunct of his own virtue.

It may also be questioned whether Jesus, in emphasizing the divine sonship of good men, in making the fatherhood of God a psychological fact instead of a figure of speech, really elevated the old idea very distinctly enunciated by the Hebrew prophets and by the Greek sages before his time. That which is named integrity, virtue, righteousness, is conformity to the law, order, and plan of nature. Out of this conformity springs highest welfare, deepest peace; so that man, under the correction of his moral sense, has come at last to learn that the path of virtue is the path of the progress of the universe, and that goodness, rather than pleasure, is the goal toward which all spiritual life advances. Now, the ancients had come to express this in this striking figure: "*Like as a father pitieth his children, so the Lord pitieth them that fear him*,* or regard the highest good. Like, the comparison is preserved, as between things not identical. God is other than man, something higher than man at his best. Could man get a stronger motive than this for righteousness? True, it comforts the struggling good man to be told he is a son of God; but it compromises his idea of God to infer that, since he is then a son of God, God is like his child. Pressing the relationship beyond the sanction of a motive and the uses of an inspiration, and comparing the reverence of a sincere and devout Pharisee with the arrogance and presumption of whole sects and generations of Christian saints who say *our Father*, might it not be feared that we have exchanged an elevating, spiritual conception for an anthropomorphic and personal Deity too nearly related to us to be reverently worshipped?

It already appears that Jesus classified men according to their kind, as children of God, and not children of God; and we have been able to determine some of the prominent characters embraced in this description. What

* Ps. ciii., 13.

were his own relations of regard and estimation toward these classes?

Among the beneficent words of Jesus that are especially remembered are these: "The Son of man is come to save that which was lost."[a] There is more joy in heaven over one sinner that repenteth than over ninety and nine just persons that need no repentance.[b] Jesus is called in the Church the friend of sinners, and his message to the world of its destruction and the coming of the kingdom of heaven is called the good news. Jesus said, when rebuked for tolerating the society of openly vicious persons, that he had not come to call the righteous but sinners to repentance;[c] and he declared that God was more pleased with mercy than he was with sacrifice,[d] leaving it plainly to be inferred that the mercy he loved in men he would not fail himself to exercise toward the penitent. But we must consider, in connection with these declarations, others of a different character. He called the civil magistrates and political authorities who would prosecute his disciples wolves.[e] He said his mission was only to the lost sheep of the house of Israel, and that it was not proper to give to heathen dogs the food the master had provided for his children.[f] The excommunicated disciple was to be to his brethren like a heathen and publican; that is, outside of their fellowship and charity.[g] The foolish virgins in the bridal procession, types of the non-elect, the rejecters of his mission, like the pretenders who had followed him, working cures and calling him Lord, he would profess that he never knew. The goats, representatives of those not his followers, and who had ministered neither to him nor his disciples, were to go away into everlasting punishment.[h] All mere worldly men, they who eat, drink, buy and sell, plant and build, they who are occupied with business, were all to be destroyed, when the Son of Man was revealed, as were the inhabitants of Sodom.[i] The importunate prayer of the elect should bring down upon the wicked not blessings, not repentance and salvation, but speedy vengeance and punishment.[j]

[a] Matt. xviii., 11.   [b] Luke xv., 7.   [c] Luke v., 32.   [d] Matt. xii., 7.
[e] Matt. x., 16, 17.   [f] Matt. xv., 24, 26.   [g] Matt. xviii., 17.
[h] Matt. xxv., 2–12, 23, 46.   [i] Luke xvii., 26–30.   [j] Luke xviii., 7, 8.

Recurring now to the parables of the lost sheep, the piece of silver, and the prodigal son, which have been accepted as expressions of the universality of Jesus' benevolence, we find their scope considerably restricted. The lost sheep was still one of the hundred that belonged to the fold of Israel. He represented not an outside sinner or heathen, but only a lapsed disciple, over whose defection the angels wept, and for whom the good shepherd was searching among the mountains. It might still be true that the good shepherd, as he said, was only sent to the lost sheep of the house of Israel.[a] The woman must find her own lost piece of silver. No strange coin could fill its place.[b] The prodigal was still a son, and heir of his father's wealth. No alien and no servant was to receive the kiss of the reconciled father weeping on his neck.[c]

So when Jesus said the Son of Man was come to save that which was lost, it was in reference to one of the lost little ones or believing disciples whom he warned his followers not to despise, and whose angels always stood before God to defend them. It is the Father's will, he said, that not one of *these little ones* should perish.[d] But like the fatherhood of God, carefully restricted by Jesus to righteous men and believers, the love and saving purpose of God toward the lost of his fold have been presumptuously extended to all men.

Nothing was more original and characteristic in the moral philosophy of Jesus than his exaltation of service and his reprobation of ambition, of love of precedence, and even of self-estimation, however just. He himself, though he called himself master and even lord,[e] came, he said, not to be served and honored, but to do service and even to give his life for others. In all secular governments, it was the prince who held and the great who exercised all authority.[f] In the economy which he should establish, the really great should be the servant of all the rest. The contentions for rank and distinction excited his indignation. He censured the scribes and Pharisees because they chose the uppermost rooms at feasts and the chief seats in synagogues, and to be

[a] Matt. x., 5, 6; xv., 24.　　[b] Luke xv., 8.　　[c] Luke xv., 11-32.
[d] Matt. xviii., 6, 10-24.　　[e] Matt. xxiii., 8.　　[f] Matt. xx., 25-28.

greeted by their fellow-men with the title of *Rabbi*.[a] In the Church, he said, let the greatest be servant, and let him that exalts himself be abased. He gave directions to his followers that, when invited to a feast, they should not arrogate their own dignity by taking the most honorable places ; but, choosing the humblest, the host himself would measure their rank, and, inviting them to a higher seat, give them honor before all the guests.[b] The sheep who were placed in the grand separation at the last day on his right hand, and admitted into everlasting life, were awarded that felicity, not more because they had ministered to him and the least of his followers when sick, destitute, and in prison, than because they had done these deeds of beneficence in utter unconsciousness and had forgotten the doing of them.[c] When once there rose a strife among the disciples which should be greatest, Jesus placed a little child before them, and said whoever received that child as his follower received him, and that the least among them should be greatest. No one could enter the kingdom of heaven till he had been converted and become a little child ; that is, till he had unlearned that ambition for precedence and honor, and reverted to the guileless innocence and unconsciousness which is a trait of infancy.[d] Of his personal attachment to his disciples, who with artless and uncritical faith had accepted him, he spake with earnest warmth. Better be cast into the sea with a millstone fastened to the neck, than give offence to one of these. Of these blessed ones, a guardian angel stands ever before the face of God ; and it is his will that not one shall perish.

Blessed, he said, are the meek : they shall inherit the renovated earth.[e] Even spiritual gifts and personal integrity were not to be arrogated ; nor was any good service, however great, to claim its reward. Will a man thank his servant, who for hire ministers to him ? When ye have done all, ye are but unworthy servants.[f] The moral man, who in his prayer remembered his good life, though to thank God for it, was condemned ; while the wicked man, who bowed his head and acknowledged that

---

[a] Matt. xxiii., 6, 7. [b] Luke xiv., 7-11. [c] Matt. xxv., 36-38.
[d] Matt. xviii., 1-6, 10; Mark ix., 34. [e] Matt. v., 5.
[f] Luke xvii., 9, 10.

he was a sinner, went down from the temple justified.[a] In the same connection, Jesus put a light estimate upon the wisdom and culture of the world, as he did upon its virtue. The innocent and uncultivated child was to him the brightest type of manhood. While the critical faculty listens and doubts and rejects, the childish faith sees, believes upon report, and is blessed. What the Father has hid from the wise and prudent he has revealed to babes.[b]

This love of children is an amiable personal trait in Jesus, that has endeared his memory to the tender heart of the human race. Painters have depicted it, and enthusiastic disciples have seized upon it to mitigate the austerity of a sublime and elevated character, stern in its devotion to duty, uncompromising in its rigorous and crucial dealings with all the weaknesses and appetites of nature. But those who have reared children know that infancy has aspects other than the morally picturesque; that their innocence is rather the absence of those passions, the force of which could not be trusted to their feeble powers of resistance; that they assert all the natural appetites they have without the will or power to control; and that virtue, which is the victory over passions regulated by conscience and reason, is a grade of character far beyond the innocence which precedes the impulses that drive men to sins. It were indeed a most deplorable picture of the human condition, if the very process of human life resulted in degeneration and moral death. If to live is to fall into fatal sin, why should we wish that our children should survive their infancy, and why should we labor to surround them with sanitary conditions, which, saving their human lives, imperils at the same time the life of their souls? A just estimate of the opportunities of life satisfies us that it is, on the whole, a salutary discipline, that all its usual and legitimate experiences are promotive of virtue, and that, bad as society is, faulty and deceptive as are individual characters, the tendency of growth is toward self-control, toward temperance, toward love of others, toward justice, mercy, and piety. Society demands and expects of aged men and aged women, those who have had the widest experiences of human fortune and the most unrestricted careers

[a] Luke xviii., 10-14.   [b] Matt. xi., 25.

of earthly prosperity, a strain of integrity and rectitude never asked of the young. With many deplorable exceptions, the demand is generally met.

It were better for the world if the followers and worshippers of Jesus had given better heed to his counsels concerning rank. They have, for the most part, set them aside as summarily and contemptuously, as they have his ideas about property. In no department has the struggle for power and precedence been so keen as in the Church calling itself Christ's. The democratic spirit, not a little inspired by the words of Jesus, has been able, in many communities and among many nations, to overthrow distinctions merely political, and to reduce society to a practical equality; but the ranks of the priesthood, the titles of reverence which they demand, the vestures and badges with which they are decorated, stand upon such an authority of custom, that the ministry has ceased to be a synonym of service, and they who represent the Son of Man come no more to minister, but to be ministered to by the deference, the compliments, and tithes of the disciples.

The example of the self-accusing prodigal is less commended by the good sense of this age than by Jesus. Not the confession of sin alone is acceptable to God. When the prodigal comes too frequently with his smitten breast and cravings of mercy upon his sin, we begin to ask that the confessed sin be abandoned. Perhaps all the Pharisee said of himself was true; and there might have been those who knew the publican, and had been the victims of his extortion, who could have uttered a hearty *Amen* to all that he said. Not always self-consciousness and self-praise are to be condemned: a man may rejoice over a well-achieved work. While we demand modesty in measuring one's own worth or work, we demand truth more. David washing his hands in innocency, Paul exulting that he had ·fought the good fight and kept the faith, and Milton in his blindness boasting of his noble work with which all Europe rang, are more heroic figures than a defaulting cashier standing up in church-meeting and repeating, *God be merciful to me a sinner.*

It has been seen that Jesus judged human character by

the ruling love. In accordance with this internal inquisition into character rather than by the test which human law applies to outward conduct, Jesus held that evil thoughts, and not the omission of external purifications, defile a man. Out of the heart, he said, proceed evil thoughts, murders, adulteries, fornications, thefts, false witness, and blasphemies.[a] No teacher has been more searching in analyzing the very springs of conduct, and finding in motive and natural impulse the basis of character. Not the fatal blow, but the malicious purpose, is murder; and he who is angry without just cause with his fellow-man has entered upon the path that leads to homicide, as he who cherishes and enjoys lust has committed adultery in his heart.[b]

The gravity and seriousness of his character, that rigor of mental integrity, which he prescribed to himself, and made a rule of living for others, was manifested in the great import which he attributed to all human speech. According to Jesus, no man must sport with his convictions, or advocate what he does not fully believe and feel the assurance of, out of levity or for the sake of argument, or to conceal an unpopular or dangerous conviction. All such tampering with the light of God in the reason of man was to him blasphemy against the Holy Ghost. It was when the Pharisees said, without conviction and with a dishonest purpose of turning against him a popular prejudice, that the devil helped him to cast out devils,[c] that, after showing the falsity of the assertion, he went on to say: All blasphemy shall be forgiven but the blasphemy of the Holy Ghost. They thus speak, because an evil heart cannot speak good things. But, for every false and frivolous word that man shall speak, he shall give an account in the day of judgment, and he shall be justified or condemned as his words have been good or evil.

He thought, too, that a man was known by his moral sympathies. The man who loved, as well as who did, rectitude was blessed in his regard. The ruling love is still the test of character. The good man in the strife between good and evil takes always the side of the good. As Paul fitly expressed it afterward: "He rejoices not in iniquity, but he rejoices in the truth." The figure of Jesus

[a] Matt. xv., 11, 18.   [b] Matt. v., 21, 22, 39.   [c] Matt. xii., 24, 31-37.

is still more striking, when he says, The man, whom God shall bless, hungers and thirsts after righteousness. If, for the sake of a righteous deed he has done, or done by another he has approved and applauded, he shall suffer persecution, his very persecution, in the peace it brings to his soul, shall be a manifestation of the favor of God, and an assurance of the blessedness he shall inherit. They, too, who reconcile the offended, who make peace between those engaged in or ready for strife, showing to souls blinded by anger the better way of forgiveness and concession, and how an exaction and an oppression may be overcome and turned to justice by submission, are especially blessed.[b] They not only live for themselves and enjoy the peace that comes from virtue, but they have carried the light of their own lives into the darkened minds of other men, and taught them by the experience of forgiveness the satisfactions of charity.

It is not to be supposed that Jesus felt confident that all violent and angry men would yield to these influences. There were still some natures so rooted in evil that the pearls of good actions were not to be thrown away upon them.[c] They would trample in derision the mild and forgiving spirit, and turn like swine to tear the hand that interposed to arrest their wrath.

[a] Matt. v., 6; I. Cor. xiii., 6.   [b] Matt. v., 9, 10.   [c] Matt. vii., 6.

CHAPTER VII.

RELIGIOUS IDEAS OF JESUS.

"It is the work of Religion to sift the primitive instincts and expectations of mankind, and see which of them can have a place in the critical intelligence.... The more of God you collect in the facts which he causes, the more consistent and sublime becomes your faith.... Why, at the very moment when Religion's first opportunity has come to make the finite prove the infinite, which she presumes, need she continue the old prescription of church extension, Bible-worship, miracles, and parish life?"—*John Weiss' Immortal Life.*

QUESTIONS relating to the first cause, including the problem of the being of God, belong to the domain of philosophy. Religion, in its stricter sense, concerns itself with considerations how fitly to placate, honor and serve the Deity. Next to the philosophical ideas of Jesus, it becomes important to comprehend what were his religious ideas; what, by precept or practice, did he inculcate as a religious cultus and mode of worship.

In all ages the ideas, which men have held in reference to the character of the gods, have dictated the forms of their worship. The savage, whose god is scarcely human — rather a monster whom he never thinks of loving or even respecting — whom he fitly represents as a serpent, a dog, or a lion, and whose power and malice he seeks to propitiate, will be worshipped by the offer of victims. Accept this slaughter, this torture of my enemy, my son, my cattle, and spare my life, is virtually the prayer of the terror-stricken devotee. When a milder and more human nature came to be imputed to the gods, worship consisted in bringing to them fruits and the incense of roasted flesh, in celebrating before them games in which they might delight as spectators, or in imitating the actions which tradition had imputed to them. Such conceptions of God could but react upon the worshipper who lived, and spoke, and thought as his gods were believed to have done.

But, before historic times, man had acquired a moral sense. This acquisition was, however, an inevitable step in his progress. Until he had acquired the faculty of considering his own actions, and approving or disapproving them, man was not likely to make any record of his living, or to leave any monuments whereon his thoughts could be expressed. When conscience began to assert itself in men's living, they began to impute to the gods the moral judgments, which they passed upon themselves, and upon each other. Before the dawn of history, before any records were made, out of which history could be constructed, religion had become moral. If, in the primeval time, the gods had been violent, revengeful, or licentious, they had all at a later epoch reformed, and a moral order had been introduced into the ideal heavens. Mixed up with mythological conceptions involving the gods in treachery, falsehood, murder, and debauchery, there had arisen in enlightened minds among the Hindus, the Egyptians, the Persians, and the Greeks the faith that truthfulness, justice, purity, benevolence constituted the basis of the divine character, and that the gods were fairly on the side of righteousness.

The Egyptian and Phœnician ideas of God, which, in modified form, were perpetuated in the paganism contemporary with Jesus, were more cheerful and attractive than the more abstract and spiritual conception which the Hebrew and some other of the Semitic tribes had cherished. The Olympus of the Greeks was a family and a home, as well as a royal court. A god married and living on terms of domestic confidence — albeit not always harmonious — with a goddess, feeling a partiality for and conferring special advantages upon his own children, was a picture which gave reality and form to the faith of the Greek. The very multiplicity of gods — a godhead capable of degrees of power and wisdom, shaded down through inferior deities, demigods, and heroes to man — mitigated the awful intensity and incomprehensibility of his idea, and better accommodated it to his feeble mental capacities.

The Hebrew stood at the head of an entirely different cultus. It cannot now be studied in its roots and principles, but rather in its full development in the Old Testament, and in the Jewish religion. It is attributed to Moses; and, as all great ideas, that have considerably affected civilization, are found to have their source in the mind of some great genius, it is quite probable that the Hebrew religion had its essence, and the germs from which it grew, in the inspiration of a single mind. The best summary of it may be found in a declaration ascribed to Moses himself: "Thou shalt prefer no gods to me; for I am a jealous God, visiting the iniquities of the fathers upon the children to the third and fourth generations, and showing mercy to thousands of them that love me and keep my commandments."[a]

For the family god, for the deities that ruled the heavens and the earth with complicated intrigue, and not a little strife among themselves, who, though they had at last attained order, by mutual submission, by a reasonable self-control, and by abstaining from the excesses of their youth, were originally preternaturally sensual and cruel, the devout Hebrew substituted a god without father or child, always pure, and raised above the appetites of men, but jealous of other gods, eager for worship, placable by gifts and offerings, and vindictive in his punishments. Such an image could inspire in men little else than fear; and, indeed, the fear of God was declared to be the prime sentiment of religion, the beginning of all knowledge.[b] To accommodate an idea of God so spiritual and abstract to the low culture of his people, Moses had two devices: one was a mode of worship with its organized and consecrated priesthood, its minute prescription of sacrifices, of holy days, of purifications and ceremonies so exacting and imposing as to keep the imagination occupied and awed, if not with the thought of God, with the zeal of his service; the other was by associating their God with their worldly thrift and prosperity, which he was believed to promote, and by connecting him with all their family, tribal, and national ambition, so that he came to be considered by excellence the tutelary deity, the power that gave them success in their invasions, victory in their battles; and that forsook them and allowed them to be defeated and enslaved, when they neglected or corrupted his worship.

[a] Ex. xx., 5, 6.   [b] Ps. cxi., 10; Prov. i., 7; Eccl. xii., 13.

Thus, Moses, or, to speak more assuredly, the Mosaic spirit, as manifested by a succession of leaders and prophets, pulled down and married to human nature a spiritual idea of the godhead, not, as the Phœnicians and Egyptians had done, by concessions to sensuality, but by concessions to family and national jealousies, and by cultivating that idea in an outward worship of sacrifices, decorations, and ceremonies. Among both races, however, as is shown by the testimony of their extant literature, the tendency was, as the moral sense became developed, to eliminate from this notion of the deity whatever was sensual on the one hand, and jealous and vindictive on the other hand; and to shape the divine conception into something corresponding to man's best conception of goodness, virtue, righteousness. God is not propitiated by libidinous rites, but by chastity and pure affections, taught the philosophers and poets among the Greeks. God is not pleased with whole burnt-offerings and sacrifices, but with mercy, justice, and integrity, taught the Hebrew prophets, growing more clear in their conviction and more emphatic in their declaration, as the nation ripened in intellectual and ethical culture. But, even in Jesus' time, the superfluous sacrifices were not omitted; and Jesus himself, when comparing the weightier matters of justice, mercy, and faith with the petty prescription of tithes of mint, anise, and cumin, could go no further than to say, "*These ought ye to have done, and not have left the others undone.*" *

It is probable too, from the sceptical tone of parts of the Book of Job, and of the prophecies attributed to Jonah, that the idea that Jehovah was the tribal God of the Jews, and had treated them with special favor among the nations, had been seriously shaken in thoughtful minds by the succession of heavy calamities that had fallen upon that people. These calamities, involving the total destruction of three-fourths of the nation, and making the remnant the sport and spoil of the great conquering races of the world, seem to have fallen heaviest upon them at the very period when they had come to be most assiduous and punctilious in their cultivation of the Jehovah worship, as well as most careful in maintaining

* Matt. xxiii., 23.

the integrity of their personal conduct. The Hebrews were ever a stiff-necked people, slow to abandon a national prejudice. They held to sacrifices after the prophets, whom they chiefly honored, had assured them that sacrifices were an offence to the Deity; they believed themselves the chosen people of God, after, in the eyes of all the world, they had become the most forsaken and down-trodden of the nations.

Jesus placed himself by the side of the greater prophets of his race in declaring the excellence of righteousness over worship; and in rebuking the national pride in Jehovah as their exclusive god. He said that upon supreme love to God, and equal love to man, rested all the law and the prophets.[a] It was doubtless in deference to his well-known opinions that an "enlightened scribe" once said to him, The love of God is better than all whole burnt-offerings and sacrifices.[b] Jesus said that a man at enmity with his brother should be reconciled before he came to the altar of God with gifts; and also that God was propitiated by mercy rather than by sacrifice.[c] But, on the other hand, he said that he came not to destroy the law, and that whoever should teach that the least of its commandments might be broken should be least in the kingdom of heaven.[d] He declared that the scribes and Pharisees inherited the authority of Moses; and told his disciples to observe and do whatever they taught.[e] Petty as was the tithe of mint, anise, and cumin, it was to be punctiliously paid; and, though the duty of reconciliation to the offended brother preceded the offering of a gift at the altar, he was careful to say that, that prime duty done, it was right to go afterward and offer the gift.

In the chapter on the Political Ideas of Jesus his judgment with regard to the pretension of the people of his nation to be the peculiar people of God has been already considered. He had in the first of his career distinctly admitted that pretension. He said he was only sent to the lost sheep of the house of Israel, and that the heathen were dogs that were not to be fed from the master's table.[f] But, later, he had announced

[a] Mark xii., 28-34. [b] Matt. xxii., 40. [c] Matt. v., 23, 24; xii., 7.
[d] Matt. v., 17-19. [e] Matt. xxiii., 2, 3, 23. [f] Matt. xv., 23, 26.

the rejection of the Jews, and the choosing of a nation that would bring forth the fruits of righteousness.[a] He had declared Zaccheus, who had with such heartiness accepted his ideas of the kingdom of heaven, a son of Abraham,[b] and had consigned Dives, a type of the covetous children of Abraham, to a place of torment.[c]

After he had fully possessed himself of the belief that he was the prophetic king of the new kingdom of heaven, he began to exercise authority commensurate with that dignity, and to deal with the law of Moses with more freedom. He used violence in expelling from the precincts of the temple the money-changers and the sellers of sacrificial victims.[d] A refined and humane sensibility might have been unpleasantly affected by the noise, the cruelty, the reek and ordure that necessarily accompanied the constant slaughter and roasting of animals,— the religious offering of an entire people collected within the enclosure of a single temple and its appurtenances. A mind that had been able to overcome its wholesome natural repugnance to such a spectacle, by the sense of its sacredness, need not have been offended at arrangements which, on the whole, tended to mitigate the horrors of a great public slaughter and sacrifice. It was this very mitigation, however, that Jesus, armed with a whip, in apparent disregard of his lesson of suffering rather than giving blows, undertook to abate.[e]

His kingly prerogative of suspending or modifying the divine and civil law is asserted in his declaration, in reply to a charge of Sabbath breach, that he was Lord also of the Sabbath days.[f] The institution of the Sabbath was a distinguishing and fundamental article of the ecclesiastical law. The Jews believed that its imposition had been contained in the *lex legum*, the central summary of the national statutes, the ten commandments written upon the table of stone, miraculously given to Moses upon Mount Sinai.[g] Even the most moral of the prophets, who had spoken disparagingly of sacrifices, insisted upon a punctilious observance of this weekly holy day.[h] Among the Jews, however, the essence of the observance con-

[a] Matt. xxi., 43. [b] Luke xix., 9. [c] Luke xvi., 14, 15, 19-31.
[d] Matt. xxi., 12. [e] Matt. v., 39. [f] Matt. xii., 8.
[g] Ex. xx., 8-11. [h] Ex. xx., 12; Isa. lvi., 22.

sisted in a cessation of labor. There was no austerity and rigor of silence and devotion as has made the day so dismal in the households of Scottish Presbyterians and New England Puritans. Amusements and relaxation were quite in accordance with the character of the day. It is therefore unlikely that Jesus gave any offence to his countrymen by travelling about the country, and going through the grain fields on the Sabbath, or by accepting an invitation to a feast upon that day, so large and so promiscuous, that the guests occupied different stories of the house, and contended among themselves for precedence.^a Since it was a Pharisee that prepared the feast, and gave the invitations, it is presumable that the customs of the most religious people were in strict accordance with his act. But the abstention from labor was insisted upon to an extent that to us seems quite absurd, not only by a whimsical public opinion, but apparently by the letter of the law itself. A tradition had found its place in the Pentateuch of a man found gathering sticks to kindle a fire upon the Sabbath day, who had been stoned to death by order of Moses.^b One of the greater prophets had declared the unlawfulness of carrying any burden on the holy day.^c What the punctilious Jews objected to — and surely they stood fairly upon the better opinion — was not that the disciples went through the fields of corn on the Sabbath or even ate the corn, but that, in preparing the food by rubbing it in the hand, and blowing away the chaff, they had worked on the Sabbath, just as the man had worked, who had gathered sticks. Jesus himself does not seem to have been able to maintain an argument against these sound opinions of the scribes. Virtually, he acknowledges that they have reason. Virtually, he admits the Sabbath breach, and justifies it, on account of his own mastery of the law. He cites to the Jews instances in which David on a certain occasion did, and the priests in the temple habitually do, *things that the law forbids*, and yet are morally blameless.^d David and the priests may suspend the law. This is the plain implication. Much more may the Son of man, Lord of the Sabbath days, suspend the law of the Sabbath.

^a Matt. xii., 1; Luke xiv., 1, 7.   ^b Num. xv., 32-36.
^c Jer. xv., 21.   ^d Matt. xii., 3-8.

As the record stands there is an inconsistency in the example and precept of Jesus in reference to the obligation of the law of Moses. He had taught that every jot and tittle of the Mosaic law was to be observed; and he had called it all a tradition of the elders.[a] He had said mercy was better than sacrifices; and yet he had directed that the pettiest sacrifices should not be omitted. He had denounced the Pharisees for their long prayers and their punctilious devotions, as children of vipers doomed to damnation; and had told his disciples to honor them, and fulfil their requirements, as the lineal successors of Moses. He had excused the breach of one of the ten commandments, and had justified himself as a sovereign might, who should suspend his own decrees.

The equivocal position of the master was destined to involve the little band of his followers in a real difficulty. When converts presented themselves from among the heathen, passing all the tests of discipleship, full of faith in Jesus and zeal for the gospel, and ready to comply with any rule of conduct, as a manifestation of their repentance, what law must be given them, by what code must their external life be regulated? If Jesus had distinctly taught that the law of Moses was either binding or abrogated, if his attitude in reference to it had been more distinct and intelligible than it now appears to us in the evangelical traditions, Peter, James and John would have stood up to declare his commandment, and his authority would have closed discussion and deliberation. But there was evidently no distinct tradition either way as to his judgment. So the apostles entertained the question among themselves, trying to decide it upon just and rational grounds, aided by a liberal interpretation of ancient scripture, and devoutly and humbly imputing their own chastened good sense to the dictates of the Holy Spirit, and concluded, "*that it seemed good to the Holy Ghost, and to us, to lay upon you no greater burden than these necessary things; that ye abstain from meats offered to idols, and from blood, and from things strangled, and from fornication, from which if ye keep yourselves, ye shall do well.*"[b] Of these four requirements, three are trivial and pertain to customs, only of importance as con-

[a] Matt. v., 17–19, 21, 27, 33. [b] Acts xv., 28, 29.

nected with a culture especially Jewish. They were directions not given by Jesus, nor had he ever indicated that he thought such matters worth serious consideration. His comprehensive declaration, that not what went into the mouth, but what proceeded from it defiled a man, showed that he thought lightly of the religious value of a special diet. The fourth requirement alone is fundamental and moral, and had the sanction of Jesus' precept, and of the ethical principles in which the Jews, and even the pagans, had been educated.

There is, besides his treatment of the Sabbatical imposition, another incident in the career of Jesus, which shows that he considered the law of the old covenant merely provisional and liable to revisions by himself, when his authority in the heavenly kingdom should be definitely set up. Coming to John to be baptized, it is told that John was quite awed by the dignity of such a proselyte, and modestly remarked, that it would be more becoming for him to accept baptism from Jesus rather than to confer it on him. The august disciple by no means repels the delicate compliment, but says: *Suffer it to be so for the present. It is proper that we should fulfil all the rites.*[a]

On the whole, it seems fairly to be inferred from the precepts and example of Jesus — as noticed by a casual observation — that he held to the obligation of the national worship, even its least and most trivial prescriptions. It was in force as a provisional arrangement, and until he himself, in his new kingdom, sovereign over the law, should revise it and complete and fulfil it. But he ably supported the opinion of the most eminent and enlightened of the prophets in declaring, that if these least things should be punctiliously done, mercy was better than sacrifice, faith was higher than worship, to do righteousness was more pleasing to the Deity than prayer, and supreme love to God and brotherly love to man were more religious than all whole burnt-offerings.

In an earlier chapter, two distinct notions imputed to him in regard to prayer have been incidentally remarked upon: one, that it must be without vain repetition or much speaking; the other, that the Deity might sometimes be moved to grant to importunate and persistent

[a] Matt. iii., 13-15.

asking, to be relieved of a personal annoyance, what he would not accord from his wisdom or his benevolence. It is somewhat singular, that Jesus' own tastes, if such an expression is allowed, did not lie in the direction of verbal devoutness. Not without satire, in the Sermon on the Mount, he had spoken of the hypocrites, who love to pray standing in the synagogues and in the corner of the streets. It was the practice of the heathen to arouse the attention of their preoccupied gods by loudly calling their names and by the repetition of petitions. Nothing is finer in the older Scripture than the contrast between the priests of Baal, calling from morning till noon, in the monotonous invocation, "O Baal, hear us," and the simple one request of Elijah, prophet of Jehovah, followed by the divine response.[a] In the enlightened spirit of the writer of the legend, Jesus affirmed that prayer was not needed to make human wants known to God, and that men were not heeded for their much speaking.[b] God is the heavenly Father, he said. Will not any good father give to his children what they need, at least, for the asking? Prayer is not a service that God needs. It is not an honor and compliment, the omission of which will offend him. Go to the heavenly Father for what you want, and when you want. Simply ask, that is all.[c] There is no account of any formal or periodical prayer practised or taught by Jesus. He did not have an evening or a morning prayer; a Sabbath day's, or a new moon's, or a new year's season of sustained and continuous devotion. His personal practice seemed strictly in accord with the idea, that the relationship of God to good men was a natural and psychological relation; and that the intercourse between children and father should be that suggested by such a relation. If one wants from a father food, raiment, favor, forgiveness, counsel, he goes and asks. He has no set times or prescribed modes of paying court to his father. So when he wants of God daily bread, deliverance from temptation, help or patience in sorrow, forgiveness for an offence, the occurring want, not an occurring season is the occasion and reason of his prayer. It is related of Jesus that he

---

[a] I. Kings xviii., 26-39. [b] Matt. vi., 1, 8.
[c] Matt. vii., 7-11.

went apart occasionally to pray.[a] Some of his ejaculatory petitions in the midst of his followers are given, sometimes taking the form of addresses to God, sometimes of communings with himself.[b] In the great struggle and darkness that involved him just preceding his arrest, when he seemed to be hesitating whether to remain and confront the evil powers, trusting only to the divine assistance, or to evade the danger by escape — which seemed easy enough, and was quite in accord with the direction he had given his followers, "*When they persecute you in one city, flee to another*," and with his own previous course — he prayed most earnestly, but still not formally, uttering one simple request for deliverance or strength, and each time using the same words.[c] The intercourse of Jesus with the invisible divine spirit, which he always called his Father, seems to have been of a realistic rather than of a poetic and ideal nature; and this characteristic method of Jesus was the new cultus he gave the world.

Only great and pure souls like that of Jesus can bear this familiarity with the Infinite without compromising or abating its ideal perfection. The development of the Jewish cultus, as depicted in the Old Testament, was from a primitive contemplation of God, that presented him in human aspects, and imposed upon him low offices, up to a conception of him as transcending the comprehension of the human understanding. Canst thou by searching find out God? was the questioning of early piety. But the tendency of this habit of thought is, that it banishes from the phenomena of nature the creative and energetic agency of Spirit, and from the conscience of man the controlling sovereignty of Will. On the other hand, the fruit of the realistic idea, especially in minds deficient in reverence and poetic susceptibility, is to bring Deity to the human level, and make God the patron and promoter of personal ambitions and antipathies.

One of the evangelists seems to assert that, having given explanations of the divine beneficence and omniscience, and of the human relationship to God, Jesus had omitted any precept as to the method of prayer. The

[a] Matt. xiv., 23; Luke xi., 1.
[b] Matt. xi., 25, 27; Luke xiii., 34, 35; xix., 41-44.
[c] Luke xxii., 39-46.

disciples once said to him, reminding him of the omission, "Lord, teach us to pray, as John also taught his disciples."[a] It was only then, that Jesus dictated the brief and memorable ejaculation which has been repeated through Christendom as the Lord's Prayer. It consists of a god-speed for the kingdom of heaven, a petition for daily bread, for forgiveness in the measure of man's forgiveness, and for delivery from temptation, and the power of the evil one.

Fasting was a service of religion in much repute with the devout classes in the time of Jesus. His old master, John the Baptist, seemed to have been rigorous in the imposition of fasts upon his followers, so that the difference in the two schools of adherents to the new kingdom of heaven was remarked upon, and explanation of it demanded of Jesus himself.[b] Primarily, the joyous character of the life of Jesus with his disciples, as contrasted with the asceticism of John, must have been due to the natural tastes of the former. He had not denied even the imputation of being a wine-bibber, a familiar of publicans and loose-living people.[c] He gladly went to feasts; and countenanced by his presence entertainments given among the class of the stricter religionists upon the Sabbath day. His infrequent attendance on the temple service, if, indeed, he ever participated in it, and the satirical spirit, in which he described the precise formalism and long prayers of the Pharisees,[d] show that his direction to his disciples: When ye fast, be not of a sad countenance, that ye may appear unto men to fast, but anoint your head and wash your face,[e] sprang from a low estimate of the religious edification of fasting. It can scarcely be said that this direction, standing alone, is equivalent to saying, *When ye fast, do not fast;* but such an inference would not be wholly illegitimate, if the fact were considered that, from his example and precepts, the cessation of fasting came to distinguish his followers from other religious schools of his time. When, however, John's disciples asked the reason of such a peculiarity, he said that, while he, the bridegroom, was with them — while the King was present with his

[a] Luke xi., 1-4. [b] Matt. ix., 14. [c] Matt. xi., 19.
[d] Matt. xxiii., 14. [e] Matt. vi., 16-18.

subjects — feasting and not fasting was an appropriate demonstration.[a] Let them fast when I shall be withdrawn from them. There will be a period of separation after these festal occasions, and until I drink with you again in my Father's kingdom. His dominant idea — the expectation that more and more occupied his soul — was the explanation he himself gave of a practice, that without such explanation might have been attributed to the natural cheerfulness of his character.

In reverting to fasting again after his death, the Christian believers were, on the whole, justified by the tradition, as it stands. The bridegroom had been taken from them, and his return had been delayed. He said that during his absence they would fast. And they are still fasting and waiting.

Baptism was a religious rite, which was, in the time of Jesus, and still is, esteemed of great utility and sanctity in the external service of religion. Both Matthew and Mark impute to Jesus, manifesting himself after his death, the requirement of baptism as a test of discipleship, — a test so rigorous that it excluded from salvation the unbaptized.[b] In discussing hereafter the tradition of the resurrection, reasons will be offered why none of the conversations imputed to Jesus after his death can be treated as having any historic significance.

The probability seems to be that, as to all the external rites, whether of sacrifices, fasts, prayers, or baptisms, Jesus was somewhat indifferent. They did not comport with that stress he laid upon righteousness or good conduct — a righteousness that comprehended the underlying motive and principle as well as the overt action. The writer, called John, reports — what tradition may have preserved — the statement that, though Jesus accompanied his disciples to their baptisms of converts, he did not himself baptize. John Baptist had declared that his baptism of water was merely emblematical of Jesus' greater baptism of the Holy Ghost.[c] To such capacious minds as those of Jesus and Paul, mere ceremonies and rites of religious service were trivial and non-essential; for Paul thanked God that he had never baptized, save in the instance of two persons and a single family. God, he

---

[a] Matt. ix., 15.   [b] Matt. xxviii., 19; Mark xvi., 15, 16.   [c] Matt. iii., 11.

said, had called him to preach the gospel, not to baptize.[a]

Still, Jesus had himself submitted to the rite of baptism. Doubtless, he expressed no dissent or adverse comment on the baptisms, on which his followers were insisting; so that, after his death, his messengers and missionaries, who, with the exception of Paul, were incapable of the large generalizations and logical inferences, with which the ethical and philosophical ideas of Jesus should have been applied, found it easy to reinstate baptisms, fastings, prayers, and even sacrifices in the ritual of the Christian Church.[b] When solicited, indeed, Jesus had given his followers a brief form of prayer; but he had expressly forbidden public and social prayer, and prayers with much speaking and repetition. He had declined to appoint fasts, as incompatible with his presence among his followers; and, though submitting to baptism, that he might be blameless as to rites, he had left no place for baptism among the services he desired to be observed.

One formality, if anything so impromptu and unpremeditated as well as casual and natural, can be called a formality, it is quite evident he appointed,— the commemoration of himself, and of his death, by eating bread and drinking wine. It was evidently the suggestion of the instant. He had eaten and drunk at one of the annual festivals with his chosen apostles. He must have had other disciples and adherents — certainly many women believed on him, and their fidelity, perhaps because it was less perilous to them, outlasted that of the men at his public trial and crucifixion. Believing children, too, had followed him from Galilee. But all these women, children, and the general body of disciples, were excluded from this last festival; and each narrative asserts that only the twelve sat down with him in the upper room to celebrate this last passover.[c] Art, that has illustrated the scene in the memorable painting of Leonardo da Vinci, corroborates and perpetuates the tradition of the evangelists. After the feast, he takes the common food and drink — the universal bread and wine, then as now the diet of

---

[a] I. Cor. i., 14-17.

[b] Acts ii., 38, 41; viii., 13, 36, 38; ix., 18; x., 47, 48; xiii., 2; xxi., 33.

[c] Matt. x.; xvi., 5, 6; Luke xxiii., 49; Matt. xxi., 15; xxvi., 20-29; Mark xiv., 17-21; Luke xxii., 14.

whole races and generations of men — and asks the twelve to drink and eat once more in memory of him — the wine typical of the blood he is about to shed, the bread of the body to be bruised and broken by the hands of cruel men. He asks them to do this simple act ever afterward, till he shall come again. He evidently contemplated only a brief separation. He believed, as he had said, that the next time he drank wine with them it would be in his Father's kingdom, not many days afterward. The act was as casual and spontaneous as it could well be, not a formal religious ceremony to be held in a temple or a synagogue, and to be performed with music, prayers, and sacrifices, but an after-part, as it was an after-thought of the family meal, the gathering of intimates at a general or special festival. It is doubtful if this tradition justified the establishment of a religious ceremony that has so far outlived the expectation upon which it was founded. It is more doubtful if a request to twelve personal friends, selected out of the mass of his acknowledged disciples, to do a certain act in memory of him till his return to them justifies the whole mass of nominal Christians, uninvited, in perpetuating the act as a sacrament.

Everything, however, that was external, everything that appealed to the senses and emotions in the practices, which Jesus originated, or to which he conformed, or which without a sharp and incisive reproof he only tolerated, his followers seem to have seized upon, perpetuated, and exaggerated. So this casual and unpremeditated expression of affection between Jesus and a few confidential friends has grown into one of the most solemn, imposing, and elaborate ceremonies of our modern worship of Christ. Fitly to celebrate it requires an order of consecrated and decorated priests, and temples so costly that the wealth gathered by centuries of human toil is lavished in their construction and luxurious furniture. To be excluded from participation in it is a manifest token of rejection and damnation;[a] while a subtle and mysterious grace emanates from its decorous performance, which it is believed changes a licentious, cruel, oppressive, and deceitful man into a saint worthy the

[a] I. Cor. xi., 26-30.

society of angels and the everlasting communion of God. While thus we find little in Jesus' words or acts, that sanctions the elaborate forms of worship, which have been for centuries perpetuated in his name,— perpetuated because of conventional ideas, the growths of earlier religions, and because his example was somewhat equivocal, and his teaching not wholly consistent with itself,— it must not be overlooked, that what he did most emphatically teach and insist upon as essential was, that the divine mind is best placated by human virtue.

Prayers have always begun with ascriptions to God of all those attributes deemed by man the noblest and the best,— power, wisdom, glory, justice, mercy, and holiness. These qualities are ascribed to the Deity, not because men think God is pleased with a grossness of adulation, that would be offensive even to a man of diseased vanity. The ascription is not so much to placate God by praise, as it is to help the rude and feeble mind of man to some adequate conception of the greatness of the Being with whom he presumes to seek intercourse. He enumerates to himself the features of the dim ideal, which he strives to make present and real to his thought; and it is not till he has recited and reminded himself of the perfections and completeness of the divine nature, that his own mind is brought up to its highest powers, its clearest perceptions, its most virtuous purposes. The prescribed prayer of Jesus, brief as it is, does not omit these strenuous efforts of the soul to lift itself toward the highest possible conception of God. "Hallowed be thy name" is a self-exhortation to reverence, as are the ascriptions with which, without much speaking, the worshipper retires from the august and serious interview: "Thine is the kingdom, the power, and the glory forever."[a] But no mere reverence, however genuine; no ascriptions of honor to the divine name, however just,— will take the place of well-doing. God is more pleased when men practise virtue than when they honor him with their words or with their offerings. Not those who have said, Lord, Lord, Jesus taught, but those who have done the will of God, will I, when I come in my Father's kingdom, recognize as loyal and favored subjects.[b] On

[a] Matt. vi., 9   [b] Matt. vii., 21, 23.

a certain occasion, Jesus said those were his nearest kinsmen, who did the will of the heavenly Father.ᵃ Forgiveness of injuries, the reconciliation of offences, is of more pressing urgency than any religious service. "First be reconciled to thy brother," he said, "then come and offer thy gift."ᵇ To be meek, merciful, pure, a maker of peace, a lover of rectitude, is to be blessed of God — to be his elect ones, to whom is given the kingdom of heaven.ᶜ Men were not to take the moral law forbidding murder, theft, false witness, adultery, in a mere legal and literal sense; they were not to watch for its omissions and defects, as permissions and sanctions of appetite and evil. They were to outrun the literal sense of the requirement with the integrity of their well-doing. They were to deal with evil deeds at the very impulse and motive whence they sprang; to arrest murder in the unreasonable anger which begat it; and to anticipate adultery in the ungoverned lust that incited it.ᵈ The good-living which, he declared, the new order of the age demanded, was not the literal conformity of the conduct to an outward decency, such as satisfied the scribes and Pharisees,ᵉ but a character with which evil-thinking, evil-wishing, as well as evil-doing, were incompatible. All violence was to be disarmed by submission, all exaction by generosity, and by thus imitating God, who sent only good upon just and unjust men,ᶠ his followers were to become the children of the Highest.

In this emphasizing virtue, in placing character above mere conduct, Jesus was working in the direction of the most enlightened men of his own race; and was teaching more plainly than had the great sages of remote antiquity, and the poets and philosophers of his own times, that the upright man is he that merits the divine favor, and that, as Matthew Arnold has epitomized the lesson of the gospel, God is "*the eternal not ourselves that makes for righteousness.*" But, like all these teachers, Jesus understood that the life of virtue was no easy road. It is easier to follow the natural passions and appetites toward indulgence, excess, and oppression, than to curb and control them. A broad road accordingly leads to

ᵃ Matt. xii., 50.   ᵇ Matt. v., 24.   ᶜ Matt. v , 5, 6, 9.
ᵈ Matt. v., 22, 28.   ᵉ Matt. v., 20.   ᶠ Matt. v., 39-45.

destruction, and the thoughtless many throng it. A strait road leads to life, and few there are that find it.[a] It is this desperate chance of salvation, that makes the effort for its attainment such an invigorating stimulant to brave souls. Jesus seemed well to have comprehended that it is ever by the survival of the fittest, by contending at fearful odds against environments substantially evil, that men have attained what they have won of mental and moral superiority to the brutes. So onward toward the angelic and divine the way is still the same. The masses perish : elect souls, striving with the might of desperation, conquer a higher life.

In an earlier chapter some misgivings have been expressed at accepting in its absolute form the imputation that God imitates men in their resentments and vindictiveness. Jesus distinctly made that imputation, in language not easily misunderstood. The only comment he made upon the prayer, the form of which he prescribed, was in reference to the petition for forgiveness, made conditional upon the forgiveness of the suppliant. It was in these words : "For if ye forgive not men their trespasses, neither will your heavenly Father forgive your trespasses."[b] Jesus not only taught, that men should forgive wrongs indefinitely and absolutely, but that, in so doing, they became like God, who did the same. But he said also that God severely punished the unforgiving. He told a parable of an indebted servant, whose debt, on account of his poverty, his master had unconditionally released, but who pursued his own debtor for the last farthing with exaction and imprisonment. Then, the before mild and merciful master became angry, cancelled the gift bestowed unworthily upon a sordid man, and put him to the torture to wring from him his once-forgiven debt. "So likewise," said Jesus, most explicitly, "*shall my heavenly Father do also unto you, if ye from your hearts forgive not every one his brother their trespasses.*"[c]

The lord of the parable cast off and consigned to a place of weeping and gnashing of teeth the servants who, while watching for the return of their master, began to eat and drink and smite their fellow-servants, or who,

[a] Matt. vii., 13, 14.   [b] Matt. vi., 15, 16.   [c] Matt. xviii., 21-35.

in other words, took occasion to punish with blows their fellows who had done them injury. But the lord of the servants was the type of himself, who, coming in his kingdom, would consign to fearful punishment the revengeful and unforgiving.*

While we are compelled to approve of mercy and forgiveness, and perceive that it is better to bless than to curse, better to reward evil with good, we also see how hard it is, by a threat of punishment, to bring the heart to that gentle mood which makes such virtues possible. Against threats only obduracy and implacability rise in an undisciplined temper. A magnanimous forgiveness, an unexpected patience under affronts, breaks down resentment, and carries a germ of gentleness even into a base soul, quite likely to grow into some word or act of mercy. But no genuine love was ever begotten by the compulsion of an exaggerated and fearful punishment, threatened as the alternative of its exercise.

But while, upon the philosophic side, this view of the character of the Deity seems to jar upon the integrity and dignity of our conceptions, on the side of worship and religion it is salutary. No passion is more inveterate in human nature than revenge. For its gratification, men have submitted to all kinds of self-torture; and no lust has been sweeter to the depraved thought, than this of deferred but complete and excessive vengeance. The religion, which Jesus taught, combated this gigantic passion in a gigantic way, and by considerations, which the victims of it could easily appreciate. So uncontrollable is this passion, that, in all ages, men have boasted of it as the very measure of their manhood. Social practices, codes of statutes, systems of religion have accommodated themselves to it, as a fact of nature — something so deeply imbedded in the conditions of human life as to be restrained and regulated rather than to be obliterated.

Jesus, true to his thorough and radical treatment of evils, commanded extirpation, and left no forgiveness possible for the vengeful. As if he had said: Well, since it is nature to hate those that hate you, to render an eye for an eye, and a tooth for a tooth, act out the natural impulse; but know that God, though loving and good,

* Matt. xxiv., 49-51.

will leave you out of the sphere of his mercy in the catastrophes that await the soul, as it goes on to its destiny of weal or woe.

This lesson of mercy, just as it stands, has been a potent influence in the culture of the human race. None of the leading principles of Jesus have been on the whole so deeply impressed upon historic Christianity; and it must be confessed that none have exerted so powerful a control over the rude and savage natures, which in the Christian era one after another have come under his influence. There have been among races of men, nominally Christian, wars, invasions, massacres, cruel punishments and vengeances, both public and private; but the image and memory of Jesus have always come, first or last, to counsel forgiveness, and to hold up a minatory finger threatening the mysterious divine wrath against the heart that bars out charity from its sentiments. If there have been prayers for calamities to befall enemies, heretics, and evildoers, they have been less inspired by the words and spirit of Jesus, than by a conception of God drawn from other and older teachers — a God visiting the iniquity of the fathers upon the children of the third and fourth generation.[a]

Though Jesus had taught the intrinsic distinction between good and bad men, and had emphasized with startling precision the different estimates in which they were held by God, and the enormous disparity in the fates that awaited them respectively, he by no means exaggerated the difficulties which lay in the way of an individual passing from one condition and destiny to the other. Strive to enter into life, he said; but with striving it is possible.[b] The favor and help of God are bestowed upon evil men, when they become penitent. There is, he declared, more joy in heaven over a sinner repenting than over many just persons needing no repentance.[c] When the profligate turned his back upon his loose life, and, with a purpose of becoming a faithful servant, returned to his father, the father not only received him, but rejoiced over him, and astonished him by the warmth of his affection and the magnificence of his gifts.[d] Penitence with Jesus was, however, *much more* than confession or sentiment. To gain the divine approbation, the profligate must be-

[a] Ex. xx., 5. [b] Matt. vii., 13, 14. [c] Luke xv., 7. [d] Luke xv 11-32.

come pure, the oppressor humane, the envious man magnanimous, the rich man must give up his riches.

Human laws have not yet been able to adopt in its absoluteness the idea, that penitence, even if sincere, is to be a substitute for punishment; nor have moralists gone so far as to hold that repentance restores to the lost integrity, what has gone out in evil-doing. The reclaimed drunkard is not so noble a man, as the man whose reason and conscience had, from his first responsible acting, easy control over his appetites. There is danger, as well as falsity, in the doctrine that an experience of sin is salutary, in that it brings the sinner nearer to the affectionate heart of the Father in heaven. The law of nature seems to be, that all departure from the line of rectitude is evil in itself, and its fruits evil; and, however grateful the human or the divine forgiveness may be, the punishment belongs to the sin, and must be borne with patience as a part of it.

Here, as elsewhere, the ideas of Jesus must be accepted as of a somewhat provisional character. He had in his mind the catastrophe of a world about to perish under the retributive vengeance of its creator. It might almost be said, that, in the immediate apprehension of such a calamity, he had to a degree lost his presence of mind. A system of religion, leading and keeping pace with the cosmical movements of society, and the gradual progress of men toward a more complete and symmetrical character, would have better fitted the actual conditions of existence. The crisis, the day of judgment, so prominent in the apprehension of Jesus, has been mercifully postponed far beyond his apparent expectation. There are no indications in the heavens or in the earth that the crisis is any nearer our own age. No real good result will be attained by gathering up the wayfarers of the highways and hedges, and filling the kingdom of heaven with mere recruits, because the good things of the feast have been provided for this time, and cannot be kept. Such scouring of the byways for guests, in utter disregard of their characters, is sure to turn out ill; and not one, but many so gathered — the most of those so coerced — will be found not having the wedding garment, and fit only to be excluded from the feast. Not sudden repentance, not a momentary faith, that cries in shallow adoration, *Lord, Lord*, but doing the will of God from a good conscience — which is impossible except for natures trained in the practice of virtue, till it has become a habit and instinct of the soul — is the salvation, of whose gradual growth Jesus himself seemed to have a distinct perception, when he said: "First the blade, then the ear, after that the full corn in the ear." "An evil man out of the evil treasure of his heart bringeth forth evil things."[a]

Undoubtedly there are natures like Paul's, like Augustine's, like Loyola's, that with passionate earnestness begin and follow courses of evil, believing that they are good. Some great revulsion, a vision of the truth, arrests them; they are converted, and carry the force of will and the fiery zeal, with which they pursued pleasure or persecution into the propagandism of a holy religion; but these are exceptional cases. It is better to be a just person that needs no repentance; for, if the angels will not rejoice over such a one, they have a certain undemonstrative confidence and respect for him, which does him no less honor; while in their joy over the lost sheep they cannot repress the misgiving, that straying is apt to become a habit, and that the sheep that has been lost once may be lost again. Rectitude is to the reclaimed sinner a struggle and a warfare against all his propensity to do evil But by steadily repressing the propensity to do evil, and by doing the strange and repugnant good, the yoke of duty grows lighter, and more and more adapts itself to the spontaneous movement of the soul. Nor does the work of regeneration end with life. By the disuse of evil, man has weakened the power of evil. That which was duty in the father becomes the habit of the child. At last a trained and strengthened moral sense becomes the trait and type of a better race, that even temptations cannot seduce from a hereditary integrity. But for these cosmical changes whereby mild and moral races have been in the long epochs developed from brutal and cruel savages, there was not time in what seemed to Jesus and his immediate followers "the ends of the world."[b]

[a] Matt. xii., 35; Mark iv., 26-29.   [b] I. Cor. x., 11.

CHAPTER VIII.

IDEAS OF A FUTURE LIFE.

"Let us reject all the human interpretations of this tendency to suppose a future life. Do not try to organize it for pain or bliss. Do not fresco our ceilings with its imagined scenery; it only draws upward our eyes to discover gaudy colors on a surface of flatness. The closeness of such particulars is stifling to the soul, who prefers the impossibility of grasping one of the midnight stars, who shuns even their far-travelled hints, and plunges from their silvery coasts into wells of blackness, where not one planet roves to measure the depth of eternity. When you bring me reports from a Hereafter, I begin to lose my faith in it."—*John Weiss' Immortal Life.*

"The nobility of the Hebrew race began when it left behind the Egyptian creed of another life, and entered on the wilderness of wandering and pain, believing only in the present Deity; when it cast aside the 'Book of the Dead,' with all that solemn ritual and imagery, and the grave judgments of Osiris beyond the dark river, and, accepting instead for its sole portion the Ten Commandments, began its bleak but valiant march."—*Joseph Henry Allen.*

SPECULATIONS about the destiny of men after death, strictly speaking, belong, too, to the department of philosophy. They are closely kindred to conjectures with reference to the pre-existence of men, whether in the human, angelic, or bestial form. Religion, which in its limited sense is the cultivation of the divine powers, viewed as higher than and external to man, or of the ideals shaped by his imagination controlled and informed by his moral sense, takes no direct cognizance of the states out of which men came to their human lives, nor of the states to which they pass upon surrendering their human lives. Both states will continue fascinating fields, inviting the exercise of the speculative fancy, till our minds, capable of looking before and after, shall learn their destiny. Philosophy that has found means to bring reliable intelligence from remote stars along the beam of light, that connects them with our sight, has found means to explore backwards and forwards upon the path of human progression, noting in the growth of the individual from birth to maturity, and thence to decay and death, the rise and development of faculties, sentiments, and ideas. Data have been gathered, upon which the just and legitimate deductions are still matters of investigation and debate. Whatever opinions from these data have been reached have been fairly reached by the exercise of human faculties in their normal activity. It may not be presumptuous to believe, that, by the patient discipline and exercise of the same faculties, men may yet master the problem of their existence in its end, as well as in its origin, with a degree of confidence quite equal to that, with which they believe the accredited facts of the physical universe,— that is, upon the basis of conjectures more or less verified by observations concurrent and repeated of uniform phenomena. Hints as to the when and how of the advent of humanity to the world are being rapidly noted and collated; and the accumulating data are rapidly evolving themselves into a science, which, if not yet acceptable as absolute knowledge, has already become a competent working theory, upon which nature may be observed, and by which individual conduct may be regulated. It is an expectation justified by history, that a highly endowed genius may yet be born among men, kindred of the great souls, whose names are pronounced with reverence and worship through successive generations and by various races, who will be able to draw an outline of a scheme of the stage of being lying next beyond the mortal life, and of the mode, by which mankind in its totality or as individuals, is connected with it. A careful scrutiny of the analogies of nature and of the tendencies and directions of human progress may be able to verify and establish this hypothesis.

That nature, having produced, after tentative efforts continued through countless ages, a creature so manifestly incomplete, so unsatisfactory to himself as man, will stop, satisfied with a result so inadequate to its cost, is highly improbable. The alternative thought of those, who hesitate to accept as verified knowledge the popular theories of the immortality of the individual, very rarely has justice done it. It is bitterly denounced as hopeless, irreligious, and atheistic,— as springing from a germ of evil and itself a germ of evil in the mind. A profound study of the problem of the destiny of man, not disturbed by the hunger of mere animal instincts, may yet discover, that this alternative thought is more hopeful to all magnanimous souls, that have become capable of preferring greatest good to personal happiness, and more consonant with what we can see of the cosmic order, than a scheme, which rashly stakes the whole success of the creation and the reputation of the Creator upon the perpetuation of the one creature, who, of all sentient existences, has thus far most signally failed in achieving any worthy ends of his being.

Religion has always claimed as its own province all investigation of the problem of a future life, and has rebuked as irreverent and irreligious all purely philosophical inquiries in the direction of the after-world. It has this justification for such claim of exclusive jurisdiction. Conduct is or may be affected by the beliefs, which are entertained as to its consequences in a life to come after this. We can forecast the result of good or evil actions as they may affect our prosperity and happiness in this life, by observing the fortunes of other men, and by reading the history of people that have lived before our time. Society has been built in the interests of morality. The greatest good is attainable only by conforming to lines of conduct, that the world has agreed to call virtuous. To do with patience, and in spite of fatigue, an equivalent share of the work of the world, to control greediness, anger, and lust, to respect the property, peace, and happiness of other men, to help the sick, weak, and disabled, and to educate and cherish the affections and sentiments, through which such good actions become spontaneous — these belong to the category of duties, the doing of which the moral sense of mankind requires and approves, the omission of which it rebukes. But to men, especially to men of strong passions, and with enfeebled or degraded conscience, the sanctions of duty are largely reinforced by anticipations of rewards or punishments. They see and feel the predicaments, in which a life of fraud, violence, sensuality, and indolence involves them, and those dependent on them; and derive from the observation salutary lessons which are great helps to virtue. When these are powerless against the stormy irruption of the passions, a new safeguard is found in the anticipations of prolonged suffering for ill deeds in hell, or of lasting joys for denied indulgences in heaven. But the ideas of a life after death are so vague and unreal in the minds of common men, that to make motives brought so far at all efficacious, the horrors of hell and the delights of heaven have been in all ages depicted with an exaggerated vividness, that has tasked the most enthusiastic imagination.

It is a curious but indisputable fact, that what the Jews in the time of Jesus had come to believe in reference to a future life, they had not derived from their own scriptures, or from any communication believed to be a revelation from Jehovah. From the fact that their literature is singularly destitute of allusions to the immortality of man, and abounds in distinct affirmations that death terminates his career, it is fairly inferrible that the ideas of a resurrection, which begin to appear in the productions of the later poets and prophets, are to be accounted for by the contact of the people in the relation of subjects and captives with neighboring nations, who are known to have had distinct beliefs in immortality. It is very apparent from the memoranda we have of the conversations of Jesus that, with the exception of a small sceptical sect called Sadducees, the notions of the Jewish people in reference to a condition of existence after death were not unlike those of their immediate neighbors, the Egyptians and the Persians, and substantially similar to the views now entertained by all the civilized races of mankind.

It is a matter of debate between scholars, where the legendary traditions of the Jews leave off, and where the historic data begin; but all archæologists agree that, as a distinct people, the Hebrews came out of Egypt, where they had been held as slaves. Even if we reject as not historical the biography of Moses, the Biblical story of his expedition and preparation for the invasion of Canaan, the several distinct codes of the national and ecclesiastical law embodied in the Pentateuch, and the speeches and exhortations with which they were explained and enforced, we can gather from other data the conjecture, that the revolt from Egypt was a religious, as well as a political revolt.

It is probable that this revolt had a leader, and that

tradition has preserved his name. Egypt, in the time of the Hebrew exodus, was a civilized country, with a highly complex form of religion, of which the doctrine of a future life with rewards for virtuous living, and terrible punishments for evil deeds, was a distinctive feature. Connected with its theories of the nature of the deity or deities was a minute system of ethics, not substantially different from that believed in by modern Christendom. Though Moses in his ten commandments seems not to have departed from the ethical ideas by which the Egyptians endeavored to regulate their lives, he utterly rejected the distinctive dogma of the Egyptian cultus of a restoration of life after death, and of a heaven for the souls of good men, and a hell for evil men. In all the words and writings imputed to him, no motive is drawn from an anticipation of any life after the present life, or from any consequences to result in that life from the conduct of this. The rewards for virtue, and for obedience to the commands and the practice of the worship of the national god are all length of life, prosperity, and large possessions in the human state. Knowing now how the belief in heaven and hell had become popularized, and how it had entered into all the literature and daily thought of the two powerful races that surrounded the Hebrews — the Egyptians upon one side, and the Assyrians and Persians on the other — we can only account for the marked absence of such ideas in all the primitive literature of the Jews by the supposition that Moses — said to have been instructed in all the science of the priesthood — broke away from the doctrines of the immortality of man, with something like the repugnance of an apostate.

Prior to the Babylonian captivity, the Jews seemed to have believed the condition of the dead, great and small, was a condition of suspended animation in an underworld, not unlike the Greek Hades. In this realm of inanition there was no moral discipline. One lot befell alike the good and evil, from whose permanent condition there was no resurrection. This is the language of the Hebrew poets in the golden age of the national literature: "As the cloud is consumed and vanisheth away, so he that goeth down to the grave shall come up no more. He shall return no more to his house, neither shall his place know him any more."[a] "That which befalleth the sons of men befalleth beasts; even one thing befalleth them: as the one dieth, so dieth the other; yea, they have all one breath: so that a man hath no pre-eminence above a beast. All go unto one place: all are of the dust, and all turn to dust again."[b] "All things come alike to all: there is one event to the righteous and to the wicked; to the good and to the clean, and to the unclean; to him that sacrificeth, and to him that sacrificeth not: as is the good, so is the sinner. A living dog is better than a dead lion; for the living know that they shall die: but the dead know not anything, neither have they any more a reward; for the memory of them is forgotten. Also their love and their hatred and their envy is now perished; neither have they any more a portion forever in anything that is done under the sun."[c]

But it is doubtful if the human mind has ever fairly mastered the real conception of death. Consciousness once begun cannot know or take note of unconsciousness: it is unthinkable. Our conception of death, as of a condition entirely beyond experience, is inadequate. The nearest we ever can come to it is remembering some profound and dreamless sleep; but, if the sleep was really a suspension of all mental activity, the memory passes over the interval to the succeeding waking, and brings us no idea of the sleep. We can think of ourselves as dead, and of others regretting or missing us; but consciousness cannot attach itself to the fact of our death, but vaults over, t'.rough a force of our own imagination, to the living thought of those that survive us. Lastly, we think of ourselves as wasting away in the grave; but that, too, is a conception of our own living thought taking note of an apprehended physical condition of what was once our body. All these, it is easy to see, are ideas not of death, but of life.

So it is found that among nearly all races of men, civilized and savage, there are expectations of a life after death; the more palpable and distinct, perhaps, in uncultivated men and people, least capable by intellectual training of abstract thought. Ideas so consonant to the

[a] Job vii., 9, 10. [b] Eccl. iii., 19, 20. [c] Eccl. ix., 2, 4, 5, 6.

human mind as those of immortality and retribution Moses seemed to have succeeded in keeping out of the minds of his people by their isolation, and by exciting in them an antipathy toward a scheme of religion, which, while it had failed to make its votaries virtuous, had made them oppressors. To maintain this isolation and antipathy, he stimulated a fierce patriotism, that regarded all association with other tribes as an abomination, and all their rites and customs as impious. After the Israelites lost their national independence and became the allies, subjects, and captives of powerful races, among whom the sanctions of a future life were powerful incentives to conduct, the isolation could not be maintained; and the primitive and eccentric faith took on a popular modification, save as it was conserved among the small, intellectual sect of the Sadducees.

Accordingly, in the apocryphal scriptures, which antedated Jesus but little more than a century, we find distinct disclosures of a belief in a life after death, with fates for good and evil men according to their moral characters, and a confidence in a heaven of everlasting happiness strong enough to make men heroic and even exultant under the cruellest tortures. When Jesus came, the idea among his countrymen of the future condition of the human race in an endless heaven or an endless hell, according as they had been approved or condemned by God, seemed to be quite as fixed and definite as it is to-day. There was a small body of sceptical men, who rejected this innovation upon the teaching attributed to Moses, whose numbers and influence were less than that of the scientific materialists, who with them say to-day that there is no resurrection, neither angels nor spirits.

John the Baptist had spoken of a wrath to come, from the doom of which he declared he had not come to warn certain Pharisees and Sadducees, that thronged with others to demand baptism at his hands. He also announced that the axe of judgment was laid at the root of every tree, and that every tree, that bringeth not forth good fruit, should be hewn down and cast into the fire. The Messiah about to come, he announced, would sift men like grain, "gathering the wheat into his garner, and burning the chaff with unquenchable fire."[a] All his

[a] Matt. iii., 7, 12.

message was terrible with the proclamations of vengeance and destruction upon a portion of mankind, but whether the catastrophe was one which was a part of the general order of the divine government, or whether it was a special judgment to accompany the appearance and reign of the Messiah, whose kingdom was about to be established, can only be conjectured.

The doctrine of a resurrection of the dead and of an endless life, in which the good are blessed, and the wicked punished or destroyed, whenever taught or alluded to by Jesus, did not seem to excite any surprise among his fellow-countrymen. Everything indicates that he was speaking from ideas generally accepted and understood. The question asked, perhaps by a disciple, perhaps by a casual listener, and which he condescended to answer literally, "Are there few that be saved?"[a] evidently implied a conjecture, too intelligible to need any special explanation on the part of the narrator, that there was some calamity of a grave character impending over the race of men, quite other than the casualties of famine and sickness and death, from which calamity a saving or exemption, for at least a part, was possible. So, too, when the young ruler asked, what he should do to inherit eternal life,[b] he evidently had in his mind some good estate in the life to come, and not an exemption from death that had befallen his fathers, and would in the end befall himself.

By way of contrasting a system of beliefs, which were wholly new to the people before whom they were explained, with these teachings of Jesus entirely in accord with the popular faith, we have but to recur to the reception which Paul met in unfolding to communities of Greeks, who, as we know, had not accepted the Pharisaic doctrine of a resurrection and judgment and of an eternal retribution. To some of the Epicurean and Stoic philosophers, who listened to his daily disputations with Jews and devout persons in the market-place of Athens, he seemed a setter-forth of strange gods, because he preached of Jesus and the resurrection. When, afterward, these philosophers brought Paul to the Areopagus, and asked him to explain his system of belief, they seem to have listened in respectful silence till he came to the

[a] Luke xiii., 23.   [b] Luke xviii., 18.

assertion, that there would be a general judgment of the dead by Jesus, who had himself been raised from the dead; and then they broke out in contemptuous derision,—[a] so alien to the cultivated Greek mind was the idea of a life after death. Some time later in his career, in Jerusalem, where the teachings of the scribes and Pharisees had long given character to the popular ideas, Paul encountered a Jewish mob furiously excited by the suspicion, that he had apostatized from the customs of the fathers, and had taught the converted Gentiles to forsake Moses; and was in imminent peril of assassination. With wonderful self-possession and sagacity, the brave missionary threw himself upon the popular sympathy, and fairly turned the predominant party in the mob to his side, by suddenly crying out: "Men and brethren, I am a Pharisee, the son of a Pharisee: of the hope and resurrection of the dead I am called in question."[b] We see, too, in how different an atmosphere we stand, when, leaving the materialism of Athens, we come to Cesarea, in Palestine, and listen to Cornelius the centurion, who, though a stranger from Rome, is a devout man, who has been attracted by the simplicity, purity, and grandeur of the Jewish religion.[c] When Peter asserts the resurrection of Jesus, and that he is a witness to it, Cornelius expresses neither doubt nor surprise. In the old literature of the people whose faith he had adopted, the resurrection was no impossibility. Elijah and Enoch, perhaps Moses, had passed into an immortal state without the taint of death. It was a destiny none too exalted for such an august person as Jesus, the Christ.

Before examining the doctrines of Jesus himself concerning a future life, it is desirable to trace further in the early Christian literature the contemporary sentiments of his age and country. For it is by no means certain that all that the apostles and evangelists wrote upon this subject, they wrote upon the authority of their Master; nor could they have done so, unless he told them much more than the memorabilia of his life have preserved for us. As the doctrine of a state of retribution after death is found well developed among, not only the educated, but the general people of Judea in the time of Jesus, as the

[a] Acts xvii., 17, 18, 32.   [b] Acts xxiii., 6.   [c] Acts x., 40-48.

hints and explanations concerning the future life given by him seem to have been received without surprise, dissent, or ridicule by those who heard him,— as the same suggestions evidently were when made known to the enlightened Gentiles,— it is fairly inferrible that the writers of the New Testament, in what they give us of the doctrine of an eternal life, spake as well from the beliefs of their time as from the special teaching of Jesus.

Paul, in writing to the Romans, speaks of a "day of wrath, and revelation of the righteous judgment of God,"[a] — expressions derived rather from John the Baptist and the older prophets than from Jesus. Wicked men, he declared, were so made by God, like vessels of wrath for destruction, that he might show the glory of his mercy on vessels of mercy made for his glory.[b] Throughout his letter, though he professes unbounded reverence and worship for his master raised from the dead, and speaks of his own commission to preach the gospel, as bearing the sanction and testimony of the Holy Ghost, he carries us back to the ideas of the Hebrew scriptures, and uses illustrations and arguments relevant and convincing only to those, who shared the modes of thought derived from his own training as a Pharisee.

Writing to the Corinthian church, he declares that *"the unrighteous shall not inherit the kingdom of God,"* and makes the declaration explicit by enumerating the classes of evil-doers included in his term "unrighteous."[c] He says he keeps under the lower passions, lest he should become a castaway, or one of the lost,[d] believing, as Jesus had taught, that eternal life was the reward of intense striving. It is a Gentile and not a Jewish church; so quite naturally, even among the converts, there are some who do not readily receive the Jewish idea — rather the Oriental idea — of a resurrection; and their doubts he sets himself to combat with reasonings which will require more than casual examination. In a second letter to the same people, he unfolds his faith in these words: "We must all appear before the judgment-seat of Christ, that every one may receive the things done in his body, according to that he hath done, whether it be good or bad."[e]

[a] Romans ii., 5.   [b] Romans ix., 22, 23.   [c] I. Cor. vi., 9, 10.
[d] I. Cor. ix., 27.   [e] II. Cor. v., 10, 11.

Knowing this terror, we persuade men to believe. That there are those who will be lost he implies in a declaration that, if his gospel be hidden or unintelligible, it is so to them that are lost;[a] while he depicts the blessedness and reward of the saved in these well-known words: "Our light affliction which is but for a moment, worketh for us a more exceeding and eternal weight of glory."[b] "If our earthly house of this tabernacle were dissolved, we have a building of God, a house not made with hands, eternal in the heavens."[c]

In a letter to Philippian converts, Paul conveys the belief that inasmuch as only the happy resurrection is at all desirable, and to be anticipated otherwise than as a terror to the soul, he had labored diligently to acquire the virtue of faith in Christ, "if by any means he might attain the resurrection of the dead,"—that is, the resurrection, which was introductory to a life of blessedness.[d]

The second Epistle attributed to Peter speaks of the present physical world, including the heavens over it, as kept in store by the divine power, reserved unto fire at the day of judgment and perdition of ungodly men, and declares, that the unjust are reserved unto the day of judgment to be punished.[e]

Regarding the narrative named as John's, as an attempt to throw into the form of dramatic fiction the modified Christian dogma of the second century, it will not be pertinent to examine it for indications of the common opinions of the contemporaries of Jesus in regard to a future life. But even the novelist takes some pains to attribute to his characters only such opinions as they were believed to hold, and the literary excellence of this wholly legitimate fiction has justly earned for it the celebrity and confidence it has ever maintained in the world. Indeed, it is its literary excellence, mainly exemplified in the vividness of its descriptions, truth to life of its impersonations, and felicitousness of its conversations, that have gained for this marvellous production a regard that unfriendly criticism has not been able to destroy. So when Martha says to Jesus, who on meeting her had told her, "*Thy brother shall rise again,*" "I know

---

[a] II. Cor. iv., 3.   [b] II. Cor. iv., 17.   [c] II. Cor. v., 1.
[d] Phil. iii., 8–11.   [e] II. Pet. iii., 7.

that he shall rise again in the resurrection at the last day,"[*] it is apparent that the writer has skilfully imputed to a commonplace person — one not in the intimate confidence of Jesus, so as to reflect his thought — an opinion which was the prevalent opinion of her country and her time.

Reviewing these citations from the early Christian literature taken mostly from Paul, whose mind seems to have been singularly destitute of impressions attributable to the personal influence of Jesus — whom he had never seen — the conclusion is fairly forced upon us that the Christian dogma concerning a future life, and the distribution of its fates to good and bad men, substantially the same as it has been held throughout the Christian era, came to its maturity independently of the teaching of Jesus.

Following our inquiry, we are now ready to examine the words imputed to Jesus, setting forth his ideas of a future life, its incidents, its duration, and the permanence of its conditions. The Persians believed that there was a judicial separation made between good and evil men after death,— the former to be received into bliss, the latter to be consigned to torture. In the Egyptian scheme of the future fates of men, the day of judgment was a most prominent feature. Before the stupendous doom to heaven or to hell was pronounced, each human soul submitted to a searching inquest into its deeds, motives, and character: so that the justice of the final sentence was conspicuously exhibited before the attendant spirits of all men, and to the conscience of the person himself upon trial. When the Jews modified their own creed and against the protest of the more strict and orthodox disciples of Moses, admitted the fearful sanctions drawn from a life after death, they, too, had a judgment, and, as we have already seen, a day of judgment, which so awed their minds by its solemnity, that it came to be spoken of in literature, and doubtless in their common speech, as *that day.* Their prophet Daniel had told them of the kingdom of the world arrayed against the kingdom of the saints of the most high God, but that, after a time of glory and success permitted to them by

[*] John xi., 23, 24.

God, the judgment should sit, and the dominion should pass to the saints, who should reign forever.ᵃ

Following the popular language, Jesus, in closing his first discourse on the mount, declared: " Many will say to me in *that day*, Lord, Lord, have we not prophesied in thy name? and in thy name have cast out devils? and in thy name done many wonderful works? And then will I profess unto them, I never knew you : depart from me, ye that work iniquity." ᵇ So searching should be the inquisition into character on that day, that not only the ostensibly wicked should be in imminent peril, but even many, who had acknowledged him as master, and drawn from the association power to do wonderful works, should find their claim to be his elect publicly disavowed, when the disavowal meant their everlasting destruction.

Afterward he told his twelve disciples, whom he sent out to proclaim the near approach of the kingdom of heaven, that the cities that refused to hear that message and to receive them, should receive in the day of judgment less lenient consideration than Sodom and Gomorrah, anciently destroyed by fire for the excesses and bestiality of their licentiousness.ᶜ Indignant at the indifference of the people of two cities, Chorazin and Bethsaida neighboring to Nazareth, his birthplace, and to Capernaum his home, to the mighty works he had done in their sight, he declared, that it should be in the day of judgment more tolerable for Tyre and Sidon — wicked cities of the heathen, which had perished, as it was believed, for their sins — than for them. And his own Capernaum, exalted to heaven in the privilege of being his home, should in the day of judgment fare worse for its contempt of him than Sodom itself.ᵈ

In explanation of the parable of the tares and the wheat, to his questioning disciples he announced, that, at the end of the world, "the Son of Man shall send forth his angels and they shall gather out of his kingdom all things that offend, and them which do iniquity; and shall cast them into a furnace of fire : there shall be wailing and gnashing of teeth. Then shall the righteous shine forth as the sun, in the kingdom of their Father."ᵉ The same segrega-

ᵃ Dan. vii., 25-27.   ᵇ Matt. vii., 22, 23.   ᶜ Matt. x., 15.
ᵈ Matt. xi., 22, 24.   ᵉ Matt. xiii., 40-43, 49, 50.

tion of the wicked and their destruction was typified by his parable of the good and bad fish as explained by himself. On another occasion, when announcing that the Son of Man would come in his kingdom before the death of some that heard him, he said, "The Son of Man shall come in the glory of his Father and with his angels; and then he shall reward every man according to his works."[a]

Answering his disciples, who had asked him for the signs of his coming, and of the end of the world, he explained, that he would "send his angels, with a great sound of a trumpet; and they shall gather together his elect from the four winds, from one end of heaven to the other."[b] It was doubtless these remembered words of the master that fixed in the minds of the disciples an incident of the judgment, of which they felt a strong assurance. Paul, depicting with glowing fancy the details of the general resurrection, seems to be treading on firmer ground, when he insists in emphatic parenthesis: "*For the trumpet shall sound.*"[c] He assures the Thessalonians also that the unmistakable signal of the great crisis will be "*the trump of God.*"[d] Further on in the same discourse, Jesus gives a graphic picture of the great judgment itself, himself sitting by the divine appointment upon a glorious throne, with an attendant multitude of holy angels, and all the nations of mankind gathered before him for judgment and separation. He even gives their treatment of himself and of his disciples and adherents as the test which is to be applied in that stupendous proceeding to determine the ultimate condition of all souls.[e]

It is a habit of modern thought to speak of the condition of the dead as one of happiness and blessedness, at least of rest. From this cheerful expectation, only a few criminals and wicked men, dying suddenly in the very flagrancy of their sin, are excepted; and even these, when they have expressed some contrition for their evil lives, or have been moved by the fear of death to some words or feelings of devotion, are let into the good condition, in which the general dead are contemplated. Jesus does

---

[a] Matt. xvi., 27. [b] Matt. xxiv., 31. [c] I. Cor. xv., 52.
[d] I. Thess. iv., 16. [e] Matt. xxv., 31–46.

not seem to have shared this feeling, or to have uttered a word upon which such vague hopes for the well-being of the ordinary dead can be based. He plainly taught that salvation was discriminate, and by no means universal. Not all the invited would be received as guests at the banquet of everlasting life. Many were called : few were chosen.ᵃ In sending calamities upon the world, particularly those calamities that precede and forebode the end of the world, he declared God had no consideration for the sufferings and terrors of mankind in general. But for the sake of his chosen ones he would destroy all flesh; and only for his elect's sake, who to some extent must share the terrors of the rejected ones, would he shorten the period of distress. The Son of Man, coming as judge, avenger, and ruler, would send his messengers throughout the world to gather together his elect; for only an angelic intelligence can detect those delicate shades of character, which mark the favor that had chosen certain men for salvation.ᵇ To the common observation, these two men working together in the field, those two women grinding together in the mill, are alike.ᶜ The judgment of the world has made no distinction between them. But God has chosen one man and one woman to the honor of an eternal life, and left the other man and the other woman to shame and everlasting contempt. What availed the afterthought of the foolish virgins? They were never reckoned among the wedding guests. The lord of the feast said unto them at last, "*I do not know you.*"ᵈ The distinctions between all nations of men of elect and non-elect, he declared, were as palpable to the divine eye, as was the shepherd's perception that he had both sheep and goats in his flock; and he could place the bad upon his left hand as easily as the shepherd could separate the sheep from the goats.ᵉ He told his hearers not to commiserate the fate of certain Galileans, whom Herod had murdered in the midst of their worship, or those others who had been killed by the fall of a tower, for without repentance they would perish, referring of course not to a death by a like casualty — which was most improbable — but to the perishing of all the unrepentant in the after-world.ᶠ

ᵃ Matt. xx., 16; xxii., 14.   ᵇ Matt. xxiv., 22, 30, 31.   ᶜ Matt. xxiv., 40, 41.
ᵈ Matt. xxv., 1-13.   ᵉ Matt. xxv., 32.   ᶠ Luke xiii., 3, 5.

All literal exposition of his serious thought, as well as the figurative and poetic imagery, in which he sought to illustrate and convey it, depict the fate of ordinary men as baleful; and the rescue of any as a favor conferred by his procurement upon those whom he chose, either on account of their intrinsic excellence, or on account of their penitence, or on account of their faith in him. If this law of discrimination is found uncertain, it is an uncertainty due to the varying character of his own utterances. This much, however, is obvious. The exemption from the calamities that impended over mankind was not indiscriminate, nor was it to be exercised toward the mass of men.

He charged his followers to wait for his coming again in the terrific glories of his everlasting kingdom, abstaining from drunkenness and sensuality, and from absorption in the cares of business; "for as a snare shall [the day] come on all them that dwell on the face of the whole earth."[a] His coming, though with power and great glory, was to be an event at which all the tribes of the earth should mourn. His disciples once asked him — evidently prompted to the question by the sombre tenor of his own speculations upon the future life — "Are there few that be saved?"[b] and he said: "Strive to enter in at the strait gate; for many will seek to enter in, and shall not be able." He also declared that the road to destruction was broad, and many walked in it. Few found the narrow road leading to life;[c] and these few were sharply interrogated at the gate, and some, who supposed themselves disciples and even did mighty works in the name of Jesus — some of the very train of friends who watched all night for the bridegroom's coming — were either publicly repudiated as workers of iniquity,[d] or, coming too late, and after the master of the house had impatiently risen, and shut the door, were driven away, because their repentance had come too late.[e]

Seeking to know what was the idea of Jesus as to the condition of the non-elect dead, in what their misery consisted, and what was its duration, we must try to gather the implications of these words of his: "It is better for

[a] Luke xxi., 34, 35.   [b] Luke xiii., 23-25.   [c] Matt. vii., 13, 14.
[d] Matt. vii., 21-23.   [e] Matt. xxv., 10; Luke xiii., 25.

thee to enter into life halt or maimed, rather than having two hands, or two feet, to be cast into everlasting fire."[a] "His Lord was wroth, and delivered him — the unforgiving debtor — to the tormentors, till he should pay all that was due unto him. So likewise shall my heavenly Father do unto you, if ye from your hearts forgive not every one his brother his trespasses."[b] "He will miserably destroy those wicked men, and will let out his vineyard unto other husbandmen."[c] "On whomsoever it — the rejected stone, himself — shall fall, it will grind him to powder."[d] "Bind hand and foot — the unwelcome guest at the marriage feast — and cast him into outer darkness; there shall be weeping and gnashing of teeth."[e] "Ye serpents, ye generation of vipers — addressed to the scribes and Pharisees at Jerusalem — how can ye escape the damnation of hell?"[f]

Most of these images are images of destruction and death. The rejected of Jesus are spoken of as the lost in distinction from the saved. The evidently literal and solemn sentence, that concludes the grand assize of the judgment as depicted by Jesus, "These shall go away into everlasting punishment, but the righteous into life eternal,"[g] does not necessarily imply the conscious existence of the punished. The contrasted condition of life everlasting is an ever continuous death,—a death from which there shall be no resuscitation or resurrection. Even the figure of fire, by which the horror of hell is so often set forth, brings to our apprehension an element of destruction. The duration is affirmed of the fire: it burns perpetually; it is not quenched; it is not cooled; it is not removed; but it destroys effectually and forever what is cast into it. In one conversation, it is plainly implied that only the good, the elected, experience resurrection, the rest of the human race being consumed, as to whatever there is of their physical and spiritual identity, in the conflagration of the world; and that is the conversation held with the Sadducees, as to the manner of the resurrection. "They *which shall be accounted worthy* to obtain that world, and the resurrection from the dead,

[a] Matt. xviii., 8, 9.   [b] Matt. xviii., 34, 35.   [c] Matt. xxi., 41.
[d] Matt. xxi., 44.   [e] Matt. xxii., 13.   [f] Matt. xxiii., 33.
[g] Matt. xxv., 46.

neither marry nor are given in marriage."[a] But other figures less frequent bring before us a picture of conscious and continuous suffering. Six different times, in speaking of the doom of rejected men at the judgment, Jesus added this delineation of the horror of their condition: "There shall be weeping and gnashing of teeth,"[b] — a fearful image of vain sorrow and impotent rage.

It is not surprising that the prevalent conception of a hell of conscious and acute and perpetual suffering finds sanction and authority in language as vigorous and terrible as this. And such has been the conception of Christendom with scarce a protest or dissent for nearly nineteen centuries. Hell has been modified and alleviated in our own age, not by the spirit of historic Christianity, not by the teachings of the primitive disciples, or what the world has preserved of the teachings of their master, but by the spirit of modern civilization. That enlarged humanity, which takes heed of the woes, wants, and sufferings of men, of the enslaved, the overworked, the oppressed, the sick, the insane, and the bereft of the faculties of sense, has carried forward its benevolent feeling to the conditions of a future life, and insisted that the inexorable and dreadful fate of the masses of mankind shall be made more tolerable to a rational contemplation of the providence of God. To be entirely true to the influence of Jesus, let it rather be said that the intolerable hell of the Christian creed, which is also the hell of the thought of Jesus and of his age, has succumbed, so far as it has succumbed, to a spirit born of the early teachings of Jesus, his sublime doctrine of the fatherhood of God, and of the perfection of his love, which flows forth to the unkind and unthankful, the evil as well as the good, before he had himself retracted these utterances under the disturbing and ambitious presentiment of his destiny to be the Son of Man, that was to come in the clouds of heaven, to receive dominion, glory, and the kingdom over all people, nations, and languages.[c]

There are two sources of the surmises and speculations, which the reflecting portion of mankind have entertained concerning the prolongation of the individual life after

[a] Luke xx., 35.   [b] Matt. viii., 12; xiii., 42, 50; xxi., 13; xxiv., 51; xxv., 30.
[c] Dan. vii., 13, 14.

death,— tradition and imagination. We have taken what other men have believed concerning an existence beyond the grave, and believed it upon their credit; and we have enlarged and developed these ideas by the powers of our own imagination. It is not certain that these traditions have any other basis than the imagination of some highly impressible person or persons, in whose minds the conception first took form, and who were so overawed and impressed by it, that they accepted it as an intuition or revelation, and so proclaimed it as a truth of the deepest significance and importance. It is not certain that such impressions may not have proceeded in some inexplicable way from a divine, angelic or superhuman communication. There has ever been a tendency in the mind of man to impute to inspiration his best and most spontaneous thoughts, those flashes of cognition, those feats of artistic performance, into which he has put the least conscious effort. The philosopher, upon whom falls some instantaneous solution of a law or process of nature, the moralist, who has embodied in a maxim of universal validity a law of conduct, the poet, who in the frenzy of an intellectual passion has expressed in musical and eloquent language a great thought, and the painter or sculptor, upon whose brain an image of ideal beauty is suddenly projected — in the modesty of nature, in the mystery which hides the methods of our highest mental activities, in that exaggerated, maternal admiration for intellectual progeny, which accompanies birth, have ever been ready to impute the origin of a work so surpassing the scale of ordinary achievement to something above themselves. It is the muse, they say; it is the dæmon; it is an angel or a God speaking.

But such is not the necessary solution of the origin of the traditions of a future life. We are not only capable of conceiving of a continuance of our consciousness after death, but it is the obvious, natural, and necessary conception. Indeed, as has been before stated, it is impossible for a living mind to master the idea of a cessation of consciousness, that being a condition of which it has not and cannot have any experience. Hence, it follows that the belief in continuous existence has been nearly universal among mankind; and was quite as vivid and definite among people, whose lives antedated the whole epoch of what is called divine revelation, as it is among the most Christianized nations of the present age. All pictures of states of reward and punishment, which are preserved in the books and traditions of the great religions of the world, betray their human origin, in that they are conditions of human experience projected on the dark wall that separates the dead from the living. The feasts, the harps, the singing, the society, the worship, the rest, the ecstasy of heaven, are all images of the dearest and purest joys we have known in our experience, or observed or imagined in the experience of more favored men. The fires, the tortures, the mourning, and grinding of teeth, are projections of the miserable experiences of a world, whose manifold sufferings have never been able to make it less sensitive to suffering. To a certain extent, we can indulge our imaginations in the hopes and fears, which those anticipations beget. We can give such details to these surmises as our experiences can furnish us with, and we strive in vain to press beyond these limits. Why should we believe that our fathers, our ancestors, the men of earlier ages, could do any more? All that we have received from them is very like what we may conjecture upon the same data.

What we know of astronomy, of chemistry, of physiology, we have learned by studying phenomena, and by accepting the results of the studies and experiments of men, in whose judgments and good faith we have confidence. What we think we know of a future life, do we know on any other authority? Nay, is not this science in a more primitive and incomplete stage — the same stage as when, during the Middle Ages, our fathers were groping blindly in the departments of medicine and astrology among theories that had no basis but tradition or assumption? They had neither the trained faculty nor the logical method correctly to note the operations of nature, nor to comprehend its laws. Those pseudo-sciences had even this advantage,— that their principles could be confirmed by plausible experiments. The sick sometimes got well in spite of irrational therapeutics; and now and then the fortunes of men conformed to their vague, astrologic forecasting. No instance, however, has been given, in which the momentous revelations relating to a life after death have been attested to by any intelligence, that has returned hither from that country, to which such a concourse have migrated. Our situation is not unlike that of the people of the Eastern hemisphere in reference to America, before its discovery by Europeans. There were oracular and poetic revelations of an Atlantis; and philosophy was beginning to speculate that the globe must be balanced by a continent upon its dark side; but no voyager had returned from it, and nothing known to be its product, whether of living man or animal or the works of either, of shrub or tree or fruit, had come across the ocean to confirm its existence. So, now, philosophy may say: to round out our human life, to balance the unjust and unequal conditions of human existence, there must be a life beyond — a world of retribution, compensation, and completion. The universal instinct of the soul of man cannot be mistaken or denied, that has in all ages refused to believe that death is the end, and that the earthly discipline of suffering, by which the race has been raised from bestiality to intelligence and a capacity for disinterested benevolence, could have been expended upon a result so trivial as the transient life of men.

From a careful perusal of the authentic words of Jesus, it is not fairly to be inferred that he approached the problem of a life after death in any other method than in the human and philosophical method. But when the Christian thinkers of the first centuries adopted the theory, that the resurrection was a new process in the divine economy, a new law of nature introduced by Jesus himself, a consummation, in the divine order, that had awaited his coming and his conquest of death — which, till his time, had ruled over the race of men from the beginning[a] — it was natural that they should seek to support it by his own declarations. Paul first gave striking expression to this theory in his well-known words, in which he speaks of Jesus, as of him "who has abolished death, and brought life and immortality to light." The world had a right to require of a being sent from God with such a commission, that he should speak from his own knowledge of the stupendous concerns of the heavenly state, whence he had been sent.

[a] Romans v., 12-21.

The Fourth Gospel, evidently the product of a time not only after the Pauline conception had been published, but after the considerably later time, when it had become incorporated into the faith of the Church, fairly met this requirement, and may well have been written to meet it. The Johannic Jesus speaks familiarly of his own previous existence as an immortal and divine being, of the heavenly state, which he left to take upon himself a mortal, human nature, of his fellowship with God, and of the relations of rank, dependence, and affection, which subsisted between them. He flashes upon us glimpses of the condition of the happy dead.

The Jesus of John tells his disciples, that they should see heaven opened, and angels of God descending upon himself and returning from him to heaven.[a] He says he was sent into the world from God, his Father, to save those who should believe on him.[b] He assures the Pharisees that he had lived before Abraham, the venerable ancestor of their race.[c] Everywhere throughout the Fourth Gospel, Jesus speaks in perfect harmony with this claim to have been the companion and equal of God, of whose existence there had been no beginning. All that he tells of God, all of the unknown past or the unknown future of man, he tells as a revelation from the sphere of a complete and divine intelligence. All that he confides of the conditions of the eternal life he communicates at first-hand, and from a personal experience. He tells Nicodemus directly, that he spoke what he knew, and testified what he had seen. "Why," he asked him, "shall I tell you, as I might, of heavenly things, when you are incredulous of the earthly things I have told you?"[d] And this knowledge, from which he spoke, was exclusive and peculiar; "for no man," he added, "hath ascended up to heaven, but he that came down from heaven, even the Son of Man, which is in heaven." He said at another time that such was the love of God toward himself, that all the divine counsels were shared with him, and in order that all men might honor the Son, the Father had deferred to him the authority of being the judge of mankind.[e] When Martha spoke to him at the grave of Lazarus of

[a] John i., 51. [b] John iii., 16, 17. [c] John viii., 58.
[d] John iii., 11-13. [e] John v., 20-23.

the hope which she, as a pious Pharisee, had, that her brother would rise at the resurrection of the last day, Jesus interrupts her with impressive warmth: "The resurrection! I am the resurrection: he that believeth in me, though he were dead, yet shall he live; and whosoever liveth and believeth in me shall never die!"[a] He had told the Jews on another occasion, that, "if a man keep my saying, he shall never see death."[b] As he had spoken of his birth as his coming from God, so he spoke of his death as going back to him; and in a conversation memorable for its pathos, and dear to the human heart for the hopes it has fed, he gives this picture of the heavenly state to which on leaving the world he expected to return: "In my Father's house are many mansions: if it were not so, I would have told you. I go to prepare a place for you."[c]

Although he sometimes betrays the inventive character of his work, through faults of style and exhibitions of a moral culture, far below the grade of Jesus, the author carries out with admirable completeness his dramatic purpose. Jesus, though he sometimes demeans himself in his methods of expression, is always true to the rôle assigned to him of a divine pre-existent and immortal being; and, when he is made to speak of the conditions of a heavenly existence, he speaks as a revelator rather than a reasoner. He does not grope his way, as men do, in the darkness of an impenetrable mystery. He narrates with the confidence of knowledge, and testifies with the positive assurance of an eye-witness. He is Columbus, after his return from his first voyage, telling with details too natural and minute to be fancied the sights he has seen, and confirming everything by the testimony of his companions, and by specimens of men and things brought back from new discovered lands; whereas every other revelation of the unseen world is Columbus before his voyage, with his traditions of early navigators, his theories of a compensating continent and a round and bounded earth, over which all but the enthusiastic shake their heads.

Now, it is just this character of positiveness, this directness of communication as of an eye-witness, that

[a] John xi., 24-26. [b] John viii., 51. [c] John xiv., 2.

the disclosures of Jesus in the more reliable biographies lack. There is a vivid picture of the great judgment, there is a perpetual allusion to a great separation and segregation of mankind into two classes, sometimes of righteous and wicked, sometimes as elect and non-elect, sometimes as believers and unbelievers — with the category of the former generously enlarged, so as to include those who had sincerely, and out of consideration for himself, done even trifling services to his followers, or only not opposed them — to which classes widely different fates are assigned. But there are no details of the joys and glories of heaven, and only brief, striking, and terrifying epithets to indicate the horrors of hell. If Jesus knew at first-hand, and from a pre-existent experience, of which the scenes of an invisible world were familiar data, a wise reticence might have restrained his disclosures. On any other consideration, we are left to the conclusion, that some men who had preceded him, and many who have followed him, have taken far higher flights into the sublime regions of devout fancy than Jesus was capable of, or than he allowed himself to indulge in. This is by no means to be said in disparagement of his genius or his wisdom. The Egyptian and Persian day of judgment, with its searching inquisition into character and into the very springs of voluntary conduct, impressed the people, who lived in hourly anticipation of it, more powerfully than the meagre glimpses of the same stupendous procedure furnished in the words of Jesus impressed the minds of his auditors. It is Paul, who, modifying and reapplying the words of an ancient prophecy, has given for the consolation of Christendom those fascinating revelations, so full of a soothing hope in what they declare as in what they withhold: "Eye hath not seen, nor ear heard, neither have entered into the heart of man, the things which God hath prepared for them that love him."[a] It is the inspired imagination of Paul, that bequeaths this picture, like an heirloom of faith, to the world: "For we know that if our earthly house of this tabernacle were dissolved, we have a building of God, a house not made with hands, eternal in the heavens."[b] Indeed, when now we stand, as mankind have always stood, dismayed and

[a] I. Cor. ii., 9. [b] II. Cor. v., i.

appalled at that chasm of death into which has just fallen some fellow-creature — it may be linked to us by ties which it is a long agony to sunder — and beat our aching hearts against the impenetrable wall, that separates him from our ken, it is to Paul rather than to Jesus that we resort for consolation. We read at the open grave Paul's argument for immortality. He, too, claimed no special revelation or knowledge. Like Plato, like Cicero, he reasons out the problem of a life after death upon such data as his mind was furnished with. He confesses himself, he has staked the whole question upon the physical resurrection of the body of Jesus after his crucifixion and burial, an incident which even a part of the twelve apostles at the time doubted to have happened, and which philosophy can only accept as something outside of the order of nature. Corollary to this confidence is the analogy derived from the generation of plants from buried seeds, in which the fervid advocate fails to observe intelligently, when he declares with warmth that no seed can germinate till it die, whereas it is well known, to even unscientific persons, that no seed, that has parted with its life, can germinate.*

But, whatever the analogy of vegetable reproduction may imply or require, it is all fulfilled in the generation of living progeny, not from dead but from living parents, by processes of reproduction which the laws of botany and physiology, wholly unknown in the age of Paul, have indicated to be substantially alike in vegetables and animals. We do not stop to examine Paul's philosophy of a resurrection, but to indicate that, with his creative fancy, Paul allowed himself to dally boldly with the theories of a future life, made present daily to his anticipation by a perilous mission which exposed him to daily death. The Christian imagination has certainly imposed no restraint upon itself in that direction, since, from Paul's time to the present the elaboration of the scenes of the final judgment, pictures of the employments, delights, and associations of the happy dead, and details of the sufferings and the wretchedness of the lost, have been themes to invite the supreme effort of the genius of the poet, and which the preacher and moralist have chiefly

* I. Cor. xv., 35-44.

relied upon as the terror of the Lord, to win men to repentance and piety. Indeed so productive have been the intellectual labors of mankind through the Christian centuries in this dread but fascinating field of inquiry, that the heaven and the hell of the popular faith with their furniture and incidents are not derived so much from the scriptures of religions, as from the conceptions of Dante, Milton, and Robert Pollok — an English poet whose reputation is confined to a strictly theological public.

Now, going back to our annals of Jesus, we find him repeating the traditions of his forefathers; and we can reasonably infer whence they were derived, without enriching or enlarging them with a single product of his own creative faculty. In Luke, he is represented as holding a colloquy with the Sadducees, who thought that a woman several times married to brothers of each other who had died would be embarrassed by a relation, the nature of which was exclusive, if all the husbands should at once assert their marital claims. The answer of Jesus was ready, if not quite complete. "There is no marrying nor giving in marriage in heaven," he said. But this did not quite meet the point. It was not a relation that was to be, but one that had been. Undoubtedly, Jesus meant to say, not only is there no marrying in heaven, but no recognition of any marriage, that had been on earth. The relation was earthly, and belonged to the necessities of an earthly order. In the resurrection, all will be as the angels. Husbands will not be the husbands of their wives, nor children of their fathers, nor fathers of their children — for all this is implied in the denial of the fundamental relation of human life — and individuals will hold relations to each other of affection, of service, of precedence, not based upon priority of birth or participation in parentage, but upon the laws of that life, as those other relations are built upon the laws of the human life.[a]

So far, the answer was complete — an extinguishment of the Sadducees, and a philosophical statement that will stand the criticism of all sceptics, that may come after them. But he went on to add that even Moses showed that the dead are raised, when he called God the God of Abraham, Isaac, and Jacob: *for God is not a God of the*

[a] Luke xx., 27, 38.

dead, but of the living: for all live unto him. It is not easy to see how God is not the God, as well of the dead, as of the living, since all are in his power; and since another scripture has declared: *If I make my bed in the grave,* God is even there. Nor would the declaration to Moses in any ingenuous mind imply anything but that God, who had in their lifetime befriended and blessed Abraham, Isaac, and Jacob for their faith would befriend and bless Moses for his trust in him. So far from implying that the patriarchs were still alive, its impressiveness would largely spring from the fact that they were dead, that their record was complete, and that no after calamity could change their happy human lot. But what is remarkable about the argument is that, just as Paul was laboriously working out the solution of his great hope, by observing the analogies of vegetable reproduction, and by assuring himself that the crucified Jesus had been seen alive by five hundred disciples, many of them then living, and by himself on his way to Damascus, so Jesus was laboring to find in a scripture, not obviously implying such a thing, and in a declaration to the first prophet of his people — who certainly made no such inference from it himself — the ground of faith in what he had no first knowledge of, and nothing but his hopes and reliance upon tradition to support. It may be said the argument, subtle as it was, was apposite to the scepticism of his questioners, who only had faith in Moses, and to whom the words of Moses were divine oracles. This is doubtless true, and would be a complete answer to the objection, if Jesus had anywhere else, in teaching the doctrine of a resurrection, unfolded any positive grounds of a knowledge of a life after death. Besides, from men whose genius and insight place them in the order of Socrates, Pythagoras, Confucius, and Zoroaster, we have a right to expect something more comprehensive than an answer which is a mere argument to the man and to the verbal form of the question,— an answer good for all time, and that shall be valid from every point of view. To avoid being entangled in a sophistical dilemma shows resources of wit; to discover a great truth in the data of nature shows resources of wisdom.

Finally, the investigation leads back to the dominant

idea of Jesus of an end of the world, a separation of the saved and the lost, a reign of himself as Messiah over the former, and the destruction or perpetual punishment of the latter. Of the day of judgment, of heaven and hell, Jesus thought and taught less than is taught in several of the older religions, less than his apostles and the poets and preachers of the Christian Church. He took up the prevalent beliefs upon these subjects, and modified them by his own grand idea of the impending kingdom of heaven. The end of the world will be presently: the resurrection I shall myself first achieve, and bring back with me to life those thought worthy. The judgment implies the judge, which I, the Son of Man, am; and heaven is the kingdom of my Father, in which I shall sit down with all whom I have chosen in an endless life. Jesus gave definiteness and date to what men had hoped or dreaded of a future life, and the words he uttered with emphasis and staked his whole veracity upon were these, which each evangelist repeats: "*Verily, I say unto you, This generation shall not pass away till all these things be fulfilled. Heaven and earth shall pass away, but my words shall not pass away.*"

CHAPTER IX.

LEGEND OF THE MIRACLES.

"In truth, the world has become mistrustful, and does not believe things till it has seen them."—*Pascal.*

"At the stage of experience where men are now arrived, it is evident, to whoever looks at things fairly, that the miraculous data of the Bible have not the unique character of trustworthiness; that they, like other such data, proceed from a medium of imperfect observation and boundless credulity."—*Matthew Arnold.*

HITHERTO, the only difficulty that has beset this investigation of the historic data concerning Jesus has been the uncertainty of knowledge, springing out of the contradictory declarations that seem to be imputed to him by the most trustworthy of his biographers, leaving to us the alternative of questioning the accuracy of the reports, or of believing that he was either careless to maintain opinions in harmony with each other, or that in some crisis of his life he changed his views and modified his teachings accordingly. But a very large part of the narratives named of Matthew, Mark, and Luke, are taken up with transactions, which, though they evidently impressed the writers as most important, are entirely outside of the probabilities that avouch ordinary events. In a sincere quest for truth, no one is bound to believe these transactions upon anything less than the strong, cumulative, and accordant testimony of intelligent and credible persons. The miracles come under this category.

What is here said upon a theme so much discussed needs no statement or even implication of a theory. Whether the laws of nature are mathematically and invariably uniform, whether a divine agency by which the visible world exists and is controlled may or may not inject into nature other methods of activity than those which mankind have concurrently observed, need not be even considered. All that need be assumed is that men have not hitherto been able to walk upon the sea; to multiply five loaves of bread and two small fishes, so that they shall feed to repletion five thousand men with an uneaten surplus far exceeding the original supply ; nor to instantly restore to health and wholeness by a word a maimed or diseased person, whose infirmity was due to other cause than some hysterical or nervous defect in the apparatus connecting volition and action ; nor by similar means to bring back to life a man, who, having been some hours dead, was being borne to his burial; nor to do several other wonderful things that Jesus is related to have done habitually and without apparent effort. If Jesus did such acts, it is proper to require that the fact be attested by the serious, if not sworn, testimony of intelligent persons of integrity, given with all the solemnity and sense of responsibility of judicial proceedings. The different statements of those persons should substantially agree, differing only in those details and circumstances, about which it is always impossible for even careful and conscientious witnesses to agree.

It is not intended to approach in any flippant or irreverent spirit the inquiry into these claims for the founder of the Christian religion to have been gifted with superhuman powers. Indeed, the propriety must be obvious to every one of treating with respect and consideration what a great majority of the best and most cultivated minds have believed and still believe.

It has been already explained why we are compelled to accept Jesus as a veritable person of history ; and the purpose of this writing is to work out, feature by feature, the details of his character and his actions, with a view of justly estimating his weight and worth. Thus far, the task has proceeded by considering the progress of history as generally uniform and natural, by regarding the men of the first century as men of like passions and like infirmities with ourselves, and by applying purely human judgments to declarations and conduct not presumably outside the influence of human motives. The result has been the dim outlines at least of a remarkable, highly endowed, and heroic soul, self-confident, self-sustained, mainly consistent with his own ideal, and pressing forward to death amid opposition and danger in the achievement of a high destiny, which he believed appointed for him, but at the same time a human soul sensitive to reproach, eager for appreciation, and saddened by the limitations with which human nature on every hand confronted his inspirations.

In the same spirit, and by the same method, let this assertion of the power to work miracles be examined. What do the most reliable documents say, what do they omit to say? How do their statements harmonize with each other? The earliest and most authentic Christian documents are conceded by scholars to be the epistles of Paul. Paul is a witness of eminent credibility and respect among his compeers. Born in Tarsus in Cilicia, while it was a province of Rome, and by that birth entitled to the consideration and privileges of a Roman citizen, he was in nationality and religion a Hebrew of the Hebrews, and betook himself to Jerusalem, the sacred city of his race, to be brought up there at the feet of one of its most celebrated *Rabbis* in the strictest principles of Pharisaism. He bore the name of the first king of his nation, in the early period of its independence and glory, selected from his own tribe of Benjamin. But he was compromising and politic enough to change his name to a familiar and distinguished Roman protonym, or else, when the change had been made by his acquaintance, readily to adopt it. He was the first considerable convert the new faith had made among the class of cultivated men of the world; and to his conversion it seems fairly due, that Christianity did not survive save as a secondary Jewish schism. When Stephen, the first martyr, was stoned to death for preaching the faith of Jesus in Jerusalem, Paul, who was an active leader in the violence, was called a young man, but as he styles himself in his letter to Philemon, believed to be written in the sixty-fourth year of the era, "Paul the aged,"[a] he would hardly have been so known and designated, if he had been younger than that era. This would make him thirty-four or thirty-five, when he assisted in the execution of Stephen, and not younger than Jesus himself. Here, then, is a witness in the best position to give testimony concerning the career of Jesus, if Jerusalem was its theatre; an enthusiastic, eloquent, but carefully educated scholar, who has learned something of logic, and understands the force of an argument;

[a] Phil. 9.

who is as nearly impartial as he can be, in that he was a fierce partisan in succession of the Jewish and of the Christian faiths, while at the same time he was thoroughly imbued with such ideas, as might have been derived from Roman citizenship, travel, and the study of pagan poetry and philosophy.

If Jesus came to Jerusalem for the first time a few days before his arrest, trial, and execution, as the narratives of Matthew, Mark, and Luke plainly imply, the brief excitement, which attended those events, might all have occurred while Paul was absent in his native province of Cilicia or upon some of the extensive journeys, by which he had familiarized himself with the civilized ancient world. The cosmopolitan spirit manifested in his writings, and the comprehensive manner in which he set about propagating, over wide regions extending from Arabia to Spain, if not to Britain, the faith he had formerly persecuted, show that he had learned the world, not only from books, but from actual contact with its different races and religions. If Paul had been then living at Jerusalem, the same fanaticism, of which he makes confession, would have attracted him to the judgment hall of Pilate and have made his voice the loudest among those, who clamored that Barabbas, the robber, should be released and Jesus be crucified. If the apostle had on his conscience the guilt of having been one of the murderers of the man, for whom he came afterward to cherish such an exalted opinion as his master and savior, that sensitiveness, which made him recur so often to his persecution of the disciples, could not have been suppressed in his correspondence. It is therefore to be believed, that Paul was not in Jerusalem at the time of the crucifixion; and it is probable — that being the only period when their two lives could have touched each other — that he never saw Jesus in his lifetime.

The early Christian records are quite full of a controversy, which arose in the early Church over Paul's pretension to be an apostle. The evangelical party seemed to have insisted, that among disciples only twelve were raised to the rank of apostleship. Only these twelve were admitted to the confidences of the last supper.[*] The

---

[*] Matt. xxvi, 20.

number must be kept full, but must not be enlarged. So when Judas fell off into apostasy and suicide, the eleven survivors met to fill the vacancy with solemn prayer and deference to the intimations of the Holy Ghost. But they are not at liberty to choose at random. The apostles were the witnesses of the resurrection of Jesus, and the selection must be made from among those, who were his companions from the time of the baptism of John till the ascension,— a requirement which would most effectually have made Paul ineligible.[a] Now then, when Paul with some warmth sets forth his claim to apostleship, based upon an oral commission from Jesus himself, if he had been able to substantiate it by adding, that he too was a witness at least of the death and resurrection of Jesus, which events happened at his home in Jerusalem,— though in his blindness and hatred he had refused to believe in the resurrection until an apparition of Jesus had appealed to his heart on the way to Damascus,— it would have given him a plausible qualification for the apostolical office. Still further, the stress he ever laid upon that ghostly interview, and his insisting that he did not care to know anything more about Jesus in the flesh, or as a living person,[b] while showing how he had been taunted with his ignorance of the person of Jesus, show also that, not having aught to meet the reproach, it had a basis of truth beneath it.

Throughout Paul's letters there is a remarkable absence of allusion to any communication received from Jesus in his lifetime, or to any personal recollection of his acts or words. When Paul anticipates the question: *Upon what authority do you speak of Jesus? Who tells you what you report of him?* he invariably answers: The Spirit. God has revealed it to me by the Spirit. The Spirit searcheth the deep things of God. The things of God knoweth no man, only the Spirit of God. I speak not man's wisdom, but as the Holy Ghost teacheth.[c] The gospel I preach I received not from men, but from the revelation of Jesus Christ, who called me by his grace to preach him among the heathen; so I went not up to Jerusalem to confer with the witnesses.[d]

[a] Acts i., 15-26.   [b] II. Cor. v., 16.   [c] I. Cor. ii., 10, 11, 13.
[d] Gal. i., 11, 12, 17.

But Paul is absolutely silent on the subject of the miracles, which came to be attributed to Jesus. If Jesus, living in Galilee, had done all his mighty works there, and, coming to Jerusalem only to be arrested, convicted, and put to death, had declined to show his miraculous powers there, otherwise than by his resurrection, as the Synoptic Gospels declare, Paul, whose absence from Jerusalem during the events connected with the crucifixion may be reasonably conjectured, could not have had personal knowledge of the miracles so occurring. But how can the fact be accounted for, that no rumor of these marvellous deeds came to his ears? How can we believe that a distinct tradition of miracles had been received among the more reputable disciples, as early as the time of Paul's writing?

It may be said, however, although Paul's writings contain no hint that Jesus in his lifetime cured diseases, cast out devils, of which many were possessed, walked upon the sea, multiplied food, transfigured his form into something angelic and divine, and in several instances raised the dead, these writings everywhere attribute to Jesus higher and even divine powers, which imply the power to work miracles. It may be added in support of this view that Paul believed in miracles, and claimed that he himself had wrought them. He narrates in one of his letters that he was caught up into Paradise, and heard unspeakable words, which it is not lawful for a man to utter.[a] In vindicating his claim to be an apostle, he says the signs of an apostle were wrought among his converts in signs and wonders and mighty deeds.[b] Miracle-working is on his theory indeed only one of the secondary gifts of the Spirit, given to the believers in consequence of the resurrection and return to heaven of the Head of the Church. He even goes so far as to give a scale of valuation of these gifts and powers in his first letter to the converts at Corinth, thus: "And God hath set some in the Church: first, apostles; secondarily, prophets; thirdly, teachers; after that miracles; then gifts of healings, helps in governments, diversities of tongues."[c] *

[a] II. Cor. xii., 1-4.   [b] II. Cor. xii., 12.   [c] I. Cor. xii., 28.

* The writer is aware of the weighty argument which makes it nearly certain that when Paul, in these and several other passages, uses the word that has been unwarrantably translated in our version *miracles*, he only refers to the *charismata* or gifts — rather spasmodic

The argument is that the silence of the apostle in attributing miraculous agency to Jesus is not significant, since he could not honor so dignified and sublime a personage as he believed Jesus to have been by imputing to him powers, which Paul felt ashamed to speak of, easily exercised by himself, and which among the new gifts of the Church he classed as inferior to apostleship, prophecy, and teaching. There is much force and pertinence in the statement, when thus put. But let it be considered that these gifts came to the world, as Paul everywhere declares, under what he characterized as a new order and *régime* of the Spirit, introduced after the vindication and glorification of Jesus as Son of God; and also that Paul, whenever he speaks of the human life of Jesus, never places him — as the evangel of John does — in the category of an exalted and divine person signalizing his authority and dignity by mighty works and miracles, but as submissive to servile conditions and the shame and contempt which he voluntarily assumed as a part of his service and sacrifice. In his letter to the converts at Philippi, he gives this view of Jesus in his pre-existence and in his human life: He being "in the form of God, thought it not robbery to be equal with God; but made himself of no reputation, and took upon him the form of a servant, and became obedient unto death, even the death of the cross."[a] This rôle of servant and contemned person, which he says Jesus assumed in being born as a man, is quite incompatible with the character of a great magician commanding the elements, ruling evil spirits, and suspending the processes of nature. It was when God raised Jesus from the dead by the working of his mighty power, that he set him at his right hand in the heavens, far above all principalities and power, and might and dominion, and every name in this world and the world to come, and made him the head of all things to the Church.[b] It was through his crucifixion and resurrection that his glory came, that he ceased to be the contemned servant, and became the head of the regenerated world.

[a] Phil. ii., 6-8.   [b] Eph. i., 19-22.

than supernatural — of which, though he possessed them himself in an eminent degree, he came to have a contemptuous estimate; and that properly there is no claim by the apostle himself that he had ever wrought a miracle. It is deemed proper to offer considerations invalidating the supernatural acts attributed to Jesus in his lifetime, that may fairly appeal to the candor even of those who believe in apostolic miracles.

In his letter to the Roman Christians, Paul declares that Jesus, who by his human birth was of the family of David, was declared to be the Son of God with power, *by the resurrection of the dead.*[a] And, in his second letter to the Corinthians, Paul writes that his master suffered crucifixion through weakness; that is, the weakness incident to the servile condition to which he had voluntarily submitted, but that he lived again by the power of God.[b] Hence, Paul everywhere and in all his writings always asserts, that he preaches Christ the crucified, or rather Christ the risen from the dead; insisting not only that the spiritual gifts, the rare powers, that came to the Church, were the gifts of the glorified Saviour, but that his own power, dignity, headship of the Church, and office of judge, were obtained through the suffering of the cross; and that the abolition of death for them who believe was wrought out by the death of Jesus, and confirmed by his resurrection. Paul denies that he preaches Jesus the moralist, or Jesus the miracle-worker, but Christ the victim, submitting to crucifixion, raised above all principalities and powers by the power of God through his resurrection from the dead. It is easy to see that with such a conception miracle-working — any display of divine powers — breaks the harmony of the part, in which he fulfils in weakness and patience the humiliation of a chosen lot of suffering and shame.

Of course it is impossible to reconcile this silence of Paul with the account in the Fourth Gospel which gives us a Jesus spending three years in Jerusalem and its vicinity, and making excursions into Galilee; holding long colloquies in the temple with the Pharisees, — the multitude attending, and generally taking sides with Jesus; healing an impotent man; and giving sight to one born blind, in the most conspicuous way; and in the presence of the assembled populace, and, strangest of all, raising Lazarus from the dead before a company of respectable and influential Jews. Even if we believe Paul, by a prolonged absence from the city, might have missed personal knowledge of these memorable events, he could not have returned without finding his adopted city full of the rumor and excitement which such works would naturally

[a] Rom. i., 4.   [b] II. Cor. xiii., 4.

occasion. He does know, and know vividly, of the crucifixion, and comes enthusiastically to believe in the resurrection. Of both these events, his authentic writings are full. He does not know of other resurrections, as remarkable as that of Jesus, preceding his, and caused by him, since his whole scheme of a resurrection gives Jesus the precedence, or, as he expresses it, makes him the first-fruits, makes resurrection impossible until Jesus has, by dying, visited the realms of death, and brought back with him from the king of death those whom he has kept in the prison of the grave.[a] He knows nothing of any miracle, or of any rank or condition of the human life of Jesus, with which miracle-working would be compatible; and so, to such powers, he makes no allusion. When Paul wrote, the biographies of Jesus were not written; what was believed concerning him was told, from mouth to mouth, among his disciples. Paul insists even, that the tradition of the last supper he received directly from Jesus himself.[b] Paul, in his writings, frequently betrays his unwillingness to acknowledge any indebtedness, even to the brothers and intimate companions of Jesus, for knowledge of the incidents of his life and principles of his doctrine, lest he should thereby degrade his apostleship by seeming to have had only a second-hand and hearsay knowledge of Christ. It can hardly be credited that Jesus in vision told him of the manner in which the communion of bread and wine had been inaugurated. It is, however, reasonably probable that there was at the time of Paul's writing no record in any form of Jesus' life and teaching, because every record, afterward appearing, had recounted this ceremony of the supper.

The argument from Paul's silence concerning miracles is negative, but it is significant. Here is a first-rate witness in the very presence of the most remarkable events that history has ever recorded, and he has no word to utter concerning them. Let us suppose that, ages hence, a question should arise whether Napoleon had been in fact a restless warrior, who had subverted governments, obliterated frontiers, and filled Europe with terror and bloodshed. Let us suppose, too, that of all the literature of our age only the writings of Goethe should have sur-

[a] I. Cor. xv., 20, 23; I. Thess. iv., 15-17.   [b] I. Cor. xi., 23.

vived. How significant would be the silence of a writer, who had lived in the very countries chiefly disturbed by the ambitious projects of the French sovereign, or only such mention of him as implied that he was a pacific ruler, chiefly interested in reforming the laws and enlarging the liberties of his subjects!

If the Epistles attributed respectively to Peter, James, and John, were written by those Galilean companions of Jesus, their omission of miracles is most remarkable. If those Epistles were written by later disciples, using apostolic names, then the first recognition of miracle-working by Jesus must be carried to a period later than the apostolic age. None of these writings speak of Jesus as a worker of wonders. Peter, if the second letter attributed to him be genuine, testifies to hearing the voice from heaven on the mount of transfiguration. But this scene was the manifestation of a power not attributed to Jesus, and of which he was the subject rather than the agent.[a] On the whole, these writers mainly agree with Paul in representing Jesus' human life as a career of humiliation, and not one that was made splendid by marvellous powers, and in asserting that his glory and honor came to him after his resurrection. Peter, in the Epistle the authenticity of which is generally admitted, speaks of the glory of Christ as following his sufferings, of God raising him from the dead and giving him glory, of his being put to death in the flesh, but made alive by the Spirit ; and asserts that, on his resurrection, he went into the heavens on the right hand of God, angels and powers being made subject to him.[b]

A reference having been made to the extant writings of Paul, also to those of Peter, James, and John, companions and witnesses of Jesus, to learn whether he wrought miracles, they give no testimony on the subject. They present a scheme of the life and office of Jesus incompatible with miracle-working. If the so-called Catholic Epistles were not written by the persons to whom they have been attributed, they are genuine literature of the early Christian epoch ; they indicate what the earliest writers considered the opinions of apostles. Who then among the believers first asserted that Jesus did miracles?

[a] II. Pet. i., 15-18. [b] I. Pet. i., 11, 21; iii., 18-22.

What works so denoted did they attribute to him? How do their statements agree with each other?

The narratives of Matthew and Mark need not be treated as distinct testimonies. Scholars differ as to which was the earlier production. The most casual inspection shows that Mark's narrative is Matthew's, with the discourses of Jesus left out or greatly abbreviated, or that Matthew's narrative is Mark's, with the Sermon on the Mount, the parables and conversations of Jesus superadded, together with legends of his birth and childhood. Whether Mark's story was first committed to writing, and Matthew's afterward, to supply its deficiencies from a more accurate memory, whether this order was reversed, and Mark's Gospel was written to abbreviate the other record, retaining only what was more surely and universally believed, or whether, as some assert, both histories are reproductions of an earlier document that has perished, are questions of secondary consequence. It is enough to note that a similarity of diction and a generally similar order of events in the first two Gospels indicate that both have adopted one version of the memorabilia of Jesus, widely credited among his followers at the time of its publication, whenever that may have been.

In this connection, it ought to be observed that the traditions of the propagandism of Paul and the chief apostles, as preserved in the Acts of the Apostles and the canonical Epistles, contain no allusions to any written memorials of the life of Jesus. It is fairly inferrible that the writing, or, at any rate, the publication of the Gospels, must have been later than the time when any of the canonical Epistles were written. In all modern missionary enterprises to propagate the gospel, even among degraded and illiterate people, like the South Africans and South Sea Islanders, the literary department is most sedulously attended to. Years of painful study are first devoted to learning the language of the barbarians, whom it is proposed to convert. If they have no written language, one is invented for them. The machinery of propagandism is wrought with infinite industry, and against the friction of an enormous expense, and by processes so slow and painful, that only a sustained and systematized enthusiasm could prosecute the task, to establish through culture an intellectual relation with the people to be Christianized. The best genius of the most ardent and scholarly men have found no shorter road than this to the heart of the heathen. All through the long labor of overthrowing a rude cultus and supplanting it with a higher one, the Bible, translated into the speech of the pagan people, the tract, the written and printed page, are relied upon as the great agency of their conversion.

Now, there is every reason why the first disciples should have taken the same mode of effort. Their task was to carry the gospel of the kingdom of heaven not to illiterate and heathen people, but to the enlightened Greeks, who, in that period, were at the zenith of their culture, and who had schools and libraries in Egypt, Syria, Asia Minor, Greece, and Italy. The gospel narratives were written in Greek, then the language of the civilized world. If the apostles possessed them, they would have used them to confirm their testimony of Jesus. They would have used them as the missionary and revivalist use them now, as effective instruments to arouse and impress the conscience of their auditors, to edify the believers under their persecutions, and as the ritual of their devotional services. We have their hortatory letters to the churches; we have in the Acts fragments of their occasional discourses; and in neither is there any mention of the Gospels, though in both, the old scriptures are used as frequently, as copiously, and for the same rhetorical purposes as in modern preaching. We even find Paul, the philosopher and scholar, when he writes to Christian communities, in such regions as Rome, Galatia, and Corinth, drawing all his doctrines and arguments from the Bible of a religion which he believed Christianity had supplanted, and keeping the minds of his heathen converts occupied with the narrow discipline, in which Jehovah had trained the Jews. It thus appears, that, if the canonical Gospels or any of them were written in the lifetime of Paul, he studiously withheld from them the sanction of his name.

All this tends to discredit in advance the testimony of the evangelists upon the matter of the miracles. We find the great and responsible men in the Christian movement silent, if not hostile, toward the claim; and we have to deal with unknown writers, whom neither Jesus nor his apostles are known to have commissioned. Long after the events they record, on their own account, and under none of the responsibility that accompanies publication under a reputable name, these writers undertake to give a statement, not of actual occurrences, but of what "*is surely believed*" among the adherents of a new faith. Luke, in the introductory note to his Gospel, confesses such motive and method of writing. The authority of a history of the events of our own century would be properly estimated upon a scale like this. First, an historian of world-wide celebrity, like Macaulay, Niebuhr, or Prescott, wrote and published it thirty years ago; it has been republished, after being subjected to the criticism of scholars for the intervening period. This would be called historical evidence of prime character. Second, it was written anonymously, as long ago, but published in a most respectable and trustworthy review, is probable in itself, and has never been contradicted. This would be called secondary historical evidence. Third, it was written anonymously, as a private letter; it is full of statements intrinsically improbable; and its authorship has never been ascertained. What would be the worth of the last-named testimony?

The story of the miracle-working begins with the account of the opening of the public ministry of Jesus, and Matthew tells that he went about all Galilee, healing all manner of sickness, and all manner of disease among the people; and that they brought unto him all sick people that were taken with divers diseases and torments, and those which were possessed with devils, and those who were lunatic, and those that had the palsy, and he healed them.[a] Taken narrowly and literally, this implies a healing of all the disorders and diseases of the province of Galilee, then densely peopled. But the narrative, written in an animated style, and with Oriental exaggeration characteristic of the age and country, is not to be so treated. It does, however, fairly imply that Jesus visited all parts of Galilee,— not to say every house or even every hamlet,— that, to all the principal centres of its population, he came, not only as a preacher of

[a] Matt. iv., 23, 24

the kingdom of heaven, but as a healer of the sick, that there were brought to him, if not literally, *all sick and disabled persons*, yet some of all kinds of such; and that as many as were brought he healed. Less than this cannot be fairly implied, if indeed the reader is at liberty to find any definite statement in the language.

Later on, the same writer gives us the picture of one day's life of Jesus in Galilee, in which by a word he cleansed a leprous man, cast out an evil spirit from the servant of a Roman centurion, cured Peter's wife's mother of a fever by a touch of his hand, and restored to sanity and healed many persons brought to him in the evening. Afterward, he stilled a dangerous tempest on the sea of Galilee, and, landing upon the pagan side, relieved two men tormented with fierce devils, that had made them a terror to the neighborhood.[a] The sequel of the last-named miracle shows how national prejudices may sometimes intrude themselves into the most serious narrative. We readily detect a popular origin — the opportunity of some local humorist to make mirth for his countrymen, at the unclean practices of the barbarians of the other side — in the consignment of the expelled demons to the herd of swine.

Returning among his own countrymen, Jesus by a command made a palsied and bed-ridden man rise and walk, cured with a touch of his garment a woman of a disease of twelve years' standing, and, taking by the hand a certain ruler's daughter, who was supposed to have just died, brought her to life. Afterward,— the writer gives no chronology, and very rarely a locality,— he is evidently recounting traditions, of which no detail is preserved,— Jesus causes two blind men to see, and a dumb man to speak, or, as the writer describes it, the man being possessed with the devil of dumbness, Jesus casts out the devil, when the man, no longer obstructed, speaks like other men. Then there follows a still more sweeping assertion of miracles, done in the mass, in these words: " Jesus went through all the cities and villages, healing every sickness and every disease among the people."[b] Still, it is not asserted that he healed every sick and diseased man in all the cities and villages; but it is fairly

[a] Matt. viii.   [b] Matt. ix.

implied that, going into all the cities and villages, he healed every kind of sickness: there was no prevalent sickness, of which he did not effect a cure.

After some time,— we are not told how long,— Jesus went into *their* synagogue on the Sabbath,— we are not told in what country or city,— and after some hesitation on account of the Pharisees, who were watching him, he restored to vigor the withered arm of a palsied man. Alarmed at the hostility, which thereupon beset him, he withdrew,— we are not told whither,— and healed all the sick among the multitudes, that followed him.[a] It is then related, that he cast out a devil, which had afflicted a man with blindness and dumbness, so that he both spake and saw.[b]

When certain scribes and Pharisees asked him to do a miracle, he told them that the only miracle he should show them was the miracle of rising from the grave after being buried three days and three nights.[c] But notwithstanding this refusal, it is again told that, pitying the multitudes who followed him to a desert place, he healed the sick among them, and with but five loaves and two fishes fed to repletion five thousand men with their accompanying women and children.[d] His disciples returned across the lake from this desert place, leaving Jesus alone on a mountain; and, in the middle of the night, he, walking on the sea, came to them as they were struggling with a storm, and at once it fell calm.[e] Then he went into the coasts of Tyre and Sidon, and there exorcised a devil possessing the daughter of a Canaanitish woman, and healed those that were lame, blind, dumb, maimed, and many others brought to him by great multitudes of people. There, too, he repeated for the benefit of a crowd of four thousand — women and children not counted — the miraculous multiplication of food.[f] Again, he refuses to exhibit his powers to scribes and Pharisees, denounces them as a wicked and adulterous generation, and says, no sign shall be given them but the sign of the prophet Jonah, whose burial in the whale for a season, to be returned alive, he will not long thereafter re-enact.[g] The sequel tells of his transfiguration on the mountain

[a] Matt. xii., 9–15. [b] Matt. xii., 22. [c] Matt. xii., 38–40. [d] Matt. xiv., 14–21.
[e] Matt. xiv., 23–32. [f] Matt. xv., 21–39. [g] Matt. xvi., 4.

and the apparition of the two greatest of the Hebrew prophets doing him homage;[a] and again of his casting out a devil that had baffled the skill of the disciples, who seem strangely to have lost the powers conferred on them, when sent out to preach the kingdom of heaven.[b] As the career of Jesus goes on, he seems to lose control of the unseen powers. His works of healing and dispossession seem to grow less frequent; and his teachings, parables, exhortations, prognostications of the future, and expositions of the polity of the kingdom of heaven fill a larger place in his life.

Still upon the multitudes, who follow him out of Galilee as far as the region opposite Judea beyond the Jordan, he exercises his powers of healing,[c] and gives sight to two blind men, who sat by the road as he came out of Jericho, followed by his Galilean disciples bound to Jerusalem.[d]

Once arrived in the city, all miracle-working ceases. The scribes and Pharisees are the rulers of Church and State; and before them, even in Galilee, he had resolutely, and with contumelious language, refused to show a sign from heaven. The only sign he will do among them is the Jonas-sign of the resurrection. True, Matthew says, the blind and lame came to him in the temple, and he healed them.[e] But Mark and Luke do not confirm the statement. Such exhibitions of power by Jesus would have been inconsistent with his avowed purpose not to show any sign, and with his determination to bring about his own arrest, condemnation, and death, which could only be effected by abstaining from any exhibitions of power, that might convince or overawe his enemies.

This is the combined testimony of Matthew and Mark concerning the thaumaturgic power of Jesus. It is to be remarked, that the power is not universal or uniform. Jesus is made himself to say that he did not exercise it arbitrarily, but in such places and upon such subjects as God pleased. There was, he declared, the same restriction of the wonderful power manifested of old by the prophets Elijah and Elisha. He gave this as a reason why he could not do in Nazareth[f] the mighty works reported done in Capernaum. The narrator in

[a] Matt. xvii., 1–8. [b] Matt. xvii., 14–21. [c] Matt. xix., 1, 2.
[d] Matt. xx., 29–34. [e] Matt. xxi., 14. [f] Luke iv., 23–27.

each of the first two Gospels asserts that miracle-working in Nazareth was obstructed by lack of faith on the part of his fellow-townsmen.[a] But, on the other hand, for what end, we are constrained to ask, were these marvellous powers given? Clearly, the writer answers that the people to whom Jesus was sent should believe that he was the commissioned messenger of God. And Jesus himself is made to avow this object, when, in the hearing of the messengers from John, he appealed to the cures he had effected, to the diseased persons restored to health and wholeness, and said: As to who I am, let works like these declare.[b] Again, in reproaching Capernaum, Chorazin, and Bethsaida, wherein most of his mighty works had been done, for not believing, he is made to admit that such mighty works were done to produce belief.[c]

This difficulty then confronts us. Here is a personage appearing in an obscure corner of an outlying province of a subject and despised country, who, having passed his youth in utter seclusion, conceives that he is a prophet, a divine messenger, the heir of an everlasting kingdom, the early establishment of which is to overthrow all earthly kingdoms, and bring the physical universe itself to an end; and he begins in his early manhood to proclaim a new era, and to ask of men their allegiance, the reward of which shall be their everlasting salvation, the refusal of which shall be their speedy and miserable destruction. He claims that he is accredited by supernatural gifts of healing, and the power of suspending, by his will and word, the ordinary courses of nature. Now, to make men believe, it is clearly requisite, according to conceptions imputed to him in these narratives, that he should exhibit these powers. And yet the reverse condition is exacted. He is made to say that he will not exhibit these powers, unless men will first believe that he can.[d] His biographer declares even, that he could not do miracles in Nazareth because of the unbelief of his neighbors. Clearly, this was the very people upon whom the miracle-working should have been essayed, in order that they might believe. A supernatural effort is superfluous, where faith, the great purpose of supernatural demonstration, has already been produced.

[a] Matt. xiii., 58.   [b] Matt. xi., 4, 5.   [c] Matt. xi., 20-23.
[d] Matt. viii., 10, 13; ix., 28, 29; xvii., 20.

Again, the message of Jesus was first to the Jewish people, to the scribes and Pharisees, who, as he admitted, sitting in Moses' seat, represented the will and thought of the nation.* I am not sent but unto the lost sheep of Israel, he said. If Chorazin ought to have believed, because mighty works were done in it, the converse is true ; and mighty works, if they tend to produce belief, as he told John's followers, ought to have been done in every city where he desired men to believe. Only charlatans and impostors ask for faith beforehand. The discoverer of some occult law of nature, some striking result of chemical experiment, says rather : I do not ask you to believe this in advance. I ask you to disbelieve it, since it is in itself ostensibly impossible and incredible; but I shall do it in the most open way before you, and I leave it to you to say, whether or not you can accept it as a fact and conform your preconceptions to it. Why, then, of all classes, did he refuse to show a sign from heaven to the scribes and Pharisees? Are not the Jews first, through their authorized guides and masters, to be proffered the grace of the great salvation? If they are unbelievers, why should not their unbelief be assailed by the divine power, given for that purpose? Why, like John the Baptist, proscribe them in advance, coming to the baptism of repentance, and refuse to exhibit before them what is so lavishly displayed before the multitudes, who throng around the heavenly messenger in the desert, and not withheld even from the dogs of heathen that feed on the crumbs which the guests of Israel drop from the table?

This insisting upon faith in Jesus as Messiah and Saviour, everywhere injected into these gospel narratives, carries us forward beyond the age of Jesus and his apostles to the period of propagandism of the new religion, to the long and ardent struggle which the enthusiasm of a young faith maintained with the philosophy, culture, conservatism, sordidness, and sensuality of the old world. In this struggle, faith was everything. Give in your adhesion to the new ideas, own Jesus as master, these were the frantic appeals of the devotees to the frivolity and indifference that abounded. " Every spirit," wrote the pseudo-John, "that confesseth that Jesus Christ is

* Matt. xxiii., 2, 3.

come in the flesh is of God"; and again he asks,—the coarseness of his language betraying the dogmatic fierceness of his spirit,— "Who is a *liar*, but he that denieth that Jesus is the Christ?" Whoever believeth that Jesus is the Christ is born of God.[a] Paul, too, wrote: *No man can say that Jesus is the Lord but by the Holy Ghost;* and Paul seems to have composed two of his Epistles to prove that faith is a substitute for virtue, and that all virtue is the fruit of faith. So great, in the struggle to inaugurate a new creed, were the eagerness and enthusiasm of its apostles.

How does Luke, the other witness, tell the story of the miracle-working? Luke says: Jesus returned in the power of the Spirit into Galilee from the wilderness of Jordan, and teaching in the synagogues was glorified of all men, and a fame of him went through all the region.[b] This indicates a fame and honor springing rather from his preaching than from miracles. The utter chronological confusion, in which the incidents of Jesus' career are told by Luke, is indicated by the statement that, coming to his own city Nazareth, he is importuned by his neighbors to do in their midst the works they had heard of as done in Capernaum,[c] no such works having as yet been recounted, as done anywhere in Galilee. Returning afterward to Capernaum, he casts out an unclean devil from one possessed; and the people are amazed, as they would not have been, if many such works had been before done among them, so that the rumor of them had spread to Nazareth.[d] He also cured Peter's wife's mother ill of fever.[e] In the evening, all the families that had sick brought them to him, and he healed them by a touch.[f] Devils also came out of many invoking him as the Son of God.[g] Afterwards, going into Peter's ship, he directed where the net should be cast, and so many fish were taken that they filled not only that, but a companion ship nearly to sinking. This marvel so impressed Peter and probably his brother Andrew, and the two sons of Zebedee, James, and John that they left their calling to become his disciples.[h] In a certain city, he cleansed a

---

[a] I. John iv., 2; ii., 22; v., 1. [b] Luke iv., 14, 15. [c] Luke iv., 23.
[d] Luke iv., 31, 33. [e] Luke iv., 38, 39. [f] Luke iv., 40.
[g] Luke iv., 41. [h] Luke v., 3–9, 10, 11.

leprous sufferer ; and then multitudes were brought to him to be cured of their infirmities. On a certain other day, he restored vigor to a palsied man brought to him on a bed, and let down through the tiling of the roof.[a] Afterward, on the Sabbath, he healed a man with a withered hand;[b] and, coming down from a mountain, whither he had gone to pray, a great multitude of people out of all Judea and Jerusalem, and from the sea-coast of Tyre and Sidon, came to hear him, and to be healed of their diseases, and they, as well as all vexed with unclean spirits, were healed. Virtue went out from him, and healed them all.[c] It was then — it is not told where — that he addressed, not to the multitude, but to his disciples, that part of the Sermon on the Mount that Luke has recorded.

Coming again to Capernaum, he cures the servant of a Roman centurion by a word, without visiting him ;[d] and the day after stops a burial procession, and restores alive to his mother in the city of Nain her only son, who was being borne to burial. The rumor of this great work went through all Judea and the region round about.[e] It is then told that, in crossing the lake in a ship, on which were the disciples and Jesus, who had fallen asleep, a great storm of wind arose ; the ship took in water and was near foundering, when Jesus awoke, rebuked the winds and a calm ensued.[f] Arrived at the country of the Gadarenes, he commands the horde of devils to go into the herd of swine, and they rushed to the lake and were drowned.[g] He afterward returned to the Galilean side, and called to life the young daughter of the ruler Jairus, who was supposed to have died ; and healed a diseased woman by the touch of his garment.[h] Luke next tells of the feeding of five thousand people upon five loaves and two fishes, of the story of the transfiguration, and of the casting out of a fierce devil from a child.[i] Then follows the casting out of a dumb devil in the presence of the Pharisees, and their imputation to him of a league with the chief of devils, with his crushing reply.[j] It is afterwards told that the multitude pressed him to show a sign, and that he told them they were an evil generation,

[a] Luke v., 12-15, 18-26.   [b] Luke vi., 6-10.   [c] Luke vi., 17-19.   [d] Luke vii., 1-10.
[e] Luke vii., 11-18.   [f] Luke viii., 22-25.   [g] Luke viii., 26-33.   [h] Luke viii., 40-56.
[i] Luke ix., 10-17, 28-36, 38-42.   [j] Luke xi., 14, 26.

to whom no sign should be given, but the sign of the prophet Jonas, raised to life from the belly of the whale, as he himself would be from the bowels of the earth.[a] After many chapters of teaching and parable, another work of healing is ascribed to Jesus upon a woman bowed together with a spirit of infirmity, so that she could in no wise lift up herself.[b] More and more the marvellous powers disappear, and the incidents that befall the great Prophet fall into the sphere of probability. Still a dropsical patient is healed upon the Sabbath;[c] on the way to Jerusalem, in a certain city, it may have been in Galilee, it may have been in Samaria, ten lepers are cleansed, but one of whom had the grace to return to give thanks;[d] and a blind man, who begged by the wayside, as he approached Jericho,[e] is restored to sight. But with this last effort the superhuman power is apparently suspended, and, resuming the weakness of human nature, he yields himself to the malice of his enemies.

How is this testimony of miracles to be treated? If it is the testimony of God, or of men inspired, informed, or directed by Him, it is to be reverently believed. But it must be so far subjected to rational criticism, as to determine whether it is to be so regarded. Both narrators agree in these general statements, that all the mighty works or miracles which they impute to Jesus, with the exception of restoring sight to a beggar, or two beggars in the environs of Jericho, were done by him in Galilee, and in the countries adjoining that province, eastward across the Jordan and Sea of Galilee, westward in the coasts of Tyre and Sidon, and southward in the province of Samaria. They both leave us to believe that the miracle-working power either left Jesus or was restrained by him, after he left his home in Galilee, and betook himself to Jerusalem, where, after his arrival, his arrest, trial, and execution speedily followed each other. Both assert that, while still in Galilee, he declined showing his miraculous power in the presence of scribes and Pharisees, and again declined, after he had come to Jerusalem, in each instance alleging that all the sign he would show to them was the sign of his resurrection after being buried

[a] Luke xi., 29, 30.   [b] Luke xiii., 10–13.   [c] Luke xiv., 2–4.
[d] Luke xvii., 11–19.   [e] Luke xviii., 35–43.

three days and three nights. Both insist that preliminary faith was a favorable condition of successful miracle-working : and that confirmed disbelief in his power would in many cases even totally counteract, at least, his moral power to accomplish a miracle.

Moreover the two narrators agree in the affirmation that in his native province of Galilee, Jesus visited all the principal centres of population, and — to take their language literally — every city and village, and healed and relieved, if not all sick, lame, maimed, and mentally deranged persons, all that were brought to him in all the cities and villages. As both writers assert that great multitudes followed him, and that the fame of him filled all the province and all Syria, they leave it to be inferred that all or nearly all the persons suffering infirmities in Galilee, were first or last brought to him, and were relieved; since all who believed in his power, and many who did not, would not hesitate to avail themselves of it, when it was so easy of access, and so uniformly efficacious.

When it comes to details there are discrepancies. Part of these may be accounted for by the consideration that each, besides special cases, gives a general, comprehensive statement of cures and restorations, of which no details are given, while in selecting some to be more fully described, Matthew chooses certain instances, and Luke selects different ones. Thus Matthew tells of one leper being cleansed, of whom Luke makes no mention, but makes amends by telling of ten lepers cleansed, which Matthew fails to report. Luke affirms that four chief disciples were won by a marvellous draft of fishes, which would seem to have given the successful fishers a new zest for their calling; while Matthew says, Jesus found the eager disciples sitting listless on the shore mending their nets, and that they gladly left a precarious business to become fishers of men. Both tell of the healing of the centurion's servant, with such agreeing details, that it is an evident purpose to describe the same transaction; but Matthew says the centurion came himself with deferential courtesy to solicit Jesus' aid, while Luke insists that, in the first instance, the centurion sent elders of the Jews to procure the attendance of Jesus, and, growing impatient, sent friends to say it was not worth his trouble to visit the patient, but that he might speak a word that would heal the servant, giving as a reason for such suggestion what is meaningless as told by Matthew, "I, too, am a man of authority, and when I speak to my soldiers, they do what I bid." Luke is silent concerning the miraculous cures attributed to Jesus in the vicinity of Tyre and Sidon, but there was a national feeling, and a theory of the blessings of the gospel being offered only to Jews at the first, which might account for the omission.

But there are variances not so easily explained as these. Thus Matthew says in the country of the Gadarenes, Jesus was met by two men possessed with devils exceeding fierce, while Luke, evidently occupied with the same tradition, says there was but one man so possessed. Luke tells of the miracle of the five loaves and two fishes feeding the five thousand people, but Matthew tells that incident, and says that it was repeated as to four thousand people not long afterward. Matthew says Jesus, having absented himself for several hours from his disciples, came to them at night, walking upon the sea, while Luke, who gives with great detail the stilling of the storm, does not mention this marvel. Both writers undertake to recount the last of the miracles, but Matthew says that it was restoring sight to two blind beggars, after Jesus and his company had left Jericho journeying to Jerusalem; Luke says it was the cure of one blind beggar sitting by the wayside before he entered Jericho. Finally, Matthew, who tells — as both tell — with detail of place and time the healing of the centurion's servant in Capernaum, wholly ignores the stupendous work wrought by Jesus the very next day in the neighboring city of Nain, in raising from his bier alive a young man, son of a widow, whose corpse was being carried to burial,— a miracle which Luke says brought fear upon all the people, who declared that "a great prophet had arisen among them, and that God had visited his people." When an event happens, it draws with it its natural and usual concomitant circumstances. Accordingly, Luke goes on to say that the rumor of this remarkable achievement went through all Judea, and throughout all the region round about. It could not have well been otherwise. In no age, among no people, in no quarter of the world, could a dead man be raised from his bier and presented alive to his rejoicing friends without creating a profound admiration for the deed, and an awful reverence for its author. The biographer says also, that it was this crowning exhibition of superhuman power by Jesus which arrested the attention of John the Baptist, and suggested to him that the Messiah, whom he believed to be near his coming, must be this worker of wonders. Why does Matthew omit all mention of a miracle in which the fame of Jesus culminated, which caused his countrymen to accept him as a great prophet, and gained John's weighty adhesion to him, as to him *that was to come;* which led to his own reluctant assumption of the Messiahship, and so precipitated the crisis of his fate? The omission of such an incident in the career of Jesus by a writer evidently undertaking to tell the whole story, and bringing us indeed to the very occasion and day, when this thing is said to have occurred, throws the greatest doubt upon its actuality.

Dr. Paley says: —

I know not a more rash or unphilosophical conduct of the understanding than to reject the substance of a story by means of some diversity in the circumstances with which it is related. The usual character of human testimony is substantial truth under circumstantial variety. This is what the daily experience of courts of justice teaches. When accounts of a transaction come from the mouths of different witnesses, it is seldom that it is not possible to pick out apparent or real inconsistencies between them.

Conceding to its full extent the principle enunciated by Paley, and by him appealed to, to support the credibility of the New Testament writers, it is obvious that it is a rule that he applies only to *human* testimony. The variance in circumstances accompanying a fact, which different witnesses report substantially alike, is usually due to the natural defects of the *human* understanding. The rule cannot be pleaded to excuse the variance in two different divine oracles. To the divine mind, however manifested, we attribute entire integrity, complete knowledge. We always speak of the infinite intelligence as something not subject to the limitations and errors of the finite intelligence. So that very rule, which Dr. Paley lays down, concedes all that the sceptical critic can ask, in conceding that Matthew and Luke are to be treated like ordinary men giving their testimony upon knowledge acquired by the defective and imperfect faculties of mere, unaided human understanding. When it is asked upon what authority are we to believe that Jesus of Nazareth wrought miracles, we are only told that two persons of common intelligence, unknown to us, have so declared in writings to which they have put their respective names.

Conceding now, that whether two men among the Gadarenes were dispossessed of devils, or only one; whether two blind beggars in the vicinity of Jericho were restored to sight, or only one, are mere circumstances, which different truthful witnesses might observe, remember, and report differently, the divine mind, the spirit of truth, an inspiration of God, could not and would not report such circumstances incorrectly. But here is not a variance in circumstances, but a variance in the substantial fact, that we have to deal with. If one witness should declare in court that Judas Iscariot in the vicinity of Jericho killed and robbed a travelling Samaritan, and another witness, being afterwards sworn, should testify that the accused killed and robbed at the same time and place two Samaritans, it would be held, that there was such a variance in the substance of the *corpus delicti*, that it could not be considered as proved by such evidence. One of the modes of protecting innocent persons against the malice of false accusations is to seclude the witnesses, and draw each in turn into a detail of circumstances, which it is hardly possible for two different imaginations to fabricate alike, and the rule applied in courts of justice is, that where several witnesses bear testimony to the same transaction, and concur in their statement of a series of circumstances, and the order in which they occur, such coincidences exclude all apprehension of mere chance or accident, and can be accounted for only by one of two suppositions: either the testimony is true, or the coincidences are the result of concert and conspiracy. We are but following the line of argument by which the credibility of events connected with the life of Jesus is supported by the most distinguished champion of the Christian faith, when we decide that the evidence of the evangelists is to be treated exactly like human evidence.

The view already taken of the Fourth Gospel prevents its being considered a third and independent testimony to the miracles. If that work is, for the reasons heretofore set forth, to be regarded as a legitimate literary fiction, the purpose of which was not to give a history of the acts and conversations of Jesus, but to develop in a vivid dramatic form the conceptions of his ideas and office to which the more advanced and philosophical believers had arrived in the age when it was written, then the writer was not obliged by the rules of his art to confine himself to the authentic facts of the life of Jesus. He could use those facts, when he found them subservient to his didactic purpose. He could imagine kindred and other facts that would best harmonize with the symmetry of his subject, and make the life of Jesus realize the ideal conception he wished to present. Thus Shakspeare, in dealing with Henry the Fourth, or Richard the Third, avails himself of the known prominent events, like the great battles, the great trials and executions, and follows history mainly in his *dramatis personis;* but he puts a purpose and a meaning into plots and projects, far more heroic and poetic than the dull facts. He brings the sharp retrospect of a more critical later age to vivify and inform the conduct of the past, and injects into the minds of kings and courtiers the consciousness, which they did not have, of the relation of their struggles and intrigues with the development of English character and of English civilization. So the Johannic dramatist does not intend to make any new demands upon the credulity of the Church. It is already believed that Jesus rose himself from the dead, and that, in one or two instances, he had restored the dead to life. The author wishing to present the doctrine of the resurrection, as it had come to be held in philosophic schools of the new faith, does it dramatically, rather than metaphysically. There was a Mary and Martha whom Jesus knew, whose names tradition had preserved. They had lived at Bethany. Jesus had lodged with them, when in daily peril of his enemies in Jerusalem, during those last days of his life. The dramatist will have a brother in this family. He graphically depicts their domestic life, homely, pleasant, but thoroughly respectable. He brings Jesus to them with their other most eminent and reputable friends. It is the pathos of fiction that death can be made to visit the creations of our fancy. Wishing to unfold the mysteries of the resurrection, he lets Jesus do it with touching eloquence over the grave whence Lazarus is summoned to return to his dim and unreal life.

Jesus did no miracles in the temple or even in Jerusalem, but he had elsewhere, and frequently restored sight to the blind. Keeping up the great controversial debate, of which all the apostolic writings are full, between the hard and uncompromising Mosaic monotheism, and the new claim that God had a son, that there are two, if not three deities, and trying to find in the old theology some implication or foreshadowing of the new, the writer enlivens the argument with marvels kindred to those already believed. He has a blind man cured in the temple, and makes it the occasion of a serious appeal to the Jews to recognize in him, to whom God appoints such works, one sent and commissioned by Jehovah. As the dramatic English kings of Shakspeare have crowded out the historic, and stand forever in the grand attitudes in which his genius placed them, so the dramatic Jesus of John has eclipsed the Jesus of the Synoptic Gospels, and is enshrined in the reverence and affection of Christian hearts.

Those, however, who accept John's story as history have to reconcile, as they can, the entirely different version of miracle-working which he gives. Not only is no confirmation given by him of the general healing of all sickness, and all disease among the people of every city and village of Galilee, of the curing of all the diseased among the multitudes that thronged around him from that province, from Judea, and the region beyond Jordan, of the great fame of such great works, that filled all Syria, so that the people at least of Galilee believed him to be a great prophet, but John asserts that Jesus did but two miracles in all in Galilee.[a] John names in fact two others;[b] but he asserts that the principal and great miracles were done in Judea and Jerusalem. He discloses that, comparatively late in the public career of Jesus as a prophet, his own brothers did not believe on him,[c] and that the people of Nazareth were only induced

[a] John ii., 11; iv., 54.   [b] John vi., 5–14, 17–21.   [c] John vii., 5; Mark iii., 21.

to accept him, after the report of the miracles had come to them from people who came from Jerusalem and Judea.[*]

In a work of purposed and avowed fiction, such departure from the historic tradition is of no significance. The only historic weight to be given to the Johannic narrative is that, at the time when the believers came generally to accept its statements as authentic, whether that was during the second century or still later, there was a tradition of the miracles entirely inconsistent with the earlier tradition. If the so-called John declared that but four comparatively insignificant miracles were done in any other province than Judea, and no others; and Matthew and Luke, or writers so called, with equal positiveness assert that no miracles were done in Judea, and that Jesus refused, on being solicited, even to attempt them, the testimony can only be reconciled by believing that both were either mistaken in saying that miracles were performed anywhere, or mistaken in denying that they were not performed in both regions where Jesus is known to have lived or visited. In such contradiction, it is obvious that we are obliged to take that alternative which is most probable and most consonant with human experience.

Considering the testimony of the evangelists as mere human testimony, we find both writers evidently groping among popular beliefs vague and uncertain and burdened with few details of time and place. It was, they say, in a certain city, at a time after some other time, itself not given, and their sequences of events by no means correspond to each other. The believers had been taught and they believed that Jesus had raised himself from the dead, and ascended to heaven. They fully accepted him as a superhuman person. One by one, the marvellous feats of curing, of walking on the sea, of creating food, of raising the dead began to be told and believed by obscure partisans of the new faith, who already had all the elements of faith in miracles, to wit: first, a belief that they had been wrought for and by the great patriarchs and prophets of their nation; second, a belief that Jesus was of superior rank to the greatest of the patriarchs and prophets. The apostles, including the sagacious and cultivated Paul, had all died, else they would have contradicted this prolific

[*] John iv., 45.

gossip,— contradicted it as inconsistent with their own evident conception of the subject and servile condition of Jesus' human life. It grew and diverged with the telling, so that, when, after the apostolic age, the annalists undertook to write for purely personal reasons, as so-called Luke did for the information of some candid pagan friend, they wrote not as historians, not under the stress and responsibility which accompanies authorship, but to tell in a vivid and striking manner what was believed at the time among the Christians.

What two or three persons nearly simultaneously undertook, many others copied. The age of action had passed; the novelty of faith had been lost; the sharp edge of persecution and public obloquy that confronted discipleship had gone by. It was not disreputable, nor greatly dangerous to be a follower of Jesus; and, in the quiet that succeeded the martyr age of the new religion, a public sentiment had formed itself, that stimulated and demanded literary expression. The poets, the storytellers, the pamphleteers, began to moralize upon the completed epoch, and to describe it, as they never do and never can, while the agony of an epoch is just upon them. So that not only these Gospels, which the Church has cherished, were produced, but a whole swarm of other Gospels, all more or less full of the picturesque and the miraculous. Something like twelve Gospels are alluded to among Christian writers of the first four centuries of the Christian era, as held in more or less repute among the Christians. These were imputed to each of the twelve apostles, and to others, known or unknown, in the canonical writings. Most of these Gospels have perished; but a Gospel of Nicodemus, two Gospels of the infancy of Jesus, and the Protevangelium, attributed to James, the brother of Jesus, are still preserved.

In the Protevangelium and books of the infancy of Jesus, whole verses are copied, the one from the other; and his miraculous birth is told substantially as by Matthew and Luke, but with more minute and gross details. Nicodemus describes the trial and crucifixion, and recites copiously the conversations between Pilate and the Jews, and between the High Priest and elders, and a small body of eminent men who favored Jesus. The conversations of Pilate with Jesus, and of the High Priests, are so similar to that given in Matthew and John, that the writers of those Gospels either copied from this narrative called "of Nicodemus," or it is copied into that from them. The earthquake and rising of the dead, which Matthew declares attended the death of Jesus, appear also in the same language in this apocryphal Gospel.[a] In the story of the infancy of Jesus, the journey to Egypt is told with much detail, and many absurd, and some indelicate miracles are recited as wrought by Jesus, while an infant in the arms of his mother, by the touch of his person, by contact with the clothes he wore, or with the water in which he had been washed. It is evident that the Nicene Council, or some other assembly of the bishops and overseers of the Church in the earlier centuries, were obliged, among a mass of writings, in which the legends of the miracles had been collected, to select those for approbation which seemed to be most creditable to his memory. Their rule of selection and exclusion seems to have been, not which of those stories are most widely believed, and which stand upon the most creditable testimony, but which are the most decent, and which will be received by the reason and taste of a cultivated and philosophical age with the readiest credence, and which will best minister to the edification of the Church. Perhaps a severer taste would have omitted, as Mark and John omitted, Matthew and Luke's story of the unnatural origin of Jesus, and left details of that kind to the condemned apocryphal writers, who seemed to have magnified it inordinately. Perhaps it would have left untold the conjuring of the devils into the herd of swine, as piquant only in that it amused a national prejudice of diet. It might, too, have considered the changing of water into wine at the wedding at Cana as not beneficial, or a work of mercy. It was the task of this primitive Christian criticism to select from the literary records of several centuries — all written on purely personal impulses by unauthorized persons, using without hesitation the artifice of imputing what they wrote to some eminent person — to reject what was trivial and indecorous, and to indorse with their sanction what was of good report.

[a] Matt. xxvii., 51-53.

As a whole, their judgment will meet the approbation of the cultivated modern mind.

The wholesale curing of disease and mental derangement in Galilee, accompanied by two conspicuous instances of feeding many thousand persons to repletion with food scarce sufficient for ten persons, the walking upon the sea, the restoring of strength to bed-ridden and palsied men, of wholeness to those who were maimed, and of life, in one or two cases, to persons who had died, could not have happened during the reign of Tiberius in any part of the Roman Empire and civilized world, without producing greater effects than the New Testament literature records. Still more true is this, if, in addition to these marvels done in Galilee, there had been miracles of healing in Jerusalem, and a man raised from the grave, after four days' burial, in the midst of a company of intelligent and reputable citizens of that city.

It was an age of comparative peace. Wealthy and educated Romans, following the armies, and employed in the proconsular governments, in official service or in the pursuit of pleasure or the study of philosophy, passed the whole length of the Mediterranean, and noted whatever was remarkable in the countries they visited. The Jews were not a barbarous people. To their own considerable culture, they superadded that of the Greeks, in whose language they spoke and wrote. They inhabited a region lying between old Greece, on one side, shorn, indeed, of its political, but still wielding its philosophical and artistic sway over the world, and Egypt on the other side, in which the culture of Greece had had a *renaissance.* The cosmopolitan Greek was everywhere, whose sole passion it was to hear and to tell some new thing.[a] Why were there not about the luxurious court of Herod, under whose jurisdiction Jesus lived and taught, curious men, Greeks and Romans, who would have taken the liveliest interest in a man with the rumor of whose wonder-works of beneficial magic, that so surpassed all that the sibyls and soothsayers and magicians of the pagan world had been able to achieve, all Syria was ringing, to carry to Rome, to Athens and to Alexandria, some report of what Jesus was doing in Galilee? In every city were philoso-

[a] Acts xvii., 21.

phers, dreamers, and schemers, who would have welcomed such a prodigy as a new revelation. And yet pagan literature has not the slightest trace of Jesus, *the wonderworker*.

But, disregarding the so-called secular testimonies preserved in literature, let us look carefully into the very records, upon which the actuality of the miracles stands, to see if they are consistent in setting forth effects, which should have naturally followed such wonderful manifestations of power as are ascribed to Jesus.

Mankind are much more inclined to credulity than to scepticism. In our own age, among such enlightened peoples as the Americans, the English, the Germans, and the French, the coarsest forms of superstition, the most puerile and whimsical speculations, the most shallow personal pretensions to sanctity or to inspiration, find swarms of believers. And yet, in all those countries, an enlightened public sentiment counteracts such tendencies to delusion, and draws men back to the sphere of reason and common sense. But if Jesus should come to the most sceptical of modern cities, say to Paris, and should there do the works of healing, dispossession, and magic, including two instances of restoring the dead to life, which tradition declares he did in Galilee, the ignorant and superstitious peasantry, the devout and fanatical world would follow him with faith and wonder. More than this, after some contempt, and a natural reluctance to admit the actuality of what transcended ordinary human experience, the philosophers would organize commissions to watch and examine him; and they, together with the scoffers and frivolous pleasure-seekers, would be coerced, by the stupendous and repeated exhibition, to accept him as a messenger of God. A palpable fact recurring so many times as to preclude all deception, witnessed by so many persons as to make defective observation impossible, is more potent than all *a priori* science. Ever since it has been observed, the sun has risen in the east and moved through the skies to the west. There is the strongest ground for believing that this movement is a permanent arrangement of nature. But if, for the mornings to come, in the sight of all rational human beings concurring in the observation, the sun should rise in the west and travel toward the east, it would be legitimate to conclude that, for that period at least, the arrangement of nature had been changed. No prepossessions of science could stand against such a palpable and evident fact.

But the first century was far more credulous than is the nineteenth. There was no logic or science which in the first century rendered miracles impossible. On the contrary, all the systems of knowledge then extant accommodated themselves to miracles, which men of all nationalities and creeds held to have happened at some time, if not in their day and sight. The Jews were not the least superstitious people of the first century, nor the Galileans the least superstitious community among the Jews.

Now, what do the gospel narratives themselves declare as to the effect of the mighty works of Jesus, upon the people in whose sight they were done? After the death of Jesus, and after it was believed among his adherents, that they were commanded to assemble and remain in Jerusalem to await some most momentous event to befall them and all the world, the number of the believers in Jesus was one hundred and twenty.[*] As even his chief, chosen apostles had previously forsaken him,— Peter, his confidential friend, denying, with oaths and anger, that he had ever known him,— it is probable, that the most of these were attracted, not so much by their recollections of the miracles done in Galilee, as by the belief that Jesus had risen from the dead and ascended into the skies.

Let it be said, this was at Jerusalem, where the public feeling was strongly hostile to Jesus. There were one hundred and twenty Galileans, who showed their devotion to him by sharing his perilous mission to the sacred city, besides the multitudes of believers that remained at home in all the cities and villages of that province. It must be acknowledged, that only a portion of his adherents — generally poor people — could leave their homes and follow Jesus to Jerusalem; and, if more than a hundred of the more ardent disciples did so follow him, five hundred or a thousand might have been left at home, who believed in him as the Messiah. But what was to be expected

---

[*] Acts i., 15.

was that all Galilee, all the people among whom he had wrought cures, cast out evil spirits, fed multitudes without any adequate provision of food, and raised the dead, should have believed in him as a divine being, or as a man specially favored and endowed by God. The records quite contradict this view. He is made to reproach the chief cities wherein his greatest miracles were done because they believed not. He said of the multitudes, whom he miraculously fed, and whose sick he wholly cured, that they followed him only to be fed by him. He called his followers, those that accepted him as of God, a little flock, alluding to the paucity of their numbers; and he said that he would not explain the parables to the multitudes, before whom he is said to have wrought his miracles, because they were not disciples, and had no right to be initiated into the mysteries of the kingdom of heaven.

Of course, as has already been shown, the miracles at Jerusalem, including the raising of Lazarus, could not have been performed without placing Jesus in such an estimation of admiration and awe in the minds of the citizens, that it would have been utterly impossible for the rulers to subject him to the ignominy of a public trial, and for the people to have madly clamored for his death, when Pilate made overtures to pardon him. They, who accept the Johannic narrative as history, have also to reconcile with the statement of the occurrence of the miracles in Galilee the other statement, that, after the period when they are declared to have been performed, the brothers of Jesus did not believe on him. It is no slight confirmation of the view here taken, that, even regarding John's Gospel as a dogmatic fiction, a writer of the second or third century should have represented the isolation of Jesus and his repudiation by his countrymen in so vivid and touching a manner.

But did Jesus possess no remarkable powers out of which the legend of the miracles naturally grew? It has been seen already upon how much less evidence this claim for him stands than does his historical identity, his teaching of a coming kingdom of heaven, and of an impending end of the world, and his ethical doctrines,— mainly of self-denial, mutual forgiveness, meekness, and almsgiving. All these facts find confirmation in the concurrent testimony of the whole literature of the age, and have entered into a faith that survives to our own time. But the miracles are told by unofficial and unauthorized reporters, whose accounts vary in substance as well as in details, who are contradicted by facts, which they themselves report, incompatible with such occurrences. Then, too, their testimony is disturbed by the fact that after them came a writer of marked ability and great celebrity, whose Gospel is either a literary fiction or a palpable contradiction of all the substance of their miraculous claims. If it be the former, it shows how miracles were injected into the ordinary annals of Jesus' career to exalt his character, and express the awe which his name had come to inspire. We cannot say that Matthew's and Luke's miracles may not have subserved the same dogmatic and literary office as those of John.

But how, then, is the wonderful influence which Jesus exerted upon his contemporaries, and which finds such vivid expression in the Pauline and other early Christian writings, accounted for? It cannot be wholly accounted for as simply the effect of his personal purity, his blameless conduct, and the cogency and impressive eloquence of his speech. These endowments would most affect persons of abnormal intellectual and moral culture. In our own times, and indeed in all times, men come to their own order and class, and find appreciation. But Jesus seems not to have powerfully affected the men of intellectual culture of his own age. He said the things he taught were hid from the wise and prudent, and acceptable to babes. He appealed ever to the simple believers, of easy and impulsive faith, and shunned those who were critical and intellectually cautious. It is certain that his earliest and most devoted followers were not men of distinguished intellectual capacity; nor do the glimpses given of their speech and conduct imply that they were gifted with fine moral susceptibilities, or had subjected themselves to the discipline of much self-restraint. The classes he principally affected were the very classes to be attracted by a feat of walking upon the sea rather than by the subtle persuasion of a doctrine of self-denial. How is such effect upon such a class to be accounted for?

To assert that the miracles of Matthew and Luke were actually performed to the extent and upon the subjects they affirm is to find a cause quite too great for the insignificant and petty effects that flowed from it. A cause is wanted consonant and equivalent to the effect, and no more; and the cause, since it operated mainly and most powerfully upon rude minds, must be something of like kind, if less in degree, than that which tradition has imputed. Miracles have been zealously affirmed in all ages. There are certain modes by which certain presences can affect persons, which, not being as yet sufficiently understood or capable of harmonious adjustment with our accredited knowledge, are pronounced marvellous, abnormal, or miraculous. There are in all communities certain persons, having no superiority over ordinary men in either physical, intellectual, or moral talent or culture, who can, by touch or word or look, exert a power over the wills or the nervous organization of other persons, which in certain diseases results in a temporary or permanent cure of such disease. It is foreign to the character of the present discussion to consider the nature of any such agency. Whatever it may be, real or imaginary, there are few intelligent persons, upon whose observation some occurrences have not been thrust, that have not been explained by any of the ordinary laws of science.

It is altogether probable that Jesus, with his sensitive and delicate organization, with a temperance and moral strength of will, that put all his impulses and appetites under the easy control of his reason and conscience, had also in his habitual self-possession, and moral force that came of a well-ordered life, a certain mastery of presence, a magnetic influence, that powerfully affected sensitive persons. His becoming aware of such power may have been the beginning of the prepossession, that, not only was the kingdom of heaven at hand, but that he was its king. Most of the miracles are miracles of dispossession, It seemed to be the belief of that age, shared by Jesus himself, that all dementia attended by erratic and violent conduct was the possession of demons, and, when the delirious strength of the sufferer was very great, that the force of many devils entered into his possession. The New Testament writers seem also, in several instances, to impute even deafness, dumbness, and blindness to devilish obstruction. The caprices of the insane are proverbial. Their intense antipathy to some persons — perhaps their nearest relatives — is sometimes contrasted with the strange and soothing power of other persons, who can allay by a word or a look their severest paroxysms. Jesus might have possessed this power even in an unusual degree. The fame, which his personal sanctity established, would increase it. Its efficacious exercise might have been, as it is now known generally to be, only temporary; for it is said of Mary Magdalene, that seven devils had been cast out of her.[a] She was insane; Jesus had spoken, and soothed and relieved her, or, in the thought of the time, *that demon is cast out.* But, the cause of her malady not having been removed, she lapses again into madness. Alas! exclaim the friends, *another demon has come: where is the great prophet?* So the cure is repeated, until seven seasons of mania have been endured and relieved. It may have been a case, wherein had happened, according to the remembered, curious diagnosis of Jesus, that fatal relapse, when seven demons have come back to a once cleansed soul. Even this new peril is safely passed under his benign treatment; and the grateful woman had become famous as a person relieved of a sevenfold possession.

It is curious to note that all this report of devilish agency comes to us from the three earlier Gospels. When we read them and take our minds back to the quaint region and remote period which they describe, we think of Galilee as a country where the torment of devils was endemic. Some lands are plagued with fevers, some with malaria, some with poisonous insects or reptiles: this land would have been wholesome and salubrious but for an incursion into it of evil spirits. Devilish possession was one of the commonest casualties of human life — the local peril that would stimulate the precaution of travellers, and excite the solicitude of mothers. Even a constitution, as well endowed as that of Jesus, was not exempt from exposure to it, and escaped the baleful influence only by the constancy of his faith.

Now, when we look through the Fourth Gospel, all this ghostly visitation disappears. The writer attempts to

[a] Luke viii., 2.

describe the same country, the same age, the same people, the career and activity among them of the same historic personage, but he knows nothing of devils entering into or being cast out of men. Seven different times the writer uses the word "devil," but always in our modern sense. He makes the Jews accuse and acquit Jesus of having a devil. He makes Jesus retort vigorously upon them that they are children of the devil.[a] But his idea clearly is to impute to bad men and bad actions, as we still do, a prompting and principle of evil, belonging permanently to such natures, and for which they are to be held guilty. The idea of the Synoptic Gospels as clearly is, that to have a devil is a misfortune, that may befall a good man, and from which he may be relieved.

How forcibly the conclusion impresses itself upon our minds, that in passing from the first three to the Fourth Gospel we have arrived at the ideas of another time and of another people! How can the Fourth Gospel be the work of an intimate companion of Jesus in all his career of exorcization in Galilee, who had witnessed the tortures of the possessed and heard their imprecations and invocations? How could it have been written by that very one of all the twelve apostles, whose thorough belief in demoniac possession is disclosed so unmistakably in the Third Gospel?[b]

But there are other forms of disease mainly affecting the nervous organization, of whose subtle law science has as yet learned little, where what, for want of better intelligence, is named personal magnetism, produces strange and inexplicable curative or alleviative results. Why cannot this paralyzed or palsied man walk or lift his arms? He is alive, his muscular structure is apparently unimpaired, his circulation unobstructed. The nervous connection between brain and muscle has been interrupted. A shock and a strong impulse of the will, such as a great joy, or a sudden peril, or a touch or word of certain persons, will restore the connection, and the imbecile patient will find himself able to walk.

It is even easy to find a basis of fact for the legend of raising the dead. New-born infants, persons rescued from drowning, have often no actual life, only the capacity

[a] John vi., 70; viii., 44, 48, 49; x., 20, 21; xiii., 2.   [b] Luke ix., 49.

of living. There is a perfect mechanism of vitality; but like a clock wound up, but not in motion, it requires an impulse to set it going. There are lungs with which to breathe, a strong heart ready to throb, a circulation ready to flow to the remotest members of the body, but they are all still and paralyzed. Without prompt external aid, that feeble infant, that pallid, drowned man will die; these flexible muscles, valves, and veins will grow rigid and collapse, and no power can reinstate the lost vitality. But a gentle pressure of the chest, a warmth and stimulus ministered to the arteries, and the pulse of life begins to beat, and strength and consciousness return to the very dead. Doubtless, in many acute diseases, the strength of the fever is abated, and the sufferer lies unconscious, apparently dead of nervous prostration and exhaustion. He is just in the situation where the slightest impulse, the gentlest beneficial shock, such as the presence of some greatly beloved or greatly revered person might bring, would start the feeble pulse and summon back the fading spirit from the very portals of death. The ruler's daughter might have been at this very crisis of her fever. Jesus himself, in perfect good faith, as we must believe, said she was not dead, but asleep, exhausted, in a state, that would become death, if no change could be wrought. His presence, longed for with the last consciousness, his touch, his thrilling word is the needful change — the slight access of nervous force, which turns back to joyful life the enfeebled will from the death, into which a fatal sleep is fast deepening. The rational result followed. Those that believed the girl was not dead, as Jesus said, rejoiced, but were not astonished. Those that laughed him to scorn insisted that she was dead, and told the story far and wide; and, after the power to raise the dead was once imputed to him by the credulous, it was easy for rumor, growing for centuries, to expand it into the raising of the widow's son at Nain and of Lazarus at Bethany.

Just this extent of power and no more, while it gives a probable foundation for the legend of miracles, harmonizes completely with the effects, which the evangelists themselves confess the career of Jesus produced upon his country and his age,— that is, a few persons, mostly among the illiterate, believed that he was the Son of God; the community generally disavowed that pretension, and either aided or acquiesced in his judicial murder. A solution, too, offers itself of the undoubted periodicity of the curative power of Jesus. All but the romantic John agree in the statement, that the miracle-working was characteristic of the earlier part of Jesus' ministry, that it abated, when he became more widely known in his own province, and that it wholly ceased, when he emerged into the broad light of history in coming into the publicity of Jerusalem. This is excused by the writers by two pleas, not quite consistent with each other. Jesus could not do miracles anywhere, where there was a serious counteraction of persons without faith. Powerful as he was, the critical and self-possessed spirit was always hostile to his energy, and rendered it inefficient. He would not do miracles at Jerusalem, because his purpose was, not to convince and convert the Jews, who would on their account have believed on him, but to deceive them and harden their hearts, that, in killing him, they might prepare the way for his return in the character of king of the world, and ensure their own condemnation and reprobation. But it is degrading the memory of a heroic martyr to associate him with that unmistakable badge of charlatanism and imposition, which always begins an effort at deception by some trick to juggle and put in bondage our common sense. And, if the last was the deliberate purpose of Jesus, it is hard to understand why the advent to the world of such a malignant spirit should ever have been considered an event over which mankind should congratulate itself.

If Jesus had once the power that in this discussion has been conjectured, it is not difficult to account for its subsequent abatement. He lost the control of his own spirit, in his later faith, that Heaven had appointed him to the dazzling glory of kingship in a new-created world where awaited him the homage of saints and angels. No longer did he maintain that fine equipoise of soul, that harmony with nature and with God springing out of the unselfish nobility of his aspirations, and making him strong in self-possession and a tower of strength to the weaker men that attached themselves to him; he could no longer speak with the spiritual force his meekness and humility had given him. "This kind," he once said, "goeth not out but by prayer and fasting."*

* Matt. xvii., 21.

CHAPTER X.

HIS ARREST, TRIAL, AND DEATH.

"The Jesus, who appears to be depicted in the original tradition of the disciples, is a Jew preaching to his countrymen the immediate coming of the kingdom of heaven, for which they were waiting, and repentance and amendment as the conditions of entrance to it; protesting against the narrow technical morality, and the absorbing ritual observances of the religious guides of the people, whose hostility he thus excites; winning at first an amount of popular favor that awakens the fear of the government, to avoid which and the hostility of the Pharisees he retires to Syro-Phœnicia; then publicly entering Jerusalem in the avowed character of the King of the Jews; renewing his conflicts with the Pharisees, and exciting the fears and the enmity of the chief priests and elders; delivered by them to Pilate as a rebel against the authority of Rome, and as such crucified. Thus viewed, his own proceedings and those of his adversaries appear natural and consistent, and his death to have been the inevitable consequence of his assumption of the character of the Messiah."—*Sir Richard Hanson's "Jesus of History."*

IT has become necessary, pursuing a method purely historic, next to consider more fully the causes of the death of Jesus. If history be conceived of as evolved according to a definite plan or by a vital growth,—one event being the seed and parent of another,—the apparently capricious actions of men seem to be parts of an orderly social and political movement, as much under the control of law as the succession of the seasons, the courses of the heavenly bodies, or the propagation, growth, and decay of living forms.

In trying to find the proximate causes of the death of Jesus, it is not necessary to deny that there were providential purposes subserved by the event, or that it has drawn after it consequences in the evolution of civilization disproportioned to its apparent importance. From the period of the Christian era, immediately succeeding the death of Jesus, to the present age, there have been devout minds that have not been able to consider the crucifixion in the category of human events. To them, it is more a conspicuous scene of divine administration, a crisis in the divine economy, which in some way brought men under the dominion of new laws and new duties, and endowed them with higher hopes and larger destinies. Paul explained to the philosophers at Athens that this crisis had occurred in his own lifetime, previously to which God had been comparatively indifferent to the sins of men, but that from that time, taking fresh cognizance of the conduct of his creatures, he had demanded universal repentance.[a] This spectacular and typical aspect of the death of Jesus, its mysterious connection with the enlarged vision, the enduring inheritance of life and happiness, which it is believed to have procured,—if not for all mankind, for all who strive to obtain the great gift,—has had some effect to lessen the world's pity for the sufferings of a heroic martyr, and its indignation against his murderers. How severely can we inveigh against the agents in a transaction so rich in the fruition of blessing and salvation to the human soul? Leaving to minds capable of large generalizations and deep insight these profound speculations,—if indeed there remains an aspect of the case that sincere faith and reverence have not already perceived and disclosed,—let us essay a more modest and less frequently attempted task.

How came such a man as Jesus, engaged in such an enterprise as he is seen to have undertaken, pursuing it by his methods and with his character, to have made himself so obnoxious to the leaders of public opinion in Church and State, as to fall under the cognizance of the civil law of his country? Why did he so far lack popular sympathy and support as to have been execrated by the mob, and forced by them to his fate, when a mild and vacillating governor tendered his release? It has already appeared that Jesus lost his life because the chief priests, elders, scribes, and Pharisees, the ruling classes in the ecclesiastical hierarchy which constituted the State, bitterly hated him; because the highest civil magistrate, the Roman proconsul, was induced by his love of popularity, or provoked by jealousy, to lend his soldiery for his execution; and because the populace wildly clamored for his crucifixion. He had no friends in either of these orders; and they embraced the whole public of Jerusalem upon which Jesus had voluntarily ventured.

[a] Acts xvii., 30.

What was there about Jesus and his methods and ideas that gave offence to the people of his nationality and religion? His gifts of healing, if possessed in the degree conjectured in these chapters, would have gained for him consideration and gratitude. If these gifts had been exercised, as the narratives of Matthew and Luke assert, in a wholesale obliteration of every form of mental and bodily disorder throughout all the cities and villages of Galilee, they would have secured for Jesus universal veneration and respect. The connection of his presence with such wonderful works as the restoration of sight to the blind, locomotion to the paralyzed, rational speech to the insane, and life to the dead, even if the mysterious agency by which he wrought was not understood, would have insured him not only against all personal violence, but also against all opprobrious or contemptuous epithets. As a worker of beneficent miracles, Jesus could not have been hated and persecuted.

As a teacher of a sublime system of ethics, Jesus could not have excited the deadly hostility of his countrymen. True, the prophets of Israel who had, along with their exhortations to maintain the established forms of national worship and the integrity of faith in Jehovah, sedulously inculcated just dealing, mercy, and kindness to the poor, and personal temperance and chastity, had been persecuted by their countrymen, and some of them had been slain. But the prophets were patriots as well as preachers; and they encountered hatred and persecution, either because the idolatrous practices they denounced so vigorously were favored by the kings or those men and women of their courts who chiefly controlled the affairs of state, or because the alliances with powerful heathen nations that more or less controlled the affairs of the little kingdoms of Judah and Israel, which the prophets sometimes favored and sometimes condemned, had more of a political than of a religious character. The prophets had suffered persecutions, as their successors have, as politicians not on the winning side. The Sermon on the Mount, though addressed to the disciples of Jesus, was listened to by the people with some astonishment at the novelty of its doctrines and at the intuitive confidence with which its principles were affirmed, but not with anything like opposition.[a]

[a] Matt. v., 1, 2; vii., 28, 29.

Yet, in that discourse, Jesus had indicated very significantly his indisposition to maintain any fellowship with the ruling classes of the Church, and had subjected to a free handling the Mosaic ten words. But all the positive doctrines of that memorable discourse had nothing in them to provoke opposition and hatred. They could provoke no other feeling than the pique with which men, confident in their own rectitude and that their standard of conduct is the highest possible, resent the implication against themselves, when a man of deeper spiritual insight and loftier virtue declares a rule of life, the comprehensiveness of which makes their own seem narrow and incomplete. Doubtless, the scribes and Pharisees perceived this implication, and returned the disparagement of Jesus with both anger and disdain. But, being above all things politic, and anxious to preserve their reputation as men of virtue, moderation, and devoutness, they would be more likely to conceal their chagrin and lay claim to the possession even of the more interior goodness which he portrayed, than to resent the establishment of a standard of rectitude too exalted for their emulation. Indeed, the history of Jesus gives us several anecdotes which show that the scribes and Pharisees never confessed themselves surprised by any of his more esoteric doctrines; but that, when he uttered any profound and ideal principle, they even affected to be very familiar with it, and claimed it as a well-known feature of their own doctrine.[a] How could they then take offence when he pronounced a blessing on the meek, the pure, the poor, the merciful, the lovers of peace, the persecuted for righteousness, upon the true successors of the prophets whom they revered; when he denounced causeless anger as murder, and a lascivious look as adultery; when he declared that it was safe to make no defence against any violence, and wise to forgive all injuries; when he said that men must give freely to every asker, and must take no thought of how the body was to be fed or clothed, asking freely of God for every needed thing, in confidence that it would be given? These principles might be criticised as impracticable and visionary; but in no age of the world, where they have been from time to time reproduced as the basis

---

[a] Mark xii., 28, 32-34.

of an ideal system of life, have they excited derision and satire, much less rage and hatred.

Did Jesus become obnoxious to the people of his time by the claim which he made to be the Messiah of the nation, and the king of a kingdom that was to supplant the kingdoms of the world and reconstruct the order of society and the constitution of the physical universe? There had been Messiahs before Jesus, and there were Messiahs after him. It was a pretension, which in itself flattered the national pride of Israel and fed the quenchless hope, that has characterized that strange race through the long history of its slavery and depression. Had the Messianic idea of Jesus been more in accord with the prophetic foreshadowing, and with the popular expectation, his claim to be the Messiah would have given him prestige and authority, at least commensurate with the pretenders that preceded and succeeded him, each of whom drew after him a numerous following.[a]

The kingship of Jesus, if it had anything ominous about it, threatened the security of the Roman power. The Jewish hierarchy, after they had come to hate Jesus, did all they could to turn the eyes of the civil power to the political dangers which his heresy portended. How futile the effort was, how utterly indifferent the sceptical, luxurious petty sovereigns, who held the vice-royalties of Judea and Galilee, were to the danger, is apparent in the Scriptural traditions. It is highly improbable that either Herod or Pilate ever made the ministry of Jesus, and his progress through their respective provinces, proclaiming himself the king of a kingdom to be established during his own generation in Jerusalem, the subject of a personal, still less of an official communication to Cæsar at Rome. If they had done this, perhaps some memoranda of him might have crept into secular history. Matthew tells, indeed, that Herod of Judea had so far interested himself in the Hebrew prophetic literature that, learning, by the exposition of the scribes, that the Messiah was to be born in Bethlehem, and by a communication from certain *Magi*, who came to Jerusalem from the far East, that the Messiah had already been born, he took the precaution to procure the slaughter of all the children of

[a] Acts v., 36, 37.

Bethlehem under two years of age.[a] But as no other Gospel contains this story, as the older copies of Matthew's Gospel omit it, and as a full history of the crimes and cruelties of Herod's reign, written by no friendly hand, does not recount this massacre, it is not likely to have occurred.

Herod of Galilee imprisoned, and afterward murdered John the Baptist, but this was the result of the fury of a wicked woman whom John had provoked by the plainness of speech with which he had denounced her incestuous connection with the king.[b] Jesus, though he was fearless in bringing home his rule of rectitude to the life and thought of the persons with whom he was in actual conference, rarely made personal application of his doctrines to particular individuals. As Herod had slain John, whose teachings so closely resembled those of Jesus, the Galilean Pharisees tried to alarm Jesus by telling him that Herod was seeking his life. The slight apprehension this, doubtless, false information caused in the mind of Jesus, and the confident and contemptuous answer he sent back show that Herod had taken no notice whatever of Jesus' enterprise.[c] It would have been apparently as easy for the king to imprison and slay Jesus, as it was to rid himself of his compatriot and master. The Roman official evidently did not suspect that Jesus was of the least political consequence.

How little the eager suspicions of the elders and chief priests affected the more mild and philosophical Pilate, the proconsul of Judea, is apparent in the Biblical record. Jesus was delivered to him as a plotter against Cæsar, a pretender for the throne of Judea; and Pilate, as the sequel will show, could not consider the empire of his master seriously threatened by a hallucination that seemed to him so absurd.

As Jesus never encountered any danger from the Roman government either of Galilee, where he lived, or of Judea, whither he betook himself, so it is to be said, that, apparently, while he remained in Galilee, he was never in any situation of formidable peril from any quarter. Luke alone tells of a fierce and sudden tumult, which was caused in Nazareth during the earliest days of his more public

[a] Matt. ii., 3-5, 16. [b] Matt. xiv., 3-12. [c] Luke xiii., 31-33.

life, when a mob seized him and bore him toward a precipice to throw him down. The provocation given by Jesus seems to be quite inadequate to cause such an exhibition of animosity, unless words were spoken which the record has not given us, though doubtless the inflammable fanaticism of those provincial Jews exceeded the limits of modern comprehension. Whatever the provocation was, and however great the tumult, it was a mere temporary excitement, only possible in an isolated Jewish village. It was not preconcerted or connected with any designs against Jesus formed among the scribes and elders of the principal neighboring cities, and it subsided as rapidly as it rose; for it seems Jesus continued to make Nazareth his home, and, so far from being ever molested afterward, must have considerably gained in public consideration, and secured in the end the good opinion of his own quite numerous kinsmen. The elders of the Nazarene synagogue were probably quite as indignant at the unwonted presumption of a young carpenter undertaking to read and interpret the Scriptures, as they were at the disparaging imputations of his comments.[a]

How much the Galilean and Judean communities were disturbed by the claim of Jesus to be the expected Messiah may therefore be exactly determined by the effect it had upon the jealous and suspicious Roman proconsulate whose business it was to watch and crush, at its first outbreak, every effort at national independence. If Rome did not care that Jesus was making a progress through the land in some kind of royal state, as King of the Jews, it may be certain that there was nobody to care.

As he was in no danger from Herod, an irresponsible and capricious tyrant, so he was in no danger from the elders, scribes, and Pharisees, during the time after his baptism that he dwelt in Galilee, generally believed to be about three years, but more probably only a few months. The Pharisees, as a general thing, treated him with deference and respect. They addressed him as Rabbi, giving full credit to his prophetic office. They extended to him social courtesies and invited him to their feasts. They referred to him questions of ritual practice, of the con-

[a] Luke iv., 16-30.

struction of their written law, of general casuistry, and of political expediency and duty; and we are not obliged to adopt the evident prejudice of the evangelists, that these questions were always put craftily and disingenuously for the sake of embarrassing and discrediting him.* It was not the practice of the bishops, canons, and curates of the English Church to form a part of the promiscuous audiences which listened in the fields and in barns to the preaching of Bunyan, Naylor, and Fox. It was never known that leading Presbyterian doctors of divinity or Evangelical presidents of theological seminaries in the United States condescended to hold newspaper controversies with Joseph Smith, or with the itinerant Second Adventist missionaries. Religious bigotry must have been far more rife in Galilee in the first century than it is in either Old or New England in the nineteenth century; and the fact that the scribes and Pharisees listened to Jesus, held colloquies with him, and frequently approved and commended his doctrines, indicates on their part a position toward him far more respectful than modern Orthodoxy maintains toward modern dissent.

While this was the attitude of the religious classes toward Jesus, what was his attitude toward them? What overtures did the Messenger and Son of Jehovah make to the priesthood of Jehovah, to that body of men who, whatever may be justly imputed against them, had been, as far as can now be seen, exceedingly zealous for the Lord of Hosts, and for the integrity of his worship. To them, it was certainly due that the last traces of idolatry had been eliminated from the cultus of their race, and that the people had been thoroughly schooled into the practice of a decorous and decent morality. When or where was the grace of the Gospel offered to scribes and Pharisees? Why should Christianity have been left to advance slowly through nineteen centuries with the emphatic protest, borne steadily against it, of the most devout and religious race the world has ever known?

The antipathy of John the Baptist to both the popular sects, the Pharisees and Sadducees, has already been spoken of. It has never been known in the world, that a reformer and teacher of a new faith did not seek to make

---

* Mark xii., 13, 14, 19, 28, 32-34; Luke vii., 36; x., 25; xi., 53, 54; xiv., 1.

converts; but, when this ascetic preacher saw multitudes of the Pharisees and Sadducees coming to his baptism, he was disturbed and disgusted. He addressed them as a *generation* of *vipers*, and told them that their damnation was so assured, that it had not occurred to him to give them any warning to avoid it.ᵃ This pre-judging of their case, this shutting in their faces the door of hope, shows how truculent and intolerant was the spirit of this ascetic prophet. Perhaps Paul, then a zealous student of the law at the feet of Rabbi Gamaliel, going, with other Pharisees, to hear what the preacher had to say, might have been stunned and repelled, and had his orthodox faith confirmed, by this ungracious rebuff. From such a master Jesus himself received baptism, and seemed ever afterward to have had his memory in reverence. He insisted that he was the most enlightened of the prophets, and that no greater man had been born of woman.ᵇ

When John had been cast into prison, Jesus began himself to preach,ᶜ and, in his first discourse, indicated his utter hostility to the whole teaching and moral standard of the Pharisees. He reviewed the ten words of the law with the expositions and deductions the scribes had put upon them, and declared them superficial and inadequate; and he said plainly: "Unless your righteousness exceeds the pattern prescribed by the scribes and Pharisees, ye shall in no wise enter the kingdom."ᵈ No more emphatic announcement could be made that the grace of his gospel was not for the scribes and Pharisees, or for any person accepting their faith and conforming to their practices. He evidently meant the scribes and Pharisees, when in the same discourse he bade his disciples beware of false prophets. They have, he said, the clothing of sheep, but inwardly they are ravening wolves.ᵉ

Early in his public career, he said, that people from all corners of the earth should come into his kingdom, but that the children of the kingdom — that is, the Jewish Church — should be cast into the outer darkness.ᶠ That the Jewish Church had a certain right of primogeniture, as the first begotten of Jehovah, Jesus seemed at times fully to recognize. Thus, when he sent out his twelve disciples

ᵃ Matt. iii., 7.   ᵇ Matt. xi., 11.   ᶜ Luke iii., 19, 20.
ᵈ Matt. v., 20.   ᵉ Matt. vii., 15.   ᶠ Matt. viii., 11, 12.

to proclaim the kingdom of heaven, he told them: "*Go not into the way of the Gentiles, and into any city of the Samaritans enter ye not; but go rather to the lost sheep of the house of Israel.*"[a] The lost sheep were the poor, the sinners, those that were oppressed and bowed under labor, those whom the scribes despised, those whom the Pharisees in their self-righteous prayers thanked God they were not like.[b] But, though Jesus sent out his disciples to make converts among the people of his own nation, he evidently had slight hopes of the success of their mission. For he said: "Shake off the dust of your feet against the city or house, that will not receive you; it shall be more tolerable for Sodom and Gomorrah in the day of judgment, than for that city;[c] and ye shall be brought before governors and kings, and scourged in the synagogues, and hated of all men as representatives of me."[d] For his own part, Jesus said, almost with the emphasis and exclusiveness of John the Baptist, that he came not to call the righteous,— meaning the religious and plausibly moral Pharisees,— but sinners to repentance.[e]

The first actual contact between Jesus and the scribes and Pharisees was, when certain of their numbers went down from Jerusalem to Galilee, doubtless as a committee of the body, to inquire into his teachings and practice. With some evident awe of his known eloquence and dignity of presence, they attribute the conduct, which they wish to censure, not to him, or to his example, but to the fault of his disciples. "Why do *thy disciples*," they ask, "transgress the tradition of the elders in eating bread without laving their hands?" Never was a reply more crushing and personal, from a mind fully prepossessed with a judgment adverse to their characters and doctrines,— "*Why do ye transgress the commandments of God with your traditions?*"[f] Then he called them hypocrites and said, they were those described by Isaiah as worshipping Jehovah with their mouths, while their hearts were far from him. So possessed was he with the resentment, which their petty prying into the trivial table manners of his household had justly excited in him, that, after the committee had left him, he denounced the whole body of

[a] Matt. x., 5, 6. [b] Matt. xi., 5, 28; Luke xviii., 11. [c] Matt. x., 14, 15.
[d] Matt. x., 18. [e] Matt. ix., 13. [f] Matt. xv., 2, 3.

Pharisees to the multitude, as blind leaders of the blind, to be let alone, and, unled and unwarned, to fall into the ditch.ᵃ

This attitude toward the leading religious sects cannot certainly be considered as conciliatory; but, during all the life in Galilee, it did not appear to have subjected Jesus to any personal danger. The invidious multitude, who like to see men conspicuous for their social position and repute, satirized and derided, and who doubtless listened to the derogatory epithets with applause, probably liked Jesus the better for the freedom of his censures; and the subjects of them, who were not left to hearsay to learn the ill-repute they stood in with him, bore them with remarkable good nature. On the whole, the record does not impress us with the idea that the Pharisees were vindictive; and we acquire confidence in the statement of Josephus, who says of them that "they follow the conduct of reason, and what that prescribes to them, as good for them they do."ᵇ

Why, then, did not Jesus remain in Galilee, where he was certainly gaining in reputation and influence, and where he was in no peril? His own rule would have justified such conduct, for he had told his disciples in sending them out, "*If they persecute you in one city, flee to another.*"ᶜ They were not to resist, but to succumb to and avoid danger. Peter, too, as we see, was quite alive to the perils of the mission to Jerusalem; and, though he received a crushing rebuke for his advice, it was evidently given with a most affectionate solicitude for his master's safety.ᵈ

But Jerusalem was not to be avoided with any thought even of saving life.ᵉ So terrible had been the silent struggles of Jesus with his own temperamental apprehension of death, as the natural result of the enmity he had already excited among that class that were all-powerful in Jerusalem, that when it arose again, albeit in the familiar voice of his admired friend, it seemed the spirit of the world — the insidious voice of Satan himself — and he set himself to crush it. He had diligently counted the cost. No king, he said, goes to war against another king until

---

ᵃ Matt. xv., 1-14.   ᵇ Jos. Antiq. xviii., 1, 3.   ᶜ Matt. x., 23.
ᵈ Matt. xvi., 22, 23.   ᵉ Matt. xvi., 25.

he first considers his own force and that of his enemy; no man undertakes to build a house until he sits down first and counts the cost.[a] Counting the cost is the very thing which kings and house-builders have ever been reproached for not doing; but Jesus was evidently putting into counsels for others exhortations he was in fact addressing to himself. He had diligently studied the prophecies, and meditated much and long upon all that the Messiahship involved. The king must go to Zion, and go, too, in the days of his humiliation, in the meekness of his servitude. But Messiah must be cut off. The Shepherd must be smitten; the sheep must be scattered. He must make his grave with the wicked. But afterward he will come as a conqueror and a judge, with legions of holy angels and the glory of his Father. So, to fulfil his destiny, he must go to Jerusalem,— go sadly, treading alone the wine-press of the wrath of God. He fears not the peril of rulers,— of the wolves in sheep's clothing,— of the priest and elders, and the powers of the Gentiles, who will scourge and put him to death. He will go to defy them, to provoke them to the very controversy, that shall insure his deliverance to death. Jesus undertook the journey to Jerusalem in order that he might die at the hands of his countrymen.

He took with him his twelve disciples, and the friendly Galilean women, who charged themselves with the expense of his support.[b] As it was the occasion of one of the annual national festivals, a considerable part of his adherents must have accompanied him with their families out of the cities of Galilee. But, as the Jews were generally at the same season going up to the Passover, there was nothing in his expedition to excite particular attention. Among the multitudes, that went up to Jerusalem, only his confidential friends knew the sad errand that took him thither. He went slowly and indirectly, crossing the Jordan and avoiding Samaria, the direct route, and doubtless the thoroughfare of most of the pilgrims. A man does not travel rapidly or cheerfully on his way to a voluntary death. No plots of the Pharisees annoyed him, and no spies from Jerusalem watched his movements. Probably the whole city was profoundly ignorant of his

[a] Luke xiv., 28, 33.   [b] Luke viii., 2, 3.

plans and unacquainted with his person. The citizens knew as little that their long-expected king and deliverer was actually approaching Zion, as that they themselves would in a few days take upon their souls the guilt of the blood of the chiefest of their prophets, and earn for themselves and their children to the remotest times the execrations of mankind.ᵃ

But, if there was hesitation, there was no pusillanimity and no swerving from his high purpose on the part of Jesus. Up through the wilderness of Jordan, where he had visited John and received baptism, where, later, curious multitudes had followed him out of the towns and villages of Galilee, and done honor to him as a prophet, he travelled, more depressed than weary, strengthening his spirit by the assurance that the Scriptures must be fulfilled, and by the silent prayer, *Not my will, but thine be done.*

In another connection, the triumphal entry into Jerusalem has already been mentioned. It was not ostentation on the part of Jesus, nor does it seem he derived any augury of hope from the demonstration. He had already made up his mind that he must be rejected of that wicked generation, and be put to death; but the Scriptures must be fulfilled, and it was prophesied of Zion's King that he should come meek and sitting upon the foal of an ass.ᵇ It was but a meagre pageant. The Galileans, that were of his company, cast palm-branches in the way, and the children shouted: "*Hosannah! blessed is He that cometh in the name of the Lord!*"ᶜ But the city itself made no responce, only it asked: Who is this? as it would not have asked had he been for months during two or three years an *habitué* of the temple, conducting famous arguments with the Rabbis, the populace inclining to his side. Jerusalem does not know his person or his name. It is answered by those of his party: "*This is Jesus, the Prophet from Nazareth of Galilee.*"ᵈ His name, which was a very common one among the people at the time, does not identify him; and he must be distinguished by the name of his town. Even Nazareth is so little known that it must be further told that Nazareth is a city of Galilee. Then it

ᵃ Matt. xxvii., 25.   ᵇ Matt. xvi., 21; xxi., 5.
ᶜ Mark xi., 8–10; Matt. xxi., 15, 16.   ᵈ Matt. xxi., 11, Revised N. T.

might have occurred to some of the more intelligent scribes,— he is Jesus, of whose dealings with the possessed we heard a while ago, when we sent messengers to observe his methods. He the Messiah! Zion's King, that was to come from Bethlehem of Judea, come out of Galilee! There is no warrant of Scripture for that.

Still considering the implications of such a procession announcing itself with such cries, it must be said that the Jews submitted to it with rather remarkable patience. But the pageant proceeds directly to the temple itself, and Jesus, dismounting at its portals, arms himself with a whip of cords, and casts out all them that sold and bought, and overthrew the tables of the money-changers and the seats of them that sold doves.[a] The conduct is somewhat inexplicable, not only that it seems to be in quite another spirit from the prophetic meekness, which he was attempting to illustrate, but because it seems to be foreign to all the ideas of Jesus to undertake any reform whatever of the temple service. He had not distinguished himself by the assiduity or punctuality of his attendance upon the temple services and sacrifices. Certainly all his influence had been in the direction of a substitution of morality for worship, and he had claimed the right in a matter, so fundamental as the Sabbath, to substitute his own authority for the letter of the law.[b] There was much in the details of such a mode of worship as the Jews had perpetuated to disgust a sensitive disposition like that of Jesus. The eager crowds of men, women and children, the jostling of the multitudes of large and smaller beasts used in sacrifices and feasts, the ungentle hand of the slayers, the terror and cries of the victims, the reek and horror of wholesale slaughter — far less concealed and mitigated than in well-regulated modern abattoirs — would seem to have moved an innovator like Jesus to denounce the whole service as superstitious and savage. But what Jesus did was to break up an arrangement really in the interest of decency, and an arrangement not only convenient and sensible in itself, but expressly permitted by the law. For it is enacted in the second book of the law, that "If the way be too long for thee, so that thou art not able to carry the firstlings of thy flocks consecrate to Jehovah, or the place be too far from thee, which the Lord thy God

[a] Matt. xxi., 12-16.   [b] Matt. xii., 3-8.

shall choose to set his name there, then thou shalt turn it into money and bind up the money in thy hand, and shalt go unto the place, which the Lord shall choose, and shall bestow that money for oxen, for sheep, and for wine."[a] These sellers of doves very properly met that want, and the money-changers were there to accommodate the sellers and buyers with coins of convenience in their purchases. Doubtless there were extortionate practices attending this traffic, which merited the punishment inflicted; but of these the record contains no hint, nor does the extrusion seem to have been accomplished upon any other ground than the abatement of a profanation of the temple service.

The scribes and Pharisees might have overlooked the triumphal entry, and the claim to be the King of Zion; but "Who is this," they asked, "that undertakes to control the practices of the temple, and overthrows the statutes of Moses?" They were seriously disturbed.[b] They still refrain however from violence. They do not arrest Jesus. They do not even interrupt him. Either moderation or timidity seemed to have influenced the chief priests and elders of the people, or this interference with the national worship would have been promptly resented. Doubtless, too, they deferred somewhat to the universal reverence, in which the office of prophet was generally held. Whatever may have been their motive, they contented themselves with a decorous inquiry addressed to the Galilean Rabbi: "*Who gave thee authority to do these things?*" Jesus says he will answer this question, if his interrogators will first tell him, whether or not the mission of John the Baptist was divine.[c] The relevancy of John's authority to the question of his own was apparently no more obvious to the scribes than it is to us; having consulted among themselves, and over-cautious to avoid the logical dilemma they might have been driven to by the keen intelligence of Jesus, they decline to answer, and, overawed by his courage and resources, forthwith abandon their inquisition into his proceedings.

But though his enemies retire dismayed from the controversy, Jesus on his side continues it, and shifts the accusation from his to their proceedings. He is evidently in no mood to make explanations, or to proffer concilia-

[a] Deut. xiv., 24-26.   [b] Matt. xxi., 15.   [c] Matt. xxi., 23-27.

tions. Indifferent to the effect his words may have to exasperate the ecclesiastical rulers, he tells against them two parables.[a] The first was of two sons, one of whom had promised obedience, but neglected to keep his promise; the other was insolent at first, but repented and complied with his father's will. This was the lesson of the story: publicans and harlots believed John, and repented; you scribes and Pharisees, professors of righteousness, repented not, when the preacher of righteousness came to you. The other parable was of the householder, whose servants, and finally whose son were slain by his wicked tenants. But the owner will come and destroy those wicked men, and will let his vineyard to those who will render him the fruits in their season. And, said Jesus, the kingdom of God, which John offered, and you rejected, shall be taken from you, calling yourselves the chosen of the Lord, and given to a nation bringing forth the fruits thereof.[*] This was a gratuitous taunt, if, when they had in fact come to John seeking his baptism, he had driven them away, saying they were children of vipers, who had never been invited to repentance.[b]

If the priests and elders were angry when they came to Jesus, they go away more angry; and they are now ready to lay hands upon him. But caution prevails.[c] They do not yet know how much support he has among the people. The demonstration in the streets, in which the Galileans were active, may have made friends everywhere among the people. It seems prudent to wait a few days to see how Jerusalem itself will receive her latest prophet. Meantime, the hierarchy attempt to embroil him with the Roman authorities or to prejudice him with the people, by asking if it be lawful to pay tribute; and Jesus in his answer plainly commits himself against the patriotic party.[d] Then, the Sadducees put to him their case against the resurrection, which Jesus evades.[e] The discomfiture of the Sadducees pleases the Pharisees, who with great show of deference ask him: "*Which is the chief of the commandments?*" evidently referring to the decalogue.

[a] Matt. xxi., 28-32.   [b] Matt. iii., 7.   [c] Matt. xxii., 46; Luke xx., 19.
[d] Matt. xxii., 16-22.   [e] Matt. xxii., 23-32.

[*] If Jesus had himself during a period of three years preached the gospel of repentance in Jerusalem, as the Fourth Gospel represents, why did he not reproach the priests and elders for the rejection of his own message, rather than for the rejection of the message of John? These words of Jesus seem to carry a strong implication that all that Jerusalem had heard f the doctrine of the kingdom of heaven it had heard from the lips of John the Baptist.

Jesus indicates neither one of the commandments as superior to the rest; but declares that supreme love to God and equal love to men — a sentiment wholly above the grade of the ten words attributed to Moses, found in a prophetic writing of a much later age than his — is the basis of the whole law and prophets.[a]

When the Pharisees and Sadducees were withdrawn, Jesus turned to the multitude and to his disciples and proceeded to utter that invective against the scribes and Pharisees which is the summary of his judgment against them. He charged them with hypocrisy, deceit, oppression, ostentation, ambition, extortion, and blasphemy. He called them fools, blind guides, children of hell, the predestined to damnation. They were full of hypocrisy and all uncleanness; and there was no future for them, but to fill up the measure of their iniquity; for he declared them guilty of all the blood of the good men, that had been slain in the world, which God would require at their hands.[b]

This ended his controversy with his enemies. He had done and said whatever was possible to make them implacable and unforgiving, and there is nothing before him now, but to take leave of his followers and explain to them more fully the nature of the new era that is about to open upon the world in which he and they are to be exalted to the right hand of power, while the glory and pomp of kingdoms and churches is to fall in darkness and condemnation.[c]

The whole narrative indicates that these events followed each other in rapid succession. Doubtless Jesus seized the occasion of so many Galileans going to the Passover to go himself with his disciples. We can understand something of the economy of the little sect. The twelve had been required to leave all and follow him. They had probably sold their possessions and paid the proceeds over to Judas, one of their number who was their treasurer.[d] The conjecture of the Johannic narrative that Judas was an embezzler of the small treasure of the company of Jesus is not approved by the more reliable biographers; but as it is quite probable that one of the twelve was intrusted with their funds, it is fairly supposa-

---

[a] Matt. xxii., 34–40.　[b] Matt. xxiii.　[c] Matt. xxiv., 3–51; xxv.　[d] John xiii., 29; xii., 6.

ble that Judas was in fact the treasurer, as John declares. The more wealthy converts supported the poorer, and Jesus was the especial charge of certain devout women who seemed to have some property. While the disciples were on their missions of healing and preaching, they lived upon the hospitality of the people who chose to receive them.[a] Such an establishment might be supported indefinitely in Galilee, where the habits of the people were simple and the means of living abundant. But transported to a populous city in a mountainous district, where everything was brought in from outlying fields and sold to the citizens who were priests, teachers, public officers, traders, artisans, and laborers, and where Jesus is not known to have secured a single avowed adherent, even the little band of believers could not have maintained themselves upon their own means for very many days,

Jesus betakes himself at night-fall to Bethany. This may have been his custom every night that he remained at liberty.[b] He takes that much precaution for his safety; not that he does not even court death, but because he will have his enemies proceed against him publicly, officially, and by daylight, and not by secret assassination or abduction.[c] Mary and Martha, friends and believers, had made his acquaintance on his way to Jerusalem; and they are now honored in having him for a guest. At Bethany, and just before his arrest, occurred an incident, of which mention must be made.[d] A woman came into his presence, and with a freedom, which seems to have excited the suspicion of the disciples, anointed either the head or the feet of Jesus with a costly perfume. By what a cruel disagreement of the annalists has she been robbed of the fame, she was assured she should have throughout the world for her delicate and sympathetic gift! For Matthew and Mark do not even give her name; and Luke casts against her the cruel imputation that she was a sinner. Only the poet of the Fourth Gospel could see in the touching incident, so contradictorily told down to his day, something to be made more pathetic by his artistic genius. So he makes the unnamed woman — the *sinner* of the Third Gospel — no less a person, than the

[a] Matt. x., 9–11. [b] Matt. xxi., 17; Luke xxi., 37. [c] Matt. xxvi., 4; Luke xx., 20. [d] Matt. xxvi., 6; Mark xiv., 3; Luke vii., 37; John xii., 1–8.

gentle and refined Mary, sister of him, that had been raised from the dead, she whose saintly devotion Jesus had, according to Luke's narrative, so pointedly contrasted with the sordid housekeeping carefulness of Martha. All the evangelists evidently refer to the same transaction, too eccentric and unique in the surprise it occasioned, too well identified in the accompanying words of Jesus, to have happened more than once.

Whether the disciples kept together, and lived upon what Judas could buy with the not-exhausted fund of the company, or whether they scattered and found friends among the poor of the city or of the suburbs cannot be known. They met Jesus every day, and must have been exceedingly excited by the boldness, with which he confronted the priests and the elders, and by the stupendous disclosures he was making to them of the events of the kingdom of heaven on the eve of being established.

When we read of those colloquies of Jesus with the Pharisees and Sadducees, we must not infer that the whole body of Pharisees and Sadducees in Jerusalem, or even the more prominent leaders and elders of the sects, took part in the discussions. It has been seen that on his arrival at Jerusalem the person of Jesus was not known to the citizens.[a] It is now to be noted, that the chief priests and elders were in the same condition of ignorance. So entirely aloof was Jesus and his company from the cognizance of these high dignitaries of the Church, that, though they had doubtless heard, that a rabble of men, led by one Jesus from Galilee, had marched in fantastic procession to the temple, where the same man had interfered with violence in the practices of the worshippers, that he had been quite too self-possessed for the wits of some of their own number, and some Sadducees, who had ventured to hold an argument with him, and had bitterly denounced themselves to the multitude, they had not seen or heard him. No description of his person had been given, whereby he could be identified among the thousand strangers from Galilee. So they were compelled to use money to induce one of his own chosen disciples to accompany the officers, and indicate him to be arrested.[b] This circumstance shows most conclusively, how really isolated

[a] Matt. xxi., 10.   [b] Mark. xiv., 10, 11.

Jesus was in Jerusalem, and how little impression his teachings and demonstrations had made outside of the little circle of men and women, who had accompanied him from his own country.

It was clearly the preference of the priests, elders, and scribes to put Jesus to death secretly.[a] But his precaution in keeping himself surrounded with a company of his followers by day, and withdrawing at night-fall, defeated this purpose, and compelled them to resort to the legal forms of procedure. Judas' treachery in the mean time opens the way, and Jesus is at last identified, on the night of the Passover,[b]—the only night, that he cannot retire from the city,—in the garden of Gethsemane outside the walls, where doubtless he knew that his enemies would be sure to trace him. Late in the night-time, he is carried before Caiaphas the High Priest, with whom the scribes and elders are assembled in anticipation of the arrest.[c] Both parties had evidently mistaken the temper of the Jewish mob. For days, the exasperation of the priesthood has been at its height, and they are ready to accomplish his assassination; but they are afraid to subject him to a public trial, lest the populace might interfere for his rescue. So they have assembled secretly and unlawfully in the night, and have sent a body, not of Roman soldiers, nor of regular police, but of hired ruffians,—an improvised gang, armed with swords and staves, having Judas for a guide—to find Jesus among the celebrants of the Passover, and bring him before them. Their further proceedings will be determined by the manifestations of popular feeling. If the multitude incline to favor him, they will make away with him secretly. If the multitude take the side of the priesthood and scribes, then they will proceed regularly, and obtain his condemnation and execution under the forms of law.

Unexpectedly, the mob have got wind of what is going on; and they join the ruffians, and go to Gethsemane with them to find Jesus. He is manifestly chagrined and disheartened by their appearance.[d] A brave and devoted man may make up his mind to die, to accomplish some lofty purpose, but he will welcome every obstacle thrown in the way of his death; and he will hope to the last that

---

[a] Matt. xxvi., 4. [b] Matt. xxvi., 47. [c] Matt. xxvi., 57. [d] Luke xxii., 47-53.

some angel of mercy from heaven may intervene for his rescue. Jesus had noted the multitude, who perhaps applauded, when, standing in the temple, he had pronounced the scribes and Pharisees a generation of vipers, the progeny of hell; and he may have drawn some augury of hope from their apparent favor. When the *posse* of the priesthood came upon him in the garden, he seems to have had no reproaches for the armed ruffians, none even for his own trusted disciple, who had betrayed to them his place of hiding; but he turned to the multitude with words like these: I sat daily with you teaching in the temple, and hoped you were not enemies, as ye laid no hands upon me; and are ye now come out with swords and staves as against a thief to take me?[a] Yes, the appearance was delusive: the mob were on the side of his enemies; and now even the courage of the twelve failed, and all but Peter fled and hid themselves.[b] He was bold enough to follow at a distance, hoping to pass himself off as one of the mob by telling a lie.[c] His Galilean dialect, however, betrayed him,—another evidence that no Judæans had believed on Jesus. Peter is in no danger: there is on the part of the hierarchy no purpose to molest any of the company but their chief and leader.

Now, for the first time, and only for a few hours, Jesus comes out from the privacy of his provincial life into such publicity as the official world of government and the courts can give to illumine his conduct. Here, if anywhere, in the evangelic narratives, we come upon veritable history. Accordingly, we find a more substantial agreement in the different traditions of his trial and execution than we find in the traditions of his doctrines or of the incidents of his preceding life. That there was a Jesus Christ, who lived among the Jews of Palestine during the earlier years of the Roman Empire, and that he was put to death by crucifixion, are the best known facts in reference to him. How uncertain all the data we have of his life, character, and teaching are, may be inferred from the grave differences in the histories, that are extant, as to the proceedings at his trial, as to how his conviction was reached, and how sentence against him was executed. It could not well have been otherwise. His trusted friends for-

---

[a] Matt. xxvi., 55.   [b] Matt. xxvi., 56–58.   [c] Matt. xxvi., 69–74.

sook him in apprehension for their own safety. None of the New Testament writers seem to have had access to any record or official documents, in which the proceedings against him, and the final judgment are set forth, if indeed there were any such official documents. As to what was *formally* charged against Jesus, by what, and what kind of testimony, it was attempted to be substantiated, and what, if any, defence was made, we can only know from the unskilled persons, having themselves apparently no knowledge of the classification of crimes, of the nature of sufficient testimony or of the methods of judicial proceedings, who have undertaken, years after the event, to tell us. As to the *informal* proceedings,— that is, what was said to Jesus, and what he said, other than in the indictment and pleadings,— we can know still less. This much is certain: Jesus himself after his arrest had no opportunity, during his life, to converse with his disciples and to disclose to them the proceedings in reference to himself before the Sanhedrim, and none of his disciples were present as witnesses. What the public of Jerusalem learned about those proceedings they must have learned from members of the Council. Doubtless, many members of the Council afterward embraced the faith of Jesus, and described his language and bearing with all the partiality of believers and admirers. Others, the majority, who retained their animosity, told the story tinctured with their own prejudices. But, between the two classes, a substantial agreement as to the main facts ultimately obtained, which formed the public opinion of the time. From a public opinion thus informed, the disciples collected their information; and it was finally committed to writing in what are called the Gospels.

It is doubtless correct as to its substance. What Jesus said, if anything, at his trial and during the suffering of his public execution, owing to the solemnity of the circumstances, and the number and character of the observers, would be likely to be better remembered and more accurately reported than any of his words. Taking the most trustworthy report of his words and of the course and issue of his trial, let us try to understand how the proceedings against him which terminated in his death were conducted. It will be necessary to consider the condition

HIS ARREST, TRIAL, AND DEATH

of the civil government, and of the criminal code, to which he was subject.

The political situation of Jerusalem and Palestine was somewhat anomalous. The Romans did not until the year 70 of the Christian era conquer the country, and make it a part of the empire. In extending their dominions, they had subdued the Greek dynasties of the Seleucidæ, and Ptolemaiæ on either side of the Jews; and the latter, who had succumbed to the armies of Alexander, had no means of resisting the armies of Pompey. In fact, Rome got possession of Palestine as an ally of one of its native princes, waging war against his kinsmen for the throne of Jerusalem.

Ever since the time of Antiochus Epiphanes, the Jews had maintained their independence. Their first revolt from the Greeks was under Judas Maccabæus, 164 B.C.; and he and his brothers, and their descendants, had not only delivered Judea, but had conquered Samaria, Galilee, Trachonitis, and part of Idumea from the Syrio-Greek kings, and had ruled over this territory as princes. In the year B.C. 104, Aristobulus, one of those princes, took the title of king. His brother Alexander succeeded him. Aristobulus and Hyrcanus, sons of Alexander, strove together in arms for the succession, and the latter, being defeated, called in the Romans as umpires; and Pompey, the general of the Senate, took Jerusalem and made Hyrcanus king. Antigonus, son of Aristobulus, made war on Jerusalem in the year 43 B.C., and tried to recover his father's throne. Herod, the son of Antipater, who had married the grand-daughter of Hyrcanus, attempted to defend the city, but having been defeated fled to Rome. The Senate declared him king, and sent him back with an army. Antigonus in his turn was defeated and slain; and Herod became king of Palestine, reigning at Jerusalem, until about the time of the birth of Jesus. On his death, the kingdom was assigned to his sons, Judea to Archelaus, Galilee to Herod Antipas, and Trachonitis to Philip; but Judea in the sixth year of the Christian era was added to the proconsulate of Syria, and governed for the Emperor by Pontius Pilate. Afterward, for a brief period, Herod Agrippa, grandson of the first Herod, ruled for a few years over re-united Palestine; but after 44 A.D. it was ruled by governors as a Roman province

As the revolt of Judas Maccabæus was not only for political, but for religious independence, and as it was incited chiefly by an attempt by Antiochus to abolish the Mosaic religion, it is to be concluded that all the Asmonæan kings were devout Jews, and zealous for the national worship and the faith of Jehovah. Hyrcanus himself was originally the High Priest, and his powerful family kept both the Church and the State well in their hands. Indeed, the very last king of the line, Herod Agrippa, seemed to have well merited the compliment bestowed on his orthodoxy by Paul, when, in the presence of his heathen compeers, he invoked him as a brother of the faith: "*King Agrippa, believest thou the prophets? I know that thou believest.*"

Coming into possession of the country by policy rather than by force, and ruling it for several years only by accepting the fealty of its own native princes, the Romans would be likely to interfere as little as possible with the internal affairs of the people, and to leave the priesthood in the complete exercise of all their ecclesiastical functions. The Jews were not required to abjure their religion, to change their forms of worship, or to contribute soldiers to the armies of the republic. They felt the loss of their independence only in the payment of taxes, rigorously exacted, and in the presence of Roman garrisons in their strongholds. After the court of Archelaus was broken up, and Pontius Pilate, a Roman knight, had been established in the palace to represent the majesty of Cæsar, the High Priest was still absolute in all matters of religion, and perhaps the court of the Sanhedrim still continued to administer justice in all civil affairs. The probability is that ordinary offences against the person, against property, as well as crimes of sacrilege and blasphemy, were judged and determined by the Council of priests and elders; while military offences, like rebellion and riot, treason and crimes against the Roman sovereignty, were tried before the Procurator as the representative of Rome. Historical critics are not agreed as to whether the power of executing sentence was allowed to the Council of the Sanhedrim, or whether, in cases of capital offences, the sentence of punishment required, as it does in England and in the United States, the warrant of the Chief Executive, who had, besides, the prerogative of pardoning.

So far as the data given in the Acts of the Apostles are trustworthy, it would seem, that after the death of Jesus, and while Judea was still under the control of Roman governors, the Council of the chief priests and elders was allowed, not only to initiate, but to complete capital trials, to declare and execute sentence. Thus, Peter and John, preaching the resurrection and faith of Jesus, after his death, and while Pilate was still Governor, were arrested and imprisoned, and brought before the Sanhedrim for trial. Peter addressed the tribunal as: "*Rulers of the people and elders of Israel.*" After listening to the defence, the Council retired and consulted. It determined indeed to threaten and release the accused preachers; and the account says, the Sanhedrim refrained from exercising their authority, not for fear of any interference by the Roman military government, but for fear of the people, who sided with the disciples.[a] The same apostles were arrested a second time, committed for trial, and were rescued from prison, but recaptured and brought before the Council. Again the Council heard the defence, again it deliberated apart, and then sentenced the accused to be beaten.[b]

The proceedings against Stephen, though doubtless somewhat irregular, were in their form judicial. Witnesses appeared; the charge of blasphemy was made; the proofs were offered; the defence was listened to, and a sentence of condemnation was passed. Stephen was executed by stoning, the witnesses attending and casting the first stone,[c] as the law required. This was the legal method of executing a capital sentence,[d] and although there was manifested in the execution all the hatred and vindictiveness, which characterized a mob, it is not lightly to be believed, that an upright man, a scholar and a Pharisee, like Paul, would have participated in proceedings, that were simply lawless and murderous.[e] Later still, after Agrippa had obtained the kingdom, Paul himself was arrested in Jerusalem, and was carried by the Chief Captain of the Roman garrison before the Jewish Council

[a] Acts iv., 1-23. [b] Acts v., 17-40. [c] Acts vi., 11-15.
[d] Lev. xxiv., 16. [e] Acts viii., 1.

to be tried. True he sent afterward a band of soldiers and recovered his prisoner; but that was because it had become known that he was accused only of some ecclesiastical offence; and that he was a Roman citizen. As military commandant, Claudius Lysias took the liberty to change the jurisdiction, and to send the case of a man not a native of the country, but a Roman citizen of the province of Cilicia, to the judgment of the Roman governor. This proceeding indicates, that, but for that interference, the authority of the Sanhedrim to proceed to trial, sentence, and execution, would not have been questioned.[*] The conclusion must be, therefore, that, in the political status of Palestine at the time, it was within the province of the Council of the elders and chief priests to try Jesus, to pass judgment, and to execute sentence upon him after conviction.

A writer in the *Contemporary Review*, in two papers characterized by intelligence and judicial candor, has undertaken to show that Jesus was subjected to two distinct trials under two widely different systems of jurisprudence, the Jewish and the Roman, both of them justly celebrated for their elaborate and effective methods of securing justice, and of preventing popular prejudice or the influence of the government from obtaining conviction in any other than clearly proved cases of guilt. The writer undertakes to show that in both of these trials the fundamental rules of the law were disregarded, and that the delivery of the accused to execution was without the requisites of a valid judicial conviction. The special points stated to show that the proceedings before the Jewish Council were in violation of the national criminal code are, that the trial, being a capital one, was commenced in the night, the law requiring all trials in criminal and in civil cases to be commenced in the day-time, though the latter only might be concluded in the night. The law also required the Council in criminal cases, unless their judgment was for the acquittal of the accused, to separate and consider their verdict of condemnation twenty-four hours, or longer, if a Sabbath or holiday intervened, before formally affirming it. It was not lawful for the Council, or any member of it, to procure the

[*] Acts xxi., 27-40; xxii., xxiii., xxiv., xxv.

witnesses, who, under the Jewish system, were also the prosecutors. The accusation and testimony of these witnesses were the only indictment,— the only setting forth of the offence that the proceedings required. The witnesses also took the initiative in inflicting the punishment. It was an outrage on all Jewish ideas of justice for these persons, who assumed the responsibility of the prosecution, to be either the magistrates who listened to the evidence, or to be suborned or procured by them. It is also maintained in the same papers, that, when the testimony of the witnesses broke down, as it is declared to have done, either because of its inadequacy to show an offence, because of the lack of credibility of the persons offering it, or on account of its contradictory character, Jesus should have been at once acquitted. The subsequent adjuration of Jesus, and the finding by the Council that his confession was blasphemous, were in direct violation of the letter and spirit of the Hebrew law, which permitted no accused person to be interrogated, and protected him from self-crimination as effectually as does the common law.

Instead of there being two trials, upon two distinct charges, there was, according to the most credible tradition, but one. The writer, trying to account for the fact that there was a reference to Pontius Pilate, a judgment by him from the Pretorium, and a delivery of the prisoner to the Roman soldiery, who led him away and consummated the execution, assumes that there must have been a trial, and methods of procedure something like what were prescribed by the statutes and customs of the Roman republic in criminal cases. But there is nothing in the tradition to indicate that any second or Roman trial was had. After reference to Pilate there was no accusation, no fixing upon a day for trial, no testimony offered under oath, no *delatio*, no argument of counsel, no deliberation or balloting of jurors, all of which were essential features of a trial conducted after the Roman methods. It is true Syria, and Judea, after its annexation to Syria, were Imperial, and not Senatorial provinces, and were ruled directly by Cæsar and by his deputies, responsible only to himself; but in those cases, where the emperor intervened directly in the trial of criminals at home, or in the provinces through his deputies — the proconsuls — the forms of proceeding were substantially the same, as when the trials were conducted before the quæstors or the special judicial magistracy in Rome. The emperor, the proconsul abroad, the quæstors at home, presided in the court; but the responsibility and judgment were with the jurors, who gave their votes for acquittal or condemnation, just like a modern jury, save that a mere majority could convict, whereas from modern juries unanimity is required.

The matter came to the judgment of Pilate because he was the recognized chief-executive power, and because the soldiers depended upon to accomplish the crucifixion were under his orders. It seems probable, as has been already shown, that this was not necessary; that the Council of Jews that had condemned Jesus had plenary power to cause their sentence to be executed, and that they might have ordered against him the same punishment of lethal stoning, to which a short time afterwards they subjected Stephen, with no more interference on the part of the Roman governor or garrison, than happened in Stephen's case.

There are two reasons way probably the Sanhedrim did not undertake, in the case of Jesus, to execute their own sentence. The first was their great timidity, of which the evangelical writers speak not only in their account of the proceedings against Peter and John, but also in the proceedings against Jesus. They had suppressed their resentment and postponed summary measures, because Jesus had brought with him from Galilee the reputation both of a prophet and a wonder-worker, and, doubtless too, of an upright, pure, and blameless life. The sect of the Pharisees, as Josephus says, never inclined to excessive punishments.[a] They dared not proceed against Jesus, until they had gained the support and sympathy of the multitude. During those few days that intervened between his arrival in Jerusalem and his arrest, their emissaries had undoubtedly been busy with false and exaggerated accusations against him in all quarters of the city. After the multitude turned out at midnight to assist in the arrest of Jesus, the chief priests

[a] Jos. Antiq. xiii , cx. 6.

first became sure, that the mob would stand by, and aid in putting him to death. But now if, having thrown part of the guilt of his plotted death upon the multitude, they can throw a part too upon the Roman administration, they believe that they can almost acquit themselves of blame. So, in a spirit of new and feigned loyalty, they carry their convicted prisoner to the deputy of Cæsar, and ask him to issue the necessary order to have him executed.

The other reason why the chief priests and elders did not insist upon a jurisdiction, about which they had generally been quite tenacious, was the fear of a military interference with their proceedings. Jesus was not a native of Jerusalem or of Judea. He was a Nazarene, and a subject of King Herod, then reigning, an independent ally of the Romans. When afterward the same Jewish Council undertook to proceed with the trial and punishment of Paul, the Captain of the garrison sent a body of soldiers to rescue him, and transferred his case by sheer military power to the Roman magistrate, on the ground, as alleged in his letter, that he was a native of Cilicia, a Roman province, and of Tarsus, whose citizens had obtained from the Senate the privileges of Roman citizenship.[a] Doubtless, in repressing riots and in collecting taxes, the officers and soldiers, partly through ignorance, partly through contempt, had roughly violated many of the local and ecclesiastical laws and customs of the country, in which they were strangers, and so rendered themselves amenable to arrest and punishment before the local courts. It would ill comport with the dignity of conquerors to permit their own functionaries to be thus molested by the tribunals of a captured country, and rescues of accused persons claiming Roman protection must have been already frequent. There were strong reasons, therefore, why the Council at Jerusalem should not arrogate against the Roman authority a criminal jurisdiction, which seemed by no means unquestionable, over the person of Jesus.

There having been but one really judicial proceeding, it becomes necessary, following the footsteps of the *Review* writer, to consider how far it was regular in its

---

[a] Acts xxii., 24-29; xxiii., 25-30.

modes of proceeding, and whether its findings were substantially consistent with what we now know to have been the facts in the case. It might be assumed, *a priori*, that, under the known circumstances of the case, the safeguards of the law would have been violated, and all the provisions which favored the accused would have been, in spirit, if not in form, overridden. A body of men so exasperated that they will, if they dare, arrest a person and put him to death in secret, if they afterward, to satisfy some of their more tender-hearted or more scrupulous associates, decide to give him the benefit of a trial, will be likely to make the trial as much as possible the instrument of effecting their predetermined malice. They will try him, not to see if he be guilty, but the more safely to compass his death. In the same spirit, in quite recent times, many famous State trials have been conducted in England, where the judges and the juries, in their judgments and sentences, have given savage utterance to the resentment of the court, whose favor they sought to win, by lending themselves to accomplish its revenge, or to the prejudice and rage of the people, from whose violence perhaps the prisoner had been rescued. During the madness of the Reign of Terror,— although executions followed the sentence of legalized tribunals, and after a summary hearing of testimony,— so prevalent was the prejudice, so cruel and ferocious the whole populace, and the government it had improvised, that history properly characterizes such wholesale punishment of innocent persons as massacres and murders.

Undoubtedly, the proceedings against Jesus were open to the condemnation, that they were unlawfully initiated in the night-time, and that a judgment of conviction was rendered early in the morning after the arrest, and a few hours before execution, which could not have been lawfully rendered earlier than the third day afterward. It has been seen that Jesus was arrested in the night, after the Passover had been celebrated in the evening — that occasion probably having been seized upon to find him in the environs of the city. According to received tradition, this was the day of the week corresponding to our Thursday. The day following, the trial and condemnation took place; and, before three o'clock on the same afternoon, the agony of his death was over. It was unlawful for the Council, who were his judges, to procure the witnesses to prosecute him; and, upon the failure of the suborned testimony to justify his conviction, he was clearly entitled to an acquittal.

The objection that, under the Hebrew law, the High Priest had no right to adjure him to make confession, nor the Council afterward to convict him upon a confession thus illegally extracted, is not so well taken.[a] The interrogation of the High Priest was not a part of the judicial proceedings. He addressed the prisoner as the public prosecutor, the judge, or any casual person might have done. He put a question he had no right to ask, the putting of which was a gross official impropriety, if not an illegality. But Jesus was not prejudiced by the question, and was neither compelled nor even called upon to answer it. It would have been the part of ordinary discretion not to answer. Jesus was by no means destitute of such discretion. His conduct in several difficult emergencies, and the directions he gave his disciples, indicate that he was a man of marked sagacity and self-possession, was rarely at loss for a wise answer, was keenly alive to what was due to his own dignity, and never betrayed himself by any inadvertence of speech. As he did answer the question of the High Priest, it must be concluded that he did so in full view of the peril he was placing himself in, and for the purpose of maintaining to the last that claim to divine authority, which he knew would offend the priesthood.

The *Review* writer assumes the proceeding to have been the trial of an accused person upon a certain charge, and the failure of the court to find legal evidence to substantiate the charge. Thereupon, the presiding justice adjures the prisoner to state whether or not he is guilty. The prisoner, in replying, uses words which the court deems to be tantamount to a confession of guilt, and it proceeds to pass a judgment of conviction. This is not exactly what the record imports, but rather, that the accusation breaking down through the infamy, incompetence, or disagreement of the testimony, the accused repeats the crime in open court, and is proceeded against *de novo* for the new

[a] Matt. xxvi., 63-66.

offence. It was as if a person were under trial for an assault with a dangerous weapon upon an officer. The witnesses to the assault are so contradictory, and of such bad repute, that the court refuse to consider the charge proved. In that stage of the proceedings, the accused, it may be with the very manacles, with which his hands are confined, assaults the officer and dangerously wounds him. The original indictment must fail; there must be a new arrest, a new indictment, and a new trial, at which it may or may not be improper for the members of the court, who were witnesses of the assault, to sit as judges. But that the criminal can be tried by some tribunal, and can be convicted upon the facts being shown, there can be no doubt. Or it was as if the offence charged had been an oral libel against a magistrate, and, midway of the trial, the accused repeats the libel in open court. Is there any doubt that, so far from being treated with impunity, the repetition and publicity of the libel, and the contempt it implies, will be considered an aggravation?

We must try to understand the proceedings. Under the Jewish law — and the Roman law was nearly the same — there was no indictment, no formal written complaint. The declaration of the two witnesses was the indictment. The witnesses — doubtless in familiar, informal language — made their declaration of what the accused did or said. The Council determined what offence was implied in the acts or words, and proceeded to try him for that offence.

In this case, Matthew narrates, that the *delatio* of the witnesses was as follows: "*This fellow said, I am able to destroy the temple of God, and to build it in three days.*" [a] Mark's version of it is this: "*We heard him say, I will destroy this temple, that is made with hands, and within three days I will build another made without hands.*" [b] Luke, very properly considering, that this charge, whatever it was, broke down, and the sentence was for the offence in open court, omits all account of it, and proceeds directly to the adjuration and the reply, deemed by the court blasphemous. But let us revert a moment to the trial as it began. The accusation, as given by Matthew, involves only a single offence, a claim to supernatural or divine power. As given by Mark, it involves that, and

[a] Matt. xxvi., 61.   [b] Mark xiv., 58.

also sacrilege, inasmuch as it not only asserts ability to rebuild the temple miraculously, but the intention to destroy it. Both of these offences were high crimes under the extant Jewish law.

Now, we may either believe that the actual statement of the witnesses was as Mark records, or that it was as Matthew records,— for there is a substantial difference between them,— or we may believe that both are correct, and that this very discrepancy was the reason why the Council determined that the disagreement was fatal, and the offence not proved. But for which of the two offences, blasphemy or sacrilege, implied in Mark's words, was the court actually proceeding? Clearly for the former. Jesus had in fact never uttered any threats against the temple; and it is not probable, that he had ever spoken the words put into the mouth of the false witnesses by Matthew. It was not a malicious purpose of destroying the temple that the Council for the moment entertained, but the presumptuous implication of the power to rebuild it in three days. He who could do that must be greater than Solomon, greater than Ezra or Nehemiah. Only the divine power could build such a structure in three days. The author of the Fourth Gospel, in the construction of the conversations ascribed to Jesus in his lifetime, has skilfully used this charge against him, and aptly indicated its significance in the minds of his accusers. "Forty-six years," said the Jews, "was the temple in building, and wilt thou rear it up in three days? But he spake of the temple of his body."[a] It is probable, too, that the author, who evidently believes Jesus had used the words alleged in the indictment, wished to extenuate their apparent impiety by the after-suggestion, that they were spoken in a figurative sense. In the contradiction between the witnesses at the trial, the Galilean evangelists, and the Fourth Gospel, it is now impossible to determine what Jesus had said. Was it something about coming back in three days, with which the synoptic writers have confused the three days of Jonah in the whale, and John a destroyed temple to be raised in three days? The real similitude indicated by Jesus to Jonah must have been, that as Jonah was a sign

[a] John ii., 20, 21.

to the Ninevites, so was he himself to his generation;[a] and his actual allusion to the temple must have been, that not a stone of it should be left upon another.[b] After the disciples began to believe that their Master had come back, after three days, from the grave, the swallowing and casting-up of the old prophet, and the destroyed temple to be restored, were thought to be parallels and prophecies of the resurrection. What a fanciful believer had appended as a marginal note to his copy of the *memorabilia* of Jesus became adopted as the text of a later transcription. What the High Priest said, with the evident concurrence of the Council, indicates that the inquisition of the court was toward blasphemy, and not toward sacrilege. "*Ye have heard the blasphemy,*" the blasphemy about which we have been questioning the witnesses; what need of further testimony, that is, of further *like* testimony, of testimony pertinent to the matter under investigation?[c]

It only remains to consider, Was the judgment itself just? It has already appeared that the proceedings were grossly irregular and illegal, both those of the court in condemning, and those of the *de facto* executive power in ordering to execution a person, whose sentence he had the power, if not the right, to review, and whom after examination he found to have done nothing worthy of death.[d] Such violent proceedings could only issue in judicial murder, and the verdict of history has been just that Jesus was put to death *without having been lawfully convicted, or regularly tried.* But a murderer may be unlawfully put to death by a mob, who are so indignant at his crime, that they have broken into his prison, and taken him thence, and hanged him. It is in the eye of the law as much murder as if the victim were an innocent man. And yet, in the case supposed, the murderer would certainly have been convicted, and the mob have only anticipated what would have been done ultimately by the officers of the law. Did the acts and language of Jesus, if they have been handed down to our times correctly by the received traditions, constitute what a conscientious and enlightened jurist of Jerusalem was

[a] Matt. xii., 41; Luke xi., 29-32.   [b] Matt. xxiv., 1, 2; Luke xxi., 5, 6.
[c] Matt. xxvi., 63, 64.   [d] Luke xxiii., 13-22.

required to consider blasphemy, or any other capital offence?

The words charged, the substance of which was that he, Jesus, had power to rebuild the temple in three days, did not seem to have been proved. We can account for the tradition of the Fourth Gospel imputing them to him, by the notoriety created by the trial, and the unsuccessful effort of an apologist to extenuate their criminal significance. For if Jesus meant by this temple this body of his,— a meaning no hearer would infer,— it was equally a claim to divine power. A temple is a human work, and may be made even in three days, with a sufficient force of perfectly organized laborers; but a dead body cannot be made alive by any power or skill of the deceased. The explanation, if admissible, is an extenuation of the offence of sacrilege. It is a confession of the offence for which he was actually tried. And if Jesus had not said those words, we know now that he had said other words, that less equivocally asserted his divine sonship and Deity, upon which the charge of blasphemy might have been as well based. He had called himself Christ (meaning the Messiah),[a] the Son of God,[b] Master,[c] King,[d] King of Zion,[e] and the Lord — the usual designation among the Israelites of Jehovah, their God.[f] He had declared himself the Judge of mankind.[g] He had claimed authority to forgive sins,[h] and to modify the law of the ten words.[i] He had said that he was greater than Solomon,[j] greater than the temple.[k] He had assured his followers that he would soon come in the clouds of heaven in glory, with all the holy angels as a retinue.[l] He had asserted that all things were delivered to him by God, and no man could know God except by him.[m] Within a few hours of his trial, he had said, that he had only to ask God, who was his father, and he would send twelve legions of angels to rescue him from the soldiers, who had arrested him.[n]

The old Hebrew law still in force in the time of Jesus was, *He that blasphemeth the name of the Lord shall surely be put to death, and all the congregation of Israel shall*

---

[a] Matt. xxiii., 8, 10; Mark ix., 41.
[b] Matt. xvi., 16, 17.
[c] Matt. xxiii., 8.
[d] Matt. xxv., 34.
[e] Luke xix., 38, 40.
[f] Matt. xii., 8; Luke xix., 31.
[g] Matt. xxv., 31, 32.
[h] Matt. ix., 6.
[i] Matt. v., 21–32; xii., 7, 8.
[j] Matt. xii., 42.
[k] Matt. xii., 6.
[l] Matt. xxv., 31.
[m] Matt. xi., 27.
[n] Matt. xxvi., 53.

certainly stone him.[*] The oneness of God had been the great idea, for which the whole cultus of the Jews stood. All around them were peoples who believed in families and associations of gods, in gods who were the husbands of goddesses, and the husbands of mortal women, in gods who were the fathers of other gods, and the fathers of heroic men. All this was an unspeakable abomination to the pure mind of the Jew. His God was neither begotten, nor did he beget, but was from everlasting to everlasting the same — never growing old, never sharing his power or glory with a son or a successor. In their piety and service of Jehovah, the Israelitish orators and poets had used the figure of fatherhood to represent the tender love of their deity for his chosen people; they had used the figure of husband to represent the peculiar and exclusive attachment, which that relation implied from the chosen people toward their deity, but always strictly as a figure of speech. No Jewish mind was ever literal or gross enough to connect anything genetic or sexual with the relation. All around them among the Greeks, the Romans, the Assyrians, the Egyptians, the Phœnicians, the gods were altogether like themselves: they married, they were given in marriage, they broke over the exclusiveness of the tie with the license allowed to great kings, and they begot offspring like unto themselves, who shared their power and immortality. One son of God had rebelled against his father and conquered from him the sovereignty of the universe. But neither as fact, philosophy, nor poetry did the prophets of Israel receive these ideas, or tolerate the least compromise with them, or with any symbols or rites, that recognized them. Perhaps they believed there were such gods, and that they lived in such practices; but their God, Jehovah, living in utter remoteness from all such compromising relations, in an awful austerity of purity and holiness, was not to be soiled by any such imputations. How hard had the lesson of the prophets been! How easy it had been for the rude people to forget their sublime faith, and to adopt gods that flattered their instinctive and family affections! And what years of famine, war, pestilence, and slavery had they suffered — as they came to believe — for their apostasies.

[*] Lev. xxiv., 16.

But now at last they have grown up to the sublime idea of their own religion; and, after the revolt of Maccabæus, the nation may have been licentious, cruel, intolerant, and turbulent, but it was no longer and never will be idolatrous or capable of being turned from the great lesson of its discipline, burned into its experience and heart,—
"*Hear, O Israel! the Lord our God is one Lord.*"[a]

Still, plain as was the prohibition of the law, strong as was the national sentiment that sanctioned and enforced it, and palpable as was the claim of Jesus to a genetic relationship and substantial equality with God to be considered in the eyes of an intelligent Jew of his time a breach of the letter and spirit of the law, it seems to be fairly implied from all that we know, that Jesus would not have been molested, notwithstanding his divine pretensions, had he remained in Galilee, or, coming to Jerusalem, had he refrained from denouncing the ecclesiastical authorities, and from violently interfering with the temple service. He would have been safe in Galilee, which was ruled over by Herod, nominally himself a Jew, but who could never have been induced to molest a prophet that abstained from denouncing his own licentiousness. The hesitation of the Pharisees and elders, and their reluctance to assume the guilt of his taking off, show that they, too, would have overlooked the legal offence, but for envy and malice, and the pretext it gave them to revenge themselves on an enemy.

There is still a law against blasphemy in England and in the United States, less severe in its penalty, but taking cognizance of the same offence set forth in the Mosaic code. There has been in this country and in England much reverent and sincere, but bold and free, criticism on matters of religious belief, which would seem to fall literally within the purview of this statute. An enlightened public sentiment prevents the law — still wholesome and salutary to punish ribald and profane libels upon the sincere faith of the great mass of mankind — from being used to punish honest and earnest inquiry, and the free expression of religious convictions, that differ from the popular standard. Should a prosecution to enforce the statute against blasphemy be undertaken in this country, it would

[a] Deut. vi., 4.

be most desirable, that it should fall under the oversight of a wise judge, who would know how to discriminate between the conscientious inquirer, who had given expression to a reverent belief, and the flippant scoffer, who had degraded a high ideal. Even as early as the first century there was a liberal spirit, then due to the influence of Greek philosophy and learning, and to the general scepticism, that was beginning to make the whole scheme of the pagan mythology slightly ridiculous, which modified the rigor of positive law, and prevented it from being put in execution, except in cases like that of Jesus, where the ostensible charge was a mere pretext to cover a concealed envy.

We are carefully considering the question from the stand-point, not of the modern reverence for the name of Jesus, but from the stand-point of Jewish law, as it stood when Jesus came from his native Galilee to Jerusalem. There is one consideration not to be overlooked. If Jesus was the Son of God he claimed to be, how is the justice of the judgment of condemnation pronounced against him affected by the relation? The legal mind is by no means unfamiliar with the privileges, which in many instances modify and change the relation of persons toward the laws. It was a maxim of the Roman State, that the emperor was raised above all liability to the penalties of the law. The English common law has always maintained the principle, that the king can do no wrong. The privilege of clergy, and of the peerage has been, and to some extent still is, a bar to ordinary criminal proceedings, and removes an accusation to some special tribunal jurisdiction. So military authority, during the exigency of a state of siege, takes away from the police and from courts all inquisition of the violent and arbitrary acts of commanders. But all cases of exemption from jurisdiction, on account of the rank, dignity, or authority of the person, must be apparent as a public fact, or must be not only pleaded, but proved. It would be impious to pretend, that the Deity, even if he should veil himself in human form, or any divine being sharing his attributes, could ever be the subject of human criminal law; and, if Jesus obviously belonged to this grade of being, his crucifixion was the most daring and blasphemous act that ever oppressed the conscience of man. It would, however, ill comport with our ideas of justice to punish or even to execrate a human tribunal that had ordered the death of a divine being, who had effectually disguised his deity in the form of a man, and had in that character committed an act, which would have been criminal in a man.

But were the Sanhedrim, according to the character in which the person of Jesus became known to them, justified in regarding him as a man? Could they indeed properly entertain any other opinion of him? Whatever demonstrations of superhuman power Jesus may have made in Galilee, he had come to Jerusalem making only such manifestations as a prophet and preacher might make. He had declined, when importuned, to give any sign to authenticate even that character and office. He had allowed himself to be proclaimed in the street as the King of Zion, and in the temple he had forcibly reproved an old custom on the authority that the temple was the house of his Father. But it was these very acts and declarations, that had seemed to the Jews blasphemies, and had led to his arrest and trial. But, as Jesus had come to Jerusalem to die, he had refused to put forth any powers, which might overawe his enemies, and prevent them from consummating their malicious purposes.[a] He had in his agony prayed to God, whose high purposes he believed himself to be accomplishing, to spare him, if possible, the bitterness of death.[b] He had in his mind vague hopes of a rescue by legions of angels at the very last moment; but now he will not show any of those gifts of healing or eloquence, by which he had won converts in Galilee, to soften the hearts of the soldiers, and turn to his cause the favor of his judges.[c] He will confront his accusers and receive and endure his sentence simply as a man. He will not even allow his followers to defend him, though this he at one time appears to have meditated. This mob, he declared, these rulers, this Roman governor with his soldiers, are all ministers of Jehovah; and they must work out, through my submission and death, those divine purposes, which lead to my glory and the salvation of my elect.[d] Having doubtless in his mind the prophetic emblem of the lamb dumb before his

[a] Matt. xxvi., 53. [b] Matt. xxvi., 42. [c] Luke xi., 29. [d] Matt. xxvi., 54.

shearers, he clearly intended to maintain entire silence, and let his foes work their will. Before the Council of the chief priests and elders, he is silent.[a] The prevarication of the witnesses, who try to tell something he had said, does not disturb him. The purely personal sense of his language — the temple he would raise being his own slain body, as explained by John — was open to his explanation; but he does not avail himself of it,— partly, because it will not take from the language the implication of blasphemy, but partly, because he will not say anything, that might constitute a defence or soften the hearts of his persecutors.[b] The Chief Priest is astonished and indignant at his silence, and at length adjures him, by the living God, to say whether he is or is not the Christ, the Son of God. Now, Jesus will speak; because his speech will not lead to his deliverance, but will, as it did, insure his condemnation; and because he has an opportunity to repeat the lofty claim, upon which he has dared to stake his life.[c] We are thus left to the conclusion, that whatever dignity or privilege may have elevated such a person as Jesus from capability of committing the crime, for which he was condemned, he studiously avoided showing that dignity and privilege, in any way that would be likely to affect his judges favorably toward himself, or take his acts and words out of the category of human conduct, for which he wished to remain absolutely responsible, in the character of a man and a subject of the State. Inasmuch as the judgment of the Council — in which there were probably some men of candor and impartiality — was unanimous for his conviction, it must be concluded that there were no misgivings, even on the part of any of them, that Jesus was other than a Galilean Jew, born into, and living under allegiance to the Mosaic law, and to the ecclesiastical authority of the chief priests and elders,[d] to be judged for his conduct in those relations precisely like an ordinary person.

In examining the different accounts of the trial of Jesus, new confirmation is found for the opinion expressed in these pages of the fictitious character of the

[a] Matt. xxvi., 63; xxvii., 14. [b] Matt. xxvi., 59–63.
[c] Matt. xxvi., 64. [d] Mark xiv., 64.

Fourth Gospel. Matthew, Mark, and Luke — these names are only used to distinguish from each other the unknown writers of the narratives bearing their names — all assert that the occasion of Jesus being in Jerusalem the night he was arrested was to eat the Passover with his twelve chosen disciples. The Passover itself was a nocturnal feast.[a] In the company of the believers, the occasion was prolonged by much conversation, by the institution, after the regular feast, of a memorial service, and by many counsels and prophecies which the presentiment of death forced upon the mind of the Master. According to each of these writers, there occurred at this time the prediction of Peter's treachery; and, according to Luke, it was accompanied by a serious warning of Peter's imminent spiritual danger, and of an assurance of intercessory prayers for his deliverance; also by the rebuke which Jesus gave to his friends about striving for precedence and the promulgation of the law of his kingdom, that he was greatest in it who served, which Matthew and Mark attribute to an earlier occasion; and, finally, by the assignment to the twelve of their splendid rank in the new order of things, in which they should sit on thrones as princes of the twelve tribes, and eat and drink at the table of the great king.[b]

Whichever account is to be taken as correct, it is evident that it must have been well into the night after the feast of the Passover had been generally celebrated in Jerusalem, before Jesus went out of the city to walk in the garden of Gethsemane. It is late; and the chosen friends of Jesus, left to their sad thoughts, cannot refrain from sleep. Before they had quitted the upper room in the city, Jesus had said to Peter, "*This night thou shalt deny me*"; and again — indicating that it is still night, and before dawn — "*Before the cock crows*, thou shalt deny me." The writers of the Synoptics all assert that Judas' overtures to the chief priests to betray Jesus were made before the Passover feast, and leave it to be inferred that they were made some interval before, during which he sought opportunity to betray him.[c]

Turning now to the account of how Jesus was delivered

---

[a] Lev. xxiii., 5.   [b] Matt. xxvi., 26–35; Mark xiv., 18–31; Luke xxii., 14–38.
[c] Matt. xxvi., 14–16; Mark xiv., 10, 11; Luke xxii., 3–6.

into the hands of his enemies, given in the Fourth Gospel, the only indication of time we find is that it was *before the feast of the Passover*. Without indicating anything that took place before the Passover, except the declaration so characteristic of the writer's mind, "Jesus, having loved his own, loved them to the end," the narrative goes on to say: "*Supper being ended, the devil having now put into the heart of Judas Iscariot . . . to betray him*," and other inconsequential considerations being named, "*He riseth from supper.*"[a] According to all other writers, this must have been the Passover supper itself, an evening feast; but John does not say so. Indeed, so far as he could indicate a time, it is before the feast of the Passover. He says that when Jesus, at the supper, told Judas: That thou doest, do quickly, some of them thought he meant, Buy those things we have need of against the feast.[b] Later on, he says that at twelve o'clock on the day that Jesus was crucified, Friday, *it was the preparation of the Passover*, which would then have occurred either the night of the crucifixion, or the next night, the Sabbath.[c] And again, after the institution of the communion service, after the admonition to Peter, after all the events that Luke dates as occurring the same evening, and after the formal discourse of the fourteenth, fifteenth, and sixteenth chapters, which no other writers have mentioned, after the scenes in Gethsemane that all other writers describe, after the trial before the High Priest which Matthew and Mark say began at night and was continued by adjournment to the following morning, we come to the bringing of Jesus after his condemnation to the judgment hall of Pilate for sentence. "They," John says, which must mean the priests and elders, cannot go into the judgment hall lest they be defiled, and so be unfit to eat the Passover.[d] But the Passover was eaten the evening before. If it is said the Passover lasted from the evening of the 14th to the evening of the 15th of the month *Abib*, there is good law for the statement. The whole period from the 10th to the 14th, or perhaps for seven days, was sacred, and only unleavened bread could then be eaten; but the Passover itself must be eaten at even on the 14th. "*In the fourteenth day of this month at even, ye shall*

[a] John xiii., 1-3. [b] John xiii., 27-29. [c] John xix., 14. [d] John xviii., 28.

keep it in his appointed season." ᵃ And yet John declares that Satan entered into the heart of Judas with the sop that Jesus gave him *at the supper*.ᵇ John does not say that all these proceedings were in the night, only we may infer that they were, inasmuch as the captors of Jesus are said to have borne torches and lanterns,ᶜ and the cock crows while Jesus is before the High Priest.ᵈ

According to John there was no trial before the Council, no examination of witnesses, no accusation of sacrilege or of blasphemy, no deliberation of judges, no judgment of conviction, and no sentence. Jesus is arrested by a band of men and officers from the chief priests and Pharisees; he is bound and led away, first to Annas, then to Caiaphas, his son-in-law, the High Priest.ᵉ Apparently, it is to the houses or palaces of these clerical dignitaries, one after the other, that he is led. The elders and chief priests are not assembled, and no formal proceedings whatever are had. It is not the case of a writer omitting what previous writers have minutely told. It is a writer, who ignores the statement of other writers, who brings the narrative to the same point with them, and then gives an entirely different account. For, instead of proceeding to try him, or to institute any legal proceedings against him, Caiaphas accosts him just as if the visit had been one of ceremony or courtesy: he asks him concerning his disciples, and his doctrine.ᶠ The captured prophet is brought to Caiaphas, not to be tried by the Sanhedrim under Jewish law, but that the High Priest might go with his captors as accuser and prosecutor to lay the case before the judgment-seat of the Roman procurator.ᵍ "*Thine own nation*," Pilate is made to say later, "*and the chief priest have delivered thee unto me.*" ʰ So here is an account of the trial of Jesus as different from that of the Synoptic Gospels, as is the whole accompanying story of the life, the character, and the teachings of the man.

Here, as elsewhere, the dogmatic and didactic purpose of the author reveals itself. He will tell nothing that comports not with his idea of the dignity of his hero. He will tell only that part of his arrest, his trial, his crucifixion, which accords with his divine ideal. But the

---
ᵃ Lev. xxiii., 5–8.   ᵇ John xiii., 27.   ᶜ John xviii., 3.   ᵈ John xviii., 27.
ᵉ John xviii., 12, 13, 24, 28.   ᶠ John xviii., 19.   ᵍ John xviii., 28.   ʰ John xviii., 35.

invention of man is less simple, less dignified, less worthy the historic fame of Jesus, than the truth as told by the less ambitious contemporaries or predecessors of the writer. Perhaps the writer of the Fourth Gospel did not wish to acknowledge that he, who was before Abraham,[a] demeaned himself, like one of the children of Israel, to celebrate the Passover, which could only be kept at Jerusalem. He had carried him often to the temple, but never as a worshipper, always as a teacher of a higher *cultus*, than that celebrated in the temple; and had made him say the hour had come, when true worshippers no longer worshipped in the high places or in the temples.[b] He gives an account of the arrest, but he cannot tell it with the simplicity of the earlier disciples. He must have Jesus overawe by the glory of his presence the very ruffians that captured him. As soon as he said, "*I am Jesus of Nazareth,*" they staggered backward, and fell to the ground.[c] When Peter valiantly drew his sword, so prostrate are his foes, that their overthrow would have been easy. But Jesus can only be bound by his own sufferance. "*The cup,*" he says, "*which my Father hath given me, shall I not drink it?*"[d]

The writer is always injecting, to the great derangement of the sequence of his narrative, some explanation of his own to prevent Jesus from being compromised. When Jesus asks the *posse* who come to arrest him, "*Whom seek you?*" the writer cannot bear to have his reader think that Jesus did not know, and he explains thus: "*Jesus, therefore, knowing all things that should come upon him,* went forth," etc. He asks the question only to reply, "*If ye seek me, let these go their way.*"[e] When the High Priest asks Jesus of his disciples and of his doctrine, he is made to say: "*Why askest thou me? Ask them which heard me, what I have said unto them: behold, they know what I have said.*"[f] The answer was considered disrespectful by the bailiff, who replies to it by a brutal blow.[g] Such an answer would hardly be considered pertinent or decorous by any modern tribunal. It was quite unlikely that Jesus would have trusted any

[a] John viii., 58. [b] John iv., 20-24. [c] John xviii., 4-6. [d] John xviii., 11.
[e] John xviii., 7, 8. [f] John xviii., 21. [g] John xviii., 22.

casual hearer among those, who had heard him in the temple, to explain to the official head of the old national faith the sublime mysteries of his doctrine Happily, although this record has stood as authentic for eighteen centuries, there have been noble spirits tried for their lives in both the ecclesiastical and political courts, who have left to the world a better example than this of patience, self-possession, and dignity. Better the noble silence of Matthew and Mark, than to open the mouth only to give expression to irritability and impatience.

Following along the Johannic fiction, we encounter only accumulating improbabilities. Jesus is carried to the judgment hall, but his accusers do not go in, for fear of being defiled; and Pilate so far accommodates himself to their scruples as to come outside to learn what the charge is against the prisoner.[a] There was no other trial, according to the teller of the story; and yet we recognize neither the formalities of a Jewish, a Roman, or even of a mere military court. It is the record of a trial conducted under great difficulties,— the accused inside, in the hall of judgment, the prosecutors and witnesses, if there were any, outside, and neither confronted with the other. We find in the mind of the writer no apparent familiarity with judicial proceedings of any kind; but what we do find is the incessant dialogue of the whole book perpetuated through the trial, and to the end of the life of Jesus,— the dialogue couched in the aphoristic, antithetic, repetitious, never-to-be-mistaken style of the first Johannic Epistle — a style made up mainly of a series of verbal catches and captious retorts upon the phrases used in the interrogations. Thus, when Pilate asks very properly and formally, "*What is this man accused of?*" the chief priests reply captiously and offensively, "*If he were not a malefactor, we would not have brought him at all.*" "Well, then," says Pilate, irritated by the flippancy of the answer, "take your malefactor and judge him according to your law."[b] Everybody seems to be waiting for everybody else to make some slip in his speech, and then to pounce on him with a sarcastic reply. In this temper, of course nothing can be done; and the petulant Jews have at last to tell whether the man is accused of robbery

---

[a] John xviii., 28, 29.   [b] John xviii., 30-32.

or theft, of a political or an ecclesiastical offence, before any progress can be made. But the immediate reply of the Jews is that it is not lawful for them to put any man to death, though we find in the sequel that this, too, is captious and untrue. They could never have truthfully so said. All the other evangelists say they had already condemned Jesus to death for blasphemy; and the Jewish law, then in full force, was that the blasphemer should surely be put to death. The same writer, earlier in his narrative, had declared that the law against adultery required the guilty parties to be put to death;[a] and in a following chapter he makes the same Jewish priests tell Pilate, "*We have a law, and by our law he ought to die, because he made himself the Son of God.*"[b] The contradiction is explained by imputing a divine direction to the language of the priests who thus brought about the fulfilment of Jesus' prediction, that his death would be by crucifixion.[c] They are made to say: It is not lawful for us to put this man to death — certainly not during these sacred festivals — but we are guiltless if he be affixed to a cross, and his death ensue — as if any judge could entertain the idea that a man dying lingeringly in crucifixion was less slain by human hands than if he were strangled, beheaded, or stoned.

When Pilate returns to the judgment hall, not having elicited from the persons, who had arrested Jesus and stood outside as his prosecutors, any information of what the accusation was, the same cross-purposes, that had irritated the disputants and prevented the trial from having any progress begin again between Pilate and the accused. Pilate asks Jesus, "*Art thou king of the Jews?*" and he replies captiously, "*Did you say that of yourself, or did others tell it of me?*"[d] Pilate loses his self-possession at the impertinence, and flings back: "*Am I a Jew? Thine own nation and the chief priests delivered thee unto me: what hast thou done?*"[e] The prosecutor will not accuse him, will not even present himself in court; so the judge asks the criminal what offence he has committed. Jesus is made to reply, "*My kingdom is not of this world, if it were: my servants would fight, that I*

[a] John viii., 5. [b] John xix., 7. [c] John xviii., 32; iii., 14; xi., 51; xii., 32, 33.
[d] John xviii., 34. [e] John xviii., 35.

should not be delivered to the Jews."[a] Every declaration of this writer is so tautological that its substance can be rendered by copious omissions. To this, Pilate: *So you are a king, then?* The question is at last answered by indirection. Jesus replies, "*Yes, for that end was I born, that I might witness the truth, and every one who is of the truth heareth me.*"[b] "*What is truth?*" said Pilate; and, getting no answer, he went outside to the prosecutors and said, I have tried the man you have delivered to me, and find no fault in him.[c] Tried him for what? For no ordinary civil offence; certainly not for sacrilege or blasphemy. The governor had asked him if he were king of the Jews. Jesus had at last admitted that he was, but explained that his kingdom was not of this world,—that he was a king only in that he had come into the world to reveal the truth; and, very justly, Pilate had determined that there was nothing blamable in such a pretension. How then, according to this writer, did Jesus suffer death? The curious story tells itself in the following chapter. Pilate, instead of discharging a person whom he had acquitted, after his only trial, forgetting, first, that *he* had power to crucify or release him,[d] asks his accusers to consent to his release; then orders him to be scourged,— this acquitted man—then tells the Jews to take him and crucify him, *for I find him innocent;* then delivers him to *his own soldiers* to be crucified, upon an outcry of the Jews, that, if he released him, he would not be a friend of Cæsar.[e] It is easy to see that, if we had no other record of the trial and condemnation of Jesus than is given in this Gospel, it would be hard to understand how it came to pass.

The whole Johannic story treats the ecclesiastical hierarchy at Jerusalem with much more leniency than do the Synoptic Gospels. Sharp colloquies are held with the *Rabbis* in the temple, and Jesus once, in the irritation of his spirit, pronounces them children of the devil.[f] But, generally, they are deferred to, reasoned with, and pressing overtures are repeatedly made to them to admit the claims of Jesus to the place he claimed in the Jehovistic dispensation. But the harsh speech of John the

[a] John xviii., 36. [b] John xviii., 37. [c] John xviii., 38. [d] John xix., 10.
[e] John xix., 12, 15, 16. [f] John viii., 44.

Baptist is omitted, as well as the censure against them in the Sermon on the Mount. They are not shut out of the kingdom of heaven as proscriptively as in the several parables and plain declarations of Jesus. The terrible invective of the twenty-third of Matthew is suppressed; and, when it comes to the crucifixion, they are not the judges and executioners of Jesus, but are made to cast the responsibility of his death upon the Roman governor, who crucifies him as a plotter against Cæsar, rather than as a person claiming a divine origin and destiny.

It ought here to be remarked that Matthew's narrative, which is strictly confirmed by Mark, again vindicates its character, as the most probable tradition of Jesus, by its insisting on the silent acquiescence of the accused in all the proceedings that culminated in his crucifixion. He apprehends the result beforehand. Toward the mob, toward the rulers and chief priests, toward Pilate and the soldiery, he makes no demonstration, and allows no defence.[a] He insists that their acts are providential and a part of the divine purpose. He will try only the effect of prayer, to modify, if possible, that divine purpose; but, if God will not defend him, he will neither allow himself to be defended nor rescued.[b] Accordingly, he is more persistently silent before Pilate, than he was before the Sanhedrim. "*He answered him never a word, insomuch that the governor marvelled greatly.*"[c] But both Matthew and Mark mean to say that Jesus said one word to Pilate, when he asked him if he was king of the Jews.[d] As he had put his great pretension in the very form, in which it was most offensive to the chief priests, when he admitted to them he was the Christ, the Son of God,[e] so now he will admit, in the most offensive form in which it can appear to a Roman governor, that he is the king of the Jews. To be a son of God was to the High Priest blasphemy, to be king of the Jews was treason to Cæsar; and he will give such answer to each, as will insure his destruction.

After this exhibition — so entirely consistent with both the character and plan of Jesus — it is impossible for us to give credence to the contradictory statement of Luke, who

[a] Matt. xxvi., 62, 63.　[b] Matt. xxvi., 51-54.　[c] Matt. xxvii., 14.
[d] Matt. xxvii., 11; Mark xv., 2.　[e] Mark xiv., 61, 62.

says that, when Jesus was adjured by the High Priest, he made the compromising and undignified reply, "*If I tell you, you will not believe; and if I also ask you, you will not answer me,* NOR LET ME GO."[a] If he asked what, what could Jesus ask the High Priest relevant to his case? Self-delivered, as he declares himself to have been, by his own voluntary act, to accomplish a stupendous destiny for himself and for the world, how could he have demeaned himself by the pusillanimous consideration of being *let go?* But Luke, too, makes him nobly silent before Pilate.[b] It is only in the Johannic drama that the whole statement of these three writers is utterly falsified, and the noble dignity of Jesus compromised. On the occasion of the arrest, that peculiar *chaffing*, so prominent a blemish in the whole book — introduced so many times in the story of the curing of the blind man, in colloquies with the Jews, in the speech of Jesus with his followers, and perpetuated even after the resurrection — reappears. But brought before Pilate, Jesus, instead of the marvellous silence, to which all his real biographers bear testimony, is made, by the writer of this masterly, but most presumptuous fiction, to offend his friendly intercessor, as he does the taste of the modern reader, by the captiousness and verbose inconsequence of his replies.

Strange to say, the writer of the articles referred to in the *Contemporary Review* evidently considers the Johannic the authentic report of the trial of Jesus, and has discovered a hidden meaning in those petulant remarks, which were said to have been considered by the officer a contempt of the High Priest. He cannot, however, understand how — the principal trial being under Roman forms — Jesus should have confessed that he was the king of the Jews, and yet have been acquitted by Pilate of any fault. He concludes that it was because Jesus had satisfied Pilate, that his kingdom was not of this world. If he had satisfied Pilate, that to be a king of the Jews was no invasion of the authority of Cæsar, because it was a heavenly and not an earthly kingdom that was claimed, then Pilate must have seriously entertained the idea that Jesus was a heavenly king. If it was an insane vagary, a sensible governor would have been as

[a] Luke xxii., 67, 68. [b] Luke xxiii., 9.

little disturbed by a peasant's claiming the political sovereignty of his own proconsulate, as he would by a claim to the kingship of the Jews in heaven: either pretension would only have amused him. The reviewer succumbs to the evident purpose of the writer of Johannic fiction to represent Jesus only in an imposing character, without seeing that in so doing he has destroyed the probability of the events he narrates, and compromised the character of the hero. For how, if Pilate had been really affected by the claim of Jesus to be a king of a heavenly kingdom, and had judicially acquitted him of treason *on that ground*, could he, while still finding him blameless, take Jesus and scourge him, and have him mocked by his soldiers, and finally have this sentence — the most remarkable in the annals of Roman jurisprudence — passed as the judgment of the court, "*Take ye him, and crucify him, for I find no fault in him*"?[a]

The fact is, the writer is misled, as is the ordinary lay and clerical mind, by coming to the study of this great trial with prepossessions, not easily overborne, of the exalted character of the person convicted. It is difficult to measure the utter isolation and contempt in which Jesus stood before the public of Jerusalem. Only the scribes and Pharisees are angry enough to be in earnest in their malice; but they reveal their utter disrespect for their victim, by the summary and hasty manner in which they proceed to his trial. He is a Galilean fanatic, in whose favor no one asks for deliberation or delay, or even a seeming compliance with the forms of law. His followers have all forsaken him at the first sound of personal danger; and his most trusted servant, lately so demonstrative in his devotion under the hope of being his viceroy and prime minister, has denied with oaths that he ever knew him.

The High Priest does not deign to make any reply to his assurance that he will come in the clouds of heaven, on the right hand of power, but turns to the Council to learn if they are not now satisfied that the blasphemy is sufficiently proved.[b] The condemnation is immediate and, as Mark reports, unanimous.[c] There was no Gamaliel or Nicodemus, or Joseph of Arimathea, or other candid

---

[a] John xix., 6. [b] Matt. xxvi., 65. [c] Mark xiv., 64.

person, to interpose any plea in mitigation or postponement of the sentence of death. It was not the custom of Jewish courts to insult the capitally condemned. In all human minds and in all ages, the doom of impending death has invested the person of the criminal with a sort of dignity and awe that has gained for him pity rather than insult. How extreme must have been the contempt of Jesus in the minds of these rulers of Israel and dignitaries of the Church, so that even the sanctity of impending death did not restrain them from leaving their seats to spit upon the face of the silently suffering man, and from brutally buffeting him with their hands, after covering his face, while they derided his prophetic character by challenging him to tell who had smitten him.[a]

When the chief priests and elders brought Jesus to Pilate, it was, as has before been shown, with the evident purpose of causing him to take the initiative in the execution of the sentence they themselves had passed, or at least to confirm it by an executive warrant. They knew that no considerations of blasphemy, no questions of mere ecclesiastical law would influence a Roman magistrate. So they falsely represented Jesus as claiming to be king of the Jews, and as forbidding to pay tribute to Cæsar.[b] It is possible that Pilate may never have heard of the Galilean prophet, and of the kingdom of heaven that he had preached. It may have been that some rumor of him had even reached the ears of the governor. The chief priests and elders, who utterly contemned the pretensions of Jesus to be the Messiah, could not honestly excite an apprehension in the mind of Cæsar, which they themselves believed to be groundless — though, if Jesus was the king of such a kingdom of heaven, as he had preached, his purpose threatened the supremacy of Cæsar, and the stability of every human state and kingdom. But, whether Pilate had ever heard of Jesus and his scheme of a kingdom of heaven or not, it took only a brief colloquy with him to convince Pilate that he need have no serious apprehension for the authority of Cæsar, and no resentment toward Jesus. "Are you the king of the Jews?" he asks. Jesus answers in all simplicity and seriousness that he is;[c] and Pilate instantly concludes that he is

[a] Mark xiv., 65.   [b] Luke xxiii., 2.   [c] Luke xxiii., 3.

dealing with a harmless monomaniac. It ill accords with his humane notions to put such a man to death. And yet, with his pity, there is a contemptuous estimation of a mind clouded, as it seemed to him, with such a fatal hallucination; and, after feeble attempts to get him released altogether as a harmless enthusiast, or to get him adopted as the one forgiven criminal that an old custom surrendered to the populace, he weakly passes the order for his execution, lest — in the minds of the envious Jews — he might seem to be wanting in loyalty to Cæsar. Still, when he proposed that he should be chastised before his release, he showed that, in all this vacillation, Jesus himself had made no favorable impression upon his mind. And the fact that he sent him to the cross — an ignominious mode of punishment reserved among the Romans for slaves and the disreputable — proved that there was no deference to his rank as an artisan or free subject, and still less to the sanctity, which he should have obtained in the office of a prophet and healer of the sick.

Neither do the soldiers nor their officers, upon whom the next cruel office fell, indicate anything but contempt for their victim. They cannot proceed in an orderly way even to put him to death. They, too, are amused with the idea of a Galilean peasant persisting that he is king. A king, forsooth! they said. Let him have a robe of scarlet! and one was found for him; and a sceptre — a reed was placed in his right hand — and, for a crown, thorns are plaited and placed about his temples. Then, they bowed the knee in mock homage, and hailed him as King of the Jews. They, too, spat in his face, and smote him upon the head with his own reed sceptre.[a] An inscription is prepared — John attributes this malice to Pilate — expressing at once the official derision and the general levity and mockery which scandalized all the proceedings.[b]

Nor does the spectacle of his suffering touch the hard hearts of his murderers. The very passers-by make grimaces, and shaking their heads at him, ask why one that could destroy and build the temple could not save himself. "Come down from the cross," they cried, "Son

[a] Matt. xxvii., 27-31.   [b] Matt. xxvii., 37; John xix., 19.

of God: save, if thou canst, thyself!"[a] The chief priests and elders could not forego the malicious satisfaction of looking upon his helplessness; and they join in the horrible ribaldry. "If he be the King of Israel," they sneer, "let him now come down from the cross, and we will believe him. He trusted in God: let him deliver him now."[b] The very thieves so far forgot their tortures, that they are swept away in the general ridicule, and cast the same words in his teeth.[c] It is certain the whole scene of the trial and the execution of Jesus, as described with every indication of probability and in complete historic harmony with itself, is not of a person of any supernatural or unusual endowments, or majesty of bearing, but of a person so ill-reputed that his judges lose their decorum and dignity in trying him, the witnesses and the officers of the court insult him with impunity, the Roman governor, who sees at a glance the incompatibility of what he deems a monstrous hallucination, with any dangerous or criminal purpose, amuses himself and amuses the multitude with his kingly pretensions; while the soldiers, the mob, the on-looking priests and elders, the very wretches, companions of his torture, mingle mirth and derision with a spectacle of fiendish cruelty, over which the sympathetic heart of humanity has shed more tears than over the great aggregate of misery which has saddened the history of the world.

It was over at last. Sensitive to suffering as was Jesus, by a nervous organization as fine-fibred and delicate as a woman's, the darkness and the peace of death came to end his tortures, long before the tough nerves of the two coarse fellows, who hung at his side, had succumbed to keen and accumulating pains. Pilate marvelled that he was so soon dead,[d] — probably because the victims of that terrible mode of capital punishment practised at Rome, upon the person only of ignoble criminals, usually held out longer. But, if the history is veracious, there were other causes of death than the agony of the nails, and the deadly torture that comes of quivering nerves and the slowly ebbing forces of life. Only Luke tells that there followed Jesus to his crucifixion a great company of people, and of women who bewailed and lamented him,

[a] Matt. xxvii., 39, 40.   [b] Matt. xxvii., 41-43.   [c] Matt. xxvii., 44.   [d] Mark xv., 37, 44.

and that, in forgetfulness of his fate, he turned to commiserate them; that he besought God to forgive his tormentors — for they knew not what they did; that one of the thieves, awed by the majesty of his bearing, prayed to him in penitence, and was assured of bliss that day with him in paradise; that he confidently commended his spirit to God at the last; that the centurion, who commanded the executioners, openly acknowledged him as a righteous man; that all his acquaintances and the Galilean women looked on from a distance; and that the people that looked on sadly smote their breasts in sorrow at his fate.[a] So Luke omits, as he must if Jesus met his death in that spirit, the despairing appeal to God, and the loud wail with which his spirit took leave of his tortured body. But Mark and Matthew report that, at the time of his arrest, all his disciples forsook him and fled; and neither of them assert that they returned to witness the crucifixion,[b] or that his acquaintance, or the women, whose sex might have given them impunity, stood even within distant view of his last agonies. According to both, the isolation of Jesus was complete, the cruel mockery and hatred of all the participants and spectators of his putting-to-death were universal; and, in the desolation of soul which came over the enfeebled sufferer at last, he declared, quoting the language of one of the hymns of the temple worship, that God, whom he had trusted as his father, had forsaken him.[c] Why did this sad refrain burst from his lips, after he had seen in brave silence all the hideous preparations for his cruel and lingering death, and, turning to the ribald crowd in vain for one pitying or sympathetic look, had uttered no word of complaint or reproach? What expectation or hope, that till that supreme moment had buoyed up his soul, of help from the skies — interposition from the Father in heaven — gave way, when that passionate and inexpressibly piteous voice made itself heard above the mockery of the soldiers and the mob, and has made its echoes heard through all later time? Can there be any doubt that this older tradition as given in Matthew and Mark is the true

---

[a] Luke xxiii., 27, 28, 34, 42, 43, 46–49.   [b] Matt. xxvi., 56; Mark xiv., 50.
[c] Ps. xxii., 1; Mark xv., 34; Matt. xxvii., 46.

history of the bearing of Jesus under the suffering to which he was subjected, and that the purpose, evident in the Fourth Gospel, is also apparent in the Third, to eliminate from the narrative whatever is indicative of human weakness? How can we help regarding the suppression of that irrepressible utterance of a great disappointment which wrung his soul, and made him oblivious of physical torture, as a concession to an ever-growing conception in the minds of the early believers of a triumphing and all-conquering deity, which more and more displaced the recollection of a meek, suffering and submissive man?

CHAPTER XI.

PERSONAL PRETENSIONS AND CHARACTER OF JESUS.

" Invective may be a sharp weapon, but over-use blunts its edge. Even when the denunciation is just and true, it is an error of art to indulge it too long. We not only incur the risk of becoming too vapid, but of actually inverting the force of reprobation which we seek to rouse, and of bringing it back by recoil upon ourselves. At suitable intervals, separated from each other by periods of dignified reserve, invective may become a real power of the tongue or pen. But, indulged in constantly, it degenerates into scolding; and then, instead of being regarded as a proof of strength, it is accepted as an evidence of weakness and lack of self-control."—*John Tyndall, on Goethe's "Farbenlehre."*

" Science, as distinguished from philosophy, has always been republican. Not that it refuses to reverence superior minds; not, perhaps, that it is altogether incapable of yielding to the temptation of trusting a particular authority for a while too much, or following a temporary fashion. But, as a general rule, it rejects as a superstition the notion that a superior mind is at all infallible ; it dissents without a scruple from those whom it reverences most."— *Natural Religion.*

A COMPLETE summary of the elements that formed the unique character of Jesus, a just estimate of the weight and import of his life, will necessarily involve the recapitulation of particulars of his history that have already been considered under appropriate categories, and a renewed reference to incidents of his career, and the implications of his extant words, that have already been in this discussion repeatedly cited. So little is known of what he said, so brief and meagre is the record of what he did, that all his words and all his acts, so far as their authenticity is reasonably certified, must be considered on every side, till their full significance has been exhausted.

It may be safest to limit the scope of our conjectures by embodying them in tentative answers to the questions that have been debated with assurance and acrimony for nearly nineteen hundred years : What did he believe himself to be ? What did his age believe him to be ? What was he ? These are substantially the questions he is said himself once to have asked: "*Whom do men say that I, the Son of Man, am? Whom say ye that I am?*"ᵃ

As has already been seen, Jesus through his whole career most frequently spake of himself in the third person, as the *Son of Man*. The epithet was not in itself specially assuming; for "Son of Man," as used poetically in Hebrew literature, means Man generically,— the impersonation of humanity. It is improbable that Jesus used the designation in this unpretentious signification. When he is heard affirming of this Man, or Son of Man, that he has power on earth to forgive sins;[b] that all things are given to him of God, who is his father;[c] that he will come in the glory of his Father, with all the holy angels with him;[d] it is to be inferred that the Son of Man is not a person of ordinary human rank, but that the term was used in a special sense, and with reference to the man whom Ezekiel saw in vision upon the throne above the firmament,[e] and to the Son of Man whom Daniel saw coming to the Ancient of Days in the clouds of heaven.[f] There would be none of the striking antithesis which marked the style of Jesus in these words of his: "Foxes have holes, and the birds of the air have nests; but the Son of Man hath not where to lay his head,"[g] if, by Son of Man, he meant only a human being. It is no uncommon lot for men to have no place of their own to lodge in; but what a humiliation for the exalted Son of Man, companion of the Ancient of Days, to be less securely sheltered than the birds and wild beasts!

From the beginning of his public career, Jesus seems to have claimed that he was aided by the divine power, and impelled by the divine spirit, and to have assumed a character and office above the grade of ordinary humanity. If the question is concluded by the chronological order of his conversations given by Matthew, it must be allowed that the claim of supreme divine authority was nearly simultaneous with his appearance among his countrymen as a teacher. For, in the Sermon on the Mount, he said that he himself would pronounce in the day of judgment the sentence of banishment upon false disciples.[h] Apparently in the midst of his mission in Galilee,

---

ᵃ Matt. xvi., 13–15.   [b] Matt. ix., 6.   [c] Matt. xi., 27.   [d] Matt. xvi., 27.
[e] Ezek. i., 26.   [f] Dan. vii., 13.   [g] Matt. viii., 20.   [h] Matt. vii., 23.

he is declared to have said, "All things are delivered unto me of my Father"; [a] and, about the same time, he claimed authority to set aside the law of the Sabbath, promulgated in the ten sacred laws of Jehovah.[b] But the chronology is not wholly trustworthy; and Luke gives a later date to one of these declarations.[c] It would have been very difficult for the evangelists, redacting the oral traditions of Jesus' words after his death, and after the Pauline ideas of his exalted character had become prevalent, not to impute to his early consciousness the exaggerated estimate of his later days. The verse found both in Matthew and in Luke, "All things are delivered unto me of my Father: neither knoweth any man the Father save the Son, and he to whomsoever the Son will reveal him," is so evidently *Johannic* in style and thought, so unlike the *synoptic* style of Jesus, that its source is to be looked for in an adoption much later than the original tradition.

As has been seen, the distinct recognition of his Messiahship, of his heirship to the throne of the kingdom of heaven, did not originate with Jesus himself. It was first imputed by John the Baptist.[d] When the unclean spirits invoked him as Son of God and as the Holy One, he rebuked them;[e] and when, at last, he communicated to his disciples the assurance to which he had come, that he was the Christ, he charged them strictly not to make it known to any man — so alien then to the modesty of his nature seemed so lofty a self-estimation.[f] He began his career as a prophet and healer of diseases; and he gained the adhesion of his first disciples as a person in whom were the spirit and power of God, rather than as the Messiah and hope of Israel.

In answering the question, what Jesus thought of himself, we must not disregard a crisis, that seemed to have changed the project and purpose of his life. This crisis occurred in the remote north of Palestine, whither Jesus had withdrawn, perhaps to avoid the enmity of Herod, perhaps to escape the inquisition and contradiction of the Pharisees. Apparently, he has got beyond the rumor of his gifts of healing — much narrower than the evangelists define it — and, unvexed by the multitude, in the presence

[a] Matt. xi., 27. [b] Matt. xii., 1–8. [c] Luke x., 22. [d] Matt. iii., 2–11.
[e] Mark i., 24, 25, 34. [f] Mark viii., 30.

of his twelve friends, he gives himself up to a survey of what he has done, and of the enterprise that still lies nuattempted before him.[a] It was an opportune time for confidence and confession. Let us consider what the gospel tradition preserves of this memorable interview.

Though hitherto not unconscious of himself, nor indifferent to public opinion, he now becomes morbidly sensitive to the opinion of the world, and in his self-exaltation he aspires to the highest grades of being. What do men think of me? in a moment of frank confidence he asks of his disciples. The answer was one which should have been grateful to a most aspiring spirit. Some, said his devoted adherents, say that you are John the Baptist come back from death. Some say you are Elijah, some Jeremiah; others, one of the great prophets. These surmises of the credulous Galileans, who had followed him out of their cities, and whose sick he had healed, seemed but slightly to move him. Is that all? "Whom say ye that I am?" is his next appeal. When Peter, in the fervor of his allegiance, replied, "*Thou art the anointed Messiah, Son of the Living God,*" Jesus was profoundly affected, and with ardor exclaimed: *Blessed art thou, Simon, son of Jonas! Only the spirit of God could give such true insight.* Thou art the rock, upon which I will build my church, and the gates of hell shall not be strong against it; and I will give thee the key of heaven, and power to bind and loose on earth as viceroy of the king of heaven.[b] But the old modesty soon comes over his spirit; and, repressing his exultation, he charges his disciples that his Messiahship is not to be divulged to any human being. For the discovery of his high office and dignity, which Peter, inspired with insight from the divine mind itself, has just made, all honors are offered to him, even to sovereign power upon the earth; but tell no man, he charges him, what God hath revealed to you; for, before my glory in the acknowledgment of God, and the plaudits and worship of all good spirits, must come my humiliation, shame, and death. So all the prophets have declared. Let the world, ignorant who I am, work its evil will, till all eyes shall see and every tongue shall confess the glory, which they have put to shame. The scene

---

[a] Matt. xvi., 21.   [b] Matt. xvi., 13-19.

is most striking and impressive, and at the same time quite human and natural. Surely never at any other time did a human soul rise to a higher level of inspiration or indulge in vaster dreams. But when Jesus, subduing and repressing his gratification at such appreciation, as had burst from the lips of his sanguine friend, with sad thoughts of the dark and dreadful path, by which he must walk to his glory, proceeds to tell how he will go to Jerusalem, and suffer the scorn and persecution there of scribes, elders, and chief priests, and even be killed, Peter, in his turn elated at the sovereignty of the Church, so generously given to him, thinks the trusted viceroy may at least advise, albeit in the affection and kindly solicitude of a friend touched with human pity at the coming sufferings of his Master. "That be far from thee, Lord," still respectful, he ventures to interpose, "that shall not be unto thee,"— not so much evidently to dictate his Master's well-considered course, as to express a motherly anxiety, that a cruel death should not befall one beloved. He had little comprehended the deep enthusiasm, to which this mysterious man had been wrought up, nor understood how that gentle spirit, when thwarted and contradicted, could flash in the lightning of rebuke.[*] For Jesus, who had said: He that is angry with his brother, without a cause, shall be in danger of the judgment, and he that saith to his brother, *Thou fool*, shall be in danger of hell-fire,[b] turned upon Peter, whom he had just declared blessed, inspired of the Holy Ghost, the head of the Church to be,— upon Peter, whose affectionate solicitude, apparent even now to the reader of the narrative, he could not have misunderstood — with these withering words: "*Get thee behind me, Satan: thou art an offence unto me;* for thou savorest not of divine things, but of human things."

Then, with firm hand, he represses that rapturous delight of himself and his followers, which had culminated in anger and cruel, contemptuous words, by calling their attention to the sufferings, which all, who would share his triumph, must first undergo. "If any man," he said, "would be a follower of me, let him follow me to my cross."[*] Do not think of saving your lives by desertion.

[a] Matt. xvi., 21-28. [b] Matt. v., 22.

[*] It is scarcely questionable, that Jesus foreboded and foretold his own death by violence. We have noted the successive steps he took to make such a result the catastrophe of his life.

If by desertion you should not only save life, but gain the whole world, what profit were it? If you lose your lives, you may thus gain the life of your souls. For, when I come in the glory of my Father and with his angels, I will reward every man according to his integrity. Nor is the reward a remote one, for some of you shall not die, till you see the Son of Man coming in his kingdom.

Jesus comes from this conference with the twelve with purposes either wholly changed or more definitely determined upon. Let the Galileans still debate which of the great prophets has come back to enlighten his people. Jesus knows; and Peter, inspired of the Holy Spirit, has learned that a greater than all the prophets is here — no less a personage than the Messiah promised of old to Israel. His work in Galilee is done. He need not ask even three days of Herod to do cures and cast out devils. That epoch has passed; and he must go to Zion, as the King of the new kingdom of heaven. The change in his purpose, in the nature of his communications, in the temper of his own spirit, even his dull adherents do not fail to notice. All the synoptic evangelists, with more or less distinctness, indicate it; and they all assign its date to the period of this Cæsarean interview. In the First Gospel, it is said: "From that time forth began Jesus to show unto his disciples, how that he must go unto Jerusalem, and suffer many things of the elders and chief priests and scribes, and be killed, and be raised again the third day." [a]

The character and scope of a pure self-consciousness it is always difficult to determine. Indeed, a man's estimate of himself varies immensely with his moods. It rises at words of commendation from other men, at honors and rewards that are spontaneously offered and under the satisfaction and exaltation which come from the accomplishment of some great task. It sinks under reproaches of those whom we esteem, under obloquy and neglect, and in the pain and mortification with which we charge ourselves with the carelessness or the ignorance or the want

[a] Matt. xvi., 21.
It is less probable, that he anticipated that the mode of his taking-off would be a form of punishment so little known among the Jews as crucifixion. After the crucifixion, the cross naturally became in the minds of his followers the symbol of suffering; and those, who recounted from fading recollection his conversations, could hardly avoid using a symbolism, that everywhere permeated the Christian speech and the Christian thought.

of skill or courage, which produce our great defeats. So with Jesus. His moods changed. He exulted over the career of power that seemed opening before him. He beheld Satan as lightning fall from heaven.[a] All things seemed to be given into his hands by God, and himself to be the only medium of knowledge of God open to the human mind.[b] In his ardor and confidence, he is ready to share his splendid glories with his humble friends. They shall eat and drink at his table in his kingdom, and have twelve thrones, and sit and reign one over each of the tribes of Israel; and whatever they loose or bind on earth shall be loosed or bound in heaven.[c] Sometimes, he even doubts if his enemies will be able to overcome him. It was in the prophetic plan that Messiah should be cut off, that his grave should be made with the wicked. But Jehovah's judgments are not absolute. When he had commanded Abraham to offer his precious son as a sacrifice, did he not stay his hand, as it was stretched forth to slay the already bound victim? And was not Nineveh spared upon its repentance, in spite of an unconditioned sentence against it? So, in the garden of Gethsemane, he goes three times to pray, "If it be possible, let this cup pass from me."[d] For a little while, as the danger thickens about him, he thinks he will arm his friends. When only two swords can be found, however, this man of peace, sickening at the thought of using them, says, "It is enough." His better thoughts recur to supernatural allies. "Thinkest thou now," he said, "that, if I so prayed, the Father would not send me twelve legions of angels?"[e] When the children of Jerusalem, who did not join the babes of Galilee in shouting Hosanna, and whom he would fain have sheltered from fast-coming calamities, as a hen shelters her chickens under her wings, shall see him again, they shall say — so he felt assured — "*Blessed is he that cometh in the name of the Lord.*"[f]

His prevalent tone, however, as he went up to Jerusalem, was one of manifest sadness. He speaks often of what is to befall him, rather as his suffering than as his glory. And, in his prayer for deliverance, he was in agony, so that his sweat fell like drops of blood to the

[a] Luke x., 18. [b] Matt. xi., 27. [c] Luke xxii., 28-30. [d] Matt. xxvi., 37-45.
[e] M. L. xxvi., 53. [f] Matt. xxiii., 37-39.

ground. For a form so delicate and susceptible as his, the sufferings of the Roman method of executing criminals must have been unspeakably terrible; and the cry wrung from his soul, succumbing to the prolonged agony of death, was by no means incompatible either with his high courage or the grand sacrifice which he believed himself to be accomplishing. The Messiah was to have been oppressed and afflicted, and brought as a lamb to the slaughter. He was to tread the wine-press of the divine wrath alone — to be esteemed smitten of God.

It thus appears, that, up to the eve of his departure from Galilee, Jesus had been reticent, perhaps uncertain, about his own function and rank in the divine economy, and that, simultaneously with that departure, he began to assume the dignity and title of the anointed sovereign of the heavenly kingdom; and, while he lived, he continued to assert it with more and more assurance.

What was the contemporary opinion of Jesus among his countrymen? All accounts agree that he was brought up to manhood in the Galilean city of Nazareth.

It is with some distrust that we adopt the chronological order of events as detailed in the first two Gospels, differing as it does from that in the Third Gospel. Adopting that order, it is found that, after the healing of all manner of sickness and disease in every city of Galilee, after the report of these miracles coming to the ears of John the Baptist had excited in his mind the surmise that Jesus was the Messiah, after Capernaum, Chorazin, and Bethsaida had been reproached for their disregard of mighty works done in them, the people of his own town, Nazareth, considered Jesus to be the son of Joseph, the carpenter, and did not believe in him.[a]

The people who came to listen to Jesus, described in the Synoptic Gospels as a great multitude from every province of Palestine, must not be reckoned among his adherents.[b] They were not of the flock — always a little one — to whom he said it was the good pleasure of the Father to give the kingdom of heaven.[c] They were not of the favored ones, to whom it was given to know its mysteries.[d] He was moved with compassion to give them food in the wilderness from the supplies of his own com-

[a] Matt. xiii., 54-58. [b] Matt. iv., 25. [c] Luke xii., 32. [d] Luke viii., 10.

pany; but he never seems to have won their confidence, nor did he gain even their inchoate discipleship.[a] He makes a distinction between the people and his disciples. The former he dismisses, the latter he sends before him on his return to Galilee. Even the disciples seemed to have failed to see anything unusual in the feeding of the multitude, for their hearts were hardened.[b]

To those who deem the Fourth Gospel historic, it is a most significant declaration that, comparatively late in his career, his own brothers did not believe in him.[c] Indeed, it is not apparent, that, with the exception of James, his family had, up to the time of his arrest, given in their adhesion to his Messianic pretensions. The mother and brethren standing without, and desiring to speak with him, instead of being within and listening to him, indicate a somewhat hostile attitude, as does his reply: "I recognize as my kindred those that do the will of my Father."[d] In that view, we can understand the stress he laid upon the sundering of all ties of kindred, as the necessary conditions of discipleship; and that, when he said, I am come not to send peace, but a sword, to make discord and dissension in families, and a man's foes shall be they of his very household, he was speaking in the sadness, if not the bitterness, of his own domestic experience.[e]

After a prophetic career in his native province — it may be only for a few months, though it may have extended over several years — Jesus undertook the fatal demonstration upon Jerusalem. As his going thither, in the mind of his followers, if not in his own, was to inaugurate the kingdom of heaven, and begin the reign of righteousness in the world,— a consummation which he seems to understand must be preceded by his death,— it is likely that nearly all who believed in him accompanied him upon his journey. The company seemed to include women,[f] and so many children, that those who applauded him in the streets of Jerusalem were spoken of by him as babes and sucklings.[g] While some real believers must have been compelled by sickness or poverty to abide the impending event at home, the faith and devotion of those who attended upon him seemed of the most precarious

---

[a] Mark vi., 35-45. [b] Mark vi., 52. [c] John vii., 5. [d] Matt xii., 46-50.
[e] Matt. x., 34-38. [f] Luke xxiii., 55. [g] Matt. xxi, 15, 16.

kind. When the city turned against him, and his arrest, quickly followed by his trial, conviction, and execution, was obstructed neither by supernatural nor popular interposition, *all his disciples*, according to the most authentic tradition, *forsook him;* and even Peter denied with scornful oaths that he had ever known him.[a]

On the day of Pentecost, however, one hundred and twenty adherents rallied to his name, influenced by the impassioned faith of the twelve disciples, that he had been seen alive, and that, by a triumphant resurrection, he had established his Messiahship.[b] All those one hundred and twenty were Galileans, as the writer Luke narrates;[c] and noting how much more rapidly and numerously converts were made to the faith by the reputation of the resurrection, than by his personal presence, with all the effect of his teaching and miracles, it may be justly assumed, that a considerable part of the company of believers were attracted to the faith by the wonder of the resurrection, which had proved efficacious enough, not only to bring back Peter to his allegiance, but every one of his fellows, whose desertion had only been less conspicuous, because their original zeal and confidence had been less pronounced than his.

This then was the impression Jesus made upon his age and people. Something like a hundred persons out of the cities of Galilee so far believed on him, as to follow him, until it became evidently unsafe to be identified with him. Then, they fled, and left him to the rage of the populace, who hated him, not because they knew aught against him, but because their fanaticism had been designedly worked upon by his real enemies, the hierarchy of the Jewish Church.

What the Galileans generally, including his unbelieving kinsfolk, thought of him cannot be certainly determined. In Nazareth, where he lived, his life was once attempted.[d] Frequently, he betook himself to uninhabited regions away from the cities and villages, either because his person was not safe among the habitations of men, or because he could not brook their indifference and scepticism. Did the favor, with which the people at first seemed to listen to him, change afterward to suspicion

[a] Matt. xxvi., 56, 74. [b] Acts i., 15. [c] Acts ii., 7. [d] Luke iv., 28, 29.

or contempt? Did they, who were first inclined to recognize him as a prophet and preacher of righteousness, fall off from him, when he began to exact more rigorous requirements of conduct, or to put forth claims to higher personal dignity? The written tradition clearly presents two contrasted pictures, one of a reformer going forth full of confidence and assurance upon a high and beneficent mission, the other of a man of sorrow, sore-hearted with disappointment, and not repressing keen complaints of withheld appreciation. The Fourth Gospel has an incident, probably historic, of the falling away from him of a body of his disciples, perplexed by some new subtlety of his doctrine, and of his mistrust of the fidelity even of the twelve.[a]

In Jerusalem and Judea there were apparently no open adherents to his faith. It seems as if there was not in the sacred city a single believing family, with which he could safely lodge. A secret friend placed his upper chamber at the disposal of the disciples for the Passover festival; but he took such care to preserve his secret that curious tradition has not been able to recover it, however much it might now redound to his glory.

Difficulties are encountered in the effort justly to estimate the character of Jesus, that cannot be met in studying any other personage of history. We must gather one by one his traits from eulogists, who will not suspend their admiration long enough for us to see the man. The Gospels, too, seem to have been written, when the controversy with the ancient Church was at its height, and when a disposition to find parallels in the fortunes of Jesus, and the providential history of the peculiar people, induced the writers to see fulfilment of prophecies in the most trivial circumstances and the most dissimilar situations.[b] However cogent as arguments these fancies may have been at the time they were published, they only serve to confuse the modern apprehension and obscure the vision of a soul, perhaps more worthy of contemplation than any that has enlarged our view of the capacities of human nature. Certain it is, that in the minds of the biographers and friends of Jesus, the prophetic destiny he was believed to fulfil quite eclipsed the most vivid impres-

[a] John vi., 66, 67.   [b] Matt. i., 23; ii., 6, 15, 18, 23.

sions of memory; and their reminiscences too often give us pictures of the trained actor going solemnly through a prescribed part, when what we ask for is a majestic and original man, speaking and acting spontaneously from the resources of his intelligence and the inspirations of his genius.

It is proper to look for the germ and primal force of whatever is original and distinctive in the complex Christian cultus in Jesus himself. A careful study of his intellectual, moral, and spiritual traits will reveal to the candid inquirer with more or less clearness the secret of his influence upon the world. In his age, the authority and reputation of a wise man stood far less than it stands now, upon stores of knowledge acquired from books and study, and the capacity of communicating truth in written words. He among the Greeks was esteemed a philosopher, and among the Jews inspired of God, who could wisely answer questions without quoting and from his own insight. If he could cover an ethical lesson under a vivid figure of speech or a picturesque allegory, or compress it into a pregnant and sententious aphorism, winged with wit, he was sure of a hearing and of the adherence of disciples. Jesus was largely endowed with this talent. His parables have stood and will ever stand in the poetic imagination as the permanent imagery and illustration of most momentous moral judgments. So deeply engraven on the human heart are his profoundly sagacious canons of conduct, that they have become for generation after generation the terms in which conscience and reason express themselves.

Happily, we feel more assurance in tracing to the mind of Jesus these intellectual creations, than we do in imputing to him any thaumaturgic work, or the domination of any controlling faith or enthusiasm. We know that the annalists, who prepared for us the Synoptic Gospels, with their easy credulity, and their limited comprehension on the one hand, and with their simplicity and general good faith on the other hand, could never have invented the allegories and aphorisms, which disclose all that we know of the mind of Jesus. The mere memory will retain for ages the substance and even the form of a fable or of a parable. Each part so depends upon another, each incident and detail so contributes to the moral or to the *dénouement*, that to forget and omit one would destroy the symmetry of the whole. Just so, those sententious maxims and popular by-words, which are handed down without writing among illiterate races, and are not indebted to the aid of writing among the most cultivated races, acquire in their repetition a certain rhythmic melody, which fixes them in the memory from one age to another.

Written, as our genuine Gospels in their first draft are believed to have been, from thirty to sixty years after the events which they describe, we find them containing those very forms of speech, in which Jesus was peculiarly gifted, and which the unaided human memory is best able to retain. Doubtless, he said many unremembered things well worth perpetuation; but he did say, and substantially as they have recorded it, what the synoptic annalists impute to him. On the other hand, it is morally certain, that the writer of the Fourth Gospel — whether the Apostle John or a much later disciple — could have found in his own recollections, or in the collated recollections of all, who had known Jesus, no data for a report of the conversations dramatically ascribed to him in that work. The unaided human memory could never have retained the form or substance of prolonged metaphysical disquisitions, flowing feebly and diffusely in vague and lifeless words, with their inadequate expressiveness eked out by repetitions, enlivened by no imaginative illustrations, and charged with no force or impetuosity of diction. The task of recalling with all the precision of question and reply the conversations with the Jews in the temple, or with the disciples in the garden of Gethsemane, would be nearly as difficult one week, as sixty years after they had occurred; and it is not pretended that the task was undertaken earlier than after the last-named interval.

Many of the replies of Jesus to questions designed to entangle him in an inconsistency, an impolicy or an impiety, while they exhibit his shrewdness and the readiness of his intellectual resources, disclose also the emphasis of his moral judgments. When the Pharisees said he cast out devils by the power of the chief of devils, Jesus rejoined: "How can a power antagonize itself? How can Satan's kingdom be maintained, if he is himself busy in seeking its destruction?" How effective was his reply to the delegated scribes from Jerusalem, who, coming to learn of his doctrines, had discovered and remarked, that the disciples sat down to eat without the ceremonial laving of their hands! "Why do they thus," they asked, "transgress the traditions of the elders?" "Why do ye," retorted the Master, "transgress with your traditions the commandments of God?" Why do ye allow an empty form of words to cancel the law of God, that requires a man to honor his father and mother?

There is philosophy, wisdom, and even wit in his answer to the Pharisees, who asked, if for any cause of dissatisfaction, a man might divorce his wife. The distinction of sex, he replied, is a distinction of nature. The union of the sexes makes a relation so consequential, that the married become one flesh, and that too by an ordinance established by God. What God hath joined together let not man put asunder.[a]

There was a conclusiveness about his solutions, that left them sticking in minds like axioms, never to be either questioned or forgotten. Of that character was his settlement of the question of precedence, which his disciples raised among themselves. It left a play for a noble ambition, and a mode of gratifying it incapable of provoking envy. He that would be the greatest among you, let him be the servant of all, and let him understand that, unlike the dominions of this world, this is to be the law of the kingdom of heaven.[b]

The personal appeal, the argument to the man, was a characteristic of his speech. The men who approached him with a strong purpose of not committing or exposing themselves, while they directed him to some purely doctrinal or speculative question, found the secrets of their hearts suddenly exposed by the keenness of his criticism, either in a direct reply, or by a palpable illustration. By what authority does the Rabbi do these things,—march in tumultuous processions through the city, disturb the lawful trade in victims in the environs of the temple?

[a] Matt. xix., 3-9.   [b] Matt. xx., 26, 27; Mark ix., 33, 35.

The Rabbi says he will not answer, but asks another question: John Baptist's Gospel, was it of heaven or of men? It is deemed discreet not to answer. Well, he says, which is the obedient son, the one that promises to obey, and breaks his promise, or he who, having refused, afterward repents, and does the thing commanded? The adulterers and extortioners repented, when John preached righteousness. Why did not ye Pharisees, who are the public professors of righteousness, repent?

In some of his replies however, verbally complete, and effectual answers to the questioner, a self-possessed intelligence may detect some inconsequence, a virtual evasion of the point, which perhaps the question itself did not fully set forth. His solution of the difficulty of the much-married woman in the resurrection, elsewhere considered, is of that character.

So, too, when he is called to meet the consequences of some of his own manifest exaggerations of speech, as when he said: "It is easier for a camel to go through the eye of a needle, than for a rich man to enter into the kingdom of heaven." Who then — probably, *what rich man* — can be saved? It is impossible with men, not impossible with God, explained Jesus, as if there were two kinds of possibility in an agency in itself wholly of God.[a]

Like men of wit, he appreciated wit in others, and was evidently gratified with an answer which manifested shrewdness and self-possession. It was not more the reverence, with which the Syro-Phœnician woman received him, and her faith and humility, than her apt retort to his brusque and unfriendly banter, that made him so gracious to her.[b] It was his own facetiousness, we must believe, rather than the expression of a coarse, national prejudice, quite foreign to his character, that made him say: "It is not proper to take children's bread and cast it to the dogs." She, with woman's sagacity, saw the gentle nature under the rough, repellent speech, but was too meek, too set upon her purpose, to resent it. "Truth, Master, but the dogs may eat the crumbs that fall from the table."

When the peculiar style of Jesus is once discovered in the Gospels, it is impossible to mistake it. The terse, piquant colloquies of the first three Gospels are as utterly

[a] Matt. xix., 24-26. [b] Matt. xv., 21-28.

unlike the turgid, garrulous, and tautological discourses of the Fourth Gospel, as two styles of men of the same time could be. The ready resource, the pungent wit, and the keen edge of Jesus do appear in that one line, wherein he is made to say: "*Let him who is without sin among you cast the first stone.*"[a] Some flavor of the sententious acuteness of the great teacher — perhaps the situation, as told, was real — had evidently come down to the writer to show how incongruous were all his other imputations. It is a singular corroboration of the view in these chapters presented of the character of the Fourth Gospel, that this very passage is deemed an interpolation.

There is traceable in his mind a fondness for intellectual puzzles; and he apparently enjoyed the confusion and distraction into which the dull apprehensions of his friends were often thrown by exaggerations, indirections, and daring figures of speech. Thus, one day, he cautioned his disciples to beware of the leaven of the Pharisees and the Sadducees. Something is at fault with the bread, reasoned the disciples. Even the popular mode of preparing it is tinctured with the general falsity and adulterating character of the dispensation. "What can the Master mean?"[b] The figure so explained has been plain enough to the modern mind; but what clew had those matter-of-fact and unpoetic minds to its hidden meaning?

They were more stupidly at a loss, when, in his pointed antithetic epigram, he told the multitude, whom the Pharisees had perplexed by insisting upon some ceremonial cleansing: "Not that which goeth into the mouth defileth a man, but what cometh out of the mouth."[c]

That too, lucid as it appears to us, was a parable to them. This stupidity even annoyed him. Are ye too, he asked, still without understanding?[d] Not food going into the mouth defiles, but those words and acts, which flow out of a foul heart: they make the man unclean.[e] He had evidently overrated their perception, when a day or two before he said to them, "Blessed are your eyes, for they see; and your ears, for they hear what prophets and righteous men had in vain desired to see and hear."[f]

His whole scheme of a kingdom of heaven is presented in figures and pictures of common things. The

---

[a] John viii., 7. [b] Matt. xvi., 6-12. [c] Matt. xv., 11. [d] Matt. xv., 16.
[e] Matt. xv., 20. [f] Matt. xiii., 16, 17, 24.

world is a field, its end a harvest. He himself is a sower, a fisherman, a shepherd, a bridegroom, a master of a feast, a landlord. The elect and non-elect are sheep and goats, wheat and tares, good and bad fish, real pearls and false pearls. When, at the instance of his friends, perplexed and exhausted by the tropical character of his habitual discourse, and apparently thirsting for some definite ideas, upon which their prosaic minds could rest with some sense of reality, he undertakes to tell them plainly of the signs of the kingdom of heaven, and of the end of the world, he manifestly tries to impose some curb upon his erratic fancy.[a] But that was impossible. From beyond the world of experience, to him, as to the most gifted men of genius, only vague and shadowy images could come. He drops into unimportant details made out of the life of his own time. It is still the local Judea — all the world, to the narrow apprehension of his hearers. A catastrophe which ought to embrace the whole universe cramps itself to the limited geography of Palestine. "Let him," he said, "who is in Judea flee unto the mountains."

In estimating the character of Jesus upon its intellectual side, his relation to the superstition of his age must not be overlooked. It is not required of a transcendent mind, that it shall emancipate itself from all traditionary beliefs, and comprehend the laws of nature as revealed in the perfected science of the world. All knowledge has come into the world by a gradual process, involving patient study, and a faculty of ascending from facts to principles and laws. It is not expected of a great philosopher or a great teacher, that he shall ignore the prevalent science of his time, but, accepting it as his stand-point, that he shall illuminate it with the light of his own spirit. He must take the general tendencies of his age as his *data*, and work out the problem of human duty upon the theory they offer. Shakspeare and Dante evidently accepted the theory of man's destiny, which mediæval Christianity taught; and Socrates, though put to death for his heresies, seemed not to have disturbed by any of his philosophy the fundamental notions of his age, that there were immortal gods, who were on the side

[a] Matt. xxiv., 3.

of human virtue, and who were to be worshipped by rites, as well as by righteousness. Admitting that Jesus stood in the same relation as men of this order to his age, and to its cardinal faiths, we may still place him in the category of the world's greatest men. The Jews, with the exception of the Sadducees, had come to believe in angelic, immortal beings, who attended upon the Deity to do him honor, and to be his messengers and the instruments of his direct operations. Jesus shared this belief. At the end of the world, he thought the actual separation between good and bad men would be effected by the angels, who would be sent forth in sufficient numbers and with divine power to assign to each of the myriad crowd of souls his proper place.[a] It was by a retinue of angels that his coming again in his kingdom was to be heralded, and honored,[b] and so precious was each believer that an angel was assigned to stand constantly before the throne of God,[c] to be his vindicator and patron. When meditating his arrest by the armed guards of the law, and when he had even caused swords to be produced, as if to resist them, he told his followers he had only to pray, and twelve legions of angels would be sent to his rescue. It is not apparent that these angels, which he believed peopled heaven in such numbers, and, like the armies of Rome, were organized in legions, to guard the divine throne, had been men.[d] The belief of the Pharisees was that the dead are still in the underworld; and the early Christians held that Jesus had spent the hours of his apparent death in the tomb in a mission to them to make such as were worthy the partakers of his resurrection.[e] Jesus evidently shared this belief; for he said that they, that were deemed worthy of the resurrection, should be in their new estate like the angels, which he would not have said, if he had not considered angels an order of beings distinct from men.[f]

According to the narratives of Matthew, Mark, and Luke, the beginning of Jesus' public ministry was signalized by a temptation of his integrity conducted by Satan himself in the wilderness, after forty days' abstinence from food. How far is the intelligence of Jesus

---

[a] Matt. xxiv., 31.   [b] Matt. xxv., 31.   [c] Matt. xviii., 10.
[d] Matt. xxvi., 53, 54.   [e] Acts ii., 27, 31–34; I. Peter iii., 19.   [f] Luke xx., 35.

compromised by the recapitulation of this incident? The question is one which the sincere minds who believe the adventure actually befell him — for whom these chapters are not written — need not answer. Can the legend be attributed to the creative imagination of the evangelists, or of the originators of the oral tradition, out of which the Gospels were woven? There appears in their narratives a strong tendency to exalt the life of Jesus, whom they believed a supernatural being above the range of ordinary human experience. The exclamations of the devout prophets and prophetesses, who welcomed his birth as of a sovereign prince, the jealousy of Herod excited in his very infancy, the visit of the *Magi* that travelled from the remote East guided by a star, to do homage to him in his swaddling clothes, and the choirs of angels singing pæans of congratulations to the world, must be attributed to this tendency. The imputation to evil spirits of an intelligence keener than that of men, enabling them to perceive his divinity, sprung from the same tendency. It might well comport with this sentiment to believe that the powers of hell were seriously alarmed at the advent of Jesus to the world, and that to counteract the beneficial agencies he came to establish, by assaulting his integrity and destroying the power he had with God, was a mission demanding the personal intervention of their prince.

On the other hand, this legend of the temptation is too dignified in tone, too complete and consistent in its incidents, to be the work of any prosaic annalist. We recognize in its masterly impersonation a genius kindred to that which had inspired a similar conception in the ancient poem of Job. Great lives, like that of Jesus, are a mingling of truth and poetry. The trial to which he was subjected was the trial of timidity and doubt, of the allurement of pleasure and ambition, which assails every heroic soul upon whom is laid the burden of a great thought or of a great enterprise. Jesus had told, in his vivid and poetic style, of purely internal conflicts, and the literal minds of his unimaginative disciples received his disclosure in the gross form of the canonical legend.

In a mind like his, in which the domain of the real and that of the ideal so overlie each other, it is difficult to detect his veritable faiths. It seems on the whole a just conclusion from all our data, that, whereas he imputed his own misgivings and hesitation on beginning his career as a prophet — as he did Peter's prudence, which later sought to avert the crisis of his career as the Son of Man that was to come in glory — to the immediate suggestion of Satan, he must have believed in the reality of devilish personalities, and in the existence of a chief of devils.

Sometimes, when desired, Jesus himself made a complete separation betwixt his ideal and poetic illustration of things and his real cognition of things themselves. Thus, when he explained the parable of the tares and the wheat, for every figure of his mind he supplied the corresponding reality in the nature of things, as they appeared to him. The sower of the good seed is myself — the *Son of Man* — the field, the world; the wheat typifies the children of the kingdom, or these little ones that believe in me; the tares are the children of the wicked, and the enemy that sowed them is the devil. In such a literal and precise substitution of facts for rhetorical figures, it would be most incongruous to find a figure explained by a figure.[a]

It was in the midst of a most literal and bald setting forth of the incidents of the judgment to come at the end of the world, that he declares the place of punishment for the accursed was prepared for the devil and his angels. There was already in the economy of the divine government an everlasting fire, which would have had its victims, though mankind had all repented, or had not been born. Suspecting, doubtless, a fidelity that had been too much boasted, he said to Peter, with all the solicitude of friendship: "Simon, Simon, Satan hath desired to have you, and sift you like wheat; but I have prayed that your faith may not fail."[b]

What domination over the mind and moral sense of Jesus did the sacred writings of his nation exercise? How far did he accept, how far did he rise above, the prevalent ideas of his time? With boldness he reviewed the great moral code of his race, then and still considered to be so complete and perfect, as to be imputed to

[a] Matt. xiii., 36–43; xxv., 41. [b] Luke xxii., 31, 32.

the legislation of God. The deeper spiritual insight, that discovered its inadequacy and imperfection, reveals the force and originality of Jesus. It is in his function of seer, teacher, and reformer, that he has most permanently and most beneficially affected the world. But along with this strength and keenness of moral intuition, that exalt and ennoble him, it is necessary not to overlook a certain conformity to modes of thought, which even, what may be called the Christian cultus, has repudiated, and an undoubting acquiescence in improbable and impossible legends, which have become, on the whole, offensive to Christian taste.

It is apparent that to Jesus, as well as to the scribes and ordinary Jews, the Hebrew prophetic writings were divine oracles, and all the patriotic denunciations and vaticinations, which modern scholarship has determined to have reference solely to political events, in the lifetime of the prophets, who wrote them, had a certain cabalistic and universal significance, and that in them one hears, not the local patriot uttering his thought, sometimes wisely and eloquently, sometimes extravagantly and even bombastically, but the divine word, making these writers the medium of a communication to all mankind.

There was a temple song in use among the Jews from an early time, beginning: "The Lord said unto my lord, Sit thou on my right hand, until I make thine enemies thy footstool."[*] It appealed to the popular ambition, exclusiveness and love of vengeance. It was the reaction of the unquenchable national spirit against the successive defeats and oppressions, which a proud but feeble people had suffered for centuries from the powerful nations that surrounded them. The Lord would say to some Israelitish prince, through the mouth of the popular devout poet of his time: *I will exalt thee, as it were, to my right hand, while thy people's enemies shall be trodden under their feet.* There had been a period of national glory, which justified such a boast; and the indomitable race-spirit assured them, that it must come again. But this boastful song had for Jesus quite another meaning. The Lord, who is to sit on Jehovah's right hand,

[*] Ps. cx., 1.

is Messiah; and, since it was David, who first sang that inspired song, how can he call him Lord who is his son? That a father should thus honor his son was much more incompatible with the old Jewish ideas of paternal dignity, than with our ideas. The scribes cannot solve the riddle; but neither he who put it, nor they who were confounded by it, seemed to have doubted that it was David who had uttered the words, and that it was by the divine Spirit that they were inspired.[a]

Accepting this view of the Scriptures of his people, we must not be surprised to find him believing in the legend of the flood and of the sudden destruction of all the inhabitants of the world, except Noah and his family. The burning of Sodom and Gomorrah by a rain of fire and brimstone and the escape of Lot were also to him historical events as unquestionable as the slavery of his ancestors in Egypt, or their conquest of Canaan.[b] We have no data for denying that there was in prehistoric times some wide-spread local flood, whose devastation is perpetuated in the story of the deluge, or that in the same period populous cities had been overwhelmed by volcanic disturbances, like those known to have buried Pompeii and Herculaneum. But the modern mind finds purely physical causes for such calamities, and does not charge God either with the cruelty of producing them or the treachery of giving no warning when they impend. Like other sentient creatures, man takes advantage of the favorable conditions of life, which a cooling planet — kerneled with fire, and turned loose among attracting worlds — affords during certain stages of its evolution; and, when some cosmic convulsion smashes his petty housekeeping, he is not required to impute the catastrophe to his own sin, or to some spirit of vindictiveness on the part of God. But when, as in the time of Jesus, the most intelligent minds contemplated the sovereign will as producing all phenomena arbitrarily, and so morally responsible for them, it was necessary to find for floods and earthquakes, storms and pestilences, a cause in the wrath of God provoked by the abnormal sinfulness of men.

Turning to the moral and spiritual side of the nature of Jesus, piety is found to be his predominant trait.

---

[a] Luke xx., 41–44.   [b] Luke xvii., 26–30.

Toward God, as spiritual father of men, as the creative, vivifying power of nature, he maintained an unbounded reverence and submission, mingled, as in no other person, with a certain affection and even familiarity born of confidence in his own exalted dignity and destiny. He was wont to go to God as to an ever-present friend and father, in a communion of spirit which hardly seemed to need the intervention of words. Though it is related that he once betook himself to a mountain and spent the night in prayer, it must be concluded that, as in Gethsemane, this was a struggle with himself, an effort to coerce a timid or reluctant will to steadfast conformity to the high purpose to which he had consecrated himself. The effectual, fervent prayer of the righteous man is often a self-exhortation.

Next in prominence to his piety it is easy to recognize his courage. The career he entered upon was full of peril. The coldness and alienation of his family, the contempt of the leaders of society in Church and State, left him nearly isolated, supported among his friends by no large or constant soul. With more than the delicacy of woman, he shrank from the physical and mental suffering to be endured, as the rejected and slain Messiah, on his way through death to the glory of an everlasting throne. His sensitive heart felt keenly the stings of reproach, was soothed by words of high regard, and responded warmly to the simplest acts of deference and courtesy. His biographers, prepossessed with the prophetic idea of an unresisting victim brought to the slaughter, who, when he was reviled, reviled not again, have characterized Jesus as meek. He once so characterized himself.[a] But when we find Moses, who, in hot anger, slew an Egyptian oppressor, and who, in uncontrollable fury, brake the tablets of the divine law, and caused the summary slaughter of three thousand of his people, called "very meek, above all the men upon the face of the earth,"[b] we know that the Jews must have used the term in quite other than the modern sense. This prophetic type, unless in this peculiar sense, seems ill to comport with the lofty courage of his convictions, which distinguished Jesus. It rather appears that his constant self-possession, the

[a] Matt. xi., 29. [b] Num. xii., 3.

superiority to other men he assumed, the authority with which he criticised the oldest traditions and the most fundamental laws; his dignified bearing before the Sanhedrim, and the assertion before Pilate of his coming glory, indicate that he wore his robe of kingship in a lofty and royal way. Whatever he may have been, it must be confessed that no man ever asserted or more consistently maintained a diviner pretension.

No view of the character of Jesus will be complete, that does not exhibit what may be called the thoroughness of his ethical methods. All qualifications of a moral principle, all restrictions of its application, all abatements of its integrity, seemed wicked and impious to his clear-sighted and loyal soul. His methods with all evils and all falsities were summary. He could see no soul of good in things evil. Reform it altogether and at once, was his comprehensive requirement. What he meant by faith — that faith, which could remove mountains, and to the force of which nothing should be impossible — was this spiritual integrity, this absolute confidence in and alliance with that supreme righteousness, which was the order and method of God, and the law of all vital progress, rather than any intellectual belief in himself, or in any abstract proposition. His strong will, his wholeness and clearness of moral conviction, and his regard of nature as something that was, or at least might be, completely subservient to the beneficent will of God, were the secret of what he did, that seemed to his contemporaries, perhaps to himself, to be miraculous. The consciousness of his own power to invoke the supreme source of all power was the first suggestion of his Messiahship. He believed he knew that a reign of righteousness was in the plan and promise of God. What the popular faith, misinterpreting the oracles of divine prophecy, had accepted as the glory of Israel, he — admitted as a son to the confidence of Jehovah — had come to understand as the kingdom of heaven. He had never once estimated the grand aggregate of happiness involved in its realization, nor distributed its satisfactions to the capacities of the great mob of sentient creatures. It was not to be a reign of happiness for the subjects, but of righteousness and justice, and of glory for the sovereign. What if its enormous compensations should inure only to a handful of elect souls! What if its stupendous results could be justified only in the inscrutable satisfactions of God himself! It is no more the thirst of virtue, that it shall find in heaven appreciation and reward, than it is the lust of evil to fly deliriously into the fascinating flames of hell and be consumed.

All great souls have looked upon the miseries, the sins, the evils of the world, as the result of some great mistake and mishap, some falling out of the perfect order of paradise. Nothing can balance the awful catastrophes which theology places at the end of human history on this planet, but some wilful disobedience and rebellion of a creature of angelic intelligence and unalloyed bliss at the beginning of that history. What wonder that these great souls have confidence that, by a word, they can summon back these angelic intelligences to their primitive allegiance, and disenchant them from the spells in which Satan has bound them!

Either Jesus learned his radicalism from John the Baptist, whose axe was at the root of every tree to cut down and cast into the fire every corrupt and false growth, or else this uncompromising spirit of the ascetic iconoclast was the secret of the attraction he exercised upon the enthusiastic soul of his convert, who so far surpassed him. It requires the judicious aptitude of Paul—that ability to see truth from other points of view, and good in worldly and even evil men—to make Christianity a fit instrumentality of civilization, and give its heavenward expanding branches a strong and lusty root in the soil of the world enriched by decaying faiths. But alongside of the politic and accommodating Pauls, there have always been the imitators of Jesus cutting with sharp repentance and reform the tangled knots of evil, which the former have had the patience to untie.

Tradition has given us the character of Jesus adorned with the lustre of personal virtues, due in him, as in most good men, to a happy endowment of nature. The Jews repudiated his lordship and crucified him, but they have not maligned him. There is no imputation, even among the enemies of his faith, that he was unjust, cruel, sensual, or envious. In him culminated that type of character —oftener found among women—strong in purity and integrity; that loves with passionless affection what is brave and heroic, and is moved with a motherly pity for a good man environed with peril or involved in excessive toil or care. He easily and by instinctive impulse conformed to the severe rules of self-control he laid down for others, so that his words, his manners, his very presence, carried with them ministrations of chastened thoughts to the profligate, and purposes of repentance to the sinful.

In the true spirit of a practical reformer, Jesus had set himself most strenuously to combat the corrupting sensual tendencies of the Greek and Semitic races, with whose vices he was conversant. With no premonitions, that, after his time, the centre of civilization would move westward; and that among chaster races the prevalent form of sensuality — the active agent in deteriorating the quality of the human race — would be alcoholic drunkenness, Jesus left no precepts against intemperance. His own habits were social, if not convivial. He used wine as a pledge of fidelity, and a symbol of the blood he was himself to shed in passing from the subordination of a despised servant to the glories of a heavenly kingdom. Contrasting him with the ascetic John, his countrymen had called him a glutton and a wine-bibber, and it did not stir his sensitive spirit to resent the imputation; for, he said, wisdom is justified of her children.

It is certain that the sober second thought of, what may be called the Christian sentiment of the world, has opposed to the radical ideas of Jesus serious qualifications and limitations. Out of the attraction of sex, which man has brought up from the inferior orders of creation, which lie behind him, have undoubtedly sprung all the domestic affections, as well as those sentiments of kinship, which dignify his nature and assert its superiority. That oneness of flesh, which the association of man with woman, resulting under the ordinance of nature in offspring becomes, Jesus perceived with a philosophic insight. But, while declaring a law for ordinary humanity he as plainly declared, that it was not a rule for himself, nor for the order of ideally perfect men, to which he belonged, and which it was his effort to multiply in the world. In the resurrection, they neither marry nor are given in marriage.ᵃ They who can undergo the ancient test proffered to the most aspiring spirits will become celibates for the sake of the kingdom of heaven.ᵇ By one of those possibilities of God, the married may enter the kingdom of heaven, but not its highest rank. The first impulse of the genuine disciple is to forsake his family. What is my mother, he asked, or what are my brothers to me? These disciples that do the will of God are my brothers, my sisters, and my mother.ᶜ The ties of sympathy in a common enterprise and in a common faith have quite outgrown the ties of natural affection, in him abnormally weak. In one of his parables, he classes the cares of avarice and the preoccupation of business along with the strength of marital fondness, as hindrances to the grace of the gospel,—"*I have married a wife, and therefore I cannot come.*"ᵈ It was not only houses and lands, that were impediments in the way to the kingdom of heaven, and for the sacrifice of which a man was to be rewarded a hundred-fold, but father and mother, wife and children.ᵉ He once told the multitude following him: If any man come to me, and hate not his father and mother, and wife and children, and brothers and sisters, and his own life also, he cannot be my disciple.ᶠ

Looking back over those spasmodic and abortive efforts, which individuals and masses of men have from time to time made to introduce a better order into the world, and to bring mankind up to some new control of the evil influences that environ them, frequent instances are found of this hostility to marriage, this contempt of the domestic relations, and repressal of the affections, that flow out of them. Too often has the spectacle exhibited itself of men forsaking wives and children for some vision of the kingdom of heaven. Why, under the pressure of strong religious enthusiasm, does it so often become apparent, that there is some incompatibility of spirit between a man and the woman, who has given him her affection, and staked upon his trusted integrity the hope and fortune of her life? It is not, as it evidently was in Jesus, a vision of a heaven of purity, that lures such a man away from his fidelity and his duty, but some abnormal access of that

ᵃ Luke xx., 35.   ᵇ Matt. xix., 11, 12.   ᶜ Matt. xii., 48, 50.
ᵈ Luke xiv., 20.   ᵉ Matt. xix., 29.   ᶠ Luke xiv., 26.

passion, which in man's nature is stored too near his devout instincts not to share disastrously in their explosions.

We look in vain through the New Testament literature for the high estimate of woman, and the chaste idea of marriage, which finds its expression in modern poetry, and in the thought and speech of well-bred men. To Paul, marriage seemed a sanctioned compromise with a natural instinct too powerful to be controlled.[a] There is traceable in the disclosures of Jesus a conception only less gross, in that it is less distinct. Shrinking from marriage himself, he delicately hints, that it is a relation incompatible with that perfection of character, which the select society of the heavenly kingdom demands.[b] Neither he nor Paul had attained that idea of wedlock, in which the animal and instinctive is absorbed in the affectional; in which two persons, preferring each other before all the world, become, by a sympathy running through their whole natures, not only one flesh, but one soul; so that what was earthly in its origin becomes spiritual in its perfection,— the safeguard of all chastity, the spring of a refined and refining love, flowing out to children and to friends, to the race of men, and to the divine ideals of the imagination.

Neither the Greek, the Jewish, nor the Christian culture brought these influences into civilized society. They had their origin in the Teutonic courtesy and honor, which among the barbarous German tribes placed woman by the side of man, equal in his confidence and respect,— that Teutonic courtesy, of which mediæval chivalry and knighthood became the later expressions, and which, especially among the English and German races, gives to woman to-day that lofty homage and respect, under the restraint of which, the rudest men grow ashamed of their selfishness and brutality.

Passing from these sins, that spring from an ill-regulated sense, let us consider those, that result from a feeble control of the reason and conscience over the thought and word. Anger is the self-assertion of the soul against assaults by injurious actions or words ; and the precept of Paul: "*Be ye angry, and sin not; let not the sun go down*

[a] I. Cor. vii.   [b] Matt. xix., 10-12.

on your wrath," wisely recognizes the natural function of anger, as well as the necessity for checking its exaggerations.[a] While anger, commensurate to the injury that it repels, adds tenfold to the energy of a man, and sometimes raises him into the aspect of sublimity, excessive anger, too long cherished, too cruelly expressed, degrades a man's dignity before all that witness it, and leaves him, in his swift remorse, weak, pitiful, and open to assaults from without, and self-reproaches from within, under the combined influence of which he is almost sure to inflict some permanent injury and shame upon himself.

Nothing can be more excellent or complete than the ethical rules inculcated by Jesus to restrain this dangerous impulse of the soul. Blessed are the meek, blessed are the reviled. Anger without cause is an offence kindred to murder. Be reconciled with your brother, agree with your adversary, before performing any religious worship. Resent not injury, and give your cheek to the smiter. Bless them that curse you, that ye may be the children of the Highest, who does good to the unkind and the unthankful. By these lofty principles, by which he invited men to rule their spirits, it cannot be invidious to judge his own.[b]

How can his antipathy to the scribes and Pharisees, and the severe invectives he hurled against them, be made consistent with this high standard? A careful study of the Jewish history and literature forces upon us the conviction, that there had been a steady intellectual and moral progress of the people from their savage, sensual, and idolatrous condition when rescued from Egyptian slavery by Moses, down to the time of Jesus. Virtuous, devout, and clear-sighted patriots and prophets had appeared among them from time to time, who saw that the uniform plan of nature indicated the unity of the deity, and that the deity was on the side of rectitude and virtue; but the mass of the people were ignorant, sensual, avaricious, and cruel. Their gods were altogether like themselves, and the decent rites, the severe virtue, the absence of images, the repression of appetite, which characterized the *cultus*, which the prophets extolled, seemed empty and gloomy, when contrasted with the joyous

[a] Eph. iv., 26.   [b] Matt. v., 5, 11, 22, 24, 39, 44, 45.

offerings, the lascivious dances, the gilded and decorated images, by which their heathen neighbors appealed to their grosser sense. It was told in the very glory of one of the Israelitish kings, when, by reason of rest from the oppression of powerful enemies, the nation was free to follow the popular tendency in religion, that there were only seven thousand worshippers of Jehovah in the whole land.* Down through the prophetic dispensation, it is evident that there is a divided sentiment — that the very monotheistic idea is antagonized by a belief, sometimes dominant even with the king and government, in the gods of the nations; and when, under such sovereigns as Josiah and Hezekiah, the monotheistic faith gets the upper hand, it is evidently only the court religion, the mass of the people remaining idolaters.

The New Testament narratives introduce us to an entirely different condition of society. Whether from the influence of the prophetic literature, or the carefully preserved and taught written law, that had taken the place of the ancient traditions; whether from the discipline of their defeats, enslavement, and exile, or from some access of new ideas from Persia, Egypt, or Greece, the Jews, after their long training, after their stiff-neckedness, — of which their great teachers complained,— had at last become fairly converted to their own religion. The cardinal evils of mankind still existed. There was luxury and licentiousness, and the degraded classes that ministered to them. There was the pride and oppression of the rich and powerful, and the envy and servility of the poor. Men were scourged, as they are to-day, by the natural punishments that follow hard upon their vices; and they were awed by the sad vicissitudes, that lie in the path of the most prosperous lives, into at least a slavish conformity to the decencies and plausible moralities of conduct. But the mass of the people lived quiet and orderly lives, true to their domestic obligations, exercising charity and kindliness toward each other, rendering obedience to the laws, and cherishing piety toward God. There are brief but graphic pictures of the common life of common men introduced among the questionable chronicles of the patriarchs of the race,

* I. Kings xix., 18.

the founders of the nation, and among the exploits and conquests of its heroes and kings. We have similar pictures of the Palestine of the Christian era; and the moral and intellectual contrast, to the great advantage of the later period, is most striking.

At the head of this movement, and fairly entitled to the honor of this renovation, stood the scribes and Pharisees. Doubtless there were among them formalists, pretenders, and hypocrites, as there have been in all ages, among the classes arrogating to themselves special sanctity and consideration as the ministers of religion and the exemplars of piety. But, as a class, they were sincere, upright, and virtuous, and shaped their lives into some reasonable conformity to the rules of the morality which they inculcated.

The old Jewish scriptures had stories, doubtless sadly true, of the debauchery of the priestly order, that ministered at the altar,[a] and of lying prophets that sold their oracles for gain or kingly favor.[b] But in all the traditions of the career of Jesus, and of the acts of his apostles, no story is told, no hint even given, that the scribes and Pharisees, the accredited ministers of religion in the time of Jesus, were either extortionate, oppressive, luxurious, licentious, bigoted, or persecuting. On the other hand, they are always introduced in such relations, and with such estimation, as to command respect and confidence. Thus the scribes and Pharisees are said to have followed John the Baptist to the wilderness, and to have asked baptism of him.[c] Before Jesus was personally known in Jerusalem, they sent messengers to him to learn of his doctrine and his works of healing.[d] As a general thing, they accorded to him the title of *Rabbi*, listened to him with attention and respect, and assented with hearty faith to many of his expositions of the fundamental matters of the law.[e]

It was a chief Pharisee that invited Jesus on two different occasions to dine with him, and whose hospitality he accepted, as he would not that of a hypocrite and extortioner.[f] John's narrative declares that Nicodemus, a chief among the Pharisees, went to Jesus by night, and gave in

[a] I. Sam. ii., 12. [b] II. Chron. xviii., 5. [c] Matt. iii., 7. [d] Matt. xv., 1.
[e] Mark. xii., 32; Luke xx., 21. [f] Luke xiv., 1; vii., 36.

his adhesion to some of the most subtle and mystic doctrines of the new faith.^a The statement is doubtless a part of the general fiction of the Fourth Gospel; but it would hardly have been made a part of the plot, if there were not instances well known of the friendly attitude of enlightened Pharisees toward the scheme of doctrine, which Jesus taught. Joseph of Arimathea, who braved the terrorism following the crucifixion, that had scattered even the twelve, to give honorable burial to the body of Jesus, was a Pharisee.[b]

But the most striking vindication of the good repute of the Pharisees is found in one of their distinguished fraternity, Paul, who became the founder of historic Christianity. The fact that Paul was not only a converted Pharisee, but that, after his mind had been enlightened, as he believed, by the divine spirit, he gloried in his Pharisaic faith, to which he still clung, as in no wise incompatible with his fidelity to Jesus, is one of the anomalies of the New Testament tradition. He declares in one of his epistles to a church — doubtless largely made up of Jews, but in a heathen city — that he was a Pharisee of the strictest sect.[c] Evidently no ill repute of the Pharisees had reached that Greek city in the time of Paul. They stood in his mind, and in the mind of his correspondents, in the high regard, in which the world holds now the Stoic philosophers and the primitive Christians. If we would know what basis there was in Jerusalem itself for the imputations cast so indiscriminately against this reputable sect, we may learn how slight it was from the fact, that Paul, when on the point of being torn to pieces by a mob in that city for teaching, as it was believed, doctrines incompatible with the laws of Moses, had a sudden access of popularity by crying out, that he was a *Pharisee*.[d] Only the names of well-reputed men are elements of strength in a popular commotion.

Last of all is the testimony of Josephus, certainly competent to corroborate this testimony of Paul's, who says of the Pharisees : —

They live meanly, and despise delicacies in diet; and they follow the conduct of reason, and what that prescribes to them as good for them they do,

---

[a] John iii., 1, 2.   [b] Luke xxiii., 50, 51.   [c] Phil. iii., 5; Acts xxvi., 5.
[d] Acts xxiii., 6.

and they think they ought earnestly to strive to observe reason's dictates for practice. They believe that souls have an immortal vigor in them, and that under the earth there will be rewards and punishments, according as they have lived virtuously or viciously in this life; and the latter are to be detained in an everlasting prison, but the former shall have power to revive and live again. On account of which doctrines, they are able greatly to persuade the body of the people; and whatever they do about divine worship, prayers, and sacrifices, they perform them according to their direction, insomuch that the cities give great attestation to them, on account of their entire virtuous conduct, both in the actions of their lives and in their discourses also.

This testimony of Josephus to the good character and repute of the Pharisees is the more weighty, in that it has been concluded that he did not himself belong to the sect, but favored the doctrines and practices of the Essenes; and because he does not speak of the Pharisees in terms of unmixed eulogy. For elsewhere he speaks of their love of intrigue and of power,— traits of character, which ecclesiastical bodies have exhibited in every age,— and says that during the reign of Alexandra, who held the sovereignty of Palestine nine years, under the Roman protectorate, the Pharisees were the real rulers, through the influence they obtained over her. But as this influence was obtained by their reputation for wisdom and virtue, and was exercised in punishing those who had been guilty of massacres and oppression under a former reign, this, too, is rather a testimony in favor of the sect.

Toward this body of men, evidently the *élite* of their nation, the attitude of Jesus was one of hostility and suspicion from the first. He, who had said so wisely: *Judge not, that ye be not judged; for with what judgment you judge, you shall be judged*,[a] had, when we are first introduced to him, judged them with a severity, that knew neither mercy nor moderation. When the wedding feast of his kingdom of heaven was prepared, he recognized the propriety of sending his invitation to the bidden guests.[b] But the Pharisees were not bidden.[c] There cannot be found in the traditions of the gospel any overtures made to the most religious men of the time to accept the new religion.

One of the purposes of the writer of the Fourth Gospel may have been to rescue Jesus from the imputation of a too uncharitable and harsh attitude toward the religious

[a] Matt. vii., 1, 2. [b] Matt. xxii., 3. [c] Matt. iii., 7; v., 20; viii., 12.

classes of his time, which the synoptic narratives seem to have cast upon him. With some such view, that writer brings Jesus prematurely and frequently to Jerusalem, and makes his chief activity consist in doctrinal and casuistic discussions, publicly conducted in the temple with representatives of the scribes and Pharisees, of which discussions the older tradition had taken no cognizance whatever. It may have been an instance of the great sagacity of Jesus, that he concluded in advance, that an order of men proud of their prestige of sanctity, complacent in their intelligence of the will of God, were not likely to submit to be taught by a Galilean carpenter how to attain the divine favor and the everlasting life. But as Garrison, when inspired with a new sense of the wrongs of the slave, went first to the ministers of a religion that taught the equal brotherhood of men; as Columbus, possessed with the presentiment that India could be reached by sailing across the Western ocean, betook himself first to geographers and adventurous navigators; so it would seem that the first mission of a new religion should have been to the reputable teachers and exponents of the old.

But this, Jesus evidently did not intend. As has been already said, he shared the prejudice of John the Baptist, who declared that the Pharisees and Sadducees were outside of the pale of mercy of his gospel, and had nothing to expect but the wrathful fire, which should consume every evil tree.[a] In a kindred discrimination, Jesus said in his first discourse that the grade of integrity, to which the scribes and Pharisees had attained, was not such as would in any event prove a passport to his kingdom of heaven.[b] Later in his public ministry, when certain scribes and Pharisees approached him with the deferential title of *Rabbi*, and would see one of his miracles, he turned upon them with the rebuke, that they represented to him the wicked and adulterous people of that time. The times are evil, the plausible public virtue is hypocritical, the seeming pure are full of adulterous desires and practices, and you, who lead the moral sentiment of the age, are no better than the multitudes you lead. But why is the generation evil and adulterous? Jesus gives himself the reason. When Jonah went through Nineveh,

[a] Matt. iii., 9, 10.   [b] Matt. v., 20.

warning it of its destruction, the inhabitants believed and repented : when he came, warning the world of its doom, it neither believed nor repented. He believed some evil spirit had taken possession of his countrymen. It seemed to have been cast out, doubtless, when so many flocked to listen to John's preaching repentance, and to be baptized, and when great multitudes followed himself out of all the Galilean cities,— as he hoped first, to listen to his words, but, as he believed afterward, only to be fed by his supplies.[a] But the wicked spirit was only temporarily expelled. He had gone through dry places seeking rest, and had returned with seven worse devils to possess the victim, whose last state is worse than his first. So shall it be with this wicked generation.[b]

When the Pharisees came again with the Sadducees, asking for a sign, he rallied them with the well-known red sunset, as a sign of a bright to-morrow, and of a ruddy dawn as a sure herald of a dull day ; and called them hypocrites, because they knew these signs, but could not prognosticate the tokens of an impending judgment.[c] The very presence of these sects disturbed his spirit ; and it was slowly, and after an effort, that he could recover its serenity. After they had left him, he told his disciples to beware of their insidious and noxious teachings and influence.[d] He recognized the elders, chief priests, and scribes as his enemies. He knew his people would never believe in his Messiahship, while under their influence ; and he warned his disciples that it was they who would seek and accomplish his death.[e]

When he came to Jerusalem, he pursued toward the Pharisees the same uncompromising course. He confronted them in the temple, and turned upon them personally their criticisms of his questionable expositions of the law. He told them that the openly vicious, who broke away from the divine commands with headlong passion, but afterward repented, were more acceptable to God than those who professed virtue and were not holy; that publicans and harlots went into the kingdom before them ; and that their rejection of him — the sent Son of God — would be followed by their own rejection and de-

[a] Matt. xii., 38, 39.   [b] Matt. xii., 43-45.   [c] Matt. xvi., 1-3.
[d] Matt. xvi., 4-6.   [e] Matt. xvi., 21.

struction.ᵃ He told them they were the bidden guests to the marriage feast, but that not one of them should taste of it, and that wayfarers from the hedges would be preferred to them.ᵇ Finally, in Jerusalem, apparently within the precincts of the temple itself, he launches against them in the hearing of his disciples the terrible invective which is preserved for us in the twenty-third chapter of Matthew. The retort of the scribes and Pharisees was the crucifixion.

The Christian world accepts this chapter as a correct delineation of those classes in Judea, which in the first century gave character to the Jewish people, and has justified itself by the high authority of Jesus for nearly twenty centuries of hatred and persecution of the living representatives of that people. The history of the wrongs and sufferings of the Jewish race has been the standing reproach of Christendom. They, who name Jesus with reverence and even worship him as Deity seem to have forgotten that he ever said: " Love your enemies, do good to them that hate you, bless them that curse you, and pray for them that persecute you." But they have not forgotten the different spirit which breathes through this pitiless chapter, contrasted with which, their bitterest hatred seems brotherly forbearance.

It was enough for the disciples of Pythagoras, to give unquestionable authority to any assertion, to say, *Ipse dixit*. A more complete deference to the name of Jesus will foreclose the candor of most minds, and except the scribes and Pharisees from the scope and regard of his own primary canon of personal judgments: *He who would not be himself judged must not judge.*

When Jesus said of the Pharisees that they shut up against men the doors of the kingdom of heaven,ᶜ the reproach is just of them and of their descendants, if it be thereby meant, that they did not accept, and have not accepted, his claim to be the prophetic Messiah of their race. A spirit of that liberal charity *that believeth all things*, in the presence of the fact that these rejectors of the Christ had been able to maintain a standard of morality and piety quite up to the level of the Christian standard, would be ashamed to impute this rejection to any-

ᵃ Matt. xxi., 23-32.   ᵇ Luke xiv., 17, 24.   ᶜ Matt. xxiii., 13.

thing but the stress of conscience and reason. When he
said that the Pharisees made long prayers to cover the
extortions they practised upon widows,[a] we are surprised,
that neither the evangelical narratives, nor any other
contemporary history has given us any details of these
extortions. We stand appalled, as in the case of the ancient Canaanites, because history has told of their terrible
punishment, but strangely omitted to gratify our sense of
justice by telling of their sin. We wonder, too, how, if
such was, among the believers of the first century, the reputation of this sect, so enthusiastic a disciple of Jesus as
Paul should have boasted that he was a Pharisee. When
Jesus said that the proselytes which the Pharisees were
so eager to make were, like themselves, children of hell;[b]
that, in paying small tithes, they neglected justice, mercy,
and faith;[c] that they were whited sepulchres, inwardly full
of all uncleanness; that they were guilty of the blood of
the very prophets they quoted and reverenced; and that
they were a brood of vipers, who could not escape the
damnation of hell,— the frightful vehemence of his reproaches do infinitely less honor to the anger that cannot
suppress them, than to the silent patience that endured
them. "*Ye are the children of them which killed the
prophets. Fill ye up then the measure of your fathers.*[d]
*Ye serpents, ye generation of vipers! how can ye escape
the damnation of hell?*" If this was the first word of
the new dispensation to the representatives of the old,
it was not the latest nor the best. Let us turn from this
spirit that curses, to that which in the magnanimity of its
fraternal affection and pity tenderly asks to be accursed.
"*For I could wish that myself were accursed from Christ
for my brethren, my kinsmen according to the flesh; who
are Israelites; to whom pertaineth the adoption, and the
glory, and the covenants, and the giving of the law, and
the service of God.*"[e] Let the Christian Church itself
declare, which of these contrasted spirits is the most
divine.

A casual reading of the first two Gospels discloses some
effect upon the mind of Jesus simultaneous with the
avowal of his purpose to go to Jerusalem in the ostensible

[a] Matt. xxiii., 14. [b] Matt. xxiii., 15. [c] Matt. xxiii., 23.
[d] Matt. xxiii., 31-33. [e] Rom. ix., 3, 4.

character of the Messiah. The observed change is in the general character of his doctrines, and in his own temper and spirit. Doctrinally, his teaching becomes less distinctly ethical. With the exception of the lesson of humility taught by the presence of the little child, there is uttered after this crisis in his career scarcely a precept that is purely moral. Carefully considered, even that precept seems to be one of docility and discipleship. "Whosoever," he said, "shall humble himself as this little child, the same is greatest in the kingdom of heaven. And whoso shall receive one such little child in my name, receiveth me; but whoso shall offend one of these little ones *which believe in me*, it were better for him if he were drowned in the sea."[a] It is not the natural simplicity of childhood that Jesus is commending, but the disciple, who, with the docility of childhood, *has believed in him*. Faith has taken, in his mind, the place of righteousness.

There had been in the Sermon on the Mount an exposition of the great judgment of mankind; and, although Jesus was himself to be the judge, it was those who had done the will of God who were to be approved and rewarded.[b] Inasmuch, however, as in the same discourse God is characterized as the benign giver of all good things, as commending and blessing the upright and the pure, and as perfect and unchangeable in his forgiving love, the discrimination among the souls of men must be considered a discrimination of character.[c] Every tree that brings not forth good fruit is hewn down and cast into the fire.[d] Every life not fruitful in good deeds is noxious or useless, and is to be cancelled from the sum of life. This distinction between the intrinsically good and the intrinsically evil harmonized with the fundamental ideas of older religions.

Just before his arrest, Jesus gave a fuller and more vivid representation of the general judgment. "When the Son of Man," he said, "shall come in his glory, and all the holy angels with him, he shall sit upon the throne of his glory; and before him shall be gathered all nations; and he shall separate them as the shepherd divideth his

---

[a] Matt. xviii., 4–6. [b] Matt. vii., 21.
[c] Matt. v., 8, 45; vi., 32, 33. [d] Matt. vii., 19.

sheep from the goats."[a] The sheep, who are accounted righteous, and received into everlasting life, are those who have rendered services of kindness to the Judge, that is, as it is explained, to his disciples. The goats, who are esteemed wicked, and sent away into an everlasting punishment, are those who have omitted to do services of kindness to the Judge, that is, to the least of his disciples.[b]

Applying to these declarations of Jesus the conventional methods of interpretation,— recasting them in the larger mould of modern humanitarian sentiment,— we may be able to find that the poor, the sick, and the imprisoned, relieved or neglected by the elect and the non-elect, represent the suffering classes of the world. Thus explained, the discrimination is not based on creeds or upon conformity to arbitrary conditions of salvation, but is between men who do acts of charity spontaneously, and those who take no heed of the great aggregate of suffering they never think of relieving. Thus improved and enlarged, the lesson becomes one of the noblest ever taught under the authority of the great teacher. It is Jesus putting himself in the place of men — feeling that their sickness, imprisonment, poverty, and suffering are his own — rewarding those who had relieved, and disowning those who had neglected them. But did he thus interpret himself? Who are "*these my brethren,*" and "*the least of these,*" whose benefits and injuries are remembered in the final separation of the nations of mankind? It is not difficult to learn the sense in which characteristic expressions were used by Jesus. It is nowhere found in the Synoptic Gospels that he applied the term *my brethren* to ordinary men. On the contrary, he expressly disclaimed the relationship toward his own natural kindred. "They are *my brethren,*" he said, "who hear the word of God, and do it."[c] "Call no man," he enjoined, "your father upon the earth; for one is your Father, which is in heaven."[d] The injunction applies by stronger reasons to subordinate relationships. The whole stress of the later exhortations of Jesus bears upon discipleship. All his precepts, the moral of all his parables, seem designed to incite acceptance of his Messianic mission, and constancy and fidelity of personal allegiance. The judgment of the great sepa-

[a] Matt. xxv., 31, 32.   [b] Matt. xxv., 34-46.   [c] Luke viii., 21.   [d] Matt. xxiii., 9.

ration reaffirms what he had said before. It was not whosoever shall give — be it only a cup of water — to the thirsty, but "whosoever shall give a cup of water to you, because ye belong to Christ, shall not lose his reward." [a] Not he that shall injure a man, but he that "shall offend *one of these little ones which believe in me*," had better be cast into the sea with a millstone about his neck.[b] "All the tribes of the earth," foreboding their impending doom, "would mourn, when they should see the Son of Man coming in the clouds of heaven."[c] Only "the little flock" to whom it was their "Father's good pleasure to give the kingdom" were to be without fear at its coming.[d] It seems scarcely capable of question that those characteristic designations of Jesus, "*my disciples*," "*my brethren*," "*the little flock*," "*these little ones*," "*the least of these*," are terms of restricted application to those who believed in him.

This tender regard for those who had given in their adhesion to him is in striking contrast to his indifference toward those who failed to recognize him and who opposed him,— an indifference that strengthened in his last days into alienation and reprobation. The reader must pardon the repeated marshalling of the same texts to illustrate the different traits of the character of Jesus. It is made necessary by the meagre memoranda tradition has given us of his words, and by the requirements of presentation in detail of his opinions and sentiments. Sending out his twelve disciples to do cures and proclaim the kingdom of heaven, he said: "Behold, I send you forth as sheep in the midst of wolves." "Beware," he warned them, "of men." They will deliver you up unto councils to be scourged in their synagogues; but it shall be a testimony against your countrymen and the Gentiles.[e] Men, common men, what in modern phrase are called the masses, were the enemies, whose hostility he dreaded. The Son of Man, he once said, "is delivered into the hands of *men;* and they shall kill him."[f] The people were not the intelligent and virtuous constituency whom it is the fashion of modern courtesy to flatter. They were the wolves who would ravage his tender fold, and into whose merciless claws he himself would fall at last.

[a] Mark ix., 41.   [b] Matt. xviii., 6.   [c] Matt. xxiv., 30.   [d] Luke xii., 32.
[e] Matt. x., 1, 16–25.   [f] Mark ix., 31.

It has been seen that, when Jesus was pressed by the multitudes, he avoided them and went up to a mountain; and that, sitting down there, his disciples came to him and he taught them. It was his disciples that he pronounced blessed and the heirs of the kingdom.[a] It was his little flock the hairs of whose heads were numbered.[b] It was his elect who could ask whatsoever they would of his heavenly Father, and it would be given to them.[c] But, when the multitudes came, he perplexed them with parables that even his familiar friends could not understand. And so they asked him why he did so, and he frankly gave this answer: It is lawful for you to know the mysteries of the kingdom of heaven; it is not lawful for them. I speak unto them in parables, because, with eyes, they do not see, and with ears they do not hear; lest they should see and hear, and so be converted and healed.[d] In describing the calamities that should precede his coming in his kingdom, he told his disciples that, for his elect's sake — involved in the suffering — those evil days should be shortened.[e] No consideration for the mass of mankind was at all relevant. They were of no account. Only the elect stand in the estimation of God.

Toward the people of the heathen nations, his attitude was still more unsympathetic. I am sent to the lost sheep of the house of Israel. It is not proper to take the children's bread and cast it to dogs.[f] The heathen represented those outside of the pale of his sympathy and thought. For, he said, the offending disciple was to be first privately admonished of his fault, then reproved by two or three brethren, then solemnly warned by the whole assembly of believers. But, if he remained obstinate in his wickedness, he was to be like a heathen man and a publican, which was for him a condition representative of utter excommunication and separation.[g] Nothing could so completely indicate how the people of the world lay out of the scope of his regard, as what he once said to his disciples,— if ye love them, that love you, the *heathen* — or, as Luke tells it, using what to him was a synonym, *sinners* — also love those that love them.[h] The heathen sinners do good to those that do good to them. It is a small thing

---

[a] Matt. v., 2, 3.   [b] Matt. x., 30.   [c] Matt. xxi., 22.   [d] Matt. xiii., 10-16
[e] Matt. xxiv., 22.   [f] Matt xv., 24, 26.   [g] Matt. xviii., 15-18.   [h] Luke vi., 32, 33.

to equal the morality of the heathen: yours must surpass that of scribes and Pharisees. All the ordinary employments of worldly men were to Jesus impious. As it was in the days of Noah, they ate, they drank, they married wives, until the flood came and destroyed them all; as it was in the days of Lot, they ate, they drank, they bought, they sold, they planted, they builded, till the rain of fire and brimstone destroyed them,— so, he said, will I come bringing like destruction to worldly men, busied with their worldly avocations.[a] That broad humanitarian spirit which has modified the severity of codes, and given gentleness to manners; which recognizes in alien faiths, for which men would once have been crucified or burned, the product of a religious sentiment as universal as conscience,— can only be considered the fruitage of Christianity, as Christianity has idealized Christ. It has presumed to extend the charity of Jesus to those to whom he was himself hostile or indifferent.

In the Acts of the Apostles is found a fragment of Peter's exhortation to the centurion Cornelius, in which he thus speaks of Jesus: "God anointed Jesus of Nazareth with the Holy Ghost and with power; who went about doing good, and healing all that were oppressed with the devil: for God was with him."[b] If this fragment could be taken as the recollection of a personal friend, it would be testimony of the greatest weight. The known literary habits of Paul, the fact that disciples, used to writing, accompanied his missions, who would gladly have made notes of his speeches, give us much confidence, that the reports are the substance at least of his addresses. What is imputed to Peter and the *"unlearned"* apostles is more likely to be the dramatic form, in which the narrator undertook to set forth arguments, generally known to the receivers of the new faith. But, whether Peter's or the author's, this language fairly represents the view, which the early Church took of the character and work of Jesus. The only miraculous power specified — that *good* which Jesus went about to do — was the relieving of men from the infestation of malign spirits.

In the writings of apostles, of whose genuineness there is a more reasonable assurance, the benevolence of Jesus

[a] Luke xvii., 26-30.   [b] Acts x., 38.

is affirmed upon still more recondite and questionable reasons. They speak not so much of the friend and master, whose companionship they had enjoyed, or of the Galilean teacher and prophet, whose acts and words are told in the Synoptic Gospels, as of Jesus the Christ, a typical and prophetic personage. Peter in his Epistle, when he wishes to appeal to the example of his Master, gives us no picture of his human life in Galilee or in Jerusalem, no anecdotes or personal traits, that an affectionate memory could not suppress, but — reverting to a prophecy of Isaiah — thus describes him: "Who did no sin, neither was guile found in his mouth; who, when he was reviled, reviled not again; when he suffered, he threatened not, but committed himself to Him that judgeth righteously." Comparing this language with the ancient prophecy, we find that, as it is inaccurate in substance as well as form as a quotation, it is more manifestly inapt as a personal description. When the scribes and Pharisees made vile accusations against him, he vigorously retorted and called them hypocrites, blind leaders of the blind, a wicked and adulterous generation; and, when he was about to suffer at the hands of the priesthood, he pronounced against them a doom that should involve their city and the whole generation.

But the view which the apostolic writings more frequently present of the benevolence of Jesus is a view of a divine being, equal with God, dwelling in the bliss of an immortal life, who so loved the world that he consented to put off this glory and become a man and a servant, and be subject to death, that the world might be saved by believing on him. This is the view invariably presented in Paul's writings, and in those imputed to the other apostles; and, when they hold up the benevolence of Jesus as an example, it is this grand and divine sacrifice and condescension, rather than acts of human charity and mercy, that his followers are exhorted to imitate.

A rational, not to say a reverent, criticism must turn alike from such prophetic and providential contemplation of Jesus to his human life as history has disclosed it. We certainly cannot enter into or measure a purely divine personality, nor admit among the beneficences of any human life, however grandly endowed, its condescension in consenting to be born. Whatever Jesus was or is, when he became a man, he took upon him the conditions of humanity, and complete amenability to all legitimate judgments of human conduct.

Leaving out of view, as we must, that office in the divine economy, which may have brought Jesus from a pre-existent glory to an exceptionally wretched human lot, what estimate of his benevolence is justly due to what is known of his life? All the traditions represent him as going through his native province healing cases of chronic disease, mostly those disorders which disturb the normal operations of the mind, and which in his time were considered to be caused by demoniac possession. In a character as nearly faultless as that of Jesus, the sentiment of pity is quick and strong. But for what these traditions assert, we should conclude that these curative works were prompted by genuine and natural pity, and gave the doer of them an eminent rank among the great benefactors of the world. Of a person, who was endowed with abnormal capacities to cure madness, blindness, paralysis, and other forms of painful and disabling maladies, by a touch, by a word, by the mere virtue of his presence, the world would require a large activity of service. If it be lawful at all to interrupt the retributions appointed in pain and death for all violations of natural laws, it is hard in a world full of misery and disease to set any limit to the responsibility of a person thus gifted less narrow than the gauge of the aggregate of misery and disease. We should hold one, who by a word could relieve the disorders of mankind, and who failed to speak it, guilty of their perpetuation. It does not either seem just to compare efforts, to lessen the complicated wretchedness of the world, that cost so little, with those long vigils, those costly months and years of help and care, of nourishment and sympathy, which — for the very reason that we cannot by our words or prayers bring instant health to the sick — we cheerfully render to mitigate their sufferings. We cannot give the same value to these local and transient exhibitions of thaumaturgic skill told in the annals of many peoples, as to organized institutions of charity established by the best governments, and under the most enlightened social arrangements, supported by a regularity of giving, or by a munificence of endowment, that makes them as permanent as the diseases they help to relieve.

Let us look again at the traditions of the career of Jesus, and see what they assert in reference to his gifts of healing. Whatever beneficent works he wrought among his countrymen, he himself avows to have been done somewhat capriciously, and not so much from pity for the suffering, as to produce a certain opinion among spectators favorable to himself. Thus he avowed that he was not sent to cure insane persons who were Phœnicians, though he consented to make an exception in behalf of a woman, who accosted him with great courtesy and tact. He declared not only that he would not, but could not, do cures upon persons who had no faith, nor in cities where the public sentiment was decidedly adverse to him, nor in Judea and Jerusalem, where an obdurate scepticism possessed the leading classes in society.

But Jesus as the loving heart of man has cherished him, the fearless martyr braving the terrors of a cruel death, the patient sufferer silently bearing the scoffs of wicked men, the pitying man quickly responsive to every form of human suffering, more than all, the sublime prophet proclaiming the glories of an everlasting life, has been a minister of comfort, of consolation, of courage, and of hope, and has become the spiritual benefactor of all devout souls. Less distinct are the traces of his beneficence in the real world of suffering and of sin than in the ideal world of faith and aspiration.

As we have found the dominant idea of Jesus illustrating and rendering consistent much that was in itself unintelligible in his ethical system, so will it be found to throw some light upon the exposition of his character. We have seen how gradually and reluctantly he surrendered himself to the loftiest ambition that ever inspired the human mind. What wonder that, with its advent, came the dawning of a self-consciousness which affected disastrously the symmetry of a soul naturally modest and self-contained. Human infirmity, expanding under the influence of a great enthusiasm to divine capacities, betrays its mortal birth in hours of despair, oftener perhaps in hours of exultation over success. When a man begins to ask, *What do men think of me?* his spiritual integrity has not been maintained, and the staff of his achievement is broken. That such a crisis came to Mohammed is plain to us, who are not the captives of his faith, though after it came converts, conquests, and the empire of half the world. We see how that crisis separates the devoutness, the gentleness, the fidelity, and the chastity of his blameless youth from the arrogance, the ambition, the ferocity, and the sensuality of his old age. Certain it is that a line drawn midway in the career of Jesus — perhaps at the memorable conference with his disciples at Cæsarea Philippi — leaves nearly all of his meekness, his pitifulness, and his self-control, as well as his wisest and most consolatory counsels to mankind, on one side, and upon the other side his self-assertion, his petulance, and his uncharitableness, along with those sombre vaticinations of impending doom by which ignorance and fanaticism have ever since harrowed the apprehensions of the superstitious.

Not the scribes and Pharisees only became the subject of his reproaches. Into the bosom of his own little flock, upon the head of Peter, whom he had honored with a burst of sublime confidence, and a largess of power enough to disturb a cooler head, he hurled the cruel epithet, *Satan*. When he came down from the mountain, where he had seen a vision of Moses and Elias, he called the multitude, who beset him with tearful prayers for his intervention, a wicked and adulterous race, whose presence he could scarcely endure,— unless, indeed, this reproach was for the faithlessness of his own disciples. Travelling to Jerusalem, he was hungry, and sought a fig-tree full of leaves for fruit. Mark is ingenuous enough to explain that it was not the season of figs; and he must be correct, since it was before the arrest and before the Passover, which occurred in April; and the fig in Palestine could hardly ripen earlier than June. But it is told that Jesus uttered an imprecation against the tree that had refused, out of the season, to supply his wants. It was near the same time that Jesus, in forgetfulness of his lessons of peace, ordered his followers to arm themselves with swords. These incidents are sufficient to show how he could not quite assure the serenity of his own spirit, in spite of the bravery with which he coerced his soul to endure the fate that befell his high mission, without imputing to him the undignified and petulant demeanor which the Fourth Gospel reports as characterizing his bearing before Pilate.

Jesus did not come back, as he confidently expected, to establish in the lifetime of his generation his kingdom of heaven. The hope he cherished, like the hope his nation cherished, has been indefinitely postponed. Magnificent as was the scheme to accomplish which he gave his life, the thoughts of God seem to have been larger and longer. But yet, if not as the Jews longed for it, nor yet as Jesus and Peter and Paul proclaimed it, there is for all believing souls a kingdom of heaven; and it is at hand. It comes with every achievement of genius and art, with every invention that enlarges man's dominion over his environment, with the disclosure of every new law that indicates the unity, the vitality, and the divine order of the cosmos, with every new moral power which man, by conforming to the sentiment of duty, has been able to add to the stock of his transmissible virtues.

Jesus did not come back to destroy the world. Happily, he had done not a little to make the world worth perpetuation. The old lessons of virtue, already accredited as the moral science of all civilized people, he reiterated and emphasized. He cast them like seed into the hearts of men, after they had been made tender and susceptible by the terrors of impending judgment and retribution. The terrors have passed away, but not till, in the warmth radiated from the fires of a freshly opened Gehenna, the good seed had germinated, and begun to grow toward an abundant harvest.

Nor need the crown even of this kingdom be refused to Jesus. Best of all who have yet lived in the world, he is worthy to wear it. Spite of the insignificant blemishes by which his relationship to us is confessed, he still leads the van in the march of man from the plain of bestial instincts to the high table-lands of spiritual discernment and power. By his purity, by the heroism of his self-consecration to the noblest aims, by the dazzling splendor of that standard of righteousness which he portrayed and exemplified, he is as yet enthroned King of humanity.

It is rare that a great organizing mind affects the world precisely as it intends, or does the precise work it conceives and proposes. The secondary effects of great lives become often more consequential than the primary and immediate effects. Columbus did not find, as he all his life believed, a new route to India; but he found a new world. Europe, united in arms, failed to establish a Christian kingdom in Judea; but it did establish in Europe a Christian civilization destined to conquer the whole world. If Jesus did not establish his kingdom of heaven in Zion, he became the inspirer of a new religion.

Man does not live by bread alone,— by that which ministers to his health, wealth, or power. He lives chiefly by his ideals. Religion, with the awful solemnities of its worship, with its stately pageantry of deathless gods, with the invitations and repulsions of its heavens and of its hells, is the verity and substance of the life of man's spirit. So the world has honored and worshipped those prophets and saviors who have enriched it with the hopes, and reinforced it with the motives of a new religion. A man's religion is a higher and better expression of him than is his poetry, his science, or his art.

Nor is a religion always the best and the purest at its inception. Of all the great religions, whose history we know, the reverse is true. When a faith, that has been the cultus of races and generations of men, ceases to express the highest aspirations of the soul, when its dogmas affront our reason, and its standards of righteousness outrage our moral sense, when the tawdry vesture of its mythology provokes more mirth than terror, it demands and receives some worthier interpretation. Stated in terms of a just and liberal thought, it revives and survives, and becomes the support and sustenance of generations. The time however comes at last, when the old garment can no longer be patched with new cloth, when the new wine bursts the old bottles. For the critical faculty grows with the creative imagination; and where the continuity and identity between an idealized image and a historical verity are at last broken, the time is ripe for a new Messiah.

Contrasting Jesus with the founders of the other great world-religions, we may be able to approximate toward his just place in human history. Moses, Confucius, Sakya Muni, and Mohammed were all men of affairs. They had experience in domestic life as husbands and fathers; in civil offices they had the responsibilities of subjects and of rulers, in military service of leaders or soldiers ; and they rounded to its completion a human life rich in all the discipline and wisdom which comes with manifold activity in conspicuous and responsible positions. In Jesus, we have a long youth of utter obscurity in a corner of the Old World, doubtless passed in those self-musings which expose to egotistic enthusiasms; a fastidious shrinking from those domestic relations out of which grow so many of the human affections, and which furnish the chief occasions for that self-sacrifice which is the foundation of all virtues; an utter distrust of all the social and political experience of men, and an impatience of those slow ameliorations of the evils of the world which come from a better ordered state. Last of all, the career of Jesus was too brief — perhaps less than a year from the time he abandoned his artisan life in Nazareth till the whole brilliant pageant was eclipsed in the darkness and terror of Calvary — to be either a comprehensive experience, out of which to instruct the teeming races of men, or to be a fair test of his personal integrity or a measure of his greatness.

Of the great world-religions, those of the Jews, of the Greeks, and of the Chinese, have been specifically practical and secular. Moses originated a cultus, theistic indeed, but most completely outward, worldly, and adapted to men, as men ; that took the fullest account of all the human instincts, the love of life, the love of the sexes, the love of offspring, the tribal sentiments, the thirst for aggression and conquest, and the passion for possessions. Confucius gave a cultus as thoroughly human, and adapted to the development of a great nation,— a rule of life, whereby the most stable government and the most permanent social order have been maintained for more than a thousand years,— but atheistic in its basis, and appealing as little as Judaism to the imagination. Christianity, Buddhism, and Mohammedanism are essentially *other-worldly* religions. They are all based more or less upon a sacrifice of the earthly life in the interest of a life to come after death. It shows how dominant over the mind of man are the ideals of his imagination, that these great religions, which more than others feed the aspirations of his soul, have supplanted and outlasted those religions that have taken solid hold of human life, and most wisely adapted themselves to the social, political, and industrial conditions of man's present existence.

CHAPTER XII.

LEGEND OF THE RESURRECTION.

"To the mind of Jesus, his own resurrection after a short sojourn in the grave was the victory of his cause after his death, and at the price of his death. His disciples materialized his resurrection, and their version of this matter falls to ruin day by day. But no ruin or contradiction befalls the version of Jesus himself. He has risen; his cause has conquered; the course of events continually attests his resurrection and victory."—*Matthew Arnold.*

"If at first it sprang out of a local miracle, and may have been little distinguished from other waves of feeling that were propagated by the religious guilds of the ancient world, Christianity is not now identical with belief in the resurrection of Jesus. It is now, and has for fifteen centuries been, something wholly different; namely, the great bond holding the European races and their off-shoots together in that sort of union out of which naturally springs a common polity. True it may be that the miracle was the essential fact, without which the union would never have been accomplished: there may have been a time when it was true that 'if Christ be not risen, our faith is vain'; but when the union has taken place, has endured for a thousand years, and though since weakened and endangered yet subsists in the form of an indestructible common civilization and sense of unity among nations, it is no longer true. The Christian Church is now the visible expression of a true cosmopolitanism, which will be eternal; and, this being so, it avails nothing henceforth against it to argue that, after all, Christ is not risen."—*Natural Religion.*

OF all the supernatural events which tradition has imputed to the agency of Jesus, or to the divine power which he was able to invoke, no one is so well vouched by respectable testimony as the resurrection. The whole Christian Church, and ultimately the whole Christian world, with an insignificant amount of dissent, came to believe and still believe, that, a day or two after his death and burial, his sepulchred body disappeared; and that on several occasions, separated by intervals of a week's duration, he showed himself alive to some of his disciples, and fully established his identity by characteristic words and actions, and by exhibiting in his hands and side the fresh wounds left by the crucifixion. When we compare the accumulation and general concurrence of the testimony, upon which the belief in the actual occurrence of this marvel rests, with the paucity and levity of evidence which support the other evangelical miracles; when we consider the significant silence of the witnesses who ignore and omit them, it seems just to conclude, that, if the credibility of the resurrection was to be determined by merely counting and weighing the supporting testimony, we have tenfold more reason for believing it than we have for believing that Jesus walked on the sea, made of five loaves and two fishes an abundant feast for five thousand people, raised from his bier the dead son of a widow at Nain, or cured by a touch in the purlieus of the temple at Jerusalem a man who had been born blind. One who should reject as unproved the tradition of such miracles might find his faith coerced by the accumulation of testimony upon which the resurrection is asserted; but one who, on a critical examination, had come to reject the dogma of the resurrection, could not give a very convincing reason for continued faith in any of the other events outside of the range of the natural order, that are asserted to have made the life of Jesus unique and abnormal.

The raising of the widow's son is told only in the narrative of Luke, and the curing of the blind man in the temple is an incident introduced among the evident fictions of the dogmatic drama of the Fourth Gospel. If real occurrences, they were too consequential and conspicuous to be omitted in the tradition of Matthew. The wonderful enlargement of the food — the recitation of which in all four of the narratives makes it evident that the omission of what other writers had told, and the telling of what they had omitted, was not the controlling purpose that dictated the composition of either of the Gospels — is not supported by the confirmation of Paul or of either of the apostles. The omission of all allusion to the miracles in the authentic and imputed writings of Paul is not only pregnant as a negation, but the theory that he carefully and always insists upon, that Jesus' earthly life was not the triumphal career of a god, or the awe-inspiring manifestation of a hierophant, but the ignominious subjection of one submitting to service and shame, for the glory that was to come after his resurrection,— a rôle entirely incompatible with miraculous powers,— made it illogical for him to believe in the miracles imputed to Jesus. But the resurrection of

Jesus is, as to the substantial fact, asserted by all four of the gospel writers. It is declared in the genuine Epistles of Paul, nay, made the very basis of his whole scheme of metaphysics and theology. The affirmation of it is imputed to Peter and James and John, as well as to Paul, in their reported speeches, which the writer of the Book of Acts undertakes to preserve, and in epistles believed to have been written or dictated by them. It was the best known dogma of the Christian creed, the novelty and peculiarity, by which its scheme of doctrine was distinguished among the heathen from all contemporaneous and antecedent faiths.

Before we institute an inquiry into the actuality of the resurrection, let us consider precisely what the assertion is, to which our assent is invited. A careful study of the tradition, as preserved in the New Testament literature, shows that the early believers were not in accord about it. We discover two distinct explanations of the resurrection not reconcilable with each other. The opinion held by the mass of the disciples was that set forth in the four Gospels, and in the statement of which they substantially agree. Let us endeavor to apprehend it.

The body of the crucified Jesus, which Joseph of Arimathea had procured to be delivered to him, he had carefully entombed in a new sepulchre, the door of which was barricaded by a large stone. The corpse thus carefully deposited and secured was also guarded, at least for two days, by soldiers. After an interval of thirty-six hours at most, a few devoted women — among them the mother of Jesus — find the stone rolled back, the body gone, though the cerements in which it had been wound are left in the empty tomb. These women report to Peter and the other apostles, not that Jesus is alive,— though even this they begin to believe,— but that his body is not to be found in the place where, under such safeguards, it had been deposited. Peter and the disciples — as if that was the surest test of the startling hope the words of the women first awakened in their minds — proceed, actually running in their excitement, to the tomb. If the body is still there, the women have deceived them. But it is not there, and immediately they abandon themselves to the joyful assurance, that their Master has come back to life.

It was the body the women went to see. It was the absence of the body, that gave them their first vague impression that he was alive. It was the body, that Peter and John went to the tomb to identify; and, not finding it, they were ready to receive other evidence, that it has again come to life. The words spoken all relate to the corpse. "*They have taken away my Lord,*" that is, his remains, "*and I know not where they have laid him,*" moaned the affectionate Mary of Magdala.[a] "*He,*" that is, his body, "*is not here,*" said angelic voices. "*He,*" that is, the body of Jesus taking back its life, "*is risen, as he said. He goeth before you into Galilee: there shall ye see him.*"[b]

There were voices and angelic appearances, but as to these the witnesses lamentably differ. It was one angel, say some; it was two angels, say others. They stood outside the tomb; nay, they sat within the tomb. There were no angels; and Jesus, instead of being away in Galilee, and first and only seen there, was all the time in Jerusalem — never went to Galilee at all — and stood by the side of his own tomb in the guise of a gardener, and spake to Mary, who recognized and worshipped him. Communications are reported to Mary, to Peter, to the assembled disciples; but the accounts differ in both form and substance as to what these communications were, and by whom and to whom they were delivered. Only as to one thing is there entire accord, and that is that the corpse of the crucified was not to be found in the place, whence it was supposed only supernatural power could remove it. The two disciples walking, on that Sunday afternoon after the crucifixion, to Emmaus tell their unknown companion, that before they left Jerusalem the same morning certain women of their company made them astonished by reporting that, being early at the sepulchre, *they found not the body* of Jesus, and that they had seen a vision of angels, which said he was alive.

To a modern believer in the immortality of man, the hope that his deceased friend still lives is in no way contradicted or lessened by the discovery of his decaying body just where it had been reverently deposited. The belief in the continuous life of the soul takes no account

[a] John xx., 13. [b] Matt. xxviii., 6, 7.

of the presence and decomposition of what was once its physical organism. But to all the evangelists, and to the disciples of Jesus, according to the evangelical records, Jesus could not be alive in Jerusalem or in Galilee and at the same time buried in a new tomb near the place of his crucifixion. So, with pertinacity and unanimity, they insist on what to us seems in no wise an essential circumstance, the absence of the body from the tomb, while they are not careful to agree, and do not agree, as to any of the substantial details of the resurrection itself.

What the resuscitated Jesus seems in all the narratives to have insisted upon was, that he was not a ghost, but a veritable body with bodily appetite more keen and gross than even in his lifetime, and with the physical marks left on his person by the cruelties of his putting-to-death. The controversialists, to complete the discomfiture of Paul and the rationalists of his school, put into the mouth of the resurrected Christ himself this declaration: "*Behold my hands and my feet, that it is I myself: handle me, and see; for a spirit hath not flesh and bones, as ye see me have.*"[a] Even the author of the Johannic drama, from whose generally exalted and spiritual conception of the personality of Jesus a better opinion might have been expected, gives the weight of his testimony to perpetuate a gross superstition, which, chiefly on his authority, has survived to the present day. For this author too portrays Jesus in a resurrection, whose chief glory seemed to be in the consciousness of a restored physique, and in the possession of an appetite demanding an anticipation of the hour of dining.[b] Written, as this production is believed to have been, about a century after Paul's letter to the Corinthians, it shows conclusively how completely, even in the minds of the more philosophic and mystic believers, the theory of a physical resurrection had supplanted the more just and credible conception of Paul.

What was this conception? It is all disclosed in the famous fifteenth chapter of the first letter of that apostle to the Corinthians in these words: " For I delivered unto you, first of all, that which I also received, how that Christ died for our sins according to the scriptures; and that he was buried, and that he rose again the third day

[a] Luke xxiv., 39. [b] John xx., 27; xxi., 4, 5, 10, 12, 13.

according to the scriptures; and that he was seen of Peter, then of the twelve; after that, he was seen of above five hundred brethren at once, of whom the greater part still survive. After that, he was seen of James, then of all the apostles. And last of all he was seen of me also."[a] Now, thus far we find nothing directly negativing the theory of a physical resurrection, and the reanimation of the crucified body of Jesus; and, were this Paul's whole testimony, it might be our duty to reconcile it with the prevalent tradition of the early Church. For each of these alleged appearances of Jesus may have been the appearance of a body with flesh and bones, demonstrating and asserting that it was no ghost. But of the last of these appearances — all classed together as similar in kind — we know somewhat, and that, too, upon the best authority,— that of Paul himself; and we cannot regard it as anything more than an apparition.

In Paul's letters, we come upon the questionable and doubtful relation in which he lived and taught toward those who, at Jerusalem, were considered the pillars of the Church. We learn how sharply and passionately the very fundamental ideas of his theology were gainsaid and contradicted by apostles who, through their more intimate connection with Jesus in his lifetime, were justly held in higher repute than himself.[b] We know how his pretension to be an apostle was scouted, and how his whole story of an appointment by Jesus himself on the road to Damascus was regarded as a fanatical delusion. It was perhaps with a view of taking from under him the foundation of his apostleship, that the tradition of the Gospels was carefully fixed, limiting, by the authority of Jesus himself, the number of the apostles to twelve, and filling, under the sanction of the Holy Ghost, the vacancy made by the falling off of Judas, not by Paul, but by Matthias.[c]

A like disposition to check the presumption of a false apostle is further manifested in the account the real apostles seemed to have sanctioned of Jesus' ascension to heaven. It is told in the Acts of the Apostles that, after showing himself in bodily shape for a space of forty days, Jesus went out into the suburbs of Jerusalem

[a] I. Cor. xv., 3-8. [b] II. Cor. x., xi., xii.; Gal. i., ii.
[c] Matt. x, 2-5; Acts i., 17, 21-26.

with a concourse of his disciples, and there in a most conspicuous way was parted from them, and taken up to heaven, and that two angels appeared, as they watched his ascension to the sky, that received him, and said: "*This same Jesus, who is taken up from you into heaven, shall so come in like manner as ye have seen him go into heaven.*"[a] That is, forty days after the resurrection the showing of Jesus to his friends definitively ceased; and it was announced authoritatively from heaven that, when he came again, it would be his final coming, as he had foretold, to end the world. After this, no apostle, no orthodox disciple, sees Jesus. They have visions, they hear voices, the communication with the upper world is frequent and intimate; but Jesus is no longer the medium. It is always the Holy Ghost or an angel of God. The Johannic narrative — on this point plainly anti-Pauline, and in the orthodox interest — brings its emphatic disapproval of Paul's interviews with Jesus, who, during the brief interval that was to separate the ascension from the final coming, was not to be seen nor to have his privacy with the Deity intruded upon. For it puts into the mouth of Jesus himself the declaration: "*If I go not away, the Comforter will not come unto you. But, if I depart, I will send him unto you.*" "*A little while, and ye shall not see me.*"[b]

The consideration is not here disregarded that an actual absence of the glorified and resurrected body of Jesus in the paradise of God was not inconsistent with an apparition of Jesus to Paul. The common faith is, that apparitions are only of those who have departed from earth; and the sight of an apparition of an absent friend brings terror to the common mind, because it is a token of his death. But it is by no means probable that this distinction between a ghost — which in scientific parlance is a strong subjective impression upon a highly sensitive organization, not necessarily implying any objective reality — and the actual presence of one who has died clothed with an immortal though physical body was a distinction that entered into the minds of the New Testament writers, or into the mind of Paul himself. To them there were two states in which human beings might exist — as

[a] Acts i., 11. [b] John xiv., 26; xvi., 7, 16.

mortals before death, as immortals after death ; but, in both states, they had material bodies with senses and appetites. So that when the Church at Jerusalem established as a canon of faith, that Jesus with a glorified human body had passed into the heavens to remain there till his final coming, they made it impossible for Paul on his way to Damascus to have seen Jesus after his ascension and before his final coming, in any form in which they could conceive it possible for him really to appear.

But Paul's testimony must be taken altogether ; and, so taking it, the conception of the resurrection of Jesus, which he held, is still more irreconcilable with the tenet of the primitive Church, and with the tradition preserved in the canonical Gospels. The heat, not to say ill manners, with which the apostle expresses himself, indicates precisely where he treads upon controversial ground. *But some will say, How are the dead raised up, and with what body do they come? Fool! that which thou sowest is not made alive, till it hath first died: thou sowest not the plant that is to be, but only the seed of it, as of wheat, or some other grain, and God giveth it a body as pleases him; for there are kinds of bodies, as of men, beasts, birds, and of fishes; so earthly and heavenly bodies, natural and spiritual bodies. And when you sow the natural body corruptible, as a seed, it is in the power of God to raise from it a spiritual body incorruptible.*[a] Paul had been evidently provoked by the gross beliefs of his fellow-disciples. He had heard, to the point of personal disgust, the stories, that afterward embodied themselves in the gospel narratives, of Jesus coming into the assemblies of his chosen friends to exhibit the wounds on his person, to vindicate his appetite, and to assert that he was something to be handled, and no apparition ; and he cannot refrain from flinging at the whole company, high and low, who were retailing these stories, and getting them believed in spite of his protest, the uncourteous epithet, *fool.*

Nor is it of consequence that the illustration of vegetable growth breaks down wholly under a better knowledge than Paul possessed of the process of reproduction. He starts with the emphatic assertion, The old body, what is that but the seed of quite a different kind of a body?

[a] I. Cor. xv., 35-44.

So far from the old body living again, the living again is not possible "*except it die.*" The reverse happens to be true. Reproduction is not possible in the case of "wheat or of some other grain " *except the seed is alive* and *keeps alive;* and, if it is dead when planted, or dies in the ground, germination becomes impossible. But no matter. It was a simile to help his thought; and what his thought was we are perfectly able to perceive, although the illustration of it was unfortunately chosen.

Further on in his letter, Paul brings out more distinctly his peculiar idea of the resurrection. " *There is a spiritual body,*" ᵃ he says, boldly yoking together these two incongruities, which is tantamount to saying: there is a bodily spirit; there is a material soul. In the order of nature, we derive the natural body by birth from the primitive man; but after Jesus, who was the first-fruit of the resurrection, we shall put on the spiritual or heavenly body; and, turning to the corpse-worshippers and manipulators of the Master's flesh, who had made him say: "*A spirit hath not flesh and bones as ye see me have,*" ᵇ he adds with warmth: " This I say, brethren, that *flesh and blood* cannot inherit the kingdom of God, nor can corruption inherit incorruption. And this mystery some of us shall live to see; for, before the natural term of our lives, these bodies of ours, in a moment, in the very twinkling of an eye, at the last trump, which will certainly sound, shall be changed from corruptible to incorruptible, and put on their immortality." ᶜ

Now, as the process of the human resurrection — for which Paul finds a place in the economy of nature, along with the order of vegetables, and the different races of animals with their reproduction, growth, and death — was also the process or mode of the resurrection of Jesus, we can gather from these details his *rationale* of the resurrection of Jesus.ᵈ It was the death of his natural body, the germination and uprising from it of his spiritual, heavenly, and incorruptible body, in which he, and all who wear his image, will be forever clothed.

He does not see how he confuses and contradicts himself; how the word "body," which he still insists upon, concedes the whole claim he is combating. What is this

---

ᵃ I. Cor. xv., 44-49. ᵇ Luke xxiv., 39. ᶜ I. Cor. xv., 50-57. ᵈ I. Cov. xv., 11-20.

change, by which the corruptible becomes incorruptible, the mortal immortal? Do we find its analogy in the germination of wheat? Very well; the wheat germ, shoot, stalk, perfect plant, though not the subject sowed, which was a mere kernel of seed unlike them, is still a body, and material, and as such capable of dissolution. Shall we with him leave the correspondences of nature and soar into the visions and speculations of the celestial world of our aspirations and hopes, and assert: *There is a natural body, and there is a spiritual body?* A spiritual body,— if such a thing were thinkable,— but still a body. Flesh and blood may not inherit the kingdom of God, but by some mysterious process these *fleshly* bodies shall at the last trump acquire some qualities and powers, that will fit them to pass over the confines of that kingdom, and — *bodies still* — put on incorruption.

The speculation was too subtle to be popular. If Paul had affirmed immortality of the soul, asserted its superiority to and independence of the body, and resolutely adhered to his own thesis,— that flesh and blood, which is a synonym for the body, could not inherit immortality, — he would have been more in accord with the enlightened beliefs of the Jews, with the teachings of other religions older than Christianity, with the educated opinion of his time, and with the prevalent speculations of modern philosophy. Taking neither the philosophic nor the popular view, his ingenious surmises of the mode of the resurrection failed to impress themselves upon the creed of Christendom, which has read his equivocal words with great eagerness, because they are the substance of all that has been taught upon so fascinating a subject as human immortality, interpreting them either in the philosophic or in the gross form; and, from want of clearness of expression, growing out, perhaps, of want of clearness of conception, they seem capable of either interpretation.

But the triumph of the evangelists and regular apostles over Paul was more apparent than real. The whole speculation of immortality belongs to the department of philosophy. It is philosophy, rather than revelation, which, gathering its data from Egypt and India, from Zoroaster, Pythagoras, and Plato, as well as from Jesus and Paul, carefully meditating upon the phenomena of psychology, and the manifestations of the moral sense, has woven for mankind its thin and gorgeous hope of an immortal life. So that, though his own age and many succeeding ages rejected the metaphysical conceptions of a resurrection entertained by the cultivated apostle, and adhered to the vulgar traditions of the evangelists, the modern world, whose faith has received the education of science and philosophy, now cherishes its precious hope in the forms and symbols of Paul. The apostle of the Gentiles has become the apostle of the resurrection. It is the fervid and confident, although still controversial and inconsistent, language of Paul, that is read to-day over every newly opened grave in Christendom; and that which he, with too much deference, said of his Master, may, if we look at the Christian records for the report, be more accurately said of himself: "He hath brought life and immortality to light." [*]

It has been conceded that the tradition of a resurrection of Jesus, though the mode of that resurrection seemed to have been the subject of dissent and controversy among the early believers, is better vouched than any of the New Testament traditions. If it stood upon authority alone, it would actually stand stronger than it does. If we should be told that Goethe and Humboldt and John Stuart Mill and Emerson entertained a belief in the manifestations of so-called Spiritualism, we should be strongly prepossessed in favor of their truth; for it does not seem probable that such capacious, candid, and cultivated minds could concur in upholding a delusion. But if, besides, these clear-sighted men should give with particularity and detail the facts and occurrences upon which they base their belief, then we should feel required to examine the facts and occurrences, and determine whether they supported the belief. Just so, if we had only the undoubted historical fact, that such men as Peter, John, and Paul, and after them the enlightened bishops, scholars, and philosophers of the Christian Church, believed in the bodily resurrection of Jesus, it would command the respect of all unbiassed minds. But when these estimable men undertake to give with scrupulous minuteness the actual occurrence of the resurrection

---

[*] II. Tim. i., 10.

LEGEND OF THE RESURRECTION 393

and tell how it happened, who were present, what was said, and what was done, we are fairly invited, nay, challenged, to look into the details, to see if they form the basis for us of a rational belief.

This is our precise attitude as candid students of history. The messengers of the resurrection seem to have gone with their message, expecting that, as it was a wholly exceptional event, it would be received with surprise, with incredulity, with disbelief. This is just what the tradition itself declares. It says, when the women told the apostles, they disbelieved; when the apostles told each other, they disbelieved each other; and, when Jesus himself stood with them in Galilee, though some recognized and worshipped him, *some doubted*.[a] Just so when the same story, preserved for us in the tradition, comes down to us, we will be at least as candid as the disciples, and hesitate and doubt and give our assent only to what seems consistent and probable. Though ready to believe much on the authority of such good and great men, we cannot overlook the fact that they insist that we shall take nothing upon their word, but take the testimony for ourselves, upon which they have believed.

Let us now recur to what seems reasonably certain as to the death of Jesus. It took place, according to Matthew and Mark, at about three o'clock on the afternoon of the fourteenth day of the month Nisan, on Friday.[b] Luke does not indicate the hour, though he says that, from twelve o'clock till three, there was darkness over all the earth, and, after mentioning this circumstance, speaks of Jesus as speaking and dying,[c] so that his account does not contradict that of the two others. Some time during the evening, Joseph of Arimathea obtained from Pilate the custody of the body of Jesus, and, having swathed it in linen cloth, laid it in a sepulchre, and rolled a stone to barricade the entrance.[d] All the narratives concur in representing that the entombment was hurried by the lateness of the hour and the necessity of completing everything before sunset, when the Sabbath began, after which even funeral rites became unlawful.

Luke says the women who came with him from Gali-

---

[a] Luke xxiv., 11; Mark xvi., 11, 13; Matt. xxviii., 17.
[b] Matt. xxvii., 46; Mark xv., 34, 37.   [c] Luke xxiii., 44, 46.   [d] Matt. xxvii., 57–60.

lee followed after and beheld the sepulchre, and how the body of Jesus was laid. Matthew and Mark, while declaring that the women from Galilee stood afar off, and beheld the crucifixion, and naming Mary Magdalene and the mother of Joses, who seemed also to have been Jesus' own mother, and the mother of James, as among them, assert that none but the two first-named women came near and looked on at the entombment.[a]

The Sabbath began, the pious rites due to the beloved remains not yet accomplished. To complete these rites, to put spices and perfumes with the cerements, as Mark and Luke assert, was the errand that brought the women, as soon as the Sabbath was over, again to the sepulchre.[b] There is no thought among them all that Jesus has not remained dead, nor the faintest anticipation of any coming up alive from the sepulchre. Sorrowfully, carefully, expensively, they make the preparations to take a final leave of the lifeless form of him they had loved and believed in. Now begin the contradictions in the story. To the interrogation, who first visited the tomb on Sunday after the body of Jesus had been put there Friday evening, Matthew says, Mary Magdalene and the other Mary; Mark, Mary Magdalene and Mary, mother of James and Salome,— a substantial agreement; but Luke answers, Mary Magdalene, Joanna, Mary, the mother of James, the women who came from Galilee with Jesus, and other women that were with them,— quite a company of women, at the least more than four.[c]

Whom did the first visitors to the sepulchre see there? To this, Luke answers: they saw two men in shining garments. Matthew affirms that they saw an angel of the Lord from heaven, sitting upon the rolled-away stone, whose countenance was like lightning, and his raiment white as snow. Mark's account is, that they saw a young man sitting within the sepulchre on the right side, clothed in a long white garment, and were affrighted.[d] These are details indeed, but they are important details; and it is only by a substantial agreement as to facts so important, that an event, in itself incredible, is to be accepted as

---

[a] Mark xv., 47; Luke xxiii., 55. [b] Mark xvi., 1; Luke xxiv., 1.
[c] Matt. xxviii., 1; Mark xvi., 1; Luke xxiii., 55; xxiv., 1, 10.
[d] Matt. xxviii., 2, 5; Mark xvi., 5; Luke xxiv., 4.

proved. There were two of these glittering men, says one witness; nay, there was but one, say the other two. The two men *stood* beside the women, as they were perplexed at not finding the corpse, says the first deponent; nay, the one man *sat within*, on the right, deposes the next; not at all, declares the third, he *sat outside*, away from the sepulchre, on the rolled-away stone.

What did these glittering men, believed by all to be visitants from heaven, say to the women? Whoever they were, they had been placed in charge to communicate to the world what transformation of the buried body had taken place. Their communication is of prime importance, and ought to have been preserved in its very words. Here is the record of it:[a]—

"Fear not ye; for I know that ye seek Jesus, who was crucified. He is not here; for he is risen, as he said. Come, see the place where the Lord lay. And go quickly, and tell his disciples that he is risen from the dead; and, behold, he goeth before you into Galilee; there shall ye see him: lo, I have told you."— *Matthew.*

"Be not affrighted. Ye seek Jesus of Nazareth, which was crucified. He is risen; he is not here: behold the place where they laid him. But go your way, tell his disciples and Peter that he goeth before you into Galilee: there shall ye see him, as he said unto you."— *Mark.*

"Why seek ye the living among the dead? He is not here, but he is risen. Remember how he spake unto you when he was yet in Galilee, saying, The Son of Man must be delivered into the hands of sinful men, and be crucified, and the third day rise again."— *Luke.*

In the first part of this message there is sufficient accord. The last writer omits the words to reassure the fears of the surprised women, and surmises the errand of the women in a different way from the other two writers, and omits a most important direction to go and give information to the disciples; but each statement affirms that Jesus is no longer in the sepulchre — a dead body — but is risen and living. When, however, we come to the latter clauses of the communication, there is a fatal variation. All declare the message was that Jesus was not dead in the tomb; but they differ both as to where he is

[a] Matt. xxviii., 5-7; Mark xvi., 6, 7; Luke xxiv., 5-7.

and where he is to be found, and what the *ante mortem* prediction of his had been concerning his reappearance. We come here upon a point over which the New Testament records declare there had been a controversy among the first believers in Jesus.

After the new faith had begun to gain converts in Jewry, after Peter and James and John, its official representatives from humble Galilean laborers, had grown to be pillars of the Church, after they had abandoned their humble avocation of fishermen, and, as the witnesses, trusted friends, companions, and kinsfolk of the Messiah, had come to be reverenced by the assembly as bishops and hierarchs, there came into the minds of the disciples an evident desire to disown as much as possible the disreputable and provincial relation of the career of Jesus with Galilee, and by giving him a closer connection with Jerusalem, the priests, and elders, the temple worship, the national polity and its representatives, to make the active propagandism of the faith more effectual among enlightened and influential Jews. The first narratives, written on the authority of the little band of provincials who had come up with Jesus from Galilee to Jerusalem, all indicate Galilee as the theatre of Jesus' glory as a prophet. He only came to Jerusalem, they say, to condemn it, and foretell its doom, and to show how complete was his estrangement from it. Accordingly, they tinge the story of the resurrection with their local prejudices. He will not show himself alive to proud and cruel Jerusalem. He is not there. He will not even tarry to speak to his mother, to Peter, or to John, whom he loved. He has betaken himself to his beloved Galilee, which believed in him. *There, only there, shall ye see him.*

As has been seen, the whole Johannic drama had for one of its designs the presentation in its most imposing light to Zion of her prophetic king, and to do away the reproach, which seems the burden of the story: "*Can any good thing come out of Nazareth? Search, and look; for out of Galilee ariseth no prophet.*"[a] Accordingly, the phenomenon of the resurrection accommodates itself in the writer's conception to this purpose. Jesus is not in Galilee, nor will he show himself first there. In the

[a] John i., 46; vii., 52.

guise of the keeper of the garden, he himself stands by
Mary of Magdala, and calls her by name; and she recognizes him as her crucified Master.[a]

It seems to give a date to the composition of the Third
Gospel, that its version of the resurrection stands midway
between the Galilean and the Judaic traditions. The
Galilean tradition, as given by the first two evangelists,
is, that, though Jesus rose alive from his tomb in the environs of Jerusalem, he first showed himself alive to the
twelve in Galilee. The Judaic tradition, affected by the
more conciliatory policy pursued by the followers of Jesus
after his death toward the Pharisees, asserts that the interviews of the risen Master with his followers were in
Jerusalem, which he expressly forbade them to leave. For
Luke carefully eliminates from his affidavit all reference
to an appointment of Galilee as the place of reunion.
We find evident indication of a dispute that must have
quite divided the opinions of the little band of believers.
The older Galilean authorities, still clinging to their local
attachments, had insisted, that, as Jesus had honored
Galilee by doing in it all his great miracles, and preaching all his fundamental doctrines, so had he recognized
it, by making it the place where he would show himself
first alive to his chosen witnesses after his passion.
They had gone so far as to put into the mouth of Jesus
a distinct and explicit prediction and direction that in
Galilee should be the place of meeting after the resurrection, as undoubtedly they had sought the sanction of
Jesus for many other points of belief, which, in the propagandism of the faith, had become to their minds of prime
importance. Luke is no sceptic, but a man of easy faith,
full of innocent wonder at the miracles he has come fully
to believe in; and it is not possible for him to deny any
tradition of Jesus, which honors his prophetic insight.
So he changes the story, or rather, perhaps,—for there is
no reason to question his good faith,— he reports a version
of it, which the Pharisaic Christians had come to believe.
Did not Jesus say himself, that he would appear alive in
Galilee? eagerly asked the party of the primitive disciples.[b] Not that he *would appear in Galilee*, say the later
Jewish proselytes, but he said *in Galilee* that he would

[a] John xx., 14-17.   [b] Matt. xxvi., 32; Mark xiv., 28.

appear. While the believers in the older story were too numerous and too influential in the Church embracing, doubtless, Peter, John, and James, and all the original apostles, to allow their testimony to be overruled, and the first tradition to be altered, it can be well understood how a policy, which we find avowed among the early missionaries of the faith,[a] would allow a contradictory tradition to be told in those countries and among those people, where it might help in winning souls to Christ. So the two accounts, though impossible of reconciliation, find the place in the Christian literature, and, ultimately, in the canon of Scripture, which they have ever since maintained.

There is another illustration in the communication, by which the resurrection was said to have been first announced to the world, of how such an occasion was seized upon to get some sanction for cherished beliefs. Matthew, writing first, says: "The angel said, Go quickly, and tell his disciples that he is risen from the dead." Mark, writing later, reports the message: "Go your way, tell his disciples *and Peter* that he goeth before you into Galilee." Was not Peter a disciple, and was he not included in the direction to tell the disciples? Can there be any doubt that here was a writer, whom tradition declares to have been the exponent and mouthpiece of Peter, endeavoring to get honor for his patron, and to get sanction for the authority, which, according to the Acts of the Apostles, Peter in his later life assumed over the faith of the Church, — an authority culminating in the enormous pretensions of the Papacy?

Thus far, we have no statement from either witness of any apparition of Jesus. Indeed, according to Matthew and Mark and the more credible tradition, such appearance at Jerusalem will be impossible; for it will not only contradict the angelic assurance, but the explicit prediction of Jesus in his lifetime. The women, whether two or many, find the tomb empty, the body they had come to embalm gone, and angels, they do not agree how many, or whether standing or sitting, within or without the tomb, who declare that Jesus is not there. But it does not appear that those angels pretended to be, nor are they by

[a] I. Cor. ix., 20–22.

any of the visitants supposed to be, Jesus or impersonations of Jesus.

Now is there any account that Jesus himself appeared to any person other than the early visiting Galilean women, at or near the tomb, where he was buried? All the narratives agree in negativing this inquiry. Even the Johannic drama is explicit in declaring that to *no man* did the risen Master appear *at or near his place of burial.*

Did the Galilean women or either of them see Jesus alive at or near the sepulchre? Matthew says, the two Marys ran from the sepulchre to tell the disciples what they had seen and heard; and that Jesus himself met them, as they went, and hailed them; and that the women clasping his feet did homage to him, after which Jesus himself renewed the angelic message, and commanded the women to tell his brethren to go into Galilee, *where they should see him.*[a] As yet there is nothing inconsistent in the two statements. When the angel told the women: *He is not here*, it was meant that he was not in the tomb. It was not declared, that he *had departed* from Jerusalem to Galilee, only that he was *going* to Galilee before his disciples, and would show himself *to them* only there, though he might show himself to his mother and his friend before he left Jerusalem. Mark declares that Jesus showed himself first to Mary Magdalene, and the context requires us to understand that this was at Jerusalem;[b] but he does not assert, that his mother Mary or any other woman was present at the interview. It seems fairly to be implied, that the other two appearances of Jesus after his death mentioned by Mark were in the vicinity of Jerusalem,— that is, to two disciples walking into the country, and to the eleven as they sat at meat;[c] and no meeting whatever in Galilee is mentioned, though this writer declares elsewhere the prediction of Jesus making an appointment of Galilee for a showing after his resurrection, and also the angelic message that the disciples and Peter should go to Galilee to see Jesus.[d]

If we reject all of the last chapter of Mark after the eighth verse, as forming, in the judgment of Tischendorf and of other competent critics, no part of his original and genuine gospel, the appearance of Jesus to any person *in*

[a] Matt. xxviii., 9, 10.   [b] Mark xvi., 9.   [c] Mark xvi., 14.   [d] Mark xiv., 28; xvi., 7.

Jerusalem stands upon still slighter testimony. The statement of such appearance by Matthew is offset by the denial of it by Luke, and remains unproved. As, however, these twelve suspected verses stand accredited in our common version of the New Testament, upon which the whole structure of this argument is built; as they have not been omitted even in the lately revised Scriptural translation,— it is deemed proper to consider them as a part of the early, if not the earliest, tradition of the resurrection. In an argument to show that all these details of communications with Jesus, after his death, must have been legendary accretions of his veritable history, it would not be apposite to disregard a part of them, because they are suspected of being later than the rest.

But, when later, Luke undertook, in a letter to his friend Theophilus, to set forth in order "a declaration of the things that are most surely believed" among us, as delivered by the eye-witness,[a] the tradition of an appearance of Jesus either to the two Marys or to Mary Magdalene alone *at Jerusalem* had ceased to be told and believed. For Luke gives, in two methods, the precise intelligence which the Galilean women conveyed to the eleven disciples; and it is something quite different. There were many women, he says, who had visited the sepulchre; and the report they brought back was, that the tomb was empty, and that two angels declared Jesus to have risen from the dead. Their story was wholly disbelieved: only Peter ran to the sepulchre, and found no corpse therein, and went away, perplexed with doubt and surprise.[b] The account of the two disciples travelling into the country is also given by Luke; and, in their talk, they report precisely what the women had told on Sunday morning to the assembled disciples. It is not that they had seen Jesus, but that they had not found his body in the tomb, and had also seen a vision of angels who said he was alive. *Him, they assert, they did not see.*[c]

Comparing these documents with each other, and applying to them the well-known rules of testing oral testimony, it seems fairly inferrible, that the appearance of Jesus alive to Mary Magdalene or to her and other Gali-

[a] Luke i., 1-4.　[b] Luke xxiii., 55; xxiv., 1-12.　[c] Luke xxiv., 22-24.

lean women *in Jerusalem* is not proved. Luke, one of the witnesses, emphatically denies it; and, while Matthew and Mark assert it, they assert with substantial circumstances inconsistent with each other, and the occurrence itself was inconsistent with an appointment, which, they say, was made by Jesus with his disciples, male and female, to show himself to them in Galilee.

Were there no other proofs of a resurrection of Jesus than these, we should not be justified in believing that it had occurred. Credulous and enthusiastic as were the disciples, upon this evidence alone it is admitted by all the historians that the disciples refused to believe. On this evidence, not reported, as it is to us, by unnamed writers, without historic method or historic integrity, but told at first hand by persons they confided in and respected, the disciples believed not.[a] Luke asserts that they listened contemptuously to the story. "Their words seemed to them as idle tales, and they believed them not."[b]

The next appearance claimed to be of the risen Jesus was to the two disciples travelling on Sunday to Emmaus. One of these disciples was Cleopas, husband of the aunt of Jesus.[c] Of course, the person of Jesus was well known to them. In the whole legend of the resurrection, Jesus is made to authenticate his physical presence to his wondering friends by challenging an inspection and handling of his body, with the marks of the crucifixion still upon it. Having been suddenly put to death when in full health, very little change could have affected his features and expression. If the man overtaken on the road to Emmaus had indeed been Jesus, there seems no good reason why his intimate friends should not have recognized him. The explanation ventured by the writer to meet this obvious inference, that *their eyes were holden that they should not know him*,[d] is clumsy and unsatisfactory. Why should their eyes be holden, when it was the evident purpose of his appearance that they should know him? But he walked and talked with them for hours. Of course, they would have known his looks, his tones, his modes of speech; and, as they did not, we should be compelled to conclude the person who walked with them was

[a] Mark xvi., 11.   [b] Luke xxiv., 11.   [c] Luke xxiv., 18; John xix., 25.
[d] Luke xxiv., 13-33.

not an acquaintance. The account says they recognized him only when he blessed and brake the bread; though what distinguishing peculiarity there could have been in this action, it is hard to understand. They think he vanished out of their sight; but, if he suddenly left them, and they did not follow him, such disappearance need not have been supernatural.

It was natural that in their excited minds, disturbed and elated with what they had heard before leaving Jerusalem, about a vision of angels revealing to the women that Jesus was alive, they should harbor the most welcome surmise that the grave and courteous stranger, so conversant with the Messianic Scriptures, was Jesus; but, when they told the story while fresh in their memory, with all its details, to the assembled disciples, *there was no one to give it credence.*[a]

There must have been at Jerusalem many secret adherents of Jesus, of the type of Nicodemus and Joseph of Arimathea, who refrained under the prevalent terror from avowing their sympathy. Doubtless, the unknown man was a scribe, who joined the two travellers, and, finding from the questions he asked that they were adherents of the crucified, thought it safe to express his secret conviction and avow the faith he held with them in common. He withheld his name; and, when he feared that, in his enthusiasm, his disclosures might have exceeded the bounds of prudence, he might have left their company to avoid the possibility of being betrayed to the hostile influences that then controlled Jerusalem.

Thus far, then, nothing is shown to have happened indicating that the dead Jesus has been restored to life, at least nothing, that the accredited tradition, as told by the three evangelists, concurrently maintains. Whatever manifestation was made to Mary Magdalene, or to the two travelling disciples, joyfully and confidently told by them, met with no credence even from those who so much wished to believe it. Of itself, it should not command for a moment our faith, though, as the disciples came afterward to recognize the resurrection as an accomplished fact, we, too, when we shall have found other reasons for believing in it, may imitate them in revising

[a] Mark xvi., 13.

our first judgment as to these equivocal and uncertain appearances. Upon what other manifestations did the disciples come to accept the resurrection as a veritable event in the career of Jesus?

Matthew says, the only manifestation of Jesus afterward was in a mountain in Galilee, where Jesus in his lifetime had made an appointment to meet his followers. He says: "The eleven disciples went away into a mountain, where Jesus had appointed them. And when they saw him, they worshipped him; but some doubted. And Jesus came and spake unto them, saying: All power is given unto me in heaven and in earth. Go ye, therefore, and teach all nations, baptizing them in the name of the Father, and of the Son, and of the Holy Ghost; teaching them to observe all things whatsoever I have commanded you: and, lo, I am with you alway, even unto the end of the world."[a] Mark — if the whole passage be not an interpolation — says: "Afterward he appeared unto the eleven as they sat at meat, and upbraided them with their unbelief and hardness of heart, because they believed not them which had seen him after he was risen. And he said unto them: Go ye into all the world, and preach the gospel to every creature. He that believeth and is baptized shall be saved, but he that believeth not shall be damned. And these signs shall follow them that believe. In my name shall they cast out devils; they shall speak with new tongues; they shall take up serpents; and, if they drink any deadly thing, it shall not hurt them; they shall lay hands on the sick, and they shall recover."[b]

Luke's account of the manifestation to the eleven is in this wise. It was at Jerusalem, where the eleven and their party were gathered together. "As they spake, Jesus himself stood in the midst of them, and said: Peace be unto you. Why are ye troubled? and why do thoughts arise in your hearts? Behold my hands and my feet, that it is I myself: handle me, and see; for a spirit hath not flesh and bones, as ye see me have." Then, he showed his hands and feet, and called for food and ate before them, and, resuming his communication, said: "These are the words which I spake unto you, while I was yet

[a] Matt. xxviii., 16-20.   [b] Mark xvi., 14-18.

with you, that all things must be fulfilled which were written in the law of Moses, and in the prophets and in the psalms concerning me. Thus it is written, and thus it behooved Christ to suffer, and to rise from the dead the third day; and that repentance and remission of sins should be preached in his name among all nations, beginning at Jerusalem. And ye are witnesses of these things. And, behold, I send the promise of my Father upon you: but tarry in the city of Jerusalem, until ye be endued with power from on high." Then he led them forth, as far as Bethany, and blessed them, and was parted from them, and carried up to heaven.*

The last words of wise and great men, their grand summing up, at the last, of the experience and teachings of life, have always been sacredly cherished among mankind, who have hoped from the verge, that bounds the fascinating mystery beyond, to get some gleam of intelligence. How much more precious is intelligence brought not from this, but the *other side* of the gulf of death! Here is one of the wisest, the purest, the bravest souls, that ever lived, returned from the grave! He has deigned to stop in his passage from corruption and the tomb, to incorruption and a conscious eternal life in the spiritual world, to show himself to his friends. He shrinks not from their questions; and, unlike the thin company of ghosts, that appall us with their austerity, he challenges their most familiar handling of his person, and precedes them to feasts of eating and conviviality. Was ever the aching curiosity of man so lavishly satisfied? Was ever such a transcendent communication made to mankind? How momentous it is! Could one man of the eleven ever in his lifetime forget the substance or even the very form, body, expression, and tone of it, for it was only a few words? Incapable of being forgotten, as it was said, in form as well as spirit, in its very words and phraseology, what presumption, what audacity of impiety to falsify it, to suppress any of it, to add anything to it; to inject into it any trivial detail, any incertitude! And yet what perplexes and astounds us in putting together these old documents, the muniments of our title to an eternal life, is to find them so contradictory, not only in form and expression, but also in substance and subject-matter.

* Luke xxiv., 44, 46–49, 50–53.

Where was this most consequential and momentous interview between a divine being, who had come back from death, to which in the form of man he had been subjected, to throw light upon the darkness of the grave? and who were allowed the supreme privilege of participating in it? It was on a mountain in Galilee, says our most trustworthy witness, upon whom we have chiefly relied for the historic details of the life of Jesus. Nay, reply two other witnesses, it was in a private room in Jerusalem. Only eleven apostles were present, maintain Matthew and Mark. The eleven apostles, and they of their party, the body of Jesus' adherents, were present, says Luke.

Let us suppose, instead of the vast stake depending upon the actuality of this appearance of Jesus and upon the communication he is believed to have made to the world, it had been simply the title to an estate claimed to have been devised by a nuncupative will. The judge inquires of the three witnesses: Where were the words, you claim to have the legal effect of a will, uttered by the testator? Two of them testify, they were spoken in a club-house in Boston; and one, they were spoken on a mountain in New Hampshire. The judge would not permit them to testify as to the words, however accordant the report might be; for he would say: *Until you can fix the time and place of the communication, I cannot permit you to give its import.* If it should be suggested that the deceased just before his death was in the company of the witnesses both in a club-house in Boston and on a mountain in New Hampshire, and in both places he talked about disposing of his estate, the explanation might let in the testimony as to the language, because the witnesses might honestly disagree as to the place where the effective words were uttered. But let us suppose that two of the witnesses persist in declaring: We know nothing about any conversation of the deceased in New Hampshire; we never met him there. He assured us that he had not been in New Hampshire for a month before our last interview with him, and that he wished to make his will in Boston, so that his estate could be administered under the laws of Massachusetts; while the third witness should insist: His devisees, his counsel, his friends, all wished him to make his will in Boston; but he insisted that he would do nothing about it till he could get back to New Hampshire, and he made an appointment with them and us to meet him there for that purpose. In such an aspect of the testimony, the disagreement as to the attendant circumstances would make it impossible that it all related to the same transaction, and the court could never come to a consideration of the words of the communication.

The proof of Jesus' appearance stands much in this way. Matthew says it was in a mountain in Galilee by express appointment of Jesus, made in his lifetime, renewed by angelic messengers stationed at his tomb.[a] Mark and Luke say it was in a room in the city of Jerusalem;[b] and the latter adds, that Jesus expressly forbade the disciples to leave Jerusalem and to go to Galilee, and that they did not go thither.[c]

But, to carry the illustration further, let it now be supposed that, in the case of this nuncupative will, the scruples of the judge about the irreconcilable attending circumstances had been overcome, and that he had definitely or provisionally permitted the witnesses to testify as to the words of the testator, claimed to operate as a devise. They recapitulate them. They are taken down, and this is their purport. One witness says: the deceased said he desired all to take notice that all his property, real and personal, was to go to his deceased wife's nephew. The next witness says: what I heard him say was, that all he left was to be given to the town of Hanover, as a fund for the support of its poor. The third witness, on being put upon oath, testifies: he said he wanted us to be witnesses that he was about to make a verbal will, and then added: whatever I leave I desire to go to Harvard College. Could either of the devisees obtain an estate from such utterly contradictory testimony?

But, as to the substance and subject-matter of the postmortuary communication of Jesus, the testimony of the written tradition is quite as conflicting. According to Matthew, he said: that all power was given to him in

[a] Matt. xxviii., 7, 10, 16; xxvi., 32.   [b] Mark xvi., 14, 19.
[c] Luke xxiv., 33, 36, 49, 50; Acts i., 4, 8, 12, 14.

heaven and earth, and that he should always be with his disciples till the end of the world. Accordingly, Matthew makes no mention of his withdrawal to heaven; nor can he do so consistently with the assurance that he had declared Jesus had given, that he had come back from death to stay with them to the near end of the world. The message he gave, according to Matthew, was, that his disciples should teach all nations to observe the things he had commanded,— that is, that they should keep his moral precepts,— a declaration quite in harmony with Matthew's view of the mission of Jesus.

Mark makes the communication consist of a reproach of the disciples for not believing what Mary Magdalene and the two disciples had told them, whereas their caution and candor seem only commendable. The charge to the disciples was not the inculcation of moral precepts at all, but to go and tell every creature that the kingdom of heaven was at hand, or preach the good news, and he that believed that, and accepted baptism, should be saved; and he that believed not should be damned. Then, he declared that real believers should be known by their power to cast out devils, to speak with tongues, to heal the sick by touch, and to drink and handle poisonous things without harm. He said nothing about a purpose to remain with his disciples to the end; for the witness declares that, after his message, he was received up into heaven, and sat on the right hand of God.*

Luke's version of the last testament of Jesus is almost wholly different with the exception of a statement of the preaching among all nations of — not the moral precepts, nor the kingdom of heaven — but of a remission of sins in Jesus' name to succeed repentance. Thus, if we ask what did the risen Master direct his witnesses and apostles to preach, Matthew says, his doctrines of morality; Mark says, the kingdom of heaven, and faith and baptism as the conditions of salvation; while Luke insists that it was the forgiveness of sins for Jesus' sake to all who repented. According to Luke, he did not chide his friends for their doubt, or attribute it to perversity, but gently reassured them with actual proofs, both of his identity and of his physical presence, with all his members, functions, and

* Mark xvi., 14-19.

appetites, and afterwards took up the debate, which constitutes so large a part of the controversial Epistles of Paul, and is dramatically reproduced in the Fourth Gospel, and labored to impress upon his hearers that his career as a prophet, his crucifixion and his resurrection, were all foreshadowed in the Hebrew scriptures. As in Mark, everything Luke says implies a withdrawal and leave-taking, and not a staying in the world till its end; and so Luke tells elsewhere of Jesus' formal withdrawing in the sight of many witnesses to heaven.[a]

It is probable that in the First Gospel we have the earliest tradition of the resurrection; but, as it did not get committed to writing till after the writing of Paul's Epistles, it contains also, what came to be believed among a part of the disciples, the story of the meeting of Jesus with Mary Magdalene, as she departed from the tomb. This must be considered an interpolation, since any showing of himself by Jesus to his disciples in Jerusalem was inconsistent with Matthew's declaration, that both Jesus and the angelic messenger had appointed Galilee as the place for such showing. It is easy to perceive how the story grew in the telling; for, brief as Mark's general biography is, it is fuller than Matthew's concerning the resurrection. Jesus, according to Mark, shows himself first to Mary Magdalene, after that to two disciples, and then to the eleven apostles, sitting at meat,—all in Jerusalem. Mark adds a distinct appearance not mentioned by Matthew, and places the interview with the eleven in Jerusalem instead of Galilee. When Luke— the date is not known, but certainly after many other lives of Jesus had been written [b]— contributes his *memorabilia*, although he discountenances the story of any appearance to the women, or to any disciple, previously to the two travellers to Emmaus, he gives the last-named appearance with vivid and picturesque details;[c] and the appearance to the eleven at Jerusalem, with a much fuller communication from Jesus to his disciples.[d] If we adopt Tischendorf's conclusion that the last twelve verses of Mark's Gospel are additions by another hand to the genuine writing, the three distinct appearances of Jesus mentioned in our Second Gospel — which is prob-

[a] Acts i., 9-12.　[b] Luke i., 1.　[c] Luke xxiv., 13-33.　[d] Luke xxiv., 36-49.

ably older than the Third, in which but two appearances are mentioned — become intelligible. So far as they are genuine, the first two evangels make mention of but one appearance, and the third evangel of but two appearances of the *risen* Jesus.

When later Luke wrote the Acts of the Apostles, he told of a tarrying of Jesus among his followers after his death for a period of forty days, and of a showing of himself alive by many infallible proofs, and of much general instruction given pertaining to the kingdom of heaven. This statement does not necessarily imply a showing of Jesus to his followers each one of the forty days; but it does imply that during six weeks Jesus was in the habit of frequent intercourse with his disciples, and gave them copious counsel and instruction.[a]

Did not this writer think these "*things pertaining to the kingdom of God*," which Jesus, returning from the realms of death and about to ascend to the counsels and companionship of the Father, had stopped to confide to his disciples, worth telling? Did he think the recitations of Old Testament stories, which make up the speeches of Stephen, of Peter, and of Paul, of so much more moment than these awful last words of the king and judge of the world? If such things had been spoken, would they not have burned themselves indelibly into each believer's heart, who would have exclaimed : —

> " Remember thee?
> Ay, thou great ghost, while memory holds a seat
> In this distracted globe. Remember thee?
> Yea, from the table of my memory
> I'll wipe away all trivial fond records,
> All saws of books, all forms, all pressures past,
> That youth and observation copied there;
> And thy commandment all alone shall live
> Within the book and volume of my brain
> Unmixed with baser matter: yes, yes, by heaven."

When Paul wrote his first letter to the Corinthians, about the year 59 — though this was probably earlier than the writing of the Acts or either of the Synoptic Gospels in their present form — the tradition, as learned by him, seemed to be of five distinct appearances of Jesus to his disciples, enumerated in this order: first to

[a] Acts i., 2-12.

Peter alone, then to the twelve, then to five hundred disciples at once, then to James, then to all the apostles.[a] It is singular that the appearance first and solely to Peter is nowhere else mentioned in the New Testament writings, not even by Mark, whose story a definite tradition imputes to the dictation of Peter, and incredible that five hundred of the brethren should have been assembled together, when the whole body of believers numbered but one hundred and twenty, and when the difficulty of assembling them all — scattered and alarmed as they were — must have been very great.[b]

The Pauline version of the resurrection however, though avowed hearsay, stands upon better authority than anything in the Christian records, having for its sponsor so respectable a writer as Paul. When we can perceive the story growing thus in the very process of its telling, when we find in what is believed to be its earliest oral promulgation not a trace of any separate appearings of Jesus to Peter or to James, or of any assemblage of five hundred brethren, who all attested it, some of them known and living when Paul wrote, we are compelled to conclude that the other details, less contradicted, are, like these, the accretions of an enthusiastic faith, which had for its support but little, if any, basis of fact. It certainly is surprising that the primitive Christians should have gone out among the sceptics and philosophers of the first century with such a stupendous announcement as that Jesus had appeared in bodily life after his burial, without having been able to agree among themselves as to where the manifestation took place, how many times it was repeated, to whom it was made, or what was the substance or subject-matter of the communication which the resuscitated Master made to his followers.

It will not be legitimate to cite the Fourth Gospel, with the critical estimate of it adopted in this paper, as a fourth distinct account of the resurrection, since it is not probable that any historic purpose or historic responsibility controlled the writer of that unique production. It is enough to remark in this connection that the risen Jesus of John, which is the prevalent Christian conception, that has continued till our time, no more resembles the risen Jesus

---

[a] I. Cor. xv., 3-8. [b] Acts i., 15.

of the older traditions, than does the controversial Jesus, holding metaphysical colloquies with the Pharisees, with Nicodemus, with Pilate, and with his disciples, accord with the Galilean prophet, announcing the kingdom of heaven and preaching the ethics of poverty, of non-resistance, and of universal almsgiving.

We have left then five testimonies to be weighed and compared with each other. Paul's, the first committed to writing, the most genuine, and, on the whole, the most respectable, asserts that Jesus first showed himself alive to Peter, that later James was favored with a private interview, and that five hundred of his disciples saw him simultaneously. But when we take up Mark's deposition, we find it disclaiming that distinction for the apostle, who is believed in the Church to have dictated the Second Gospel. Mary Magdalene, it says, saw Jesus first. Peter only saw him later with the other eleven. Matthew's Gospel, believed to be the written form which the original Galilean tradition of Jesus assumed some time during the first or second century, of all others ought to know about an appearance to James, who, in his Epistle most nearly expresses the Galilean gospel of good works and poverty; but it does not make special mention of him as present at any reported conversation of the resurrected Jesus. All the other deponents ignore the manifestation to the five hundred brethren, and Luke gives a statement which makes such a manifestation impossible.[a] On the other hand, Paul ignores any manifestation to Mary Magdalene or to the two travellers to Emmaus, and by classing these appearances with that to him *in vision* on the road to Damascus, and by his exposition of the nature of the spiritual body,[b] most plainly indicates that all these appearances were apparitional, and not actual.

Everything before the appearance to the eleven rests upon the credit of Mary Magdalene, whose account, freshly told, the apostles themselves disbelieved, and of the two travelling disciples, whose conjecture that Jesus had walked and talked with them seemed an idle tale to their fellow disciples; and, when we consider its details, we are forced to adopt their suspicion. As to the appearance to the eleven, besides the hopelessly irreconcilable statements

[a] Acts i., 15.   [b] I. Cor. xv., 50.

as to where it occurred and what was the matter communicated, we have the *naive* avowal, that, of the eleven to whom it was said to have been manifested, *some doubted*.[a] The whole Church, including these disciples, came afterward to believe and persistently to maintain that Jesus had come back to his earthly life. We ought at least to maintain the candor of these ardent men, and conclude that a personal manifestation that could not coerce their faith cannot now secure ours in its contradictory and confused telling by irresponsible annalists.

But an argument, that builds itself upon what may be called a professional and cunning cross-examination, does not press with the weight of assured conviction upon large and liberal minds. For such minds, these considerations are apposite. Why should Jesus have appeared alive after his death on the cross? Such an appearance was wholly outside of his own anticipations and prognostications. His dominant idea was of a kingdom of heaven, of which he came to have an assured faith, that he himself was king. He believed that his human life was his sending from the Deity to the chosen people, the Jews, to give them their last dispensation of grace and salvation. First, the Lord of the vineyard sent his servants, the prophets, but, last of all, his son. But the wicked husbandmen, who had stoned and disregarded the servants, will reject and slay the son.[b] The son of God and king of heaven must submit to shame and death. But, after death, he will come again, not as before in weakness, still less in secrecy, but in power and glory, with all the holy angels with him. His coming will need no proclamation, nor will men say: *Lo here, or lo there is Christ;* for, as the lightning in the east flashes through all the heavens, so shall the coming of the Son of Man be. All the earth shall be astounded at the brightness of his coming, and all the tribes of the earth shall mourn because of him.[c]

After the legend of the resurrection, against some protest, had established itself among the believers, Jesus himself is made to give sanction to it by precise predictions of it in his lifetime. Thus, in Matthew's narrative, after the famous conference with his disciples at Cæsarea-Philippi,

[a] Matt. xxviii., 17. [b] Matt. xxi., 33-44.
[c] Matt. xxiv., 23-31; xxv., 31; xxvi., 64; Luke xxi., 25-36.

Jesus is declared to have begun to show to his disciples, that he must go to Jerusalem, and suffer many things of the elders, chief priests, and scribes, and be killed, and be raised again on the third day.[a] Coming down from the mount of transfiguration, he charges his disciples not to tell of the vision of Moses and Elias, till after he had risen from the dead.[b] Again, before leaving Galilee, Jesus said to his followers: "The Son of Man shall be betrayed into the hands of men; and they shall kill him, and the third day he shall be raised again."[c] While going up to Jerusalem, Jesus took the twelve apart, and told them: "The Son of Man shall be betrayed unto the chief priests and unto the scribes, and they shall condemn him to death, and shall deliver him to the Gentiles to mock, and to scourge, and crucify him; and the third day he shall rise again."[d] Finally, in his last interview with them, before he was betrayed, having told them his time was at hand, he said: "It is written, I will smite the Shepherd, and the sheep shall be scattered abroad. But after I am risen again, I will go before you into Galilee."[e] Mark reports the same communications, as made on the same occasions, with such similarity of language that one account is evidently copied from the other.[f] Luke reports the first three of these communications in quite similar language.[g]

That Jesus foreboded his death at Jerusalem from the malignity of his enemies, whose animosity he had determined to provoke by severe denunciations, has already been seen. He believed himself to be the Shepherd, who was to be smitten, the Messiah, whose grave was to be made with the wicked, and that this suffering and shame must needs precede his coming as Judge and Conqueror and King. The manner of his death, by whom and in what form it was to be inflicted, and the minute details of his mockery and scourging, as he could not have foreseen, must have been added to his actual declarations after the event, as was also the expectation of a resurrection after the third day. That he did not predict his resurrection the third day is evident from the fact that the Old Scriptures, though certain of them in

---

[a] Matt. xvi., 21. [b] Matt. xvii., 9. [c] Matt. xvii., 22, 23. [d] Matt. xx., 18, 19.
[e] Matt. xxvi., 18-32. [f] Mark viii., 31; ix., 31, 32; x., 32-34; xiv., 28.
[g] Luke ix., 22, 44, 45; xviii., 31-34.

the fanciful interpretations of the time, were believed to indicate that Messiah could not be held by the powers of evil forever in the under world, did not indicate *three days*, as the period of his sojourn in those realms of silence. The grotesque story of Jonah's living burial for three days in the belly of a whale, which evidently came to be credited as a veritable adventure befalling one of their national prophets, might have been seized hold of by the evangelists and disciples, as typical of the death and resurrection of their Master. But we cannot impute this whimsical fancy to Jesus without involving him in self-contradiction.* The second coming of the Son of Man was to usher in the kingdom of heaven. Jesus could not have indicated three days after his death as the opening of an epoch the day and hour of which he declared he did not know.ᵃ

But the *naïveté* of the evangelists' narration quite confutes them; for all accounts of the resurrection — those claimed to be historic and those avowedly or apparently dramatic — represent the surprise of Jesus' disciples at his resurrection to have been complete. The Marys and the company of women, larger or smaller, went to the sepulchre early on Sunday morning — Matthew and John say only to see the sepulchre, the burial rites having been completed Friday evening — Mark and Luke say to complete the burial rites, by adding ointments and spices to the cerements. But no reader of any of the depositions can fail to notice that the women went *without the slightest expectation or hope of finding Jesus alive*, though

---

*The opinion here arrived at in reference to Jesus having predicted in his lifetime a rising again in three days after his death is the result of balancing conflicting testimony. It is quite probable that Jesus did speak of himself as fulfilling some function or office of the prophet Jonah. Was the similitude that of a temporary death and a resuscitation after three days? So the disciples and evangelists evidently came to believe. A rumor seemed to have got abroad, that he had said if the temple were destroyed he would build it again in three days; and for this saying, as blasphemy, he was actually tried. But we must remember that this testimony broke down, and was discredited even by his enemies. What Jesus did say of himself in connection with Jonah is probably just what Matthew and Luke agree in reporting: —

"This evil generation desire a sign. No sign shall be given it but the sign of Jonas the prophet; for, as Jonas was a sign to the Ninevites, so shall the Son of Man be to this generation; for the Ninevites repented at the preaching of Jonas, but this generation have not repented though a greater than Jonas has preached to them."ᵇ

But the very name of Jonah suggested to the ancient as it always does to the modern mind the adventure of the whale, which effectually swallows up his fame as a prophet and reformer; and when, after the death of Jesus, it came to be believed, that he had risen again on the third day, a new and striking similitude was found between him and Jonah, to whom in wholly other respects he had likened himself.

ᵃ Matt. xxiv., 36.   ᵇ Matt. xii., 41, 42; Luke xi., 30–32.

Sunday was the third day after the crucifixion. Neither his mother, nor Mary Magdalene, nor the sympathetic and affectionate women, who stood afar off at the crucifixion, after Peter, James, and John had fled, *appeared to know anything about a resurrection.* The two disciples speak of his death, and say that they had hoped it was he that would have redeemed Israel, but speak sadly, as if that hope had perished on his cross. Though they had even heard that his body was gone, and that angels, coming in a vision, had said that he was alive, they have evidently no such hope. When Peter and the other apostles are told that the body is not in the grave, and the two disciples are full of excitement in the belief that the gracious and learned scribe whom they met on their journey was Jesus himself, they are not helped toward belief by any the slightest anticipation in their own minds of such a happening as a rising of their Master from the dead.

How is this to be accounted for? Had Jesus on four different occasions taken his followers aside, and with the plainest and most literal speech he ever used told them of his violent death, and of his coming again to life on the third day, and yet are none of them — not Peter, nor John, nor James, nor his own mother — found at the sepulchre, waiting with beating hearts to welcome him back to life? With a hope — and Jesus' plain words ought to have been an assurance to his disciples — that on the third day death would restore their leader and master to them, would the disciples have fled at his arrest, would Peter have denied him? And yet, strangest of all, while the disciples and family of Jesus have most evidently not the slightest expectation of his resurrection, though Jesus had told them plainly of it at least four times, repeating it the evening of his arrest, Matthew represents that the chief priests, who had not been told, who could only have heard of it from the lips of the disciples, seemed to be so aware of the resurrection, or of something that might be told to the credulous as such, that, with the assistance of the procurator's government, they had provided an extraordinary guard to watch over the sepultured body of Jesus![a]

This utter faithlessness of the disciples in the resurrec-

[a] Matt. xxvii., 62-66; xxviii., 4, 13-15.

tion as an event to be expected, the narratives of Mark and Luke, in their attempt to account for it, confirm. The thought evidently occurs to the writers or to some transcriber or editor: If Jesus told beforehand all the particulars of his resurrection, why did his friends, to whom he made the communication, not look for his resurrection? Why did they receive its first intelligence with scornful unbelief?

Mark says, when Jesus told his disciples that he was to be killed and rise the third day, they understood not that saying, and were afraid to ask him. Luke declares: "The disciples understood none of these things, and this saying was hid from them."* How could it be hid, when so plainly told? As Pharisees, they believed already in the resurrection of the dead. They believed their greatest prophets had gone to heaven in their bodily forms. They believed that the bones of the revered Elisha had given life to a dead man. Did they not believe that Jesus by a word had recalled from death the ruler's young daughter in Galilee? Can it be possible, if these men had stood by at Bethany a few days before, when Jesus had illustrated his ideas of the resurrection by calling their friend Lazarus from the tomb, that they could not understand how the man, who had shown such power over death, could not remain subject to it?

If the estimate of the character of Jesus held by mankind were made to depend solely upon the words and actions, which tradition imputes to him after his resurrection, it is easy to perceive that it would not be so high as that now entertained. Fascinated and excited, as we may have been, with the earnest assurances of many apparently sincere people, that under difficult and capricious conditions they could establish between us and certain celebrated persons, who have died, intelligible communications of question and answer, the general impression made upon us by these communications has been of disappointment and indifference. When the spirit of Daniel Webster is presented to us by an impressible medium, it has none of the characteristic eloquence and simple cogency of statement, which characterized the great orator in his lifetime. Franklin comes back to

* Mark ix., 31, 32; Luke ix., 45.

us with none of his practical sagacity; Humboldt, with none of his comprehensive intelligence; and Channing, with none of his elevation and purity of spirit. All the ghosts present themselves to us with their mental peculiarities cancelled and their individuality suppressed, steeped alike in the atmosphere of sentimentality and cant, in which, as in a dreary limbo, they seem to have lived. They assure us that they are happy; but we never can quite understand how they can be, in such a sphere of wearisome vapidity and platitude.

If the intercourse of Jesus with his followers after his death is an unverifiable tradition, then the undignified and unheroic conduct imputed to him, the feeble language, shorn of all the sententious pith and pungency of his known style, the insisting upon trivialities, and the prominence given to dogmas in which he had no credence are easily explicable. The narrators compromise Jesus in exactly the measure that they presume to report his words, and every sensitive reader feels instinctively that the majestic character suffers the least from him who undertakes to tell the least.

Matthew, true to the confidence he has earned by the general simplicity, probability, and orderly sequence of his narrative, only puts into the mouth of Jesus these words already quoted: "Be not afraid: tell my brethren that they go to Galilee, and there shall they see me." In Galilee, he only said: "All power is given me in heaven and in earth. Go ye, therefore, and teach all nations, baptizing them in the name of the Father, of the Son, and of the Holy Ghost; teaching them to observe all things I have commanded you: and, lo, I am with you always to the end of the world."[a]

When Mark's story, as we now have it, obtains publication, the communication of the risen Jesus has quite changed its character, and becomes, first, a chiding of his followers for their hardness of heart in not believing Mary Magdalene, who claimed to have seen him, and the two travellers to Emmaus, who had seen a person who did not look or speak like him, and who could not have been he, if he had truthfully declared that in Galilee his disciples should see him; second, an assurance that belief and

[a] Matt. xxviii., 10, 18-20.

baptism are necessary to salvation, and that real believers should be known by their power to cast out devils, to speak with new tongues, to take up serpents, and drink poison without harm, and to heal the sick by touching them.[a]

Luke elaborates and extends every thing. The reassuring word, "*Be not* afraid," becomes: "Why are ye troubled, and why do thoughts arise in your *hearts?*" and, along with a showing of his wounded hands and feet, an emphatic avowal that what the disciples see is no spirit, but flesh and bones — a veritable corporeal presence. While they believed not for joy, he calls for food, further to assure them that he is no ghost, but has the appetite of a living man. Then follows an exposition of ancient scripture, and the repetition of the arguments he is said to have elaborated before the travellers to Emmaus, with the announcement that repentance and remission of sins are to be preached in his name among all nations, beginning at Jerusalem, and a distinct command that his disciples, instead of going to Galilee to meet him, must tarry at Jerusalem, till they should be endued with power from on high.[b]

Regarding all that is told of Jesus' acts and words after his death as the fruit of the Christian imagination justifying its excursions by a dogmatic purpose, it is legitimate to allude to the Johannic narrative, even if it was originally produced as an avowed fiction. In that, the story of Jesus still expands itself, gathering the accretions the legend has received in more than a century's telling, and growing still more grotesque. Still, the dramatic power of the writer does not desert him. The narrative becomes in his hand as vivid, as picturesque, as personal, as are the conversations at Jacob's well with the Samaritan woman, or the minute details of the talk, that accompanied the restoration to sight of the man born blind. It is the man of constructive genius reciting his vivid poem alongside of the matter-of-fact annalist, and never losing his consciousness of poetic effect. Mary Magdalene touchingly recognizes him as "*Rabboni.*" Jesus looks at her with the familiar, affectionate address of "*Mary.*" Not all the disciples, only hard-hearted Thomas — if, after the gentle

[a] Mark xvi., 15-18. [b] Luke xxiv., 38-49.

reproaches before all the brethren, he is not ashamed to do it — must handle the Master's feet and hands, to learn that he is not a spirit. But Mary Magdalene must not even touch him. It is the requirement of the Johannic mind, that Jesus must give a reason for everything which he does or says; so this reason is given for the prohibition: "Because I have not yet ascended to my Father." Of course, the writer cannot tell why that should be a reason for *not* touching Jesus, and not a reason *for* touching him; nor why, if it were a reason why one disciple should *not touch* him, it was not a reason why the others should *not handle* him. John further says that Jesus breathed upon his disciples to impart to them the Holy Ghost, which Luke declares was not to be given till after a tarrying at Jerusalem after his ascension, and that he not only commissioned his disciples to preach and to baptize the repentant, but to remit or retain at their discretion all the sins of the human race,— an enormous concession of spiritual authority.[a]

The details of the twenty-first chapter — by many good scholars believed to be a palpable corruption of the text of the original writing — containing the marvellous story of the great catch of fish through the divination of Jesus, the gross demand for food, and the eager precedence of Jesus in the passage to the prepared viands, the chaffing of Peter as a piece of after-dinner divertisement, and the gossiping fortune-telling of the fates of Peter and John, are not to be laid to the discredit of a composition on the whole so unique, consistent, and spiritual as the Fourth Gospel.

In courts of law, forgeries so perfect as to deceive the most cunning experts have been exposed by discovering water-line impressions, which indicate that the paper upon which they were written was manufactured after the date they bear. In these imputed communications of Jesus, are there any indications of a similar anachronism? In the three avowedly historic narratives there is one command of the risen Jesus, as to the terms of which there is a tolerable accord among the writers; that is, the command to offer the privileges of the gospel of Jesus to all mankind. Matthew reports it: "Go teach all nations,"

[a] John xx., 11-29.

baptizing them in the three divine names. Mark declares the word to have been: "Go ye into all the world, and preach the gospel to every creature"; and Luke puts it into the form of an acknowledgment of a divine preordination, that repentance and remission of sins should be preached in the name of Jesus among all nations, the first overture being to Jerusalem.*

It was taking a liberty with language not warranted by the fidelity of history, to give this brief message of so revered a person as Jesus even such varied expression as this. But we are forced to recognize the perplexing fact, that the reporters come nearer to agreement on this than on any point. The founder of our faith appeared alive after his death, and spake to his trusted followers. *What did he say?* asks the eager world. We have not been able to agree, say those who report the stupendous event, *except that in terms*, about which the recollection of the witnesses differ, *he did direct that the benefits of his gospel of a kingdom of heaven were to be offered to every human being, to all nations and to every creature.* The words of Jesus, if all were said, were not too many for the memories of ordinary men; but is it to be supposed that the only words, the substance of which all the witnesses were able to remember, should have been within half a dozen years after his death forgotten or disregarded? And yet, if they had been uttered, we are forced to that conclusion.

For it seems from a narrative of the beginnings of Christianity by Luke, one of the gospel writers, that a certain Roman military officer, named Cornelius, who was a devout Jewish proselyte, had heard of Peter preaching the doctrine of the resurrection and repentance, and desired to listen to him. Peter apparently knows nothing of a command of his risen Master to "*Go into all the world, and preach the gospel to every creature.*" Peter does not think it lawful for him, a Jew, to seem to keep company with this devout proselyte of his own faith, or to visit a man who is of another nation. He avows frankly that he would not have presumed to do so, save that a voice of God had come to him in a vivid day vision, and thrice warned him that what God had cleansed was not to be

* Matt. xxviii., 19; Mark xvi., 15; Luke xxiv., 47.

deemed profane. Nor is he reassured that he has not committed an audacious sacrilege, till he further observes that the Gentile converts not only believed his Gospel, but attested the genuineness of ᵃ their faith by exhibition of the gift of tongues.

Peter's authority, immense as it is, will not sanction so grave a departure from the rigid exclusiveness, which prevailed among the body of the disciples. They contended with and denounced him for a heretical practice. To overcome their prejudices he must needs tell them of his vision, and of the gift of tongues shared by Gentile believers.[b] At length, they open their charity to embrace the alien brethren, their scrupulous minds reassured by remembered words of Jesus: "*John indeed baptized you with water, but ye shall be baptized with the Holy Ghost.*"[c] The language was scarcely sufficient to warrant the belief that Jesus had ever cancelled his express declaration: "*Go not into the way of the Gentiles*, and into any city of the Samaritans enter ye not."[d] If Jesus — a divine and immortal being — standing before Peter, had said in his hearing: "*Go ye into all the world, and preach the gospel to every creature*,"[e] would he have waited for a vision to invite him to visit a devout and praying man? and if the Church at Jerusalem, within less than ten years from the resurrection, had a tradition, that Jesus had explicitly commanded his gospel to be preached to every creature in all the world, would it have sought for a precedent in words spoken by Jesus in his lifetime, and only been able to find one in words in fact spoken not by Jesus but by John the Baptist?[f]

According to the same writer, when Paul began to preach, he recognized fully the prior rights of the Jews and their proselytes to the grace of the gospel. "Men and brethren, children of the stock of Abraham, and whosoever among you feareth God, to you is the word of this salvation sent."[g] When the Jews contradicted him and blasphemed, he with great boldness said to them: "It was necessary that the word of God should first have been spoken to you; but seeing ye put it from you, and judge yourselves unworthy of everlasting life, lo, we turn

---

ᵃ Acts x., xi.   ᵇ Acts x., xi.   ᶜ Acts xi., 16.   ᵈ Matt. x., 5.
ᵉ Mark xvi., 15.   ᶠ Matt. iii., 16.   ᵍ Acts xiii., 26.

to the Gentiles."[a] And this bold step he justified on the authority of the Lord, speaking through the lips of the prophet Isaiah.[b]

But the whole Church was disturbed by this innovation of Paul's, and came together to consult about it amid sharp dissensions. In the end, both Peter and James approved of the new departure — Peter appealing to the mode by which his own repugnance to the Gentiles had been overcome by his vision, and by the manifestation among Gentile converts of spiritual gifts, and James finding a prophecy of Amos, that seemed to include the heathen in the mercies of the latter-day restoration.[c]

Now if there had been at this time, when the crucifixion of Jesus was a recent event, a tradition among any of the disciples, that the Lord, whom they expected soon from heaven to establish his kingdom, had appeared alive on his way to Paradise, expressly for the purpose of laying upon his followers the solemn charge of preaching his gospel *among all nations to every creature*, and that his coming again could not take place till this work was done, would Paul or Peter or James have hesitated to invite the willing heathen to the privileges of the great salvation? If they had presumed to give this invitation, would they have justified the act by citing obscure, equivocal, and poetic passages from the Hebrew prophets, when the imperative and implicit commands of him, whose servants they claimed to be, were yet solemnly ringing in their ears?

It is true that Biblical critics have expressed grave misgivings as to the historical accuracy of the narrative of the Acts, particularly of its earlier chapters. But that the expansion of the gospel pale, so as to embrace the faithful and penitent among the heathen, was resisted by the exclusive spirit of the Jewish Christians, and yielded to only after dissensions, that threatened the unity and the very existence of the new Church, is everywhere apparent in that part of the literature of the gospel, about the genuineness of which no questions have ever been raised.

When an honest and irrepressible distrust of the authenticity of those communications imputed to the risen Jesus

---

[a] Acts xiii., 46, 47.   [b] Isa. xlii., 6.   [c] Acts xv., 7-21.

has, by considerations like this, been once fixed in our minds, we find much more to confirm our suspicion.

We cannot understand why Jesus should have come back from the realms of death with an exaggerated estimate of the efficacy of mere baptism. Yet, so Matthew and Mark have represented him.[a] We have the best reason for believing that in his lifetime he thought lightly of that rite, as he did of Sabbath-keeping. He claimed that it was his distinction that he did not baptize, except metaphorically, and with the spirit. John, he said, baptizes with water, but my baptism is one of fire — of persecution and suffering, which my heroic followers shall share.[b] Undoubtedly, the Fourth Gospel indicates a tradition that survived till the period of its composition when it declares that "*Jesus himself baptized not, but his disciples.*" [c]

The doctrine of the Trinity, which never had the sanction of Jesus' living testimony, gets an indorsement from his apparition,— an indication that it belongs to a development of the Christian scheme of mythology, later than those revelations of his Father in heaven, which characterized the earliest preaching of the Galilean reformer.

Of course, there was an admirable opportunity to gain for those doctrines, over which there had been vehement controversies in the Church during the earlier centuries, such sanction as could be derived from words imputed to Jesus — words all the more awful and weighty in that they were uttered after he had come back from death. Accordingly, we find, that Jesus is made to pronounce most emphatically against what was everywhere considered the heretical theory of Paul, that the resurrection was not of the material body, that flesh and blood could not inherit the kingdom of God. "*Handle me, and see ; for a spirit hath not flesh and bones*, as ye see me have," said the risen Jesus. What are we to believe, that Paul deliberately set himself up to gainsay with his metaphysical speculations the plain declarations of his revered Master, or that, when Paul wrote his letter to the Corinthians, there was no generally held tradition among the believers, that Jesus had uttered words like these?

[a] Matt. xxviii., 19; Mark xvi., 16. [b] Matt. xx., 22; Luke xii., 50.
[c] John iv., 2.

There was among the believers a more vital issue than concerned the Trinity, or the process and mode of the resurrection. The three evangelists have told us, that the gospel of Jesus, at least in its earliest proclamation, was an evangel of righteousness — that it related to conduct, not the outward act indeed, but to the whole of conduct, including the motive from which it proceeds; that its great word was: *He that doeth the will of God shall enter the kingdom of heaven.* James, the brother of the Lord, the pillar of the young Church in Jerusalem, had insisted that, by good works, and not by faith, a man is justified.[a]

Paul had argued with great subtilty and warmth that by works of righteousness no man is justified, but by faith only; that the good men had not lived by their virtues, but by their faith; that faith produces good works, and, whether it does or not, its salutary influence cannot be lost.[b] There was much in the later conversations of Jesus himself to give sanction to the view of Paul. Peter had dissembled, siding sometimes with Paul, sometimes with James. He too, like Paul, had had an experience as a missionary among the heathen, that modified somewhat his Galilean orthodoxy.[c] So there were schools among the disciples sharply inculpating each other.

It is curious to see that Matthew, who gives most entirely the primitive gospel of righteousness, or good living, when he undertakes to summarize Jesus' last charge to his disciples in sending them forth among all nations, declares that it was to "*teach them to observe all things whatsoever I have commanded you.*" That is, they were to preach a gospel of the observance of good works — not outward good works indeed, but good acts, done from sincere and pure motives — to do the will of God in hearing and doing the sayings of Jesus, that is the condition of salvation.

Luke, more completely than either of the evangelists, wrote the Pauline Gospel; and, true to his school, he maintains, that what Jesus charged his disciples on taking leave of them was: "*to preach in his name repentance and remission of sin,*" or the doctrine of faith, as the condition of salvation. While Mark, supposed to have

[a] James ii., 24. [b] Rom. iii.-vii.; Gal. ii., 11, 12. [c] Acts x., 28; xi., 3.

written Peter's gospel, declares, or is made to declare, that Jesus distinctly insisted that baptism, as well as faith, is necessary to salvation, and that the genuineness of faith will be attested by miraculous and spiritual gifts. It shocks all ideas of historic fidelity to find each of these schools putting into the mouth of Jesus what it deems the essential article of its creed.

Some basis of fact undoubtedly lay under the rumor of the resurrection. Paul, who was liable through physical weakness to powerful impressions of the imagination,[a] undoubtedly saw an apparition of Jesus.[b] Manifestations to both sight and hearing of the personality of dead and absent individuals to certain peculiarly endowed nervous organizations are too well authenticated in history to be declared impossible. Such manifestations may be purely subjective, and do not necessarily imply the actual presence of real persons. Spite of the constant correction by our waking thoughts of the illusions of sleep, our dreams have in them always the perfect sense of reality.

What Paul saw on his journey to Damascus, some one or more of the disciples might have seen at Jerusalem, within three days after the death of Jesus. It is not necessary to conclude that any other than Mary Magdalene had such a vision, and the reputation of having been possessed with seven devils indicates that she might have been constitutionally the subject of hallucinations. The rest of the story grew with the telling, and, since we see in the literature of the new religion the exact rate of its growth, it is legitimate to trace it back till it had only this basis of hallucination; and we may now eliminate from it its improbable and conflicting adjuncts, till we arrive at its substratum of truth in a feminine vision.

One theory is certain. Few men, that have ever lived, could be so little affected by death as Jesus of Nazareth. His life was a spiritual life: whatever he may himself have anticipated, his real kingdom was not a kingdom of this world; the powers to which he appealed are the permanent forces of this universe. Only sordid and sensual men wholly die. The far-sighted poet, the sagacious moralist, the wise philosopher, the genuine good man, when they die, do not cease to live. You might in

---

[a] II. Cor. xii., 1-5.   [b] Acts xxvi., 13, 14.

no corner of the universe find the identical form, within which their continued individuality is comprehended. When he lived, you might have found Shakspeare by getting introduced to his house in Stratford, and you would have been disappointed when you saw how common he looked, and how trivial was his speech. After his death — now two hundred years — he is more real. No Stratford house contains or limits his enormous personality, and no mind misses the complete effect of his emancipated genius.

Jesus, when he lived, was a peasant of Galilee, laughed at and tortured by the mob of Jerusalem. After he died, his fame began to fill the world. No man ever lived, who has so much affected the development of history. His spirit pervades the world, and has been the companion, the support, and the solace of all suffering and devout souls. There is no sign that his spiritual influence will ever wane.

CHAPTER XIII.

INFLUENCE UPON HISTORIC CHRISTIANITY OF PAUL AND JOHN.

"The fervid imagination of the East constructed Christian theology. It is not difficult to follow the gradual development of the creeds of the Church, and it is certainly most instructive to observe the progressive boldness with which its dogmas were expanded by pious enthusiasm. The New Testament alone represents several stages of dogmatic evolution. Before the first followers of Jesus had passed away, intricate systems of dogma and mysticism began to prevail. His disciples, who had so often misunderstood his teachings during his life, piously distorted them after his death. His simple lessons of meekness and humility were soon forgotten. With lamentable rapidity, the elaborate structure of ecclesiastical Christianity, following stereotyped lines of human superstition, and deeply colored by the Alexandrian philosophy, displaced the simple morality of Jesus."—*Supernatural Religion.*

"No religion is born complete: the interpreter is as necessary to it as the interpreted; the society that realizes the ideal, as the ideal that is to be realized. And the process of interpretation or realization, while it may seem one of formal or even radical change, is yet one of real, though variously conditioned, historical development."—*Contemporary Review.*

IF Jesus were the sole factor in that complex problem which we call Christianity, its solution would be comparatively simple; but such is very far from being the case. Not only have we to discover what were the ideas of Jesus, but also how much that is taught and believed under the authority of his name is the accretion of the centuries since his age. Thought and speculation, making use of the moral and spiritual experience of mankind, have ever busied themselves in the effort to find how best to live, how to meet the demands which an ever-expanding moral sense makes upon our wills, to repress evil ways and evil thoughts, and to bring our whole conduct, external and internal, under the law and order of righteousness. Men of great spiritual insight, enamoured of virtue, devoted to the love of God and the service of mankind, have risen from age to age, who have been able to find fresh and deeper meanings in old formulas of faith, and to burnish with an ideal lustre the rude and imperfect conceptions of sainted prophets and teachers. The Christianity of to-day — it is said to its glory, not to its reproach — is infinitely better, purer, and more adapted to the wants of humanity, than was the Christianity of Jesus, of Paul, and of John; because it has added to their discoveries the spiritual experiences of good men for nearly two thousand years. To indicate and unfold all these accretions, whereby the cultus which names itself after Jesus, and of which he was the prime source and spirit, has expanded to the capacities of civilized and enlightened men, would be to undertake a work that would task the research of a lifetime — to write, what only in these last ages has commanded the attention of scholars, the history of civilization, the evolution of the moral sense.

A more modest and restricted task has been proposed in these chapters; that is, to try from the most authentic traditions to discover who Jesus of Nazareth was, what was his character, and what enterprise he courageously sacrificed his life to promote. But the tradition having been long ago lapsed from the memory of men, or being preserved in faiths and forms of uncertain origin and authority, the world has been forced to study primitive Christianity in its Scriptures, and particularly in those Scriptures, which contain its most authentic traditions and its earliest expositions of doctrine. For us of this age, neither Jesus speaks nor any of his confidential friends and disciples. If we would know aught of him, we are driven to literature, — to the records that survive; and these indicate, not so much what Jesus was in himself, as the impression that he made upon the minds of the Galilean peasants among whom he lived, and of a few magnanimous Jews, who either witnessed or learned, after the event, the circumstances of his public trial and death at Jerusalem. This literature embraces the free-hand and evidently exaggerated narratives called the Synoptic Gospels, and the Acts of the Apostles, the controversial and hortatory Epistles of the apostles and first preachers, and the dogmatic drama called John's.

The first of this series has been the basis of the studies and discussions embraced in these essays. Their structure is simple, their style direct. There is no attempt in them at eloquence, pathos, or philosophy. They are in their genuine substance authentic reports — unhappily, too remotely connected with the events they record to be accurate — of what was believed, not by scholars and persons of responsibility, but by common men, who had come to regard Jesus as a supernatural person, and his career on earth as a new divine revelation. But what is to be remarked in reference to these narratives is, that they are pure reports. The authors neither put their personality nor the weight of their opinions into their writings. Authorship never so slightly magnified itself, nor betrayed its consciousness. It is unknown who wrote these narratives. It is not claimed that they are written by any persons upon any commission to write, or that the names of the writers, even if correctly imputed, give any special weight of authority to their testimony. But their very simplicity is their chief excellence; and they hold up to all ages the picture of Jesus, as it shone in the minds of his enthusiastic adherents, without the shadow of the personality of the writers to eclipse or obscure it.

But Christianity found greater instrumentalities to propagate itself than these humble annalists, or it would never have been heard of outside of Palestine. Two men of greatest genius were embraced among its early converts, who, for the influence they have exerted on the development of the new religion, may rank as peers with Jesus himself. These men were Paul, and the unknown author of the Fourth Gospel. It is necessary, in order to complete the sketch undertaken in these papers, briefly to consider the character and work of each.

As soon as it became probable that the stupendous cataclysm, the foreboding of which both saddened and inspired the last days of Jesus, was not to occur, that the course of history was to go on, mainly in the old order, not seriously disturbed or accelerated by the ideas that he had promulgated, then whoever could obtain a prominent place in the literature of the new epoch was sure of power and growing influence in all time. Jesus was not a writer. His teachings were all oral, and he had been utterly improvident in securing any trustworthy record of them. Besides, they had been largely provisional, and adapted to a transient period of waiting for a revolution, that was to overthrow all the relations of men to each other, and to the world in which they lived. His feeling was that the time is at hand. Those few whom he had warned of the catastrophe, that should make all things new, need not write his warning.* He would come again. Every eye should see him; and the brightness of his appearing would be as the lightning shining from the east to the west.

But the coming again was unwarrantably delayed. Then, different accounts began to obtain currency of what he had said about coming again. The witnesses of his works, the auditors of his words, were beginning, one after the other, to die; and those, who told of him at second-hand, began to mix extravagant and trivial things with the accounts of his works of healing, and to report his solemn counsels with admixtures of their own prepossessions. Full late and inadequately,—perhaps after the death of the twelve apostles,—obscure persons —mere volunteers, like Luke—began to collect the marvellous stories together in private letters to their friends; and they upon whom had fallen the oversight of the faith selected from among the mass of volunteer biographies of Jesus, those which seemed to them the most decent and most edifying, and rejected the rest as heretical. This work had evidently not been done while Paul preached and wrote. So Jesus got into literature, and got himself accredited to posterity, not by his own genius, but by the admiring after-thought of a few unpretentious and unknown men, kindred to the first Galilean disciples, and heritors of their faith.

But Paul, who contributes more than any one mind to the canon of the New Testament scriptures, is a man of superior order. He is something of a scholar, and accomplished, according to the standard in vogue in his time, in both rhetoric and logic. He is thoroughly devout and orthodox, declaring himself to the last a Pharisee of the Pharisees, and holding his faith in Jesus in strict subjection to his belief in Moses, and to a conception of the universe that made the Hebrew Jehovah the Creator and God of the world,—a conception that recognized the peo-

* Rev. x., 4.

ple of his own race as the chosen favorites of heaven, and their historic fortunes and destinies as, in a special sense, a divine providence. Upon these rooted and inveterate prepossessions he had engrafted, by a subtle and arbitrary speculation, the economy of a Messiah, a kingdom of heaven, a general proselytism of the heathen, a restoration of Israel to its favor and primacy. But the glory of the chosen race, enlarged by the privileges of faith, was to be shared with the favored of the Gentiles, and was to be established in the New Jerusalem, whose coming king he hoped in his own lifetime to welcome.

To these grand ideas and hopes he brought a devotion and enthusiasm that persecution only kindled, a tireless zeal, and an intense ambition, that drove him from one end of the Mediterranean to the other, until at his death the religion, which in the lifetime of Jesus was a despised provincialism that could not command a respectful hearing in Jerusalem, had established its churches in the cultivated cities of Greece and Rome, and had the civilized world waiting for its law.

Paul's right to be considered a man of transcendent genius — one of the great intellectual forces that has largely contributed to the culture of mankind — rests upon the fragments that literature has preserved of his letters and speeches. The Epistle to the Romans, believed by Renan to have been a circular letter prepared for all the principal churches he had established, is a summary of the great apostle's theological conceptions, and sets forth his theory of the divine economy and providence. It is dialectic rather than hortatory,— an argument rather than a revelation; but its cogency and eloquence fairly entitle it to an honorable place among the sacred scriptures of the world. It is not the highest order of composition. It can never touch the heart like the old Hebrew Psalms, nor stimulate to noble self-denials and daring efforts of virtue, like the Sermon on the Mount. Controversial writings, of which this is a masterly specimen, rarely survive the transient questions, whose interest calls them forth. But there are comprehended in this great argument so many ideas of universal and permanent import, that it has outlasted the local and national conceptions which gave it its basis and reason of being. It has not failed of appreciation. Read in the larger sense of a competent philosophy, with the copious interlineations with which a subtle and trained criticism, stimulated by superstitious reverence, has enlarged and generalized its naked formulas, it has justly taken its place among the worthy contributions to the metaphysical science of the world.

In his development of the method of the resurrection, in his first letter to his Corinthian converts, Paul displays the powers and resources of his speculative imagination, so that nearly all the hopes of Christendom of a life after death are built upon his assurances and reasonings. Either Jesus had far less creative and suggestive fancy than Paul, or — what is possible — he deemed the speculations in which Paul seemed to delight of little value in themselves, and, on the whole, enervating in their influence on conduct.

In the same letter, in the midst of much practical and sensible advice,— on the whole depreciatory of those spiritual gifts of tongues and of prophecy, which seemed to have marked the beginnings of a new faith,— he breaks out into a glorification of charity, as greater than almsgiving, more estimable than faith, and more to be desired than gifts of tongues, power of miracles, or fidelity of discipleship. This placing of charity, which is human in origin and in object, before all correctness of doctrine, all powers of the intellect, and all manifestations of inspiration, is fairly in the spirit of Jesus, who declared that love to God and man is the whole substance of the law, and was level with the highest insight of the later prophets of the Israelites, who had declared that God loved mercy and justice more than worship and sacrifice. The substitution in the late revision of *love* for *charity* may be a more literal translation of the original word; but it less correctly expresses the thought of Paul. Love belongs in its most concrete sense to the attractions of sex — to those natural instincts that prefer offspring and kindred. Wider than this, the word defines the preferences of friendship; and, highest of all, the devotion, adoration, and awe which under all forms of religion a few exalted spirits have felt toward their ideal of God or of the gods, growing sometimes from a controlling sentiment to an uncontrollable ecstasy. Charity, as Paul eulogizes it, is not quite either of these. He defines it himself in the familiar language, "Charity suffereth long, and is kind; vaunteth not itself, is not puffed up, doth not behave itself unseemly, seeketh not her own, is not easily provoked, thinketh no evil; rejoiceth not in iniquity, but in the truth; beareth all things, believeth all things, hopeth all things."[a] It is a certain geniality of character, that makes a man in the best sense, and to the best persons agreeable,— tolerant of their conduct, tolerant of their opinions — disposed to see the best side of men and things. In fine, for want of a better word, it is the quality of being a gentleman.

This chapter of charity sets forth Paul's ideal of a perfect manhood. It was the standard of excellence, which, with the impediment of a fierce impetuosity of temper, exasperated by the suspicions and accusations of men, participators with him in a sacred enterprise, he tried to attain, and toward which he more and more approximated. It is less descriptive of the vehement and intense spirit of Jesus, of the radical thoroughness of his methods of dealing with the sins of men and of the world, and of the intolerance and exclusiveness with which he regarded all other reformers, and all systems of culture other than his own. In certain features indeed, the contrast between the two pictures is quite striking. Jesus had said, "If you have faith, you might say to this mountain, *be removed to the sea*, and nothing should be impossible for you." Paul declares: "Though I have all faith, so that I could remove mountains, and have not charity, I am nothing." "Strive to enter in at the strait gate," Jesus exhorted. It is better to enter life with the loss of a hand, of an eye, than to be cast whole into hell. But, supplements Paul, though I give my whole body to be burned, and have not charity, I have made a bootless sacrifice. "Sell all that thou hast and give to the poor, and thou shalt have treasure in heaven," was the thorough method of the Master. Nay, interposes the wiser disciple, "*If I bestow all my goods to feed the poor, and have not charity, it profiteth me nothing.*"

There are two fragments, which in the judgment of

[a] I. Cor. xiii., 4-7.

many are better expositions of the genius and heart of Paul, than even these, although their authenticity is less well attested. These are the touching and eloquent words he addressed to his converts at Ephesus, when, on his way to Jerusalem, he became involved in the controversy and accusations, that drew after them his arrest and imprisonment, and ultimately his death,[a] and his sermon at Athens.[b] Both of these were unwritten speeches; and as Luke, or the writer assuming that name, nowhere indicates any literary capacity himself to originate such eloquence or comprehensiveness, there is no circumstance to invalidate the genuineness of these reports, except the difficulty necessarily attending the reproduction in their identical language of the form or substance of the discourse either by a listener of good memory or by the speaker himself. The probability, therefore, inclines quite strongly to the substantial accuracy of the report.

The farewell address at Ephesus is chiefly noteworthy for its pathetic tenderness and eloquence, and for its self-conscious but pardonable assertion of the indomitable courage and devotion of the heroic apostle. The apology spoken in the Areopagus is especially remarkable as a manifestation of the liberality of Paul's culture and the catholicity of his charity, and of that tact, which, as a man of the world, he possessed in an eminent degree, to adapt himself to the modes of thought of races and men alien to his own lineage and training. Our admiration is enhanced by the picturesque grandeur of the situation,— the new religion with all the future before it, represented by its most eloquent and cultivated convert, confronting, amid the most splendid monuments of antiquity, the old religion and the old philosophy, represented by the men who had given them their best exposition and examplars. This is Paul at his best. It must be confessed that he discloses qualities both of mind and character less admirable. He is contentious and passionate. His resentments are sudden, and not well under his control; and he launches them hotly and hastily against men, whom he loved and esteemed. He himself is the first to feel their recoil, and his apologies are profuse and sincere.[c] He is self-conscious even to boasting, and, while believing

[a] Acts xx., 17-38. [b] Acts xvi., 22-31. [c] II. C r. ii., 1-5; vii., 8; Gal. i., ii.

that he is depreciating himself, always leaves the impression that he is fully aware of the value of his services and the power of his intellect and presence. If he seems ever to humble himself, it is almost with a piteous appeal to others to vindicate and exalt him. He ever magnifies his office, and insists, against all questionings, upon the prestige of his apostleship.[a]

He liked to recall, what seemed to him the highest distinction, his training in the schools of Jerusalem.[b] Notwithstanding the bigotry and nationality of its teaching, "*the feet of Gamaliel*" was, in the first century, the best school in which an enthusiastic devotee of wisdom like Paul could study the problems of philosophy and religion. He is daring in his flights of speculative philosophy, and, more ambitiously than Jesus himself, confronts and endeavors to solve the whole mystery of God and the creation. We catch in his illustrations oftener than elsewhere intimations of his ideas about physical laws, and find that they by no means agree — as none of the surmises of his wisest contemporaries agreed — with the results arrived at by the observations and experiments of science. We are perplexed at his metaphysics, and find that his philosophy of the faculties and processes of the human mind is as foreign to the best teachings of our times as is his philosophy of nature. Even where his great strength lay, in his dialectics, we are unable to surrender our judgments to his arguments, because sometimes we see no axiom or accredited fact at the bottom of the enormous assumption of his premises, and a *non sequitur* where he attempts to overwhelm us with the assurance of his conclusions.[c] Often too, where the premise is tenable, and the conclusion legitimate, the intermediate ratiocination is either fallacious or sophistical.[d]

Comprehensive as was the survey which he took of mind and matter, of things visible and things invisible, of the past and the future — and it was much wider than any of his fellow-laborers in the gospel were capable of — it was still the comprehensiveness of a Jew fettered by the prejudices of his race and sect; and, doubtless, when he tried to convert the philosophers of the Areopagus

[a] II. Cor. x., xi.   [b] Acts xxii , 3.   [c] Rom. ii., 12; vii., 7-9; v., 13.   [d] Gal. iii., iv., v.

by turning upon them a quotation from one of "their own poets," he felt for Socrates and Plato and the sublimest speculations and purest precepts of the Stoics and Epicureans all the contempt and pity which might be expected to fill the breast of a Pharisee, skilled in the traditions of his school, and imbued with the ideas of Hillel and the most virtuous of the scribes. This Jewish cultus was the basis of all his thought. The vision of Jesus, which he scorned to authenticate—as he might have done—by communion with the surviving kinsmen and intimate friends of the Master who had frequented the mountains and lake-sides of Galilee, did not so much eclipse and supplant his hereditary Pharisaism, as adapt itself to it by a certain complicated order and succession, which the Jewish Christians of his time disowned, and which the converts from alien religions could never quite comprehend.[a] When an overpowering vision, shining with a brightness that darkened noonday, seemed to announce in his astonished ears: "*I am Jesus whom thou persecutest*," these must have been the reflections of that vehement, fierce, but tender and deeply repentant heart of Paul: Jesus in heaven! A vision, not of the Jehovah of our fathers nor one of his angels, but of this Galilean malefactor whom I have hated and maligned, now exalted to companionship with God! Paul discloses to us how this vision modified all his theologic ideas. Jehovah does not disappear, nor Moses, nor the law, nor the old economy of a chosen race; but the purpose of Jehovah, cherished from the first, to exalt his people, and through them to subdue and conciliate all the nations of men, takes a new impulse and a new direction, and uses a new and more divine instrumentality. For three years, in solitude, away from the haunts of men, aloof from the fishermen, who are repeating to admiring listeners the parables and the stories of the exorcization of devils, Paul studies the scheme of divine providence and world-ordering, until he can find in it a place for the newly revealed divine being, who has spoken to him from heaven.[b] At length, he perceives the order and symmetry of the whole scheme of salvation, and how Jesus was foretold by the prophets, and was the

[a] Rev. ii., iii.; II. Pet. iii., 16; I. Cor. iii., 12, 13. [b] Gal. i., 17-20.

great antetype, toward whom the mysteries of the ancient rites and sacrifices pointed,—the providential man, who comprehended in himself the whole purpose of God, and accomplished the fulfilment of all the promises to his nation; and how, besides, he was the seed of Abraham, in whom all the nations of the earth should be blessed. So Christianity decked itself in a Hebrew costume, and went out among the perplexed people of the heathen world clothed with the ideas and giving its sanction to the mythology of the older religion, which was foremost in persecuting and opposing it. Its literary rather than its traditional form was that in which it survived, and its literary form was mainly shaped by the constructive genius of Paul.

Paul had unbounded confidence in his dialectics. What he had worked out as a syllogism for himself he believed he could make every mind accept. His whole method of propagandism was argumentation. He believed that, with space to deploy his premises, his firstly and secondly, he could force the most obdurate and sceptical reasoner to his conclusions. Accordingly, he is nothing, if not logical. On the largest and smallest occasion, he is always formidable and ponderous with the weight of his polemic armor. He seeks to conquer faith, not as Jesus did, by direct appeals to the moral sense, intuitive of right and truth, but by mining under the outworks of the understanding. He is the father of all the schoolmen, the great prototype of dogmatism; and his influence and his school have been in the world for eighteen centuries, often drowning with the clamor of disputation the voice of him, that never gave reason or logical basis for primal truths, but spoke nevertheless with authority, and not as the scribes.[a]

It is not surprising that Paul should have so completely ignored the doctrines and the personality of his Master, when it is considered that he knew Jesus only as a vision, and that he drew all his rhetorical illustrations from the Hebrew Scriptures, working out the details of the new order of things, under what he called the dispensation of grace, in distinction from the dispensation of law, that had preceded it, and from manifestations of the divine character and purposes, in the, to him, historical inci-

[a] Matt. vii., 28, 29.

dents in the fortunes of the patriarchs, heroes, kings, and prophets of Israel. For, though we find much concerning Adam and Abraham, Sarah and Rachel, Moses and Elijah, in his hortatory writings, addressed, in part at least, to intelligent Greeks and Romans, in whose mind such mythical and national names must have been a contemptible reminiscence, we find very few allusions to the sayings of Jesus or to the incidents of his life.

Paul is too great a man to leave any work of his incomplete. It was the necessity of his mind that he should give the evangel he preached a balanced and symmetrical form. So, while he seems to have ignored the ethical system of Jesus, he gives a complete ethical system of his own. If it be asked, what did Paul do to entitle him to be ranked as the equal and collaborator of Jesus in originating what is called Christianity, the answer must be; first, he constructed its theology; second, he modified the rigor of the ethical precepts of Jesus, so as to adapt them to the exigencies of this world—to some kind of relation to the existing and developing political society.

Paul would have resented with eloquent indignation any insinuation that he lacked deference to the name and authority of the Master, whom he almost deified. He placed Jesus in so exalted a sphere above all men, all angels, all principalities and powers,[*] that it was an easy and natural transition for the Church of a later age to arrive at the dogma of his equality and co-essentiality with God. But it is apparent now that, in the very measure that Paul exalted Jesus to heaven, he banished him from the world, and left it the more open to his own constructive and innovating control. With a Christ whose only memory was an apparitional interview on the road to Damascus, whose activity was shut out from the world by the beatific glories of the upper skies, he could work harmoniously. But, when we remember the aloofness which the great apostle ever maintained toward the confidential companions and kinsmen of Jesus—the men who kept the tradition of his words and works—the conjecture intrudes upon us, that he would have found the world too narrow for himself and the prophet of Nazareth,

[*] Phil. ii., 9-11; Eph. i., 20, 21; Col. i., 15-20.

and that the latter would have encountered in him a more intractable temper than Peter's, whose headstrong impetuosity alternated, as Paul's never did, with a childlike and utter contrition and submission.[a]

There is related in the Acts of the Apostles an incident of adventure befalling Paul on the travels he undertook by land and sea to propagate the faith to which he had devoted himself, which fitly illustrates both his character and work.[b] He was nearing Malta on his voyage to Rome under arrest, taking an appeal to the emperor. There had been three days of tempest, and in the supreme hour of peril a panic ensued. The soldiers, the active men, whose aid was necessary to save the ship and passengers, are about to desert in the boats. Both the maritime and the military commanders appear to have lost their authority. Just in this emergency, a hero appears from an unexpected quarter. This scholar, this fanatical preacher, this tiresome theological disputant, a prisoner too, exhibits powers of command and of self-control, that make him the sovereign of the occasion. His assurance that safety is possible allays the fears of the terrified voyagers; and, through his advice, order and discipline are restored. The passengers, worn with sleeplessness and fatigue, refresh themselves with food, and with instinctive recognition of his superiority place themselves under his control. Though the ship is wrecked, every life is saved.

Paul found the young Church in a like peril. Its founder and leader had perished on the cross. The special enterprise, upon which he had staked all, had thus far palpably miscarried. His latest words had been of his own speedy coming, and of catastrophe and doom for the world. The coming of the Son of Man, he said, shall be like the coming of the flood, sweeping away the unforeboding children of men in the midst of their eating and drinking, marrying and giving in marriage. Your Lord, he had said, will come in an hour when ye think not, and will cut down the careless, drunken, and contentious servants, and consign them to a place of weeping and gnashing of teeth.[c] The cruel spectacle of Jesus' murder had enhanced the panic. What wonder that the common people were ready to believe the world itself

[a] Gal. ii., 5.   [b] Acts xxvii.   [c] Matt. xxiv., 37-39, 44, 48-51.

could not outlive so great a crime ; and, when Peter began to exhort the multitude to save themselves from the doom that awaited that "*untoward generation,*" they were cut to the heart, and cried out, "*Men and brethren, what shall we do ?*"[a]

Paul shared the alarm, and lived in the expectation that the catastrophe, which was to overwhelm the world, would befall in his own lifetime.[b] But Paul was heroic, and never lost his presence of mind. Since the departure of Jesus, the world had endured for twenty years. It may still endure twenty years. First of all, he said, let us have discipline, and perhaps it were as well to take some refreshments. "*Set thy house in order, for thou shalt surely die*" was the prophetic warning to an ancient Jewish king. Paul was of those orderly souls who would set his house in order, and, as far as he could, set the world in order, and have it lie down covered with decency to await the conflagration, in which it was soon to perish.

But, first of all, the tangled thread of providence must be unravelled. The world is the creation of God, and men are his creatures. What are God's plans ? What fate has he appointed for men ? To what consummation is this mystery of human life and world-history tending? To fit Jesus, his death, his resurrection, into the divine plan, to find a place for him in a scheme of providence that included Adam, Abraham, and Moses, that completed and fulfilled the law, and left a superfluous grace for the faithful among the Gentiles,— this was the intellectual task, toward which the very nature of Paul's mind impelled him.

Accordingly, we find in Paul's writings, not indeed the connected scheme of salvation that fettered the Scottish and New England mind of the last century, before humanitarianism and science had assaulted it, broken its sequences, and marred its integrity, but links of all that concatenation of dogmas,— the masterpiece of scholastic ratiocination,— at which, in their turn, Augustine, Anselm, Calvin, and Jonathan Edwards have wrought. These links may be briefly indicated in these terms : the eternity and self-existence of God ; the eternal relationship to him of a Son who was born into the world as

[a] Acts ii., 37, 40.   [b] I. Thess. iv., 15; I. Cor. xv., 51.

the man Jesus; the creation of the world, with the heaven overarching it, for the use of man and the glory of God; and the creation in innocence of a primal pair, whose speedy sin involved all their posterity, the whole race of men, in guilt, condemnation, and death; the separation from the general wicked of the descendants of Abraham, and the attempt — on the whole, unsuccessful — to rescue them by the teachings of a divinely enacted law, and by a system of sacrifices in no value of themselves, but efficacious, in that they represented a sacrifice of the Son of God, to be afterward made for the sins of all that believe on him; the coming into the world in the fulness of time of this Son of God, to grow up a servant and a man of sorrow, who, being killed, ostensibly by the wickedness and malignity of men, was in reality self-delivered to death by the eternal decrees of God to be a propitiation for the sins, first of the chosen race, then of all men who believe, whose faith is to be accepted in lieu of obedience to the divine law — an obedience which, from the innate wickedness of mankind, had been in reality from the first impossible.

This comprehensive and elaborate system might have been learned at the feet of Gamaliel. Such ambitious speculations suited admirably the philosophic genius of Pharisaism. We only know that Paul could not have learned it from Jesus: first, because he emphatically disclaims all knowledge of the philosophic, ethical, or theological ideas of Jesus, through the only source from which they could have been learned, the twelve witnesses;[a] and, second, because there is not a trace of this system in the authentic tradition of the doctrines of Jesus. Indeed, the surprise is that, considering how far Paul's zeal had impregnated the new faith with such ideas, we find so few traces of them in the preserved discourses of Jesus, memorized for us and committed to writing, after Paul's time, by believers, some of whom are believed to have been Paul's disciples.

The innovations introduced by Paul in the ethical system of Jesus are quite obvious to all who read his preserved writings. As has been seen, the attitude of Jesus toward the state was, on the whole, hostile. He seems

[a] Gal. i., 11-22.

to have hesitated whether he could so far recognize the legality of the Roman power as to pay taxes to it. "Of whom do the rulers of the earth," he asked his friends, "exact tribute, of their own children or of strangers?" They said: "Of strangers." Then are children exempt from tribute, he concluded.[a] But to resist physical power was contrary to his idea, that all exactions were to be submitted to. While asserting his right, he would not insist upon it. He that had commanded that the blow of the *private* ruffian was to be submitted to without retaliation, and the depredation of the *private* spoiler was to be borne without reprisal, could not resent the claim of the *public* tax-gatherer, backed, as it was, by the power of imprisonment. So he paid his tax under protest, and said: "If you have recognized Cæsar's sovereignty by using Cæsar's coin, you may use it also in paying for the government you have recognized."[b] But, to his view, the rulers of this world did not belong to God's order. They were the wolves.[c] Cæsar's department is one thing, God's is another. Paul taught quite otherwise: that the powers that be are ordained of God, to which every soul must be subject, and that to resist them was to resist the ordinance of God, and to incur damnation.[d]

Jesus invited men away from worldly care and labor, and told them that all anxiety for subsistence was faithless and useless.[e] Paul, on the other hand, was himself thrifty and industrious, that he might not be a charge upon his converts, and might have the means of joining them in gifts to the saints. He exhorted men to industry and diligence in business, and declared that the idle and improvident should be left to starvation.[f]

Jesus excluded rich men from the kingdom of heaven, and imposed as the first condition of discipleship the abandonment of all property.[g] Paul admitted rich believers to his churches, and only required that they be liberal in charities out of the good gifts God had given them to enjoy.[h]

Jesus, as he thought it a slight effort of virtue to abstain from murder, because even causeless anger toward

---

[a] Matt. xvii., 24-27. [b] Matt. xxii., 20, 21. [c] Matt. x., 16, 18. [d] Rom. xiii., 1, 2.
[e] Matt. vi., 25-31. [f] Rom. xii., 11; II. Thess. iii., 7-12.
[g] Matt xix., 21, 23, 24. [h] I. Tim. vi., 17, 18.

a brother was of itself the germ of murder, had said: "If ye love them that love you, what merit is there in it? The publicans do as much as that."[a] Paul, recognizing the fact that many men find it easy to forgive their enemies, and are torpid and patient under insults, who, in daily intercourse with their families and friends, do not always abstain from petty annoyances and affronts, nor preserve themselves from that peevishness or censoriousness, that so much embitters social life, added this noble precept: "Be kindly affectioned one to another, in honor preferring one another."[b] Paul did not pretend to accept Jesus' principle of non-resistance to wanton evil, but substituted for the precept to resist not evil the more practical one: "*If it be possible*, as much as lieth in you, live peaceably with all men."[c] Like Jesus, Paul exhorts to patience in tribulation, constancy in prayer, the retaliation of blessing for cursing, sympathy for those in sorrow, humility of spirit, and the overcoming of enmity by persistent and profuse well-doing,[d] though his language seems neither quoted from, nor suggested by Jesus; and, where he seeks to strengthen his authority by a quotation, it is not the Sermon on the Mount, but the older Scripture, that he cites.

Jesus was out of relation to all the political authorities, the social customs, the merely conventional and civic obligations of his time. Paul was politic, and in a certain sense conventional. He respected human laws as divine ordinances. He vindicated his rights and privileges as a Roman citizen, and his rank and birth as a respectable and orthodox Pharisee of the lineage of Benjamin. He treated with uniform courtesy and deference the High Priest, the viceroy of Cæsar, the military commanders, and the men and women, whose learning and social position gained his respect. His comprehensive direction was: "Render to all men their dues, whether of tribute, custom, fear, or honor."[e] It was to have been expected that a man carefully and religiously reared, like Paul, should represent in his conduct and in his principles the highest virtue of his age. The cultus of the Jewish people, under the tuition of the Pharisees, was one

[a] Matt. v., 46.   [b] Rom. xii., 10.   [c] Rom. xii., 18.
[d] Rom. xii., 6–21.   [e] Rom. xiii., 7.

that would favorably compare with the moral standard of the most advanced people of modern times.

The New Testament traditions introduce us to an age and people generally devout, chaste, and humane; and Jesus and Paul, themselves men of marked spiritual strength, might be expected to be in advance of the standard of virtue of their time. Accordingly, we find in Paul's writings, as in the preserved words of Jesus, a quite comprehensive summary of all that constitutes upright and blameless conduct in our own age. Adultery and all kindred disorders, murder, private vengeance, enmities, hatreds, and retaliations are forbidden, just dealing is insisted upon, extortion is censured, and piety and active charity are enjoined.

Paul, like his Master, inherited an exemption from those carnal instincts, the excesses of which have eclipsed the spiritual vision of man, and dragged him down from the angelic heights which he was approaching by his intellect and genius to the gross animalism whence he may have sprung. But Paul had too much sagacity and knowledge of human nature to hold up absolute celibacy as the ideal state, which all who would perfect themselves must attain.[a] The only warning he gave against marriage, from which he found it easy to abstain, was based upon the cares — incompatible with the high duties of discipleship — it would entail, and upon the incongruousness of a relation, which the new order of the regenerate world would so soon interrupt.[b] For those who were already wedded, he prescribed fidelity and constancy; and there were certain types of character, not deemed wholly incompatible with a certain qualified form of godliness, for whom he not only permitted, but enjoined marriage. But all that Paul has written indicates that he had the same contempt for woman in her maternal office that monks, Shakers, and other conventional celibates have ever had; that he failed to see a pure affection in the marriage relation, and looked upon the tie, out of which the domestic attachments grow, as an unworthy compromise with instincts which the wisest and best men deny and suppress.[c] Out of this contempt for woman, and the gross regard of her as the servant and convenience of man, sprang the idea,

[a] Matt. xix., 12.   [b] I. Cor. vii.   [c] I. Cor. vii.

to which he gave frequent expression and emphasis, that in the order of society woman was as far below man in worth and attributes as man is below the Deity. This conception, which he everywhere enforced with a feeling alien to all modern courtesy and chivalry, and which indicates that he was little touched by the tender deference and confidence he himself inspired in the hearts of many "honorable women," whose characters, conversation, and faith so belied his hard theories, prompted several unreasonable and absurd prescriptions and prohibitions. The gifts of inspiration seem to have fallen upon women as upon men; and, in charity and hospitality, women were specially distinguished. Paul, in his letter to the Corinthians, seems at first to have yielded to the power of the spirit to express itself through the voice of woman, but it was with ill grace; and he will have his prophetess veiled, and wearing some badge of her servitude to man.[a] But, later in his letter, he declares that it is not permissible for a woman to speak in the assembly, and in his Epistle to Timothy that he "*will not suffer a woman to teach or usurp authority over men, but that she must be silent.*"[b]

Thus, we see that Paul, besides constructing the creed and faith of the Church, undertook its edification and instruction, as the minister and apostle indeed of Jesus, but by no means confining himself to Jesus' doctrines, or, when agreeing with him in his precepts, repeating them upon his authority. As the letters of Paul were read as circulars in all the churches, while the works and words of Jesus were repeated from lip to ear as a fading and already uncertain and disputed tradition, it is easy to understand why Paul, and not Jesus, became the supreme authority in fixing both the creed and practice of the Christian Church.

By his eloquence, zeal, and imperious temper, and above all by a large-minded enterprise, which left the other missionaries of Christianity mainly to the narrow theatre of Palestine, Syria, and Asia Minor, Paul was able to maintain the prestige of his authority and doctrines during his lifetime. It is doubtful if Peter and the pillars of the Church at Jerusalem would have had the courage to push

[a] I. Cor. xi., 5. [b] I. Cor. xiv., 34; I. Tim. ii., 12.

this propagandism outside of the pale of Judaism, if they had not been startled and provoked by the boldness and success of Paul's proselytism in the Greek and Roman provinces. It would even seem, as if they followed Paul, more to counteract him and correct his heresies, than with an assured confidence, that all the world was to be allowed to share the promises of the gospel. But even Paul's preaching, as has been seen, was a glorification of Moses and of the Jewish policy. He maintained a relationship with the see of Jerusalem, whose primacy was necessarily recognized; and for all the traditions of Jesus, of his character, his teaching, his works, his death, and his resurrection, he was obliged to give all inquisitive neophytes references to the witnesses grouped about Peter and John. While he was preaching and founding churches in Greece, with large designs of pushing his operations to Italy and Spain, emissaries from the twelve apostles seduced his converts in Galatia from the freedom that he claimed to be in Christ into bondage to the Jewish law; and in a letter to his friend Timothy he complained pathetically, that all Asia had fallen away from his faith.[a]

After his death, the apostasy widened; and the early Church, so far as it was controlled by personal influence and the voice of the preacher, inclined more to the creed and domination of Peter, than to the counsels and theories of Paul. But Paul was able by his learning fully to indemnify himself for this temporary eclipse of influence. His place in literature had been assured; and as the oral traditions grew doubtful and obscure, and the reverend apostles were succeeded by narrow-minded, illiterate, and even irreverent priests, whose characters lent no sanction to their teachings, the influence of Paul became again superior; and finally, when Protestantism arose, appealing to interpretation and to the authority of the Christian literature, as against the distorted traditions and borrowed forms preserved in the Church, the Pauline plan of salvation became the creed of reformed Christianity, and has remained its creed till our own time.

If Christianity, undoubtedly inspired by the doctrines and enthusiasm of Jesus, had had no other literary expression than that given to it in the writings of Paul, it

[a] II. Tim. i., 15.

would have been a barren dogma, or at the best a dogma supplemented by an ethical code, having a standard of virtue not materially higher than that which the Jewish and the Greek cultus had, before the Christian era, established among the most civilized races. Those rules of conduct found in the traditions of Jesus, which his own immediate followers did not at once modify or set aside, had been largely anticipated by the teachings of the wisest of the heathen philosophers, and of the most eminent of the Jewish scribes. Then, as now, the world did not live according to the rules of its best teachers; and it is probable that popular virtue, like popular intelligence, was far less diffused among the community of men in the first, than it is in the nineteenth century.

Something else was wanting; some better reminiscence of Jesus than Paul's highest conception of him, not so much to teach as to inspire. The exigency was met by the advent of a man of dramatic genius, of mystic insight, capable of emotion and affection, who could not contemplate such a character as that of Jesus from a merely critical and dogmatic point of view. This was the unknown author of the Fourth Gospel. When and where he lived and wrote is not known, though it seems to be tolerably well ascertained, that he was of an age later than Paul and the twelve apostles. He might have been one of the Greek proselytes of the Alexandrian school, who had found in Jewish monotheism and the Hebrew conception of a pure God — author of the universe, and patron of righteousness — so much in accord with the teachings and implications of Plato. In his Gospel, he always speaks of the Israelites and of their long established national customs just as a native would not, and he cannot mention the Passover without explaining that it was a *"feast of the Jews"*;[a] while Paul, borrowing the Passover as an illustration, in one of his exhortations to his Greek converts of Corinth, does not find it necessary to make a similar explanation.[b] The evangelist avoids mentioning, and sometimes makes palpable mistakes in naming, places where incidents in the life of Jesus happened, just as a foreigner might do, who was groping among localities of which he had no personal knowledge.[c]

[a] John ii., 13; vi., 4.   [b] I. Cor. v., 7.
[c] John i., 28, 29, 35, 38, 43; iii., 23; iv., 5, 45, 54; vi., 3, 15.

It does not seem necessary to suppose that, in writing what is now known as the Fourth Gospel, this poet and mystic of the new religion had a historic purpose. His work is an exposition of Christian doctrine. But he did not wish to unfold the Christian ideas in a controversial or didactic form. That task had been already sufficiently accomplished by Paul. Traces of the Pauline influence are everywhere apparent in the production. Indeed, the Johannic Gospel would not have been possible, until Paul had systematized the Christian faith, and fixed the status of Jesus in the divine economy of the universe. It required a great man to take a comprehensive view of the work and character of Jesus, and none of his personal associates seem to have been capable of this. After Paul had done it, the task of the writer of the Fourth Gospel became comparatively easy.

The first certain recognition of the Fourth Gospel as an extant work seems to have been toward the close of the second century, though a portion of the critics have zealously contended for a recognition some fifty years earlier. It was early imputed to John, the son of Zebedee; and tradition asserted that he wrote it at Ephesus in his extreme old age. This tradition of authorship seems to rest upon an indirect claim in the final chapter of the book itself — now generally believed not to have formed a part of the original work [a] — upon the evident similarity of style between it and the Epistles of the canon, believed also to have been written by the same John; and upon the statement in the Apocalypse, that the writer of the vision was, at the time of its manifestation, John, "a companion in tribulation, and in the kingdom and suffering of Jesus in the isle of Patmos,"[b] a small island off Ephesus, in the Ægean Sea.

It is credible that the John, characterized in "Acts" as "an unlearned and ignorant man,"[c] who seems to have always allowed Peter to be spokesman, when they together propagated the Gospel, might have written or dictated this unique production, called in our Scriptures "The Revelation." Its lurid pictures, the monotonous horror of its plagues and torments well accord with that truculent spirit, which imprecated fires from

[a] John xxi., 24.   [b] Rev. i., 9.   [c] Acts iv., 13.

heaven upon the unsympathizing Samaritans;[a] while the theologic hate, fertile in coarse maledictions that breathe through its earlier chapters,— directed, as many competent critics have maintained, against our heroic Paul,— shows that the seer could never learn, notwithstanding the caution of his Master, not to forbid those who were casting out devils in other fellowship than his own.[b] But it is simply incredible that the person, who had thus attested the inveterate traits of his character, could also have written: "*He that dwelleth in love dwelleth in God, for God is love;*"[c] *The life of God is the light of man, and this light illumines every man that is born,*[d] — sentiments which in spirituality and catholicity are kindred, if not superior, to any the same writer has been able to impute to Jesus himself.

There are reasons for allowing the tradition to stand, that imputes to Ephesus the origin of the Fourth Gospel. It was his beloved Ephesians who had fallen on Paul's neck and kissed him, sorrowing most of all that they should see his face no more.[e] He had preached among them two years; and they, if any among the people of Asia, had entered into the large liberty of his faith.[f] It was his beloved Ephesians whom Paul addressed in his Epistle as *the faithful in Jesus Christ, no more strangers and foreigners, but fellow-citizens with the saints, and of the household of God, built upon the foundation of the apostles and prophets, and Jesus Christ the corner-stone, into a habitation of God through the Spirit.** Now, it is just this conception of Jesus and of his system, which this Epistle of Paul foreshadows, that the author of the Fourth Gospel afterward embodied. He sets forth a habitation of God, in which the apostles take precedence of the prophets as foundations, and of which Jesus, not Moses, is the corner-stone. During Paul's lifetime such views of the exaltation of Jesus may have been suspected as heretical by the *Pillar Apostles* at Jerusalem; and, after his death, the general defection of Asia seems to have reached even Ephesus — the triumphant tone of the *Revelator* indicat-

---

[a] Luke ix., 54.   [b] Luke ix., 49.   [c] I. John iv., 16.
[d] Prologue to Fourth Gospel.   [e] Acts xx., 38.   [f] Acts xviii., 10.

* The Pauline authorship of this Epistle has been most seriously questioned. It lessens the authority of this characterization, if, instead of the work of the master, it is the tribute of one of his admiring disciples; but, coming from the latter source, there is no reason to question its truthfulness.

ing how completely the seven churches had become entangled again in the yoke of bondage. But years after the death of Paul, after the intolerant seer of Patmos had himself passed away, after the idea of the *logos*, derived from the Greek philosophy, had made more comprehensive the metaphysical concepts of Christianity, and after the controversies, with which the New Testament canon is rife, had been composed, at least among the body of believers, the Johannic Gospel was demanded, and it came forth. Was it the fruit, or was it the cause of the reconciliation?

In it, the high estimate of Jesus, to which we have seen Paul constantly rising, is not abated. It is advanced. He, who was to Paul exalted above all principalities and powers, and who contained in himself the fulness of Deity, shone on the Johannic page as the glory of the only begotten of God, full of grace and truth. The calling of Israel is not denied; salvation is of the Jews, but it is only their pre-emption. The rejection of the Jews will not defeat the beneficence of God. The mission of Jesus is no longer to save the lost sheep of the house of Israel, but to take away the sin of the world. The command of Jesus is no longer: Whatever observances the scribes and Pharisees, sitting in Moses' seat, prescribe, those perform and do. All observances of the law — the older national rite of circumcision itself included — are become too trivial to mention. Faith has become the end of the law for righteousness to the believer in Jesus. But, on the other hand, the scribes and Pharisees are not denounced as hypocrites doomed to the damnation of hell; nor is the standard of righteousness in the kingdom of heaven placed above the capacities of their virtue. As for the prestige of Jerusalem in the new order of the Spirit it has entirely passed away in a cultus, that neither at Jerusalem nor on Mount Gerizim worships the Father in spirit and in truth.

The eschatology of the Fourth Gospel is quite unlike that disclosed in the Synoptics and in the Pauline letters. It differs still more from that, which the true John of Patmos seemed of all the primitive disciples most to have emphasized. The second coming of Jesus was a hope too universal, a tenet too fundamental in the Church, to be denied at once; but its whole character is changed. It is no longer the Son of Man coming in the clouds, with all the holy angels, in the lifetime of his own generation — every eye to see his presence gleaming as the lightning from the east to the west, and all the tribes of the earth to mourn because of him. The coming again is asseverated, but with uncertain, even equivocal meaning. The Spirit will come in my place, Jesus is made to say; and again: *I am myself the Spirit.*[a] Instead of a scenic showing to the world, he will manifest himself to his own, and not to the world; making his abode in the hearts of those who love him.[b] In the last chapter the writer does not contradict the current saying, that Jesus had promised that John, already dead, should tarry till his coming; but he virtually says: The only coming of Jesus is the advent of the Spirit, and that John lived to see.[c] In the body of the work, what that coming really imports is left quite uncertain. The writer seems to be holding on to a fading faith. Sometimes, as in his first Epistle, when he talks about having confidence and not being ashamed before him at his coming, of seeing him as he is, and being like him when he shall appear,[d] and in his Gospel when he puts into Jesus' mouth this explicit assurance: *"I will see you again, and your heart shall rejoice,"*[e] he seems to be declaring that the emphatic predictions of the Master must be fulfilled. Again, when he talks of the chosen of Jesus being indefinitely in the world, but kept from the evil of it by the dwelling in them of the spirit of the Father, which is the true manifestation of Jesus, we seem to see an irrational expectation succumbing to a philosophy of the permanent order of the cosmos, or yielding to a natural impatience at a long-deferred hope. This uncertain tenure of and preparation to surrender a prime article of the primitive Christian creed points to a period later than the lifetime of Paul, later than the later period of the most modern of the Synoptic Gospels.

After the revered presence of the kinsmen and personal friends of Jesus had disappeared from the world, the Pauline ideas, which their influence had rigorously

[a] John xiv., 16-18.   [b] John xiv., 22-24.   [c] John xxi., 20-24.
[d] 1. John ii., 28; iii., 2.   [e] John xvi., 22.

repressed throughout Asia, would naturally revive. Paul's brilliant career was itself a fascinating memory among his converts and their children ; and his letters survived, and were everywhere read in the assemblies,— the only literature of the new era. In that very epoch, when the Pauline theology, supported by the memory of his eloquence and the affection of his converts, and appealing to the powerful persuasion of his letters, was contending against the older creed, with — after the death of the twelve — only a tradition to uphold it, the Synoptic Gospels seem to have been produced. Their contradictions are attributable to the circumstance, that they were called out as testimonies in the pending controversies and disputes of the believers. It was a perfectly legitimate literary enterprise, according to the known standard of intellectual integrity at the time, for a writer to give an exposition of the doctrines of Jesus in the form of a fictitious sketch of his life. Indeed, the primitive Gospels with many of their kind, that have perished, were not at all unlike our modern *Lives of Jesus*, that have abounded in the present century,— mere points of view, theories of his character and office, worked out with more or less of detail. And we note how Paul himself came to characterize his own summing up the functions of Jesus, as "*my gospel*," and to speak of other views deemed by him erroneous, as "*another gospel.*"[a]

The early appreciation of the Fourth Gospel was doubtless due to the effect it had in composing controversies and giving unity to the faith of the Church, and this effect could not have been very much lessened by the knowledge of its fictitious character. Converts had come into the Church from the schools of Greece. With what literature shall they be edified ? Tradition had preserved the " Sermon on the Mount " and the parables of Jesus, but they were mixed up with predictions of the end of the world ; and the whole career of the great teacher in Galilee was compromised with the exorcization of devils. Wise words, and not signs and portents, attracted the Greek mind. When the sublime enthusiasm of Jesus, outlined by the eloquence and philosophy of Paul, had been illuminated by the poetic and mystic imagination of

[a] Rom. ii , 16; Gal. i., 5-8, 11 ; II. Cor. xi., 4.

John, then first the new Christianity became conscious of an ideal worthy of its most cultivated converts, and of a record fit for a place among the older scriptures of mankind.

The Greek convert,— Greek in culture, if not in birth,— who wrote the Johannic Gospel, evidently deferred to the talents, learning, and metaphysics of Paul; and his work shows where he follows and where he supplements his forerunner. Like Paul, he has a scheme of the divine economy, in which Jesus, whose pre-existence is assumed, has a most eminent place. Paul had believed that, in order to give Jesus, who was the first-born of the creation, pre-eminence, God had committed to him the creation of all things visible and invisible;[a] and although this pre-eminence was so great, that Jesus might without arrogance claim equality with God, it was all derived, and, in the end, would be restored to the Supreme, who would be all in all.[b] Thus, to the complete divinity of Jesus, there were in Paul's mind two important limitations. Though the agent of the whole creation, he was himself created; and his honors and supremacy were to be held temporarily, and were, in the end, to be surrendered to God.[c] We can see in his own letters how Paul had been borne along in the tendencies of his age from a lower to this high conception; and the larger conception of John — by which name we may, without misleading, designate the author of the Fourth Gospel — fairly indicates the later age in which he wrote. For the latter will not consent to consider Jesus a created being, nor indicate any period, however remote, when his authority and supremacy shall be surrendered. He has adopted from the school of the Neo-Platonists and from the Hebrew writer of the Proverbs the idea, that, as the process of the creation was by a *fiat* or word, Jesus was the word or wisdom of God, and thus too closely allied with the divine essence ever to have been created by it, and too essential to its perfection ever to be absorbed by it. He says: In the beginning,— that is, from the first,— the word was with God, and was God. Being essential life, it only could give life to men and all creatures. In men, the divine life was light, and that light had ever been in the world, though not recognized; for the

[a] Col. i., 16.   [b] Phil. ii., 6.   [c] I. Cor. xv., 28.

world, though made by the word, which was the life of men and the light of their spiritual intelligence, *knew him not*. Then this word, thus unrecognized and inefficient, because ignored and rejected of men, was incarnated in Jesus, in whom men beheld the glory of the only begotten of God, who would give to all that believed on his name power to become children of God, being born into that relation directly by the will of God.[a] This august being, with God from the beginning, the agent of all creation, the light of the world, the life in itself, needs no conception, no birth, no infancy, no growing in wisdom and in stature, as the Galilean legend had declared. He appears in the world,

"like the herald Mercury,
New-lighted on a heaven-kissing hill."

John the Baptist, wisest of the prophets, alone of men recognizes him as the Son of God, who baptizes with the Holy Ghost.[b] He recognizes his disciples before they come to him; and they welcome him as Son of God and king of Israel, and he announces that they shall see heaven opened and angels descending to wait upon him.[c]

Like Paul, John is well disposed toward the Pharisees,— perceives perhaps that they are a sect kindred to the Stoics. Early in his story, he endeavors to bespeak a favorable consideration for that class, who had so seriously provoked the resentment of Jesus, by personating them in a character introduced as Nicodemus, "*a man of the Pharisees, a ruler of the Jews.*" Nicodemus is timid and cautious, as a man high in office and in the esteem of fellow-citizens is apt to be; but he is measurably enlightened, candid, inquisitive of truth, and readily receptive of the mystic ideas which Jesus is made to communicate to him. The remonstrances which Jesus encountered from the scribes and Pharisees, elders and chief priests, and which drew down upon them the most offensive of the parables, John puts into the mouth of "*the Jews.*" In the conversation with the Samaritan woman, Jesus is made to affirm a most narrow view of the divine providence; for he tells her: The Samaritans worship they know not what, for salvation comes from the Jews. The writer does not

[a] John i., 1-14.   [b] John i., 33, 34.   [c] John i., 50, 51.

seem to be aware of Jesus' special antipathy to the Pharisees, nor of his standard of morality that left them outside of the kingdom of heaven. The whole Church had evidently, before the time of this writer, accepted the politic ideas of Paul, that the Pharisees, who in their monotheism, their exceptional morality, their belief in a divine revelation, in the soul and its immortality, had a faith in common with the new religion, were to be conciliated rather than antagonized. For it is perceived that the writer had so far compromised his original conviction that salvation was of the Jews, as to admit farther on in his work that there were other sheep, not of this fold, which the Good Shepherd must also bring with him.[a]

In vividness of description, in the dramatic naturalness of his dialogues, in the consistent and orderly unfolding of his great character, the author of the Fourth Gospel may justly demand a very high rank among the writers of the Christian Scriptures. The marvellous story-telling genius of the East, whose earliest productions were the idyls of the garden of Eden, of the migrations of the patriarchs, and of the checkered fortunes of Joseph — surviving even in the tales of the *Arabian Nights* — has yielded nothing to surpass the wedding at Cana, the colloquy at Jacob's well, and the raising of Lazarus from the dead.

But, throughout the whole work, the art is less complete. It is impossible to disenchant the solemn monologue of the Johannic Jesus of the illusion of inspiration. Strung in accord with the human heart, it has rung in sympathy with it for seventeen centuries. If it could be so disenchanted, it would be confessed that the human infirmity betrays itself everywhere in the imperfect creation. The dramatic talent does not equal the descriptive aptness, nor fulfil the didactic purpose of the writer. For though the attempt is made to represent the career of Jesus dramatically, to make John the Baptist, the leading disciples, Nicodemus, and the Jews speak each in his or their own character, they all, as well as Jesus himself, express themselves in the peculiar and unmistakable dialect of the author of the First Epistle attributed to John, and fall inevitably into his mannerisms and platitudes. Let us

---

[a] John x., 16.

examine this style more closely, and note its peculiarities.

An affirmation, sometimes an inconsequential one, is repeated. Among very many instances let these be noted in which the superfluous statement is indicated by *italics.* " In the beginning was the word, and the word was with God, and the word was God. *The same was in the beginning with God.*" [a] "All things were made by him, *and without him was not any thing made that was made.*" [b] "The same came *for a witness,* to bear witness of the light. He was not the light, *but was sent to bear witness of the light.* And he confessed, *and denied not, but confessed:* I am not the Christ." [c] " He that cometh from above is above all ; he that is of the earth is earthly, and speaketh of the earth ; *he that cometh from heaven is above all.*" [d] " The hour is coming, and now is, when the dead shall hear the voice of the Son of God, and they that hear shall live. *The hour is coming when all that are in the graves shall hear his voice, and shall come forth.*" [e] "This is the Father's will that sent me, that of all which he has given me I should lose nothing, but should raise it up at the last day ; *and this is the will of him that sent me,* that every one that seeth the Son and believeth on him, may have everlasting life ; *and I will raise him up at the last day.*" [f] " Except ye eat the flesh of the Son of Man and drink his blood, ye have no life in you. *Whoso eateth my flesh and drinketh my blood hath eternal life. He that eateth me shall live by me. This is the bread that came down from heaven; he that eateth this bread shall live forever.*" [g] "I am the good shepherd ; the good shepherd giveth his life for the sheep. *I am the good shepherd, and I lay down my life for the sheep.*" [h] " The Father who sent me, he gave me a commandment what I should say, *and what I should speak : whatsoever therefore I speak, I speak even as the Father said unto me.*" [i] " That which was from the beginning, which we have heard, which we have seen *with our eyes, which we have looked upon,* which we have handled of the word of life (for the life was manifested, *and we have seen it,* and bear witness, *and show unto you* that eternal life, which was with the

[a] John i., 1, 2. [b] John 1., 3, 7. [c] John i., 20. [d] John iii., 31.
[e] John v., 25-29. [f] John vi., 39, 40. [g] John vi., 53, 54, 58.
[h] John x., 11, 14, 15. [i] John xii., 49, 50.

Father, and was manifested unto us); that *which we have seen and heard* declare we unto you." [a] Here, the assertion that the word of life, the meaning of the phrase being set forth in the first chapter of the Johannic Gospel, was seen by us, is made four times, besides the equivalent assertion, thrice repeated, that *it was manifested to us, and that we have heard it*,—all in the compass of a single sentence. How ill-fitting a vehicle of any really elevated sentiment is such clumsy verbiage! "I write no new commandment, but *the old commandment, which ye had from the beginning. The old commandment is the word which ye have heard from the beginning.*" [b] "He that hateth his brother is in darkness even until now. *But he that hateth his brother is in darkness, and knoweth not whither he goeth, because that darkness has blinded his eyes.*" [c] "I write unto you fathers, because ye have known him that is from the beginning; I write unto you young men, because ye have overcome the wicked one. *I have written unto you fathers, because ye have known him that is from the beginning; I have written unto you young men*, because ye are strong, and the word of God abideth in you, *and ye have overcome the wicked one.*" [d]

Feeble and undisciplined minds are apt to seek to strengthen their asseverations by superfluous affirmations. Such expletives as, "*That is so*," "*There is no mistake about it*," and other even more reprehensible phrases, betray a depraved taste, but are never used by good writers, except with the obvious purpose of portraying a vulgar character. The Johannic writer has not been able to avoid literary faults even of this character. Thus, having affirmed in his prologue that all things were made by the Divine Word, he compromises the grand idea by this feeble iteration, "*and without him was not any thing made that was made.*" [e] He makes his hero interject into the delightful disclosures of mansions in the Father's house, prepared for believers, this impertinence, which we almost recognize as a coarse phrase of the street: "*If it were not so, I would have told you.*" [f]

There are the strongest reasons for believing that this was not the style of Jesus. It is incompatible with the

[a] I. John i., 1-3.   [b] I. John ii., 7.   [c] I. John ii., 10, 11.
[d] I. John ii., 13, 14.   [e] John i., 3.   [f] John xiv., 2.

dignity of his historic character. It is farthest removed from that terse, epigrammatic, and sententious speech, which none of the artless narrators of his life could have invented. Lastly, we happen to know that such weak tautology, such efforts to eke out an incomplete conception by the duplication and triplication of a meagre outfit of epithets and figures, would have been specially offensive to him; since he had classed simplicity and directness of speech among the cardinal virtues, and had declared that whatever is superadded to a naked affirmation or negation "*cometh of evil.*" [a]

It is another peculiarity of the author's mind to offer irrelevant and inconsequential reasons for propositions which seem to stand upon observation, intuition, argument, or authority. These instances will be remembered: "He [the Father] will show him [the Son] greater works than these." Why? "*That ye may marvel.*" [b] "He hath given him power to execute judgment also, *because he is the Son of Man.*" [c] Why is judgment a function of the Son of Man? Though in the same conversation, from which these words are reported, Jesus says: "I receive not honor from man," [d] he is made to give as a reason why the Father has committed all judgment to him,—"*that all men should honor the Son even as they honor the Father.*"[e] "Greater works than these [miracles] shall ye do, *because I go to my Father.*"[f] Why should his power to confer upon his disciples miraculous gifts be greater away from them than with them? When the Son of Man shall come (the second time), he will, he says, reprove the world of sin, because they disbelieved in him; but why of judgment, because the prince of this world is judged? Or how reprove the world of righteousness as well as of sin; and, if the[g] world is to be reproved of righteousness, why so, because Jesus goes to his Father and his disciples see him no more?

Another peculiarity of the Johannic style is the frequent recurrence in it of mixed metaphors. We have seen how, in the philosophic prologue, the life becomes light, and the light a man, and how both the word and the light are successively credited with the work of crea-

---

[a] Matt. v., 37. [b] John v., 20. [c] John v., 27. [d] John v., 41.
[e] John v., 23. [f] John xiv., 12. [g] John xvi., 9-11.

tion. It is not unlikely that the author so far deferred to the traditional reputation of Jesus as an allegorist, as to have attempted his manner in the so-called parable of the Good Shepherd. It is certainly far from being rhetorically a successful attempt. The writer is too intent upon his didactic purpose, too much involved in his own dominant and mystic modes of thought. He cannot surrender himself to the illusions of his own fancy, or rather the illusions of a feeble fancy have none of the vitality and naturalness which characterize the creations of Jesus. It is no parable at all. The Good Shepherd, instead of maintaining his rôle, degenerates into the door by which the sheep enter the fold, reversing the conduct in "Midsummer-Night's Dream" of the wall that insists upon taking a part in the dialogue. In developing the dogma of the sole doctrinal authority of Jesus, the whole story, without plot or catastrophe, sobers into a sermon. In the parable of the vine and the branches, less was attempted, a mere simile; and, accordingly, the chapter is worked out with less pretension and more skill.

A rudeness of style sometimes degenerates into rudeness of thought. Thrice, in the first Johannic Epistle, the historic gentleness of the evangelist is compromised by the direct imputation, that certain persons who pretend to love God *are liars.*[a] In the Gospel, this infelicity of speech is put into the mouth of Jesus himself: "*If I should say I know him not, I should be a liar like unto you,*"—the Jews to whom he was speaking.[b]

Sometimes, contradictions break the consistency of the revelations. Thus, Jesus is made to say: "If I bear witness of myself, my witness is not true";[c] and not long afterwards to declare: "Though I bear record of myself, my record is true";[d] and again to return to his former declaration: "If I honor myself, my honor is nothing."[e] So, too, he says: "For the Father judgeth no man, but hath committed all judgment to the Son," though he had already announced: "I judge no man,"[f] and afterwards had repeated that statement, with the explanation that he "came not into the world to judge the world, but to save the world."[g]

---

[a] I. John ii., 4, 22; iv., 20.   [b] John viii., 55.   [c] John v., 31.   [d] John viii., 14.
[e] John viii., 54.   [f] John viii., 15.   [g] John xii., 47.

Besides these specific blemishes, we find in this composition and in the scriptures of the same author, a paucity of ideas, with a wealth of sentiment,—much to excite and soothe devout feeling, little to interest and employ the critical understanding. A mystic, delicate, and exalted sentiment, couched in epigrammatic terseness and simplicity, as it sometimes is, is too often repeated and explained until its beauty is marred and its impressive force abated. The writer is always hopelessly illogical and diffuse; and, though some of his descriptions are so pathetic that the very trivialities of detail intensify their naturalness, and though some of his ideas are so grand that repetition deepens their significance, it cannot be asserted that, in the long controversies which Jesus is represented to have held with the Jews, his own part is so well sustained, as to merit what must be taken as a self-encomium,— "*Never man spake like this man.*"[a] In the more confidential discourses to his friends attributed to Jesus, we find a very few primal ideas, made the foundation of a mystic philosophy and theology entertained by the author, strung upon a thread of prolix talk, full of unintelligible transitions and perplexing contradictions, in no logical connection or recognizable order of thought.

Did Jesus utter these discourses of the Fourth Gospel, and did his disciple and intimate friend become so possessed with admiration for his Master as to adopt his peculiar philosophy, together with his mannerisms of style and methods of ratiocination and expression? To assert this is to account in one way for the similarity in style, philosophy, and modes of thought betwixt the discourses of Jesus in the Johannic Gospel and the writer's own language in the prologue and in the Epistles. Who, then, was the Jesus of the parables, of the Sermon on the Mount, and of the terse and natural conversations of the Synoptics? To impute to Matthew or to Peter or to Luke the striking apothegms, pregnant with meaning, of the first three Gospels, is to find in those men a grade of genius, which their simple narratives indicate to be quite beyond even their comprehension. No obscure disciple could have first uttered the "beatitudes," or such germs of transcendent virtue as "*Love your enemies,*"

[a] John vii., 46.

"*Do good to the evil and unthankful,*" "*He that doeth the will of God is my brother, and sister, and mother.*"

On the other hand, if it be asked, Could an obscure disciple originate such thoughts as these: "God is a spirit, and they that worship him must worship him in spirit and in truth"; "Except a man be born again, he cannot enter the kingdom of God," we must remember that the disciple was only obscure because he imputed to another the work that would have made him more famous than Paul. One who had read Paul's letters, who lived after the sublime ethics of Jesus had been informed by the theology of that great apostle, and harmonized with the philosophic speculations of Plato, might have uttered every sentiment imputed to Jesus in the Johannic Gospel. Indeed, what the writer could himself do in the enunciation of pure and profound sentiments he has disclosed in writings avowedly his own. In his prologue, he declares: "*There is a light that lighteth every man that cometh into the world*"; and in his Epistle: "*God is love, and he that dwelleth in love dwelleth in God, and God in him.*" The writer has not been able to rise to a higher grade of thinking than this, in any revelation he has imputed to Jesus. Having found,— as it were, *in situ*,— in the mind of this mystic poet, specimen fragments like these of his intellectual vein, why should not all the ore he exhibits — so unmistakably homogeneous — be accredited to the same quarry?

Of this we can be assured, that the Sermon on the Mount and the parables did not emanate from the same mind that originated the illustrations of the vine and branches, and of the Good Shepherd, and the discourse beginning: "*Let not your heart be troubled.*" For, if these last are in the style of Jesus, some other hand has improved the Sermon on the Mount. It is derogatory to the memory of Jesus to suspect this. The probability is much greater that the mind that produced the Epistles and the Johannic prologue produced also the Johannic discourses. It is impossible to trace any of the predominant intellectual traits of Jesus disclosed in his conversations in the Synoptic Gospels in the dogmatic disputant of the Fourth Gospel, who is incapable of imaginative creation, the arrangement of whose thoughts is as incoherent as the conclusions of his arguments are inconsequential, and whose meagre types and illustrations so inadequately serve the completeness of his expression, that he seems compelled to repeat them, and enfeebles them in the repetition.

Jesus' style is allegoric. He illustrates his ideas by pleasant apologues. John's style is typical. Certain terms of sense stand for him as representative of certain spiritual states; and, like Swedenborg's types, they shift so suddenly and so arbitrarily, that it is not easy to follow their metamorphoses. Thus, the word and the spirit become impersonations and powers of creation and generation. Life abstracts itself from its accredited sense, as the condition of living organisms, and becomes one of the original uncreated essences. But it will not keep its own estate, but is changed into light in the soul of man, and, shining into the opposing darkness of the world, becomes a person, the person who has created the world, already made by the word. So that, unless there have been two creations and two creators, light and the word are one, and were made flesh in Jesus, whose office it is to give to all that receive and believe in him the power to become sons of God, and to inherit eternal life. But no will of man determines who shall receive the incarnated light and word which give light. Only God's will designates such, and gives them to Jesus to become the recipients of his grace and salvation. In this scheme, faith is everything. But faith is by no means a matter of will or choosing on the part of the believer, since no man can come to Jesus but by the Father's drawing; and no man can even say that Christ has come in the flesh but by the power of God in him. The world is the kingdom of evil and of darkness. History is nothing, nature nothing. There is no history but the history of the advent of Jesus to the world, to save those that believe. All that is of consequence in the divine dealings with one people are the intimations God had given them in prophecies, in a typical worship, and in the providences of their national history of the great salvation; and, that salvation having come, those things that signified it have become as shadows.

This vision of all history and all providence through the

single medium of a spell-bound faith is the inspiration of the Epistles ascribed to John, and the controlling influence, under which the prologue to the Fourth Gospel was written. The controversy of the new religion with the conservative Judaism, out of which it sprung, the record of which is left to us in the canonical Epistles and in fragments of the preaching of the apostles and first missionaries in the book of the "Acts," John puts into the mouth of Jesus himself. Day after day, he is represented as standing in the temple at Jerusalem and pleading with the Jewish hierarchy — the official heads of the established Church — for recognition as the counterpart and fulfilment of their Biblical revelation.

Like the other evangelists, however, this one in no way offends us by extraordinary pretensions. He does not represent that the discourses which he imputes to Jesus were particularly successful or even intelligible as efforts of persuasive oratory. On the contrary, he declares that for a considerable time his own brothers were quite averse to the claims of Jesus to be a prophet;[a] and that the effect of one of his most spiritual and profound discourses was to offend a large part of his adherents, so that they abandoned his faith.[b] He discloses that many of Jesus' explanations, which seem quite comprehensible to us, were not understood by the twelve, who repeated them and pressed him to make them more intelligible. Finally, he declares that, near the end, Jesus himself, speaking of these discourses, admitted that they were proverbs which had not been well understood, and promised that, *in that day*,— that is, of his second coming,— he "will no longer speak to his disciples in parables, but will show them plainly of the Father."[c]

But what must be said of the marvellous success of this production, and of the eager interest and satisfaction with which its revelations have ever been cherished by all devout minds in the Christian Church? This success cannot be denied. Toward the close of the second century, the Gospel of John began to be noticed by writers of the time; and its publication could not long have antedated that period. It was too striking and powerful a work to remain long unnoticed; and it soon took its fore-

[a] John vii., 5.   [b] John v., 44–66.   [c] John xvi., 25.

most place, as the authentic and complete life of Jesus. Among scholars and the better informed Christians, its fictitious character was doubtless at first well understood; but there were many circumstances which tended to establish for it an historic reputation.

The incidents of the life of Jesus up to his appearance at Jerusalem were exceedingly obscure, and much disputed about among his adherents. The wholesale miracle-working in Galilee attributed to him, as has been already shown, did not seem to have been credited by Paul, nor by the chief apostles. The account of these miracles, that ultimately became written, seemed to have been kept in abeyance till after the death of the companions and confidential friends of Jesus. With Paul, perhaps with his compatriots, Peter and James, the essential thing was Jesus come in the flesh as the Messiah, crucified by the malice of men, glorified through resurrection as the Son of God, and as the saviour of the world through faith. Dwelling on this grand scheme of his life as the exposition of the wisdom and power of God unto salvation, the incidents of his history and the traits of his human character became insignificant,— a theme for the idle gossip of the curious and the subtle fancies of the poetic imagination to employ themselves upon at will.

The removal of the discussion over Jesus, who he was, where he was born, where he lived, and what he had done as a man, to a different public from that, that had seen and heard him,— that is, to the communities of Asia Minor, Greece, Egypt, Syria, and Rome,— favored the introduction of marvellous legends on the one hand, and fanciful speculations on the other hand, into the traditions of his career. This process was all the easier, in that, during the first century, great political changes were going on, which finally obliterated the Jewish state, destroyed its monuments, its temples, and its wealth, interrupted the culture of its people, and arrested the production of its literature; so that, when enthusiastic disciples went about Asia and Europe, telling of stupendous things, that had been lately happening in Galilee and Jerusalem, there was no body of intelligent people left in the scene of the wonders to confirm or to contradict the report. If now wholly exceptional events should be alleged to have lately happened in Belgium, in Scotland, or in Ohio, reference would be had at once to the intelligent people of the vicinage, to know if such events had occurred. The legends of primitive Christianity obtained credence and currency, in part, because political revolutions had rendered a like reference impossible. There must have been a period, not long after the crucifixion, when Christendom knew less of the life of Jesus, than it knows now after eighteen centuries. In that very conjuncture, a little too late for any story to be either verified or contradicted, ages too early for any historical responsibility to be felt, or historical method or accuracy to be possible, this Fourth Gospel appeared, and the world received, cherished, and gave it credence. This is not surprising. The dramatic Henry the Eighth of Shakspeare is a more real person to the English race, than the little-known, much-disputed-about, historic Henry. Very vivid, very authentic must that history be, which will be able to efface the heroic glamour which Shakspeare's genius has thrown around the reign of nine English kings. Critical research and the sober judgment of scholars have labored in vain to obliterate in the gallery of fame the beautiful myths of William Wallace and of William Tell. In many respects, the fictitious Jesus of John is a more interesting character than the real Jesus.

The place that the Johannic biographer obtained among his collaborators at first he has retained to the present age. The preacher, the theological writer of to-day, draws his picture of the person of Jesus from the delineations of John; and, when he undertakes to set forth what Jesus taught, he will take two passages from the Johannic idyl, where he will take one from the synoptic narratives. Even those preachers and theologians whose critical judgment has succumbed to the arguments which recent scholarship has accumulated against the historic character of the Fourth Gospel continue thus to support its authority.

Why, in spite of such faults of rhetorical execution, and the fact that the dramatic design of the writer is so palpably unfulfilled in the achievement of his work, has his composition gained this high estimation? It is because, in this sketch, defective as it is in a literary point of view, he has given to faith what an eloquent and devout preacher happily characterizes as "*the heart of Christ*"; because, like a man of genius, he has been able to conceive of an ideal person, not bounded by the limitations or marred by the defects, that robbed the historic personage of that supreme consideration and that complete success which belong to nothing human. All large human lives are capable of such treatment. As the portrait of the great artist is a truer delineation of a human countenance in its best capacities of expression, than is the photograph of the mechanic, who has caught the face in one of its aspects of pettiness or weakness, so the ideal life is sometimes truer than the real one.

The Jesus of the Galilean tradition was born in poverty. He grew in stature and in wisdom. He said wise words and did great works, but he was despised, derided, rejected. Few believed on him; and, in an attempt to win the chief city of his nation to his cause, he fell under suspicion, was arrested, tried, condemned, and summarily executed by the government,— the populace being incensed against him, and his own disciples taking oaths that they had never known him.

John's Jesus alights on the earth as one sent from heaven. A dove, which is the Holy Ghost, descends upon him. The greatest of the prophets and all good men recognize him as Son of God and King of men. He dies indeed; but he dies because he lays down his life, that he may take it again, and, coming back glorified, may give eternal life in heaven to those who have adhered to him. John's Jesus talks much of himself, of his estate before he lived in the world, of the glory that awaits him in the after-life, when he shall return to the Father, who had sent him, and when he will munificently share that glory with his humble followers. How assuring and consoling must have been such revelations of the heavenly state, and of its compensations for all the toils, sufferings, mockeries, and persecutions of the primitive disciples! How precious in all ages to the believer's heart must have been those soothing words he is believed to have uttered: "Let not your heart be troubled. Ye believe in God; believe also in me. In my Father's house are many mansions. I go to prepare a place for you." In all the Synoptics, we cannot find anything more pathetic than these words attributed to Jesus by Luke: "*Fear not, little flock; for it is your Father's good pleasure to give you the kingdom.*"[a] The Fourth Gospel is full of such tender assurances. It is not eloquent. It is not rhetorically artistic. It abounds in feeble platitudes. It is monotonous with a phraseology, that were it less venerable would become offensive. There is no wealth of illustration in its meagre symbols, which so frequently change into other symbols in defiance of all correct rules. But it is confidential, familiar, and affectionate. We are ashamed to repeat even to ourselves, much more to write, the incoherent murmurings of our deepest sentiments,— the endearing epithets we bestow on those we love. A scanty vocabulary, the same old homely epithets, pregnant with the heart's deepest experiences, serve well enough for vehicles of the ever new affection, of which the critical understanding takes no cognizance.

John's contribution to the new scriptures was like the Psalmist's contribution to the older scriptures. Until the tender sentiment to and from God found expression in the temple songs, what was the Jehovah of the law and the prophets but a stern judge or a jealous partisan? Until John found and touched the heart of Jesus, what was he to the world but an impractical moralist, or a wrathful king taking vengeance on his enemies?[b]

John's work was a more complete idealization of Jesus than Paul's. Paul would not go to the companions and kinsmen of his deified Master to learn about his life and sayings. The Jesus after the flesh, of whom they could tell him, might eclipse the grand vision of him which he believed the Holy Ghost had revealed to him. But Paul was too much of a scholastic and metaphysician to be capable of a really poetic idealization. That was the great work of John.

John's free handling of the life of Jesus, though it was bold, was for Christianity its greatest service. It was the beginning of a treatment which made the new faith capable of universality and permanence. His life, says the fervent evangelist, is the light of men! Behold the Lamb of God, that taketh away the sin of the world! We

[a] Luke xii., 32. [b] Luke xix., 27.

beheld his glory as of the only begotten Son of God, full of grace and truth! John was the forerunner and inspirer of all devout souls,—souls that have worn out enfeebled bodies in the sublime ecstasies of their love and devotion. Of his order are Fénelon and Madame Guyon, Tauler and Baxter.

If we had only the matter-of-fact annalists of Galilee to tell us of Jesus, Christianity, instead of being an inspiring and vital faith that puts man in relation with an ideal and invisible world, would have been a superstitious Millerism, ever distraught with the coming end of the world, and employing the interval of waiting for a tediously delayed catastrophe in vain efforts to make practical ethical rules repugnant alike to natural instincts and social laws.

If we had only the metaphysical conceptions of Jesus, to which Paul attained,—a Jesus playing his rigid rôle in a prescribed and fatal plan of salvation, leaning backward into the remote ages to clasp the hand of Moses, and to adjust himself to the caprices and jealousies of Israel's national God,—the fruition would have been a dogmatic Protestantism, quoting and splitting texts, the dreary predestinarianism of Jonathan Edwards, the jejune moralities and casuistries of the Jansenists. In the freedom of the spirit, out of which all serious doubt and all the breadth of modern thinking upon matters pertaining to God and the soul have grown, John has put to flight all the quoters, the literalists, the dogmatists, and the formalists, and initiated a handling of the facts of the origin and development of the Christian ideas, under which they are able to adapt themselves to the widening intelligence and expanding civilization of the world.

If Jesus may be likened to the fountain of that new element in civilization called Christianity,—the mountain lake into which it poured as rain from heaven, and welled up from springs deep in the earth,—Paul and John are the twin rivers flowing side by side like the Tigris and Euphrates, that have poured the accumulating volume of its waters to the sea. Paul has interpreted the ideas of Jesus in terms of thought, John in terms of feeling. The constructive genius of Paul has taken the wild cry,—the fire-alarm of John the Baptist in the wilderness: "*Repent, for the kingdom of heaven is at hand,*" echoed after him through the cities of Galilee by Jesus and his twelve messengers,— the whole burden of the primitive gospel,— and elaborated from it a complicated plan of salvation, a metaphysical scheme that harmonizes in a certain way the aspects of history, and gives a certain consistency to our conceptions of God and his providence. The ethical rules of Jesus, which his auditors could not receive, which seemed to them like the cutting off a right foot, the plucking out a right eye, John has made a delight, by kindling a devout enthusiasm, and by inspiring the ardor of a human love, responsive to the divine love. But what these highly endowed minds have achieved in the development of the Christian *cultus* is less valuable for us in the results than in the methods. They best learn of Paul and John, who, not accepting as finalities their inferences and conclusions, in their free spirit and with their broad sense enlarge and interpret the narrow facts. The value and permanence of Christianity as a religion is that it is capable of this idealization. It can only endure, if its creed does not cramp and imprison its spirit.

But as the Sadducees quoted the authority of Moses to deny the hope of immortality, as the Pharisees adhered to a worship of sacrifices against Jesus' idea of a worship of righteousness, as the Ebionite Christians and the "*pillar apostles*" set their narrow salvation of the Jews against Paul's calling of the Gentiles, so do the literalists of the Papal and Protestant schools to-day protest against all new interpretations of old formulas of faith made necessary both by the expanded intelligence and deeper piety of the age. Paul called the Church the body of Christ.[a] But a body lives only by the death of the living cells of which it is built. Not the gross mass alone, but the most delicate and vital organs — lungs, heart, brain, and nervous fluids — are involved in the decay and reconstruction. When the organism has lost the power to vitalize and assimilate to its structure and functions new aliments, it has ceased to be alive. So the Church,— Christianity as represented in the minds and spirit of its votaries,— when it can no longer assimilate into its faith the most comprehensive thoughts and deepest insight of capacious

---

[a] I. Cor. xii., 20, 27; Eph. iii., 6; iv., 12; Col. i., 18.

minds, or into its charity and modes of activity the most daring and revolutionary projects of reform, has ceased not only to lead, but to live.

Primitive Christianity, when interrogated by the inquisitive spirit of man, had an answer uttered from the lips of Jesus and of Paul, which seemed to solve, both on its practical and philosophic side, the riddle of human existence. At least, the answer served well enough for a petty and passing world lying in terrible proximity to the dim vaults of the underworld beneath it, and the near throne of an anthropomorphic God just above it. It serves less well for an infinitely expanded cosmos and a Supreme Ordainer, whose large plans and vast purposes, hinted at in a more closely studied nature, have become past finding out. But the inquisitive spirit of man, like the ancient Sphinx, still propounds its question; and Christianity must answer it, or confess that it is not sent of God, and so die out of the reverence and obedience of the world. What is this overture of Religion to divide with Science the domain of knowledge but a confession that the prevalent form of religion cannot answer the Sphinx's question. Neither Religion nor Science can surrender the universality of empire without abdicating. If the facts of religion are realities, if they are not falsehoods or illusions, they are elements of knowledge, and capable of statement in the terms of the science to which they belong. On the other hand, Science cannot claim exemption from the dominion of the moral sense; and all knowledge is nugatory that does not show men how best to live. Religion cannot be divorced from Science; nor will any decree, however judicial or authoritative, ever compel them to live apart, girding at and recriminating each other.

But it is on the side of morality, as well as on the side of intelligence, that the failure of help and guidance has been exhibited. When Jesus was on the mountain-top, receiving the homage of the great shades of the older prophets, there was brought to his disciples in the valley below, a man possessed with a devil, and they could not cast him out.[a] So, now, when the disciples are occupied in paying divine honors to the author of their faith, offering him the adoration of prophets, poets,

[a] Luke ix., 40.

and sages, there are brought to them the devils of war, of poverty, of intemperance, of lust, and of slavery, and the disciples cannot cast them out. Heretics devise the temperance pledge, and prick the conscience of legislators with a vivid recital of the cruelties of slavery, till they decree its abolition; unchurched rationalists build upon old despotisms free and popular governments, while atheists and agnostics agitate to supplant the oppression and competition of the social and industrial order with the veritable kingdom of heaven preached and practised by Jesus, but contemptuously discontinued and denied by his official successors. Instead of a godspeed for their beneficent work, these secular reformers are *rebuked* by the modern Johns, *because they follow not with them*.[a]

It is told that messengers came once to Jesus, and asked him: "*Art thou he that should come, or do we look for another?*" to whom he replied: *Behold the things I do. The blind receive their sight, the lame walk, the lepers are cleansed, the dead are raised up, and the poor have the gospel preached to them.*[b] To the organized Christianity of our day, the same question is propounded: Art thou the last evangel of truth and good, or must we look for another? It must give place to another, unless it, too, can point to its miraculous and beneficent works. It must be able with truth to declare: I am bearing the light of intelligence into the dark corners of delusion and superstition; by my healing touch, the disabled in the struggle for life are made to keep abreast of the strong and cunning; by my sanitary lessons, the moral and physical diseases, that spoil the brief lives of men, have been cleansed; dead enthusiasms, dead hopes, and dead heroisms have been raised to life by my inspirations; and the gospel of genuine peace and good will has cheered the fainting hearts of the poor.

[a] Luke ix., 49.   [b] Matt. xi., 2–6.

www.ingramcontent.com/pod-product-compliance
Lightning Source LLC
Chambersburg PA
CBHW051853300426
44117CB00006B/380